The
Good Holiday
Cottage Guide
2007

The
Good Holiday
Cottage Guide

2007

Edited by
Bryn Frank

'We arrived after dark, but there was no-one around, and there were no lights on at all, let alone an outside light. The car slithered into a ditch while we were trying to park, so we had to call out the AA first thing in the morning to give us a tow. We had rejoiced in the idea of an open fire, but the grate had not been emptied of ash, so that was another chore. We do like things 'cosy', and hated the fact that there were no reading lights, only overhead ones. So we went to a car boot sale the following day to buy a couple. The bit in the brochure about the huge garden was true, but it was very overgrown, so much so that we could hardly see the famous view. There was an ancient cream Aga, but no instructions on how to work it, and there was a rickety central heating system, but it went off at nine pm and we couldn't seem to override it. But at least we managed to find a pile of rather dusty hot water bottles...'

**Distilled from reader reports of a cottage in Co Durham
that is not featured in this edition!**

The help of the following in preparing this guide is gratefully acknowledged: Leyla Ali, Richard Bamforth, Carole Frank, John Harrison, Jan James, Stephen Joyce, Nicky Phillips, Paul Phillips, Debbie Richardson, John Ruler and Gillian Thomas.

Bryn Frank, Hertford, December 2006

Printed by Stephen Austin & Sons Ltd, Caxton Hill, Hertford SG13 7LU. Telephone 01992 584955.

Distributed by Portfolio Ltd, Unit 5, Perivale Industrial Park, Perivale, Middlesex UB6 7RL. Telephone 020-8997 9000. Fax 020-8997 9097.

Front cover

Top left: Podere delle Rose (Page 284: Interhome)
Top right: Cobweb Cottage (Page 211: Dorset Coastal Cottages)*
Bottom: Sutton Court Farm (Page 224)

Back cover

Top: Eastwell Mews (Page 221)
Left: Vere Lodge (Page 46)*
Right: Pant Farm (Page 148)**

* also featured in Colour section A, Page 1
** also featured in Colour section A, Page 5

Please note.
Page 82: Eyam/Hope. The properties at *Hope* are known known as 'Laneside Farm'.

Page 94: the geographical reference at the top should read: Roxburghshire: map 4/153...../Lanarkshire

Page 177. Bottom left (Classic Cottages). Caption should read: 'Man O' War' – not featured – has long been one of our favourites in the seaside village of Cadgwith.

Yes, we're still here!

We'll hardly forget 1983, and the year or so before that. That was the time when (*yes – 25 years ago*) we were putting together the very first edition of this guide, scouring the rural byways of Devon and Cornwall, the shingly beach side hamlets of East Anglia and most other corners of Britain for worthwhile holiday cottages. With a small number of exceptions, we'd hardly recognise the interiors even of properties that in the mid-'80s were considered to be the bee's knees. Orange and brown curtains and carpets were king, about one in two cottages had a TV, and half of those were small black and white portables. The catch phrase among most owners looking to clear out old items of furniture was 'It'll probably do for the cottage', and many a mattress smelled ever so slightly of wet dog.

But in 2007 things have gone much further even than (in many cases) the last word in comfort. Some owners will say 'Most of our guests expect to be not just as comfortable as they are at home but even more so. And for lots of them, at a certain economic level, the price they are asked to pay is almost irrelevant'. Hot tubs, surround-sound TV and newly installed Agas seem to have become part of a lifestyle-statement, even a world-view. In 2007 the best properties are often those owned and looked after by well-heeled owners who've forsaken high-flying careers and chosen to bring their children up in picture-postcard rural Dorset, Norfolk or Wales.

But things are moving on still further. Until a few months ago the words 'cottage' and 'green' used together usually had to do with wellies on a wet day, grass that needed cutting, children getting car sick on the long journey home. Now, if a cottage owner isn't at least thinking about 'going green', he or she is (or so we're told) in some danger of losing a part of the potential market among the-chattering-classes.

We're generally open to new trends, and like to think we are as environmentally aware as most, but we *have* taken the step of banning the newly coined cliché 'carbon footprint' from our office.

See also Page 9

Approximately two thirds of the cottage owners featured in this guide accept dogs, and acceptance of dogs usually but not always means other pets too (a small number exclude cats). Most owners charge extra – usually between £15 and £20 per week per dog – for the inevitable extra wear and tear on properties, though this is without exception much less than kennels would charge. Please don't arrive with more dogs than you have permission to take, and please don't sneak a dog into a cottage where it's not welcome.

Interhome from home...

Interhome, featured on Pages 19, 284 and 296 of this guide (and on the cover!), is one of Europe's largest providers of privately owned holiday-homes, and PropertyQC, overseas property specialists fronted by BBC1 TV's 'Homes Under the Hammer' presenter Martin Roberts, recently announced a partnership.

The two companies have joined forces to offer consumers seeking to invest in a property abroad free, expert advice through PropertyQC, as well as an established and well respected outlet in the form of Interhome through which to rent their property as a holiday home and earn an income.

Interhome has added a link to its website directing clients to a dedicated section of the PropertyQC website, where they will be guided though the property purchasing process and introduced to a selection of property investment opportunities within Europe. Equally, PropertyQC is now recommending Interhome to clients seeking to make an additional income from their overseas property purchases, as the ideal portal through which to rent it.

Says Interhome UK Managing Director Madeleine Winship: 'We're sometimes asked by our clients, who love renting holiday homes with Interhome and may have found the location of their dreams, how to go about actually buying an overseas property, so the partnership with Martin Roberts and his team at PropertyQC is ideal. PropertyQC provides a professional and much needed service that will be of great benefit to our clients. It's great news for holiday-makers too, as the joint venture means even more exciting additions to Interhome's already extensive collection of privately owned rental properties.'

Says Martin Roberts, 'Interhome clients will now be able not only to rent excellent quality accommodation, but also buy it. The properties they buy will then end up forming part of the Interhome rental offering, with all the advantages that implies...'

advertisement feature

We're always impressed in this day and age of 'don't you realise we have huge overheads, old chap' by the number of owners we feature who take great pride in paring their prices down to the minimum, and are happy furthermore to have their properties singled out as 'inexpensive'. Here is a short list of those who have asked to be included – not a comprehensive but, we hope, a useful selection:

Jockey Cottage, Page 27

Jenny's Cottage, Page 44

Carpenter's Cottages No 6, Page 55

Stubbs Cottages, Page 60

Sarah's Cottage, Page 76

Long Byres, Page 125

4 Green Cross Cottages, Page 134

Hockadays, Page 175

Chapel Cottages, Page 171

Cider Room Cottage, Page 192

The Little Cottage, Page 249

'En route': Hartwell House

One of the incidental pleasures of producing this guide is featuring hotels we have come across that are nicely placed, en route, for people travelling to their holiday cottage. Previously we've featured hotels and outstanding 'b and b's on people's way to the Dales, the Highlands, and elsewhere. It now seems that Hartwell House, a magnificent stately home in ninety acres of landscaped parkland near Aylesbury, in Buckinghamshire, has its fans among our readers. If you are en route from, say, the Midlands or East Anglia to a holiday house in the Cotswolds, lunch at Hartwell on, say, Friday or Saturday in the handsome dining room, looking out over manicured lawns, is a delight (you can have just one dish from the à la carte menu, and say a glass or two of wine and be comfortably on your way). Even better, one of our Norfolk-based readers, whose favourite holiday house in Gloucestershire has a Friday to Friday booking policy, very neatly arranges to spend a sumptuously comfortable night at Hartwell on the Friday on the way home.

www.hartwell-house.com

Alamo Rent A Car

Renting a car is easy with Alamo Rent A Car. With over 40 models of car – *all less than six months old* – and over 150 locations in the UK, we offer choice, convenience and competitive rates. Travellers can take advantage of our special offers, including 7 days for the price of 5, and 3 days for the price of 2, to make a break away all the more affordable.

Whatever they need, whether a city run-around such as the new Corsa or a nippy VW Golf, or a larger vehicle such as a Vectra or a Passat, customers can rest assured that all of our 40,000 vehicles are fully serviced and maintained to manufacturer specifications and covered by 24 hour break-down assistance.

Alamo is one of only a few vehicle rental organisations with a minimum age of just 21 and *no maximum age limit* for the vast majority of our locations in the UK, ensuring rental can benefit anyone with a short-term vehicle requirement.

And for those planning a trip further afield, don't forget Alamo has approximately 3,800 locations in over 80 countries, giving customers a wide choice of locations to explore.

Just log on to www.alamo.co.uk or phone 0870 191 6992 for more information or to book a car.

advertisement feature

Turning green

In Cornwall (it seems) the grass is greener. We hear that cottage owners in Scotland are becoming more 'environmentally aware' than most, but it's several in the West Country that we know more about.

Bosinver, Cornwall – See Page 164. Says owner Pat Smith: 'Fresh air, clean coasts, unpolluted countryside. In Cornwall we work hard to look after the environment for our own and others' enjoyment. At Bosinver visitors are firmly encouraged to recycle and compost during their stay. Cottages are fitted with low energy bulbs, cleaning materials are low phosphate and we actively encourage bike hire, walking and the use of public transport. We are as green as our lovely rural setting, which is why visitors love Bosinver as much as they love Cornwall.'

Pollaughan, Cornwall – See Page 166. 'Pollaughan Cottages, on the stunning Roseland Peninsula, in Cornwall, were the first to be awarded at Gold level in the Green Tourism Business scheme and our passion for the immediate and local environment informs everything we do. We like to think Pollaughan is a good example of combining a sustainable ethos with cottages that are both high quality but more importantly a real home from home. Recycling, local purchasing, energy and water conservation, encouraging visitors to explore the beautiful coastline by boat and foot and wildlife focus on site, are all part of the success of this popular family run business'.

Compton Pool, Devon – See Page 204. 'Hot on the heels of achieving Five Stars for all the cottages and the Gold Award for the best tourism website in the South West, Compton Pool Farm have achieved yet another top honour. The first Five Star self-catering property in Devon to be awarded the Green Tourism Award has been as a consequence of a major review of energy use, waste management and care for the local environment. A new environmental policy has increased aware-ness of the owners, staff and guests to the sensitivity of this area of outstanding natural beauty. It has always been a key objective for the farm to be a fully sustainable business'.

A possible source of information for people, including owners, who want to know more about all this is the Green Tourism Business Scheme. This organisation says 'We are the largest and most successful environmental accreditation body of tourism related businesses in Europe, and have over 500 members in the UK, including among others, accommodation providers, visitor attractions, tour operators and conference facilities.

www.green-business.co.uk

The Times Holiday Handbook

The size and comprehensiveness of *The Times* newspaper, notably since it settled down into its compact form a couple of years ago, is a joy. So it's appropriate that *The Times Holiday Handbook*, written and researched by the paper's long-established travel editor, Cath Urquhart, should be be so extraordinarily wide ranging and complete. We like the tone – never pompous, always skilfully walking that fine line between presenting useful facts and offering interesting opinions. It's a long time since I found a (mostly) factual compendium virtually un-putdownable: in fact I sat reading it late into the night, ending up as bleary-eyed as if I'd stumbled off a long haul flight scrunched up in an economy seat. (And yes, of course, there's good advice here about how to get a better deal in the air.)

Within its 440 pages it really does cover 'the whole picture'. At random, there are good thoughts on the hotelier's mantra about clean towels ('Save the planet by re-using your towels': well, maybe). About phones: don't forget the good old phone booth. About learning to wait – and wait, and wait some more – in countries not used to the same instant gratification as people in the west. And, of course, that so-vital low-tech item that astonishingly few people think of – earplugs (more comfortable to wear than they used to be).

Naturally we turned to the section on self catering, where good sense prevails. Beware close cropped pix of villas in brochures that may be concealing a power station in the background. When booking a villa on the internet pay by credit card so that you can call on the credit card company should anything go wrong. And in the UK and overseas, the advantages for a large party in not taking one big property but several smaller ones close at hand, so that at the end of the day you can close your own front door.

We liked the Top Ten Travel Tips, which include not over-planning (leave room for serendipity), remembering that if you find something you need or really like, you should snap it up (my own travel reminiscences are littered with thoughts of original paintings and drawings I should have bought). Be a generous tipper: I'd qualify that a bit, and say 'be a generous tipper on arrival in a place where you'll be staying for a while'. Cath Urquhart also suggests that if you see a clean lavatory, use it: 'You never know when the next one is coming along'. This suggests that she has impressively more control over her bodily functions than most of us!

As with most of the best travel books, you get the feeling that the author would make a congenial travelling companion – humorous, well organised, a bit adventurous but not foolhardy. **BF.**

From bookshops (£12.95) or www.navigatorguides.com

Contents

13   *Bed and breakfast/hotel accommodation: brief descriptions of 'b and b' or hotel accommodation in the same ownership as self catering places featured in the guide…*

27   *East Anglia*

59   *Cambridgeshire, Lincolnshire, Nottinghamshire*

62   *Yorkshire and The Peaks*

84   *Northumberland and Durham*

92   *Scotland*

122   *Cumbria and the Lake District*

138   *Wales*

156   *Cornwall/The West Country*

216   *South and South East*

222   *Cotswolds, Heart of England, Home Counties*

256   *Ireland*

265   *France, Italy. Spain, Cyprus, Germany, New England. Another of our ventures into 'Europe' for a brief look at properties that we know or have been recommended by readers, plus profiles of a number of the agencies we trust.*

297   *'At a glance': facilities/special characteristics, in which we respond to requests for certain easy-to-digest detail. (UK only.)*

303   *UK Maps*
       A rough guide, with a few towns/villages noted just for reference: no complaints, please, from Boston (in Lincolnshire) or Melbourne (in Derbyshire).

312   *A listing of 'web only' cottage owners, plus UK Index.*

Colour sections: Pages 193-200 and 233-240.

THE COTTAGE COLLECTION

This fine collection of British properties has really made an impact in the last couple of years. You can check the availability of all the cottages on-line or speak to the Call Centre to book one without spending time contacting owners who may be full.

Impressively, Cottage Collection's Chairman Robert Dossor has doubled the choice in his portfolio in just two years, and created for the discerning holidaymaker a tempting choice of coastal or rural retreats where seclusion and privacy can easily be dovetailed with activities such as walking, climbing, horse-riding, fishing, golf or watersports, as well as visits to nearby attractions.

'Romantics' will be spoilt for choice, with everything from a coastal Cornish cottage to a delightful Derbyshire Peak District retreat (Churchdale Farm, in the Peak District National Park, is a beautiful, quiet location). Or they can wake up in a castle in Wales: Snowdonia is just a stone's throw from Bryn Bras Castle, where there are six apartments available through The Cottage Collection.

Cottage accommodation that offers that great luxury of today, 'peace and quiet', can be pinpointed in The Cottage Collection's 2007 brochure. Properties are located in every Area of Outstanding Natural Beauty around Great Britain, and families, as well as other large parties, can be readily accommodated in a number of places.

With 'Pets Welcome' signs at most locations, and those with disabled facilities also in the portfolio, we suggest you send off for the 2007 brochure, or visit the impressive, inter-active website.

Spending time on The Cottage Collection's website brings one in touch with special offers, particularly off-peak promotions, which might include gourmet meals or cream teas on arrival – say, at Yapham Cottages, in Devon.

Brochure request line: 01603 724809 – or go to:
www.the-cottage-collection.co.uk

Bed and breakfast/hotel accommodation

We often receive requests from readers wanting somewhere to stay en route to distant cottages and for friends and family to base themselves for a night or two while visiting people staying in a holiday property. They are sometimes able to book in as 'extra people', but – as standards have improved and zed-beds are not so popular – not usually. So here below is some information (mostly in the owners' words) about self catering places linked with hotels and 'b&b'...

Alderton Hall, Suffolk. See Page 31.
Having spent all too many nights in poky bed and breakfast places (writes Stephen Joyce) we are always alert to staying in a spacious 'hall'. At Alderton Hall in Suffolk, a medieval Grade II listed country house with good access to the coast, and where Suffolk Cottage Holidays is based, there is a fascinating Tudor dining room and three lovingly restored, newly refurbished and extremely comfortable double bedrooms, all ensuite, which make up the house's south wing.
Contact: Lizzie Hammond, Suffolk Cottage Holidays Ltd.
Telephone 01394 412306, fax 412309.
www.suffolkcottageholidays.com

Gladwins Farm, Suffolk. See Page 32.
'Home-from-home farmhouse B&B in a typical Suffolk farmhouse; en-suite rooms, direct dial telephone, lounge area. From £65 per night B&B for 2. Amid Suffolk's rolling 'Constable Country', with great views. Heated indoor pool, sauna, hot tub, tennis court. **'Visit Britain' Four Stars**.
Contact: Robert and Pauline Dossor, Gladwins Farm, Harpers Hill, Nayland, Suffolk CO6 4NU. Telephone 01206 262261. Fax 263001.
Email: GladwinsFarm@aol.com www.gladwinsfarm.co.uk

High House Farm, Suffolk. See Page 37.
'Beautifully restored 15th century farmhouse on family run arable farm. Featuring exposed beams and inglenook fireplaces, spacious and comfortable accommodation. Explore the heart of rural Suffolk, local vineyards, Easton Park Farm, Framlingham and Orford Castles, Minsmere, Snape Maltings, Woodland Trust and the Heritage Coast. B&B from £22. Reductions for children.'
Contact: Mrs Sarah Kindred, High House Farm, Cransford, Woodbridge, Suffolk IP13 9PD. Telephone 01728 663461. Fax 663409.
Email: b&b@highhousefarm.co.uk www.highhousefarm.co.uk

Cressbrook Hall, Derbyshire. See Page 79.
'Perched high on the south facing Wye Valley, overlooking Cressbrook
Mill and adjacent to beautiful Monsal Dale, historic Cressbrook Hall
(circa 1835) is an impressive family residence standing in rural grounds.
Elegant en-suite B&B is offered in rooms with spectacular views around
the compass. Bakewell five miles, M1 20 miles.'
Cressbrook Hall, Cressbrook, near Buxton, Derbyshire SK17 8SY.
Telephone (01298) 871289. Fax 871845.
Email: stay@cressbrookhall.co.uk www.cressbrookhall.co.uk

Cote Bank Farm, Derbyshire. See Page 83.
'Wake to birdsong, stunning views and the smell of freshly baked bread.
The same care and attention given to guests in Cote Bank Cottages is
lavished on them in our farmhouse. Two doubles, one twin, all en-suite,
TV, tea/coffee trays. B&B from £33. Open March to November.'
Contact: Pamela Broadhurst, Cote Bank Farm, Buxworth,
High Peak, Derbyshire SK23 7NP.
Telephone/fax 01663 750566.
Email: cotebank@btinternet.com
www.cotebank.co.uk

Holmhead Farm and Guest House, Northumberland. See Page 84.
'This 19th century former farmhouse (AA/**'Visit Britain' Four Stars**) is
within the Hadrian's Wall World Heritage Site, with panoramic views
over part of the Northumbria National Park. Stay at Holmhead and
experience delicious food and comfortable ensuite bedrooms. No
smoking; tourist information; sightseeing planning – especially Hadrian's
Wall.' Tariff from £35.
Contact: Brian and Pauline Staff, Holmhead, Hadrian's Wall. Greenhead
CA8 7HY. Telephone 016977 47402.
www.holmhead.com

Machrie Hotel and golf links, Isle of Islay. See Page 118.
'The "Machrie" lies close to its 15 self-catering cottages. Along with 11 twin rooms and five double rooms, it has two bars, a dining room, a function room and a private dining room. The food is predominantly local, with Islay beef, lamb and shellfish a speciality. Bar meals are served both at lunchtime and in the evening.'
Contact: Machrie Hotel, Port Ellen, Isle of Islay, Argyll PA42 7AN.
Telephone 01496 302310. Fax 302404.
Email: machrie@machrie.com
www.machrie.com

Bailey Mill, Roxburghshire. See Page 136.
'Friendly farm holiday complex offering bed and breakfast from £25 per person, per night or self catering courtyard apartments (short breaks available). This is an ideal location for walking, cycling or horse-riding through the beautiful Scottish/Cumbria border country. Guests are welcome to relax in our jacuzzi, sauna etc before enjoying a drink and/or meal in our cosy bar.'
Contact: Bailey Mill, Newcastleton, Roxburghshire TD9 0TR.
Telephone: 01697 748617.
Email: pam@baileymill.fsnet.co.uk
www.holidaycottagescumbria.co.uk

Land Ends Country Lodge, Cumbria. See Page 124.
'Enjoy a real country experience at Land Ends. Our converted farmhouse and barn are in 25 acres with lakes, pretty courtyard, fishpond. We have ducks, moorhens, red squirrels, wonderful birdlife. All rooms en-suite. 'Visit Britain' **Three Diamonds.** From £30. Doubles, twins and singles.'
Contact: Barbara Holmes, Land Ends Country Lodge,
Watermillock, near Ullswater, Cumbria CA11 0NB.
Telephone: 017684 86438.
Email: infolandends@btinternet.com
www.landends.co.uk

Trevorrick Farm, Cornwall. See Page 175.
'In our family home there are two double rooms and one twin, all with en suite bathroom with bath and shower-over, TV, tea and coffee making facilities. There is a separate lounge for guests with colour television and video/DVD. Guests have the use of the swimming pool during opening hours from Easter to October and the games room. There are two local pubs and a beautiful 45 minute walk into Padstow, along footpaths and the Camel trail.'
Contact: Melanie Benwell, Trevorrick Farm Cottages, St Issey, Wadebridge, Cornwall PL27 7QH.
Telephone/fax 01841 540574.
Email: info@trevorrick.co.uk   www.trevorrick.co.uk

Delphi Lodge, Co Galway. See Page 263.
'You don't have to be a salmon fisherman to enjoy the exquisite and peaceful surroundings at this well known but never overrun place (never overrun because accommodation is limited). In addition to the authentically restored, cosy cottages, there are twelve guest rooms. The place is organised in house-party style, so there is no room service, and guests generally eat communally in candlelight around a fine, huge dining table. It's a bonus for lone travellers or people from overseas wanting to make new friends.'
Contact: Peter Mantle, Delphi Lodge, Leenane, Co Galway.
Telephone 00 353 95 42222. Fax 42296.
Email: stay@delphilodge.ie   www.delphilodge.ie

The editors of *The Good Holiday Cottage Guide* welcome personal calls and emails from readers about properties in the British Isles or abroad, and about things to see and do in the area that is of interest. Every property featured in this guide has been seen by at least one inspector, sometimes two or three of them, but there may be specific questions readers want to ask that are not covered in individual write-ups or round-up agency features. We are always very pleased to link people up with properties that may suit them, and there is no charge...

Telephone 01438 869489.
email: info@goodcottageguide.com

Recommended Cottage Holidays*

Over the years readers have told us how much they appreciate the regional agencies. This also applies to the relatively new but meteorically successful Recommended Cottage Holidays: the organisation has grown beyond its original boundaries and gone country-wide, but has its roots in Yorkshire.

Specifically, in a very handsome house close to the centre of the lively, ancient town of Pickering (callers are welcome). And naturally there's a strong Yorkshire programme. Near Driffield, for example, situated on a working farm (delightful for visiting children), there's an exceptionally comfortable barn conversion that even offers on-site chalkstream fly-fishing. It **sleeps 6**. Ref M64. **'Visit Britain' Four Stars**.

Norfolk is known for its sympathetic barn conversions, and there's a stylish example of one of these at Sculthorpe, near Fakenham, a focal point in that gloriously unspoilt county, only about ten miles from the coast. The spacious brick, flint and tiled single-storeyed barn conversion **sleeps 8** and has a woodburner in the handsome high-ceilinged sitting room. Ref E54. And should the beautiful but chilly North Sea be a bit daunting, the hot tub might appeal.

In rural Shropshire, handy for sought-after Ludlow, a series of barn conversions has created accommodation that can **sleep 22** – a great opportunity for families or groups of friends. Grouped around a prettily landscaped, south-facing courtyard, each cottage has its own character. Here too there's (coarse) fishing in the grounds. There are four properties available, **sleeping respectively 6, 6, 4 and 6**: Refs T65/66/67/68. Four Stars*.

This beauty near Driffield (Ref M64) actually offers chalksteam fly-fishing!

This spacious barn conversion in Norfolk (Ref E54) sleeps 8 and has a woodburner.

And near Westbury, Wiltshire, a good point from which to visit, say, Longleat, Bath and Stonehenge, there's a very comfortable, spacious, detached family house **sleeping 10**. Equipped to the highest standard, it features four bedrooms and a modern fitted kitchen with French doors leading out on to a rear patio; the perfect spot for enjoying a leisurely barbecue. A super place with, not surprisingly, five agency stars*. Ref B31.

* These are the agency's own grading, but based on **'Visit Britain'** criteria.

Details and an excellent brochure from Recommended Cottage Holidays, Eastgate House, Pickering, North Yorkshire YO18 7DW. Telephone 01751 475547; fax 475559.

www.recommended-cottages.co.uk
email: sales@recommended-cottages.co.uk

Dales Holiday Cottages*

Pour a glass of wine and put your feet up. For a browse through the Dales Holiday Cottages brochure is like taking a tour through the best of England's North Country – with detours into some of Scotland's most scenic corners. Wild moors, hidden valleys, tree-lined rivers, ancient market towns, villages that seem hardly to have changed for 300 years, little-used roads snaking up into the hills: all this is 'Dales' territory.

We know much of Yorkshire, Derbyshire, Cumbria, Northumberland and Scotland, but this agency is full of topographical surprises. Among so very many gems are *The Bothy*, near Nenthead, which is in turn near Alston – a hilltop delight that's just inside Cumbria but close to the most beautiful part of underrated County Durham and to the 'best-kept-secret' that's the South Tyne Valley. Within an outstandingly attractive detached stone barn that embraces three properties, *The Bothy* **sleeps just 2** in a king-sized bed, and among many good things has a jacuzzi and fine rural views. Ref 4313.

Deep among the Yorkshire Dales, in the sort of location we love (along a quiet lane in a village), *The Bull Barn* – another skilful conversion –

Beckhouse (not featured) is a classic, substantial Yorkshire beauty. Ref 3179.

Viewfield, in Scotland, is a classic in its way, but 'cottagey'. Not featured. Ref 3677.

sleeps 6 in great contemporary style. There's a woodburning stove and, indicative of the attention to detail and comfort, underfloor heating. Also, for example, there's a TV in each of the three bedrooms. This is a delightful corner of Yorkshire, just two miles from Malham Tarn. Ref 4329.

There are yet more barn conversions, again exquisitely located, this time in a Derbyshire village. Dating from about 1750 in Kniveton, near Ashbourne, *The Creamery* is one of three, thoughtfully and charmingly furnished, with lots of attention to detail. It **sleeps 2**. Ref 4164.

Over the border, among so many appealing Scottish properties, newly built, detached *Magnelia House* – **sleeping 8** – has great views and the advantage of being situated within the owner's spacious grounds. We know this part of Scotland well, and yet again the location is terrific. The 'capital of the Highlands', Inverness, is just 15 minutes away, as are glorious routes to the north west. Ref 4293.

The Dales Holiday Cottage website is attractive and very user-friendly, but happily is enhanced by a busy and attractive brochure. Copies of this and other details from Dales Holiday Cottages, Carleton Business Park, Carleton Business Park, Carleton New Road, Skipton, North Yorkshire BD23 2AA. Telephone 01756 790919; fax 797012.

www.dales-holiday-cottages.com
email: info@dales-holiday-cottages.com

Interhome* (Great Britain)

Widely known and admired for its huge but carefully monitored range of self catering accommodation in mainland Europe and elsewhere in the world, Interhome now has a healthy UK portfolio too.

We know a number of the properties on the company's books, and in other cases, even if we don't know the property, we know the location. For example, within a terrace of cottages with a fine view of Cardigan Bay. two-storeyed *Ty Cerrig Cottage* stands in a quiet location above New Quay and just a mile or so from the beach. There's shared use of a lawned area for sunning yourself, a garden with garden furniture and a barbecue, with shops and a restaurant also about a mile away: just a nice distance on foot on a sunny day. **Sleeps 6;** one dog welcome. Ref G6170/102.

In Morebath, about ten miles from from Tiverton, in Devon, and on the edge of the Exmoor National Park, a quietly situated terraced house called *Beech Cottage*, **sleeping 4**, makes a good West Country base that's not, however, 'a million miles from London'. Ref G5400/100.

On the edge of the Exmoor National Park, Beech Cottage is, however, 'not a million miles from London'.

An apartment in Kingston-on-Thames is very nicely situated in its own right and handy for the train to central London.

Of course, one of the strengths of this impressive organisation is its range of properties in or within easy access of major cities. One example is a comfortable, modern two-room first floor apartment in a new three-storeyed apartment house in Kingston-on-Thames, just about ten miles from London. In a central, quiet position, about 300 yards from the Thames, on a side street, it is not 'suburban', but enjoys all the facilities of what is effectively a lively (and historic) market town in its own right. Trains from Kingston to London Waterloo take approximately 35 minutes. **Sleeps 4**. Ref G1000/520B.

But these amount to nothing more than a snapshot of what's available. Interhome has an extraordinary reputation for competitively priced accommodation and for efficiency – we hear from readers who use the company regularly, and say things like 'We are Interhome people'.

Telephone 020 8891 1294, fax 020 8891 5331, or see the Great Britain pages of the Interhome website: **www.interhome.co.uk**

(on line booking possible; short breaks and bookings of flexible duration available)

See also Pages 19, 284 and 296.

Hoseasons Country Cottages

We're impressed by the range of holiday properties on offer from this famous agency. Just for starters: thatched cottages, one-time barns, pubs, chapels, farmhouses, manor houses, converted watermills, schools, stables and coach houses!

Hoseasons have always been based in East Anglia, so it's not surprising that they offer a particularly good choice there. One of these is *Kingfisher Lodge,* a lovingly converted former boathouse, **sleeping 2**. Ref 3053. Readers also appreciate thatched cottages such as the pretty, Grade II listed *West Barton*, at Thorverton, near Exeter, in Devon. The beamed sitting room has a log fire, the dining hall has a woodburner and there's an Aga. **Sleeps 7** in two double bedrooms (one ensuite), a twin and a single. Ref E3072.

One of Hoseasons' grandest properties is *Ormathwaite Hall,* near Keswick, in the Lake District. Once home to the renowned Cumbrian

Ormathwaite Hall offers stylish living at the very heart of the Lake District.

Grade II listed West Barton is a cottage to fall for, very well located for touring.

doctor and scientist William Brownrigg, it's an 18th-century mansion (**sleeping up to 13**) in three acres of grounds, with glorious views of the Skiddaw mountain range. With an intricately carved oak staircase and features like an art deco bathroom, the houses oozes quality yet still feels like a comfortable family home. It has four double bedrooms (two with four-posters), a twin and a single. The grounds include lawned terraces, a walled kitchen garden, a cascading stream and woodland where deer and rare red squirrels can be seen. Ref E3157.

In Wales, *Globe House* is a Grade II listed building (**sleeping 10**) in the Pembrokeshire National Park. Just a short walk from a sandy beach, it's ideally placed for exploring the lovely coastal path and also for bird-watching as the cliffs are home to seabirds such as cormorants and fulmers. Ref W7142.

If you fancy some monster spotting, one of the *Loch Ness Cottages* or *Ness-Side Cottages,* four miles from Drumnadrochit, would be ideal as they have a glorious panoramic view across the famous loch. Three cottages **sleep 2** in king-size four-posters and two **sleep 4**. Ref S4104, S4249, S4105, S4077 and S4351.

Details from Hoseasons Holidays, Lowestoft, Suffolk NR32 2LW. Telephone: 0870 534 2342. Fax 0870 902 2090.

www.hoseasons.co.uk   Ref C0003.

Sykes Cottages*

This highly regarded independent agency, based in Chester, has an impressive portfolio of over 900 properties throughout the UK, including the South West, Northumberland, Yorkshire, Scotland, Wales and the Heart of England.

It was started over 25 years ago by the mother of owner and managing director Clive Sykes. Each cottage is inspected and carries either its local tourist board grading or the agency's own rating. Also, you can see what previous holidaymakers thought of each property by looking it up on the agency's website (www.sykescottages.co.uk).

Signal Box (Ref 1304) is in Newtonmore, in the Scottish Highlands. Quirky, and with a sauna, it sleeps four people.

South Cottage (Ref 1568) is near Reeth, in the Yorkshire Dales. With a real 'Dales' personality, it sleeps six people.

For those who like their rural retreat with a bit of luxury thrown in, *The Red Barn* (Ref 1562) near Longframlington, Northumberland, is ideal. A magnificent 18th century brick barn conversion, the accommodation is immaculately presented, and includes limestone floors and granite work surfaces in the kitchen, oak flooring and a woodburning stove in the sitting room, and a garden room with views over landscaped gardens. The owner has even thrown in bathrobes for use with the en-suite bathrooms each bedroom benefits from. For coast or country, this makes an ideal base for enjoying Northumberland.

If accessibility is key, then *Cat and Mouse Cottage* (Ref 1714) in Sleights, on the North Yorkshire coast, offers the ideal base. This detached stone barn conversion boasts modern open plan living accommodation, including exposed beams, and a large sunny garden. Better still, the village shops and pub are just a few minutes' walk, as are the nearest bus stop and train station. With the attractions of the coast and the charms of the moors within easy reach, this is the ideal opportunity to leave the car at home.

For original features seamlessly combined with modern comforts, look no further than *The Mews* (Ref 1928) in Hollington, near Ashbourne, in the Peak District. This fabulous brick built barn conversion provides bright and airy accommodation, including a spacious sitting room with feature fireplace, beamed ceilings and a roll-top bath. To top it all off, guests can enjoy exclusive use of the hot tub in the rear garden – ideal after a day spent hiking or touring the local countryside.

Details from Sykes Cottages, Lime Tree House, Hoole Lane, Chester CH2 3EG. Telephone 01244 356896. Fax 321442.

www.sykescottages.co.uk   email: info@sykescottages.co.uk

Stately Holiday Homes*

We have rarely come across a portfolio of holiday properties so perfectly 'up our readers' street' as those handled by Stately Holiday Homes. As readers might have noticed, we're keen both on holiday houses of comfort and character and 'the stately homes of England' (as well as Wales, Scotland and Ireland). Courtesy of this splendid organisation and their impressive contacts the two elements come together delightfully.

In the summer of 2006, for example, we saw two of the most desirable inland holiday homes in Northumberland: more details on Page 85.

Essex is full of surprises: you can stay within the grounds of Castle Hedingham.

A classic rural scene, at Glanusk Park. Three super cottages are available.

Other notable locations include, for example, Haddon Hall, in Derbyshire. Three miles from 'the big house', *Rock Cottage* – **sleeping up to 5** – is a fine, clean-cut, greystone house with a most attractive interior: it's interesting to note that so many of these estate properties are understated and easy on the eye, both inside and out. In a peaceful location (another big bonus), the house has **Four Stars** from **'Visit Britain'**.

Coniston Water is one of our own favourites among Cumbria's 'Lakes', and two properties converted by the owners of Nibthwaite Grange, in the hamlet of Nibthwaite, near the southern tip of the lake, make most enviable homes-from-home from which to enjoy this very special corner of England. *Peat House* and *Nibthwaite Studio* respectively **sleep up to 4** and **up to 2,** the former being a two storeyed stone cottage, the latter also on two floors, but primarily a spacious living/dining room with a double bed. The wife of the owner of Nibthwaite was brought up at Holker Hall, and a nice touch here is that holiday tenants have complimentary admission there.

The 4500 acre Houghton Estate in Norfolk has been the home of the Marquesses of Cholmondeley since 1797. (The Queen, at Sandringham, is a next-door neighbour.) There are three cottages on offer: *The Water House* has a super walled garden, *Bunker's Hill* is especially cosy in all weathers, with central heating as well as log fires, and *The South Lodge* is as neat and pretty a traditional roadside lodge (but very quiet) as we have ever seen on our travels. *See also Page 43*. We saw these during 2005, and loved them. We also visited *Snape Castle*, in North Yorkshire, and admired a warm and sympathetic conversion of a part of the main castle building. *See also Page 75*.

There are several Stately Holiday Homes properties in Scotland, Ireland and Wales. *Glanusk Park*, in the Brecon Beacons National Park, is very popular. Three traditional, stone-built cottages have stunning views over the estate and the Black Mountains. Each is single storeyed, fitting most harmoniously into its beautiful surroundings. *Library Cottage*, for example, has an especially impressive outlook, *Garden Cottage* has a memorable walled garden, and *The Kennels*, which is very quiet and peaceful, has a small stream running close. Garden ideally **sleeps 2** in a twin, but a single room is also available. The other two **sleep 4** in a twin and a double. All three have an open fire.

Among so many other good things, outstanding even in this exalted company, *Mead Cottage*, in the grounds of one of the most elegant, sumptu-

Mead Cottage, in Castle Combe, is at the heart of a classic 'picture-book' village.

Belle Isle: a super base for exploring beautiful, underrated Northern Ireland.

ously comfortable manor-house hotels in Britain, is eye-poppingly 'last word'. It's in Castle Combe, one of this country's most photogenic, most unspoiled villages. There is for example a charming and unusual divided 'double-living room' in which on one 'more formal' side there's a Scandinavian wood stove. The delightful small dining room used to be an ice house – but have no anxiety on that score: it has underfloor heating. **Sleeps 4** in great comfort.

Much less exalted than Castle Combe, but actually one of (much underrated) rural Essex's 'best kept secrets', the village of Castle Hedingham is dominated by the mainly 12th century castle. Within the castle grounds – accessed via a private gravel drive – *Garden Cottage* is a red brick, red tiled two-storeyed beauty **sleeping up to 5**. There's also *East-* and *West Lodge*, **sleeping 2/4 and 6/8** respectively.

A bonus here is that complimentary tickets are included for cottage guests to the popular jousting and 'medieval' events held at the castle.

Not yet seen by us but high on our schedule for 2007 is *Gilar Farmhouse*, close to the edge of the Snowdonia National Park. This is a real one-off, a remarkable survivor (**WTB Five Stars**) from the past, full of original features: it dates back partly to about 1660 and has, among so many memorable features, a seven-foot-wide four poster bed.

In Ireland *Belle Isle Castle*, Co. Fermanagh, is perfect for larger groups. **Sleeping up to 14**, with seven bathrooms, the mansion stands in a 470-acre estate consisting of eight separate islands.

For the company's brochure, telephone 01638 674749; fax 663995.

www.statelyholidayhomes.co.uk
email: admin@shhl.co.uk

National Trust Cottages

When holidaying in a National Trust property it's a bonus to know that the rent you pay helps preserve Britain's heritage of great estates and glorious countryside. Over 350 properties are available, scattered across England, Wales and Northern Ireland. Furthermore, as you'd expect, the choice encompasses many unique buildings.

Each is helpfully graded with an Acorn rating which ranges from one up to five. This covers the environment (the location, setting and exterior of the building) and the interior (style of decoration, furnishings and fittings, allowing for any normal wear and tear).

Readers of this guide who in 2006 were first-time visitors to the Isle of Wight stayed in *Knowles Farm Cottage* (3-Acorns). **Sleeping 3**, it stands close to the lighthouse at St Catherine's Point – there's no foghorn! – and

The Birdcage, in Port Isaac, Cornwall is quite something. Sleeps 2 (small) people!

Mill Cottage is on the Blickling Estate, in Norfolk. Pretty as a picture, sleeping 6.

as you'd imagine there are fantastic views. Ref 001005. And a visitor from Germany who joined English friends staying in *Darnbrook Cottage*, (3-Acorns, **sleeping 3**) on Malham Moor, in North Yorkshire, enthused about the views and the open fire, among much else. Ref 020020.

The two apartments (both **sleeping 3**) in the 400-year old Fountains Hall at Ripon in Yorkshire are 4-Acorns. *Proctor,* on the third floor, is furnished and decorated in the style of Charles Rennie Mackintosh; *Vyner,* on the second floor, follows the style of Edwin Lutyens. Ref 020016/7. Nearby, in the Studley Royal Deer Park, a 5-Acorn property, *Choristers' House* (**sleeping 10**) is available. Its has three double bedrooms and two twins. Ref 020022.

One of the 'quirky' category that particularly intrigues us is *Doyden Castle* (**sleeping 3**), which stands on the cliff-edge mid-way between Polzeath and Port Isaac in North Cornwall. Graded 4 Acorns, it's actually a small two-storey castellated folly rather than a real castle. With views of Lundy Bay, it was built in about 1830 by a local bon viveur for nights of feasting, drinking and gambling. Guests can drive to it via a cliff-edge track to unload, but cars have to be parked five minutes' walk away. Ref 011030.

Anyone who dreams of a romantic stay in a secluded thatched cottage would be enchanted by *Wood Cottage* (2 Acorns) at Durgan, beside the Helford estuary in south Cornwall. Originally an apple store, this tiny timber-built bungalow (**sleeping 2**) now has a cosy open-plan kitchen/dining/sitting room and double bedroom. The National Trust's Glendurgan Garden and Trelissick Garden are both nearby. Ref 011026.

Holidaymakers staying in *East Cottage*, near Dover, on the famous White Cliffs have an incomparable view of shipping passing to and fro in the Channel with (on clear days) the French coast. At the foot of the South Foreland lighthouse, it's a former keeper's cottage (3 Acorns) which **sleeps 4** in two bedrooms – a double and a single. The lighthouse itself, no longer operational, is open to visitors on a limited basis. Ref 021003.

Close to another popular coast, *Mustard Pot Cottage* (**sleeping 4**) is on the Felbrigg Estate in Norfolk, about three miles inland from Cromer. In its own fenced garden at the end of a woodland track, it's a simple two-storey octagonal building (3 Acorns) with ground-floor extensions containing kitchen, bathroom, twin bedroom and a conservatory. What makes it special is the original part, with sitting-room (open fire) on the ground floor and above it, up narrow winding stairs, a double bedroom. Ref

Mortuary Cottage, near Barnstaple, is a really cosy hideaway for just two people.

Also for two is The Old Coastguard Station, in Yorkshire. Sea views assured!

010019. Three other cottages and two apartments (**sleeping 2 to 5**) are also available on the estate whose grand 17th-century house and grounds are open to the public on most days. Ref 010015/6, 010026, 010034/5.

For a really 'rustic' holiday amid wonderful scenery, *High Hallgarth* is a 17th-century stone cottage (**sleeping 7**) in a remote location overlooking Little Langdale Tarn, in the Lake District. As it has no bathroom and the toilet is an earth closet in an outbuilding, it is the sort of place children will find really exciting and remember all their lives. Ref 009002.

Murlough Gate Lodge, at Keel Point in County Down, Northern Ireland, is a charming stone cottage built in 1870 beside Dundrum Inner Bay, on the edge of the Murlough National Nature Reserve. It enjoys glorious views of the Mountains of Mourne, which provide some of the best hill-walking in Ireland. **Sleeping 4**, it has 4 Acorns. Ref 019014.

There is a user-friendly website where you can see all the cottages inside and out, check availability and book:

www.nationaltrustcottages.co.uk (please quote promo code HCG07W)

Or call 0870 458 4411 for a brochure or 0870 458 4422 to book: please quote code HCG07B.

A voluntary contribution of £2 towards production, postage and packing of the brochure will be requested.

The Vivat Trust

Without wanting to seem sentimental, it's organisations such as Vivat that make us a bit 'proud to be British'. The charity is devoted to rescuing, restoring, letting and managing a range of historic buildings that are (generally) available for luxury self catering holidays. These tend to stand out as very well-cared-for, combining a feeling for the past with comfort and style.

After visiting several of the properties ourselves, we have not been surprised to get enthusiastic feedback from readers who've also stayed in Vivat properties. A reader from Buckinghamshire was much impressed by the apartments in the late 16th century *North Lees Hall*, Derbyshire (she stayed in one, peeped into the other!), which, incidentally, is also familiar to readers of Charlotte Bronte. Another reader was very taken by *The Cloister House*, at Melrose, in the Scottish borders. It is an elegant, early 19th century manse in the precincts of Melrose Abbey.

We ourselves remember being charmed by *Mill Hill Cottage*, a throwback to the 1750s and a rare survivor of the 'mud and stud' style, on the edge of a prettily situated Lincolnshire village. Another little jewel, *Church Brow Cottage*, lies on the outskirts of the small town of Kirkby Lonsdale, in Cumbria. It is eye-poppingly situated on a steep bank above the River Lune, with panoramic views over the valley. It boasts an irresistible sitting room with open fire, which leads on to a formal garden terrace.

The geographical spread of properties could be the makings of a voyage of discovery for holidaymakers with an interest in history and architecture.

Church Brow is one of our favourites: it's beautifully situated, full of character...

The Summer House is all that remains of a great country seat. Amazing views...

To name several, there's the early 14th century stone-built *Chantry*, at Bridport, Dorset, a 17th century Elizabethan 'banqueting tower' called *The Summer House*, Shropshire, and a 17th century 'gentleman's residence', *Stonegarthside Hall*, in Cumbria. Vivat's portfolio also contains several fabulous restored tower houses, including *Liberton Tower*, just outside Edinburgh, *Thistlewood Tower*, in Cumbria, and *The Tower of Hallbar*, in Lanarkshire.

Despite the seriousness of the purpose behind Vivat, there is nothing austere about the accommodation. The properties feel like lived-in homes, not museums, and for added comfort most have open fires or woodburners.

For an outstandingly good brochure contact The Vivat Trust, 70 Cowcross St, London EC1M 6EJ. Telephone 0845 0900194. Fax 0845 0900174.

www.vivat.org.uk   email: enquiries@vivat.org.uk

East Anglia, East Midlands and The Shires

Who'd have thought that shingly beaches and stiff winds off the grey North Sea would come to symbolise one of the most desirable corners of England among cottage fanciers? We're thinking mainly of Suffolk, but Norfolk especially – even in the 21st century – benefits from a degree of remoteness, even wildness. A maximum of three hours' drive from London or about two hours by train brings one into the best of East Anglia. From Scotland, it takes about four, from the Midlands perhaps two. There are 'bucket-and-spade' family resorts with end-of-the-pier shows, the North Norfolk steam railway (with links to regional rail services). Roofs are thatched with Norfolk reed that lasts up to about 80 years. Churches the size of cathedrals dominate the skyline, meandering rivers are the haunt of wildfowl. Even if you are holidaying near the coast, visit Norwich: the cathedral, the castle, the open-air market. Even if you are staying in a self catering cottage, you can hire a boat on the Broads by the hour or by the day. To the west lie the prosperous farms of Leicestershire and Northamptonshire, underrated counties of golden limestone villages and elegant churches. To the north are the Lincolnshire Wolds and the haunting, flat fenland, and well into Lincolnshire are some of the finest sandy beaches in England, where without exaggeration you can be virtually alone during a sunny Bank Holiday.

Dalham Vale, near Newmarket
Jockey Cottage (map 1/1)

Many years in this guide, lots of praise.

In the heart of a village close to the Suffolk/Cambridgeshire border, a few easy furlongs from horsey Newmarket, this most attractive and 'traditional' thatched cottage is well placed for exploring the best of rural Suffolk, a good part of Norfolk, Cambridge, Ely and the low key but fascinating Fen Country. Handy for a good village pub, it is one of those places that makes a really pleasant base to return to after touring (we have heard this from a number of overseas readers). Standing well back from the quiet road through this pleasant off-the-beaten-track conservation village, it has been tastefully and considerately restored and furnished. For example, there is a skilful blend of country furniture and top-notch contemporary soft furnishings, plus a new kitchen and a dishwasher. It has a woodburning stove in an inglenook fireplace, and **sleeps 4**. Remote control television. You'll find a welcome pack, a payphone and a garden.

Pets are possible by arrangement. Linen and towels are included. Cost: about £260 to £360. Weekend breaks are available from about £130. Further details from Richard Williams, Scorrier House, Redruth, Cornwall TR16 5AU. Telephone 01209 820264.
email: rwill10442@aol.com

Throcking, near Buntingford
Southfields Cottages

We've had a good number of calls from readers who have discovered and stayed in these cottages. It's rarely because they are in love with the delights of rural Hertfordshire (debatable), more often because the cottages are so well located for people who want to be within half an hour's drive of Cambridge and within reach – best by train, via Stevenage – of London. They are only occasionally available for holiday letting, but worth the effort. On a working (but not noisy or smelly) farm, well away from the main road, each of the semi-detached but private and self-contained pair enjoys good views and is pleasant and unpretentious.

Charming and unpretentious. Falling into the increasingly rare 'traditional cottage' category, they are also inexpensive. Each sleeps up to 5.

Among the details that impressed us were bright, cottagey bedrooms, (plain white walls in most cases), some traditional knick-knacks, a sitting-out area at the rear. There is central heating, linen is provided and, although electric fires are installed, you can have usually have an open fire too. Not suitable for dogs. TVs.

Details from Mrs I Murchie 07913 480095.

Stoke Tye, near Dedham
Louie's Cottage   map 1/2

'Constable Country', a rural survivor in the face of relentless development on and around the Suffolk-Essex border, contains within its low hills and exceptionally fertile farmland some delightful surprises. The tiny hamlet that surrounds this classic thatched and 'pargetted' cottage (that is, adorned by traditionally intricate plasterwork) is one such delight. The house itself is used by the owners for their own holidays and weekends,

A classic thatched cottage: rural Essex is one of southern England's surprises...

and is suitably 'lived in', containing family antiques, charming knick-knacks, chintzy covered armchairs, a rocking chair and, for example, an upholstered window seat: very much our sort of place. We noticed an open fire, a separate study, a standard lamp, lots and lots of books – not just in one room but in several. There are two twin bedrooms with fitted carpets, chintz curtains, and – in one of those wide corridors that we particularly like – even a Victorian rocking horse! **Sleeps 4.**

TV. Dogs welcome. No linen provided. Central heating throughout.

Details from 01438 869489.

Dedham
The Tallow Factory

On a very warm early summer day we arrived at so-handsome Dedham, right on the Essex-Suffolk border, to see a property we'd heard many good things about. It did indeed turn out to be sheer delight: a classic, timber-framed piece of East Anglian history, full of nooks and crannies, with every room seemingly more interesting than the last. Authentically painted too - that dark russet 'Suffolk red' that fits so harmoniously into the rural and urban scene.

We arrived while the house was being spruced up for a group (lucky group!) arriving for the weekend, so we wandered first into the little enclosed garden, well tended, backing on to a small wood and therefore very private, and with space to sit on a hot day.

Then into the house via the neat kitchen (good quality wooden units, stone flagged floor, all the appliances you'd expect at this level) into the main sitting room that opens via french windows on to the garden. That good sized room is inviting without being prissy (deep sofas and armchairs, rugs and carpets). There's TV and video.

We really liked the dining room, especially the fine oval dining table - very convivial. This is also effectively a second sitting room. (There is, throughout the house, a most appealing combination of 'country furniture' and antiques.)

The first floor master bedroom, via a landing with a wide selection of good books to get stuck into, is a joy, so spacious that it could double as a private drawing room when a bit of peace and quiet is called for – perhaps when a large group gets a bit lively! There are four other bedrooms, two doubles and two twins, including a most appealing room on the second floor – especially light, bright and airy, looking out over the garden.

Just before going to press we were very pleased to hear that the house on the opposite side of the almost-enclosed courtyard (not seen by us inside) is also now available. This, called *Brannam*, like Tallow **sleeps up to 10**: the two properties taken together can therefore **sleep up to 20**.

Not suitable for pets. Non smoking. Linen included, towels available at an extra charge. Cost: (Tallow) about £625 to £1300; (Brannam) about £550 to £1100. Details from 01206 393711 or 07799 413779.

www.tallowfactory.com email: info@tallowfactory.com

This is an extraordinary house in a sought-after spot on the Suffolk border.

As 'master bedrooms' go, this is surely one to remember (or even dream about).

29

Edwardstone, near Lavenham
Grove Cottages

During the last few years we've watched this charming, skilfully, lovingly converted group of 300-year-old cottages become established as one of the finest of its kind in East Anglia.

It's just two hours' drive from London (and therefore great for short breaks): but as you meander along West Suffolk's sleepy country lanes you might feel you are 200 miles from any big city. The location is ideal for walking, cycling (free bikes), exploring the beautiful River Stour on canoes (for hire), horse-riding, golfing, touring and 'pubbing'.

We have admired and noted so many good things. Such as charming 'ragged' walls, an original bread oven in *The Bakery*, original brick walls, wooden floors, beams. Plus personal touches such as fresh flowers, locally hand-made soaps, fridges stocked for you with the makings of a full English breakfast, a communal fridge-freezer.

We met several guests enjoying the afternoon sun in the beautiful orchard garden. They were planning a barbecue – barbecues are provided, as well as a party-sized barbecue with refectory tables – and had enjoyed the owners' home produced honey. One couple spoke of the friendly welcome they'd had from owner (and film director) Mark Scott, as well as that from his dogs and ducks.

Early in 2005 we called again to see *Don's Barn*, a most sympathetic conversion **for a couple only** – a five feet wide bed: excellent – of a property that dates from the early 1700s. There's period furniture and – a joy – a big log fire. **'Visit Britain' Four Stars**.

If you can drag yourself away from all this you will not want to miss picture postcard Kersey and a remarkable throwback to the medieval age,

With a great commitment both to the history of the properties and to 21st century comfort, these are very special.

All the (very pretty and cottagey) main bedrooms have five-foot beds, and four of the five cottages have an open fire.

preserved-in-aspic Lavenham. Bury St Edmunds and Cambridge are an easy meander (avoiding main roads) and Norwich is not a lot further.

Sleep from 2 to 6. TV, stereo, CD player, selection of music and books. Spacious power showers, no baths. Finest cotton linen and towels provided. Pets welcome. Non-smokers or very considerate smokers preferred. **'Visit Britain' Four Stars**. Cost: about £193 to £853. Details and a brochure from Mark Scott, The Grove Cottages, Priory Green, Edwardstone, Suffolk CO10 5PP. Telephone 01787 211115. Fax 211220 or 211511.

www.grove-cottages.co.uk email: mark@grove-cottages.co.uk

Woodbridge and around
Suffolk Cottage Holidays *

One of the bonuses of a recent trip to coastal Suffolk was to renew our acquaintance with this much admired local agency, most of whose properties fall within an 'Area of Outstanding Natural Beauty' (AONB). Among several memorable places we saw was chic, stylish *Bala Cottage* at Felixstowe Ferry (a passenger ferry still runs, as it has done for hundreds of years). This is the oldest part of Felixstowe (fishing boats, yachts, two good old pubs, excellent walking routes): full of character. The cottage has spectacular views across the River Deben and the coast. **Sleeps up to 8**.

Willow Farm Cottage is a converted barn in the charming village of Lower Ufford.

The Pump House is a fabulous property in (a favourite of ours) coastal Orford.

Across the Deben, in Bawdsey, on a quiet country lane, *East Lane Cottage*, **sleeping 8** is much bigger than it immediately appears. It's a classic roses-round the door rural delight, with a charming garden.

Further up the coast, at Orford, Suffolk Cottage Holidays have a cluster of lovely cottages, including *The Pump House*, a fantastic conversion of one of the most photographed cottages in the village that offers really luxurious accommodation **for up to 7 people**. Also in Orford, with views over the estuary, the sea and the beautiful marshes are the much admired Chantry Barns, an inspired conversion of disused farm buildings. Light pours into the *Bothy, Stables, Hayloft* and *Granary*, each **sleeping 4**. All four exude the warmth and beauty of old Suffolk bricks and beams, with fine contemporary elegance, comfort and lighting.

Among other notable properties (but we hear from several sources that there are no duds) is the *Anchorage* at Thorpeness, just north of much sought-after but much busier Aldeburgh, while for people who prefer a quieter country location *The Black Barn* at Brampton – cosy and quirky – is still within a ten minute drive of Southwold and the sea.

There is an excellent brochure and an exceptionally good website. Details from Suffolk Cottage Holidays Ltd: telephone 01394 412304, fax 412309.
www.suffolkcottageholidays.com

For details of the sister company, which is called Big House Holidays (superb properties sleeping 10 people and more):
www.bighouseholidays.co.uk

Dedham Vale, near Nayland
Gladwins Farm Cottages

Gladwins is so easily accessible – less than two hours' drive from London, less than three from Birmingham – that you might be surprised by how deeply rural it is.

This extraordinarily well situated group of cottages, in which guests are well placed for exploring east and west Suffolk and, say, the Norfolk border and Norwich, has consistently high standards and excellent facilities, and we have seen for ourselves the warm welcome from the Yorkshire-born owners, the far-reaching country views, the splendid indoor pool, and, of course, the sheep and the pigs!

All but three properties face on to a courtyard. *Chelsworth Cottage*, **sleeping 8**, is very private and has spectacular views over the Vale of Dedham, an Area of Outstanding Natural Beauty. It has a four-poster bed, TV and ensuites in *all* bedrooms, a log burner, central heating and stereo. And it even has its own hot tub! A real bonus is that it has a specially adapted ground floor twin room for disabled people. *Wiston Cottage,* **sleeping 6,** has three en-suite rooms, all with their own TV, its own garden and the same impressive views. Pets are welcome here.

Hadleigh **sleeps 4/5** and is attached to the owners' home; *Constable* **sleeps 6**, *Gainsborough* and *Dedham* both **sleep 4**, *Lavenham* **sleeps 4 'plus 1'**, *Melford* **sleeps 2** in a four poster 'for that special occasion' and also has its own hot tub. *Kersey* **sleeps 2 plus 1**. All could be described as 'little showhouses' with their cosy, comfortable interiors, woodburners, modern pine, good fitted carpets and local pictures. (There's another hot tub adjacent to the pool buildings for all the other cottages to share.)

There is access to 22 acres, an air-conditioned pool and sauna building, an adventure playground, an all-weather tennis court and a trout lake.

Excellent facilities and an outstanding situation in Constable Country'...

Interiors have been sympathetically done: this (appropriately!) is 'Constable'...

Pets welcome, except in Lavenham and Hadleigh. Small-screen TVs/video/DVD players. Cost: £265 to £1880. **Sleep 2 to 8**. Open all year; short breaks. Chelsworth and Wiston are suitable for accompanied disabled visitors. On-line availability can be checked via the website.

Further details from Pauline and Robert Dossor, Gladwins Farm, Harpers Hill, Nayland, Suffolk CO6 4NU. Telephone Nayland 01206 262261, fax 263001. Bed and breakfast is also available.

www.gladwinsfarm.co.uk email: GladwinsFarm@aol.com

Brundish, near Framlingham
Potash Barns

We've rarely come across such a deeply rural, family-orientated arrangement of cottages. Children love the Hebridean sheep, the ducks and the goats, as well as a variety of hens that, when given the chance, can be as mischievous as puppies.

A reader from Buckinghamshire who joined family and friends for a couple of days here spoke glowingly of the accommodation. She knew the coast but not the deeply rural interior of Suffolk.

Of the three cottages, which we ourselves visited in 2005, *Cartlodge* is free-standing and just a step away from the other two, *Old Oak* and *Goat Willow*. These two are linked via a large central hall with sofas and a fireplace: ideal when renting both cottages.

Each cottage has a different layout, incorporating two bedrooms, a comfortable living room, and a well-equipped kitchen. The decor is both stylish and rustic, with solid wooden beams, elm or terracotta floors, and high quality fittings. The solid wood kitchens all have large fridges, dishwashers, ranges and porcelain sinks.

We admired the magnificent flower arrangements in each cottage, and the fresh, top quality organic veg and groceries that owner Rob supplies win accolades too. He can also arrange for a meal to be waiting in the oven. Each cottage has an outdoor eating area with BBQ, and there's a separate games room with table tennis, table football and a variety of games.

The cottages each **sleep 4 or 5** plus two on double sofa beds in each living room. The master bedroom at Old Oak has a huge glass skylight, enabling you to lie in bed and gaze at the stars. Cart Lodge is laid out on one floor, and has a walk in shower as well as a bath – useful for less mobile guests. Each has TV, video, DVD, washer and dryer, bath and power shower, a CD player, books and games, a woodburner and central heating. All three cottages are **'Visit Britain' Four Stars**. Children have their own play area with swings and trampoline. Most pets can be accommodated in Cart Lodge. Cost : about £250 to £665.

Details from Rob Spendlove, Potash Farm, The Street, Brundish, Suffolk, IP13 8BL. Telephone 07747 038386. Fax 01379 384819.

www.potashbarns.co.uk
email: enquiries@potashbarns.co.uk

We were wowed by the rural location, the animals, the easy-going comfort...

Colleagues still enthuse about a stay they arranged for a group of friends.

33

Woodbridge, Orford and around
Mrs Jane Good (Holidays) Ltd *

This family run, long established agency must have the most exquisitely situated offices we know: right by the yachting marina and The Quay that are a major draw in Woodbridge, which is certainly one of the most attractive market towns in England.

It's a fitting base for an agency with (in many cases) exceptionally well situated properties – a number of them of great character – that deals exclusively with rural and coastal Suffolk. Regular readers will know how highly we rate it: it is thoroughly reliable and features a notable number of classically pretty and highly photogenic cottages.

Lavender Cottage, sleeping 4 (but spaciously) offers a rare chance to be at the very heart of delightful Woodbridge.

Litle Oakland sleeps 2/4 in a quiet location in the much sought-after village of Waldringfield, near Woodbridge.

Appropriately, Mrs Jane Good (Holidays) Ltd have a number of properties very close to the water in Woodbridge itself.

Among several holiday homes on the agency's books in the town is *No 12 St John's Terrace*. Near the centre of town, with a neat garden, it has been lovingly restored. Close to the fine parish church (one bedroom overlooks it), it **sleeps 4** and is just three minutes' walk from the charming, effectively pedestrianised Thoroughfare, at the heart of the town. Another well presented (and Grade II listed) terraced cottage in Woodbridge – **sleeping 3** – is *Treetops*.

One of our favourite small towns in the whole of Suffolk is Orford, nicely 'on the way to nowhere', and happily the agency has a number of properties there. These include, on a quiet private track near the quay, *No 6 Coastguard Cottages*. From the rear bedroom – the Victorian terraced cottage **sleeps up to 4** – there are glimpses of the River Alde. The cottage has central heating *and* an open fire. Also in Orford, a recent addition to the Jane Good portfolio is *Oxo Cottage*, **sleeping 8**, which 'oozes period charm' and also has the bonus of inglenooks and a big garden.

Among a sprinkling of gems in inland Suffolk, we are fond of *The Nest* at Badingham, just a short distance from the A1120 Yoxford to Stowmarket road. Absolutely pristine and lovingly cared for, this little semi-detached cottage has retained a number of original features. **Sleeps 4**.

Between the villages of Brandeston and Cretingham, about five miles from the historic market town of Framlingham (do see its famous castle, where Mary Queen of Scots was a prisoner), is *The Potash*, a detached, mainly 16th century, thatched house. There is a large garden and views over fields and the upper reaches of the River Deben. Original features such as exposed beams and wooden floors add to the character, and the spacious sitting room has a wood-burning open fire and a grand piano! **Sleeps 8** in two doubles and two twins.

Within striking distance of famous Aldeburgh, and of the 'heritage coast', heaths, forests, rivers and bird reserves, *Ivy Lodge*, on the outskirts of Tunstall, is a most interesting and comfortable folly, bigger than it first appears, which was originally a gatehouse for Rendlesham Hall. **Sleeps 4 'plus 2'**.

Just two miles north of Aldeburgh lies Thorpeness, which we know well: a charming seaside place, created as a holiday resort by the Victorians. *Westdene* is a very handsome half timbered house **sleeping up to 8**. It is

The Lifeboat House is in a fabulous location facing the North Sea at suitably-named Shingle Street. It sleeps eight.

The Brink, near much-loved Orford, is nicely secluded, and has the makings of a memorable holiday. It sleeps four.

accessed via a little-used unmade track, and has an open fire. Also in Thorpeness are two very substantial houses that will suit birdwatchers. *Bittern* and *Crossing Cottage* respectively **sleep 10** and **8**. Bittern is a handsome family house on the banks of the Meare, has a private jetty, is adjacent to the golf club and is notable among other things for a full size snooker table; there is easy access from both properties to the RSPB's North Warren bird reserve, and in fact Crossing Cottage is within it. That bright, modernised house **sleeps 8** and is very family-orientated.

We are fond of the wooded landscape around Eyke, just four miles from Woodbridge, where people seeking absolute peace and quiet who also like the idea of being close to wildlife will appreciate *Stone Hall*. **Sleeping 4**, it is very much a traditional cottage, up a long drive and with an open fire.

We like the agency's handy A5 brochure detailing all the 75 or so properties on their books, and the star rating each cottage gets: a very honest assessment in our experience, from five stars for 'excellent' to one for 'basic'. Even most of the expensive properties are sensibly priced, and many that we know to be perfectly acceptable and big enough for a family are only a little over £300 a week during high season. Dogs are welcome in about half the properties – unusually (in almost every case) at no extra charge.

For a copy of the brochure (always a good read) contact Penny at Mrs Jane Good (Holidays) Ltd, Little Bass, Ferry Quay, Woodbridge, Suffolk IP12 1BW. Telephone/fax: 01394 382770.

www.mrsjanegoodltd.co.uk   email: theoffice@mrsjanegoodltd.co.uk

Hacheston/Badingham
Lodge Cottage/The Mill

With the bonus of the handsome river-side market town of Woodbridge just ten minutes' drive away, distinctive *Lodge Cottage* (Ref BJD) stands close to the owners' substantial country house. 'B and B' is also available in the main house. We arrived to see the cottage in the summer of 2005 as it was being spruced up by a team of cleaners in readiness for new arrivals. We admired the spacious and stylish

The Mill is a very special property, a memorable family base from which to enjoy the whole of magical Suffolk.

sitting room/dining room and loved the way the well lit, very comfy bedrooms are a few steps down on a lower floor: a rather cosy arrangement. Guests have use – shared with the owners – of the heated outdoor swimming pool, the gardens and the paddocks. There is even a small football pitch! **Sleeps 5 'plus 1'.** Also of note in this part of Suffolk, at Badingham, close to the small castle-town of Framlingham, *The Mill* (Ref BQW) is a substantial country house, worth seeking out for itself but, as a bonus, also just half an hour's drive from the coast. **Sleeps 8.**

Details from English Country Cottages, Stoney Bank Road, Earby, Barnoldswick BB94 0AA. For bookings and brochures, telephone 0870 197 6890.

www.english-country-cottages.co.uk

Bruisyard, near Framlingham map 1/9
Margaret's Cottage

On a warm afternoon in August we turned off a little used country lane to a haven of peace that has been created from the coach house, stables and outbuildings of nearby Cransford Hall – *see also the opposite page*. We loved the combination of tall, shady trees and manicured gardens, and much admired the Edwardian walled garden that originally belonged to 'the big house'. Effectively one wing of the owners' substantial house, Margaret's

There's a shared swimming pool and a games room with snooker. A fine base from which to enjoy mid- and coastal Suffolk.

Cottage is a real charmer. We loved the light, bright, spacious lemon-coloured main bedroom, the deep terracotta armchairs and the green sofa in the spacious sitting room, the well equipped solid oak kitchen, the wood-stove that guarantees a cosy autumn or winter break. There's an exceptional shared games room, with the joy of a full size snooker table, and access to a shared open-air heated pool. **Sleeps 4** in a double and a twin. Cost: about £350 to £650. Not suitable for pets; no smokers. Linen and towels included. Details from Mr and Mrs Roberts, The Clock House, Bruisyard, Saxmundham, Suffolk IP17 2EA. Telephone 01728 663512, fax 663301.

www.theclockhousebruisyard.co.uk email: cherianroberts@yahoo.co.uk

Bruisyard, near Framlingham
The Clock House

The pool is just one of the attractions here.

It seems that every time we think we know 'every stick and stone' of rural Suffolk we come across another hidden gem. Thus via narrow, leafy, silent lanes a few miles to the north of Framlingham we happened on a quartet of cottages – three of them handled by English Country Cottages (long a leader in the field of rural properties of character) in well-wooded grounds and set off by manicured gardens. It's a fine combination of the sociable sort of place to make new friends (say around the neat, heated open air pool or in the excellent games room, which is graced by a super full sized snooker table). *The Pottery* (**sleeping 6,** Ref BES) and *The Foundry* (**sleeping 4,** Ref BER) are two separate halves of a substantial single-storeyed property in a tucked-away woodland setting; *Gardener's Cottage* (**sleeping 3,** Ref BEX) is separate, in a corner of the rare Edwardian walled garden that originally belonged to 'the big house'. A nice touch: home cooked gourmet meals can be delivered to your door.

Details from English Country Cottages, Stoney Bank Road, Earby, Barnoldswick BB94 0AA. For bookings and brochures, telephone 0870 197 6890.

www.english-country-cottages.co.uk

Cransford, near Framlingham
Wood Lodge   map 1/8

A readers' favourite for many years...

A 'cottage guide' classic, tucked away and quiet, this spacious cottage is a long-time favourite of ours. We remember detouring from the historic town of Framlingham for a recent revisit, and meeting cottage guide readers sunning themselves in the big lawned garden. We like the deep armchairs, the big wood stove guaranteed to create a warm and cosy atmosphere, off which the central heating runs, its masses of space, its character, its history (it dates from about 1800), and its attractive pictures. It even boasts a complete Encyclopedia Britannica 'of a certain age'! The kitchen is well equipped, and includes a dishwasher, the dining room is inviting, bedrooms are spacious. **Sleeps 8** plus cot. **'Visit Britain' Three Stars**. TV and DVD/video, stereo and CD player. Dogs by arrangement. Free logs. Cost: £250 to £700. Linen and towels for hire. 'B & B' available. Details from Tim and Sarah Kindred, High House Farm, Cransford, near Woodbridge, Suffolk IP13 9PD. Telephone 01728 663461. Fax 663409.

www.highhousefarm.co.uk
email:Woodlodge@highhousefarm.co.uk

Southwold and beyond
Suffolk Secrets*

We've been pleased to observe the gradual extension of the admirable Norfolk Country Cottages (see Page 41) into Suffolk – over 100 properties now – and during 2005 we spent some time looking at properties in and near Southwold that come under the umbrella of that part of their Suffolk operation known as 'Suffolk Secrets'.

Firstly, just inland from the daytime hustle and bustle of Southwold (at Reydon) we admired an absolutely pristine modern house – many of our readers choose these in preference to 'olde worlde' properties. Finished to a very high standard, and under the same discriminating ownership, *Cherry Trees* – **sleeping 6** – is a very quietly situated jewel, with a superb standard of finish both inside and out. It has off-road parking and for example (just the sort of detail we would have expected) king sized beds in the main bedroom.

Almost close enough to the sea to try angling for fish, *Shrimp Cottage* is a pretty, pastel and white coloured 'bijou' delight, an absolute classic seaside cottage, complete with seasidey knick knacks and charming pictures. (We love one particular detail in the agency description: 'there's a sea view from the sitting room– even when you're seated'.) **Sleeps up to 4 'plus 1'** in two doubles and a small single – two rooms on the second floor via very steep, narrow stairs.

From a rear window of another property we were delighted to find ourselves gazing at one of the most famous views in Suffolk: Southwold across the marshes, hardly changed for a hundred years or more, an attractive skyline against a background of scudding clouds in a pale blue sky. *Blackshore Corner*, **sleeping 6** in three bedrooms and **'Visit Britain' Four Stars,** is a remarkable house, very close to the beach and next door to a pub of character. (On a summer day it's a bustling scene, but calmer and more beautiful 'after hours'.) The spacious sitting room is on the first floor to make the most of the *front* view of river and sea.

Details from Suffolk Secrets, The Old Water Tower, The Common, Southwold, Suffolk IP18 6TB. Telephone 01502 722717.

www.suffolk-secrets.co.uk

email: holidays@suffolk-secrets.co.uk

Thorpeness is a desirable, rather low-key seaside place about two miles to the north of Aldeburgh. This is No 2, The Dunes.

Westleton is one of our favourite Suffolk villages. (Among other good things there's a super bookshop.) This is Garden House.

Wortham, near Diss
Ivy House Farm

Very well placed for exploring much of the best of Suffolk and of Norfolk, these properties are pleasantly situated on the edge of the 2004 'Suffolk Village of the Year' (very close to the Norfolk border). Well back from a quiet road, there are three cottages in a row, a detached cottage and, across the yard, a historic Suffolk 'long house'.

A much-liked set-up, on the rural edge of a Suffolk village by the Norfolk border.

The fine detached modern cottage, built to high specifications, is designated as the owners' retirement home. **Sleeps 6.** The three places opposite have mainly open plan living areas and comfortable bedrooms. Each **sleeps 4.** The 'long house' is packed with character: we've long admired a cosy kitchen, an inglenook log fire in one sitting room, a superb dining room, spacious bedrooms (the 'master bedroom' is triple-aspect), good views from all bedrooms. **Sleeps up to 10.** The leisure centre has pool and table-tennis tables and a full-sized snooker table, and there's an excellent indoor swimming pool. Dogs welcome. Fuel, linen and towels included. TVs, videos, CD players. Cost: £240 to £1640. Details: Paul and Jacky Bradley, Ivy House Farm, Wortham, Diss, Norfolk IP22 1RD. Telephone/fax 01379 898395.
email: prjsbrad@aol.com
www.ivyhousefarmcottages.co.uk

Cranworth, near East Dereham map 1/19
Holly Farm Cottages

Very quiet, very much the pride and joy of owner Jennie McLaren, these semi-detached cottages make a comfortable, inexpensive base for discovering much of Norfolk. Just a few yards from the owner's house they are nevertheless private, overlooking fields. Everything is done to very high standards, and it is typical of the conscientious owner that she offers a choice of feather/down or

A bonus: golf, fly fishing and coarse fishing are all very close at hand...

more conventional duvets, or even sheets and blankets. Each is a mirror image of the other but *Cottage No 1* has a king sized bed and *Cottage No 2* has zip-link twins which can make a lovely 6 ft double. Each also has a sofa-bed in the uncluttered, maple-floored sitting room. Kitchens are excellent, and new, and the quietness of the location is a tonic. Children will find that their own pets are welcome. There's a paddock for a visiting horse or pony. Linen/towels included. Cost: about £180 to £375. Details from Jennie McLaren, Holly Farm, High Common, Cranworth, Norfolk IP25 7SX. Telephone 01362 821468.

www.hollyfarmcottages.co.uk email: jennie.mclaren@btopenworld.com

Norfolk, countywide
The Great Escape Holiday Company*

Run by the energetic Marian Rose-Cartwright, 'The Great Escape Holiday Company' has made its name by concentrating on properties of style, most of which are used from time to time by the owners themselves.

We have looked at a number of the places they have on their books. Norfolk has an especially wide range of cottages and houses of character, and this is reflected by what's available through the agency.

The Dovecote at Docking is just ten minutes' drive from the sea, but nicely inland for peace and quiet. It's a place for a large family to get together and to get away from each other when togetherness palls. With a very big living room, an excellent, very modern kitchen and masses of space everywhere, this listed building is exceptional. It overlooks open fields, there's free use of a tennis court, a games room with table tennis, deep, squishy armchairs and much more. **Sleeps 11**, plus two cots.

Another one to note is *Holly Lodge*, another high ceilinged, recent restoration and extension of an old building, surrounded by open countryside and in its own third of an acre, highly recommended for a family or large group to get together well away from city cares. The master bedroom may be the biggest any of our inspectors has seen on their travels! **Sleeps up to 12 people.**

In Holme-next-the-Sea, *The Cottage at Tudor Lodge* (a property we know well) is quite memorable. Accessed delightfully via electronic gates off the country lane that leads to the sea, it is a sumptuous, light, bright and spacious house, **sleeping up to 5**, within the owners' extensive and secure grounds of over five acres. We liked the big open-plan living area, and admired the fine, expensively fitted kitchen. This is an example (there are a good few on the agency's books) of a delightful property in a fabulous location. We always think about how nice it is in such places when day visitors have gone and holiday tenants virtually have the place to themselves.

Properties of great character in North Norfolk, with some impressive interiors.

A Great Escape 'home from home': pretty as a picture, both inside and out.

Further details/brochures from Marian Rose-Cartwright, The Great Escape Holiday Company, The Granary, Docking, Norfolk PE31 8LY. Telephone 01485 518717. Fax 518937.

www.thegreatescapeholiday.com
email: bookings@thegreatescapeholiday.com

Norfolk and beyond
Norfolk Country Cottages*

With about 300 properties covering the whole of Norfolk and North Suffolk, this hugely successful letting agency is based just off the well-preserved market place of the attractive small town of Reepham (visitors are welcome in the office).

We have visited a number of pin-drop-quiet cottages in deeply rural inland corners of the county and some cosy and convenient cottages (and more modern houses) in the much sought after family resorts of the north coast.

Among inland villages we especially remember Aldborough, which until our visit in 2006 we'd never seen. It was 'well worth the detour', because

Woodmill Lodge is at Southrepps, near Mundesley. Sleeping 'five plus two', it's in an especially peaceful rural locaton.

Green Side Cottage is in one of our favourite villages, Thornham. Sleeping 4, it's just a short walk from the sea.

we saw the delightful *Virginia Cottage*, right on the big village green: a picture book snapshot of 'olde England'. **Sleeping 5**, it's pristine and modern inside, but altogether inviting. (the original very steep stairs remain!) We noticed among other good things stylish real-wood flooring, a wood burner and a king-sized bed.

In Reepham itself, just a few yards from where this enterprising agency is based, single-storeyed *Church View No 3* is an unexpectedly bright and light little hideaway **just for 2** owned by the antique dealers who live (and have their shop) next door. But it too is modern, not ancient, in style. A pleasant base, we thought, for the noticeable number of self caterers who like a small town or 'large village' base.

And then to an absolutely top notch recent conversion close to but completely separate from the owners' house. This is *The Old Forge* at Frettenham, near Coltishall. Done to the highest specification, it has **Five Stars** from 'Visit Britain' (we'd have thought Ten!), combining a good degree of 'cottageness' with an impressive range of mod cons. There's a very comfortable beamed sitting room, with a deep sofa and armchairs, and a really charming big kitchen/diner. **Sleeps 8.**

Details/brochure available from Norfolk Country Cottages, Carlton House, Market Place, Reepham, Norfolk NR10 4JJ. Telephone 01603 871872. Fax 870304.

You can check property details and availability online at:

www.norfolkcottages.co.uk

email: info@norfolkcottages.co.uk

Castle Acre, near King's Lynn
Heron Cottage

Castle Acre is a little gem: very much 'in Norfolk' but in the south of the county, and easy to get to. The famous coast is only about 45 minutes' drive, Sandringham say 25. In the autumn of 2006 we met the new owners here. They have transformed an already pleasant cottage, just a few feet from a fine 13th century 'bailey gate' at the heart of the historic village into a delight,

A recent upgrading of a fairly modern house in a historic location.

with for example cool cream walls, pleasant 'seagrass' matting, a top-flight kitchen-diner, a bigger than average bed in the main bedroom, a top of the range shower (there's no bath), an open fire in the sitting room that runs the central heating, plus storage radiators. There is (such a luxury in this sort of location) a lock-up garage, plus a small garden yard.

Sleeps 4 in a double and a twin. Not suitable for dogs. Linen included but not towels. Cost: about £190 to £350. Available all year; short breaks possible. Further details available from Marian Sanders: telephone (in France) 00 33 546040166.

email: marianatmoreau@hotmail.com

Castle Acre, near King's Lynn
Peddars Cottage   map 1/22

In the autumn of 2006 we revisited this cosy, rather 'traditional' cottage, used occasionally (as many readers like) by the owners themselves. Fitting well into its historic surroundings (see our photo!) the house has had an ongoing makeover that includes a refurbished and much admired honey-coloured bathroom and shower and redecorated bedrooms, with new soft furnishings. The cosy interior incorporates an

Castle Acre is just off the beaten track, and this too makes a delightful base...

open fire, repro oak furniture, a traditional 'cottage suite', old local prints, a modern fitted pine kitchen. There are attractive table and standard lamps and lots of books. There are carpets virtually throughout. TV. One pet possible. Garage. Linen and towels included. **Sleeps 6** in a double, a twin and an adult-sized two-bunk-bedroom. Cost: £300 to £350. Details: Mrs Angela Swindell, St Saviour's Rectory, St Saviour, Jersey, Channel Isles JE2 7NP. Telephone 01534 736679. Fax 727480.

www.castleacre.org also **www.castleacre.org.uk**
email: angelaswindell@googlemail.com

Burnham Thorpe
The Corner Pightle

A classic Norfolk country cottage situated – better yet – in a famous village.

There's masses of competition, but among the many peaceful, unspoilt villages of rural Norfolk Burnham Thorpe – birthplace of Lord Nelson – could well be our favourite. It's very close to Burnham Market, but half-hidden away. We recently visited this traditional, cosy, rather rambling house in pristine flint set off prettily in white and with one of those pantiled roofs that add so much to the charm of the region, about 20 minutes' drive from, say, Hunstanton and just about three miles from the famous sands at Holkham. **Sleeping up to 6** in four bedrooms, overlooking the village green towards a pub named after local-boy-made-good Lord Nelson, it has so many good things going for it, such as a safely enclosed south-west facing garden, a wood-burning stove, a downstairs bedroom for convenience, a number of original beams. As with the Hunstanton properties in the same ownership (see Page 56) it is sympathetically lit, comfortably furnished and full of tender loving care. Linen and towels included. Not suitable for dogs. Cost: about £350 to £750.

Details from Nicky and Angus Runciman, 8 Luard Rd, Cambridge CB2 2PJ. Telephone 01223 246382.

www.sunnyhunny.com email: angusrunciman@hotmail.com

Boughton Hall, near Sandringham
The Water House, South Lodge, Bunkers Hill

Houghton Hall (**map 1/27**) stands in many-acred splendour about seven miles from Royal Sandringham and about fifteen from the north coast at Holkham, Brancaster and Burnham. With two holiday cottages, one as pretty a gatehouse as you'll ever find, only recently available, this is a peaceful holiday base. Most of the time cottage guests will feel they have the vast estate, the woods and the herds of deer to themselves: delightful. The cottages themselves are real

Bunker's Hill is just one of the delightful holiday cottages on the Boughton estate.

charmers. While 'bijou', recently available *South Lodge*, **sleeping 4**, is a gem, we'd find it hard to decide – for peace and quiet and a memorable escape from everyday cares – between *Bunker's Hill* and *The Water House*. These respectively **sleep 4** and **5**. Among many memorable features we appreciated comfortable 'cottagey' interiors, a sense of colour – we love the painted wooden furniture – the 'country antiques', the well chosen lamps and pictures, the rugs – all combined with a feel for history.

See the Stately Holiday Homes feature on **Pages 22-23**.

Brancaster
Sussex Farm Holiday Cottages

Many years in this guide, the five cottages at Sussex Farm are ideally located. One reader who stayed recently thinks so. She wrote: 'We love the way you can have a day on the coast, perhaps on a sandy beach, and then leave all the crowds behind to escape to your own quiet little hideaway among the trees'. There's the detached *Park Drive*, *The Pheasantry* and *One Hundred Acre*,

Both deep in the country and near the sea.

and the semi-detached *Apple Tree* and *Beech Tree*, **sleeping 10, 8, 7, 8 and 8** respectively. They are spacious and full of character. Two are suitable for people of limited mobility. We have always found the cottages clean and tidy, with original features that add to the charm, with good carpets, microwave ovens, radio cassette players, washing machines, TVs and videos. All have dishwashers and large freezers. All have central heating *and* open fires (logs included). Linen and towels included. Dogs (one per property) welcome. Cost: about £450 to £1200. Short breaks welcome. Details/brochure from Sue Lane, 4 Stiffkey Road, Warham, Wells, Norfolk. Telephone 07885 269538 (mobile). Fax 01485 210261.

www.tbfholidayhomes.co.uk email: info@tbfholidayhomes.co.uk

Blakeney
Jenny's Cottage   map 1/28

This cottage is a rare (and inexpensive) jewel at the heart of not-to-be-missed Blakeney. It is one of the most loved places on the North Norfolk coast, notable for the beauty of the tidal shore, the walks to Blakeney Point, the birdlife, boat trips to see the seals. Comfortable holiday cottages are hard to come by here, but happily this is a small-scale, Grade II listed, flint and tiled gem (dating from 1839), with a pretty courtyard garden that in summer overflows with hollyhocks. In the heart of the village, near a welcoming pub and a well stocked shop, it is

A rare chance to stay in the centre of famous Blakeney.

ideal for a couple with a small child (a double and small single). It's full of charm and comfort: a wood burner in an inglenook fireplace, well arranged lighting. Though space is limited, the main bedroom, via steep and narrow stairs, is quite a good size, and there is even a bath (we approve) in which serious walkers can ease their aching bones. We thought this would make a good and inexpensive base for a winter holiday. Well behaved dogs are welcome. Linen and towels can be hired. TV. Non smokers only. Cost: about £200 to £350. Further details from Simon Flint, Sherwood, Sandy Lane, South Wootton, King's Lynn, Norfolk PE30 3NX. Telephone 01553 672208. **email: Simon@flint2.fsnet.co.uk**

Brancaster Staithe
Vista Cottage/Carpenter's Cottage

We have had so many enthusiastic reader reports about these two well cared for cottages, memorably situated right on the North Norfolk coast. They glow with 'tender loving care'. Each has **'Visit Britain' Three Stars**: we'd have thought Four.

In both *Vista* and *Carpenter's* you can almost reach out and touch one of the most beautiful coastlines in Britain. To be exact, you can walk down the cottage gardens right on to the salty marshes and join the coastal footpath, or make your way somewhat more directly towards the water.

From the back windows of both the properties in the ownership of the Smith family, muddy inlets dotted with yachts and fishing boats snake as prettily as in any sailor's favourite picture out towards the North Sea. Bring your binoculars!

Being on the A149 Cromer to Hunstanton coast road (mostly local or day time traffic) they are not remote or irritatingly difficult to find after a long

Vista has a big garden, unforgettable views out to sea and (it's not always the case with coastal properties) immediate access to the water. It's also very cosy...

Carpenter's (also with some marvellous views) is a pretty 'upside down' cottage for 2.

journey. There is a patio with a gas barbecue, and two good pubs nearby.

In Vista Cottage, **sleeping 6**, we met a family who were enjoying spending time in a 'family-friendly' kitchen/diner with original stone flags and excellent fittings, such as washing machine and dishwasher. There is a very cosy sitting room with open fire. On the first floor, via a steep staircase, there is a double, a twin and a bunk bedded room (adult sized). The house is well carpeted and there is plenty of heating.

Next door is Carpenter's Cottage, set back from the road by a small, safely enclosed courtyard. In the owners' family for over a hundred years, it is a delightful 'upside down' house with a sitting room/kitchen/diner on the first floor and a very cosy, 'compact' double bedded room on the ground floor. The original fireplace has been restored: a lovely focal point on an autumn or spring evening, and there is a well planned window seat from which to enjoy those fabulous views. **Sleeps 2**.

Dogs are welcome in both. Linen and towels are included. Cost: approximately £240 to £750. (Pro-rata off season short breaks are available, for a minimum of three nights.) TVs.

Details from Mrs G J Smith, Dale View, Main Road, Brancaster Staithe, King's Lynn, Norfolk PE31 8BY. Telephone/fax 01485 210497.

South Raynham, near Fakenham
Idyllic Cottages@Vere Lodge

We have stayed here from time to time, and it is always a joy: the absolute peace and quiet, the beautifully kept gardens (especially the manicured, sweeping lawns) the pristine tennis court, the 'Secret Garden', the indoor swimming pool, and more.

During a recent visit we stayed in *Pump Cottage*, a private-seeming and plushly comfortable **Four Star** delight **just for 2**. Though it has no garden, it looks on to lawns. It has a most cosy sitting room and a charming, rather 'feminine' double bedroom.

Family members staying at the same time with two small children greatly enjoyed *Honeysuckle Cottage*. Their main reason for liking it was not hard to discover: they were literally a 30-second patter of tiny wet feet from the doors of the pool!

There is a magic to this place which even the detailed and colourful brochure fails to capture. Children relish the eight acres of freedom, the company of new friends, the daily feeding-round of the many tame animals and birds. Parents can relax, knowing their young ones are safe and happy.

Vere Lodge is ideally placed for exploring. Vast sandy beaches backed by sand-dunes or pinewoods are barely twenty minutes away, as are coastal resorts which range from the picturesque to the larger, more commercial

Vere Lodge is a place for all seasons.   *Rose Cottage is handsome and relaxing.*

holiday centres. Within easy reach are dinosaur parks, steam-engine exhibitions, stately homes such as Holkham and Blickling, and scores of other attractions: one of our own favourites is the steam museum at Thursford.

An impressive leisure centre is the icing on the Vere Lodge cake. There's a large, very warm covered pool (36 feet by 18), with a shallow end with steps for children, and a slide.

There's a sauna, solarium, games room with table tennis and pool table, and a centrally heated lounge looking on to the pool. Doors open on to two grass and paved sun patios, so that on hot summer days this effectively becomes an open air pool.

There's also a small shop, a launderette and a range of home-cooked frozen foods. If you *are* considering a break between, say, October and March, you'll find the pool as warm then (80° plus) as in high summer, and all the other facilities are available.

We have always appreciated the 'little touches' – good pictures, stylish flower arrangements, pretty ornaments – which help to set Vere Lodge out of the ordinary. Not surprisingly, Vere Lodge enjoys a high tourist board grading.

Secret Garden and *The Robin's Nest* are two spacious single-storey cottages built on what was once the kitchen garden to Vere Lodge. We thought them delightful, noting especially masses of space and privacy, deep sofas, good carpets, a combination of character and comfort. Both are extremely quiet and secluded with about half an acre each of garden, mainly lawn, surrounded by high flint walls. They **sleep 6** in three bedrooms – one double, two twins – and have an impressive lounge with an open fire. They are approached via Church Lane, a narrow and barely-used lane which forms the southern boundary to Vere Lodge and leads only to the tiny church and former rectory. On the other side of the lane lie the leisure centre and the seven acre grounds.

The other properties are more part of the Vere Lodge 'family'. *Apple Cottage* is a spacious and entirely self-contained ground-floor apartment, plush and comfortable, which faces on to a large landscaped courtyard. Suitable for retired couples, young couples with a baby, or the elderly or partially disabled. **Sleeps 3**. *Dahlia* and *Thyme* are two cottages which face west over fields of corn or bright yellow mustard. They therefore enjoy not only lovely views but also all the afternoon and evening sun. This is particularly true of Thyme, an 'upside-down' cottage, with a large upstairs living room, while Dahlia has the advantage of an upstairs en-suite bathroom. **Both sleep 6**. Both have their own sitting-out patios.

Apple, suitable for the partially disabled.   *Children and animals are welcome here.*

The Dolls House is a small, simple 'budget' cottage, the ground floor of which was once a part of a gun room. Complete with huge doll, it looks out over lawns to the horseshoe of beeches and flowering cherries beyond. It is warm, comfortable and compact. **Sleeps 4**. *Dove Cottage* is furnished to a standard not generally found in a holiday cottage. It has panoramic views of the grounds, woods, and surrounding countryside from the upstairs living room which opens on to its own completely private roof-terrace. We very much like the cool, soft, grey blue ambiance, and the open fireplace. **Sleeps 2 plus 2**. *Garden Wing* is undoubtedly the most popular of all the cottages: ground-floor through-out, it is especially suitable for the disabled. The large and elegant sitting-room looks out over the croquet lawn to woodland beyond. **Sleeps 4**. *Lavender Cottage*, large and west facing, once housed coaches and a harness room. It is a long raised-level cottage, outside which is a large terrace screened by a hedge, with a flight of steps up to the front door.

It's furnished in log-cabin style, but to standards such as original log-cabins never enjoyed with, for example, carpets on polished wood floors. **Sleeps 6**. *Possum's*, once a full-size billiard-room, is a spacious and unusual apartment called after Miss 'Possum' Smith, who cared for the Bowlby children for over thirty years. Tall Georgian windows face on to formal yew-hedges and flower borders flood-lit by night. **Sleeps 3**. *Pump Cottage* was purpose-built and 'incorporates the lessons learned from 25 years' experience of self-catering'. All the accommodation is on the ground floor and is suitable for the elderly or partially disabled. Open fire-place here too. **Sleeps 2**. *Rose Cottage*, the largest of all the cottages, is south-facing and therefore very sunny, with its own private walled garden. It is bright and airy, with deep, comfy armchairs and sofa, an open fire and a downstairs shower and loo. **Sleeps 7**. *Rowan* and *Honeysuckle* are an identical pair of 19th century cottages. An unusual feature is the central fireplace, raised for the protection of young children, with a log-burning fire facing into the lounge and behind it an electric fire to warm the dining room. Both are furnished in 'country-style', with a raised south-facing terrace in front of each.

Among the many things they do so well at Vere Lodge are short breaks in autumn, winter, spring or early summer. To enhance that 'baby it's cold outside' mood, several cottages have open fires. Better yet, prices even in these very comfortable properties for a three-day break – starting or finishing on any day of the week – can be as low as £18 per night per person (6 persons), which includes the use of the leisure centre.

Vere Lodge is something of an animal sanctuary, too, delightful for young

Lavender Cottage once housed coaches.

The most popular cottage is Garden Wing.

children. At feeding time (9.00 am daily) there are freshly-laid eggs to be gathered, often from under an indignant hen. In the centre paddock, tame and gentle miniature Angora goats stand on their hind legs against the fence awaiting their turn, while Mingo the donkey, and Toby the docile pony, await theirs.

Children will also love the Enchanted Wood. We certainly do, but we won't spoil the surprise!

Dogs are welcome, and remote-control videos, televisions and clock radios are standard throughout. Details and a copy of an impressive full colour brochure from Vere Lodge, South Raynham, near Fakenham, Norfolk NR21 7HE. Telephone 01328 838261. Fax 838300.

www.verelodge.co.uk
email: major@verelodge.co.uk

Bylaugh, near East Dereham
Bylaugh Hall Holiday Homes

Deep in rural Norfolk, Bylaugh lies amid unspoiled farmland. Here the restoration of a fine country house is hand in hand with the creation to a superb standard of substantial self-catering properties. We're bowled over by the quality of the work and the enthusiasm of the owners. Large groups can stay, yet smaller parties have privacy. To appreciate the range and quality of accommodation, look

A fabulous base from which to explore deeply rural inland Norfolk...

on the website for *The Coachman's Lodge, The Brewery, The Stables, The Smithy, The Courtyard Mews, The Front Mews* and, separate from the others, *The Manor,* a superb modern house that **sleeps up to 17**, *Old Heath House* (**sleeps 17**) and *The Oaks* cottages. Individual houses taken together can accommodate groups of up to 80. Note the splendid main hall and Orangery for a super wedding, party or conference venue. Adjoining the main hall and Orangery, the new Wintergarden restaurant is perfect for those who wish to take a night off self catering!

Details from Bylaugh Hall, Bylaugh Park, East Dereham, Norfolk NR20 4RL. Telephone 01362 688121. Fax 08701623993.

www.littlebigben.com or www.bylaugh.com email: info@bylaugh.com

Tunstead, near Wroxham   Colour section A, Page 1
Old Farm Cottages map 1/34

In the summer of 2005 we revisited (via quiet, ever more rural country lanes) these beautifully converted and painstakingly run former barns. They make a fairly central point in rural Norfolk from which to explore the Broads – Wroxham, for example, is close – the exquisite North Norfolk coast, the more family-orientated east, the city of Norwich itself, and even

Peaceful Norfolk is all around, but the coast and the Broads are handy...

more beyond. A number of readers have commented on how much they enjoy the covered indoor pool at the end of a day's touring. This excellent pool is set off nicely by a gym, a spa, a solarium and a games room. Each of the six properties has its own enclosed patio and barbecue. There's a high degree of privacy in these spacious, pristinely cared-for conversions, but children also have the chance to make new friends. **Sleep 2 to 6**. Linen included, towels for hire. Dogs welcome in most. Cost: from (short breaks) £252 to (full weeks) £465 to £867. **'Visit Britain' Four Stars**.

For details, telephone 01692 536612.

www.oldfarmcottages.com   email: mail@oldfarmcottages.fsnet.co.uk

Hunstanton, Brancaster and beyond
Norfolk Holiday Homes*

This much admired – even much loved – agency has featured in our guide every year without a break since our first edition in 1983. In (yes!) 25 years we have never once had any kind of complaint, have visited and revisited many times, have stayed in several properties, and never seen a dud. This would be admirable in a private cottage set-up – in an agency of any size it is a remarkable accolade.

Norfolk Holiday Homes specialises in the north west corner of the county: fine sandy beaches, tranquil villages, lonely church towers, the traditional seaside resort of Hunstanton, excellent bird watching and much more. We know from our correspondence that many readers have discovered this delightful county, which never disappoints, through the agency.

During a recent visit we were very impressed by *Courtyard Cottage* and *Norfolk House* in the quiet, just-inland village of Docking. With lots of evidence of the absolute dedication of the owners, far beyond the normal requirements, and their good taste and an eye for detail, the **Five Star** property (you can take them as one or separately) is, simply, stunning. **Sleeping respectively 5 and 4**, together they make a memorable holiday home **for 9 people**.

There are several properties in Old Hunstanton, which has all the advantages of a slightly old fashioned seaside atmosphere with easy access not only to a glorious sandy beach of its own but also to the bright lights of the lively 'family resort' of Hunstanton-proper, with its new pier. There are clean, bright modern houses (which always have a certain following) and others with a more 'cottagey' style.

Spindrift for example, is literally a minute's walk from the beach, and also pubs, restaurants and shops. There is a pretty, enclosed courtyard garden as a bonus, and the property **sleeps 5 'plus 1'** (there is a king size double in the main bedroom). *Sandbanks* is a superb, large, detached family residence (**sleeping 8,** on the outskirts of the town in a very desirable area, yet

Norfolk House, in Docking, has one of the most stylish interiors we know. We are not surprised it has Five Stars.

The Old Coastguard Lookout is an extraordinary place: you'll have to get your booking in early!

within easy reach of the cliff tops and the beach). There are rural views from the front and distant sea views from the rear first floor rooms.

Ashdale House is an exceptionally comfortable detached house tucked away in quiet surroundings, but still close to the beach, golf course and other holiday amenities. The garden is fully enclosed and there is ample parking. Furnished to a very high standard throughout, the property offers spacious accommodation **for 7 people**.

Finally, but still only scratching the surface, *The Old Coastguard Lookout*, overlooking the clifftops near the lighthouse, has been thoughtfully restored since it was built in 1906 as a Marconi Wireless Station. It has associations with both World Wars, was once a maritime museum and spent its 'last years' as the Coastguard Lookout. It has unique accommodation on three storeys, and enjoys superb, uninterrupted panoramic views of the Wash and the coast. There is immediate access to the wide sandy beaches that make this one of the most popular resorts in the east of England, but you are well away from the brasher part of the town, with its fish and chip shops and amusement arcades. **Sleeps 3**.

Linzel Cottage is a superb, 17th century, chalk and brick cottage just off the village green at Thornham, which has been tastefully restored to a very high standard to reveal its original beauty and charm. **Sleeping 6**, the accommodation incorporates a galleried hall and landing, bathrooms with cast iron baths, Yorkstone flooring and terracotta floor in the kitchen plus a multitude of other interesting features. Not to be missed!

It's worth remembering – especially if you don't already know Norfolk – that even a cottage that on the map appears to be well inland is probably just a few minutes' drive from the coast. Some coast! The wide sandy beaches, typically set off by pine trees, are remarkable, but everyone comments on how quiet they are even at the height of the season.

There is lots going to appeal to the whole family: children will especially like the entertainments at Thursford, the North Norfolk steam-railway, and the narrow gauge railway that puffs through idyllic, unspoiled pastureland between Wells-next-the-Sea and Walsingham.

Dogs are welcome in over half the properties on the agency's books, and several cottages have open fires, which can be the makings of an autumn or winter break. Also, short breaks and discounts may be available. All properties are inspected and graded by 'Visit Britain', and a number have ground floor accommodation suitable for disabled people.

Ashdale House, in Old Hunstanton, is exceptionally comfortable. It is close to the beach and the golf course.

We have stayed in Linzel Cottage (see also Page 56). It is a real charmer, and sleeps six 'plus baby'.

An exceptionally good brochure, fully illustrated in colour, is available from Sandra Hohol, Norfolk Holiday Homes, 62 Westgate, Hunstanton, Norfolk PE36 5EL. Telephone 01485 534267/fax 535230.

www.norfolkholidayhomes-birds.co.uk
email: shohol@birdsnorfolkholidayhomes.co.uk

Horning (Norfolk Broads)
Little River View

Of all the bustling villages that are a focal point for visitors to the Norfolk Broads (it's not all lonely creeks and wildfowl-haunted marshes), our own favourite is Horning. And at its very heart, opposite a 100 year old pub of character and handy for a range of village shops, stands a pretty, charming cottage that – always a good sign – is occasionally used by the owners themselves. We noted two comfy, deep sofas in the very cosy sitting room, a 'proper' bath in the (downstairs) bathroom, a spacious double and twin bedroom on the first floor, an inviting kitchen/diner. This is one of those places in which the owners' concern for their guests'

As neat and pretty a cottage as we've seen in East Anglia.

comfort is apparent, with, for example, books, games, information folders, etc. Note too that landlubbers may hire a day boat nearby to get a flavour of life on the Broads. This is a rarity in such a sought-after location! **Sleeps 4.** TV/video/DVD. River views. Not suitable for pets. Cost: about £219 to £539. Short breaks. Linen, towels and gas/electricity included. No smoking. Details from Victoria Free. Telephone 07801 288822 or 07759 125919.

www.littleriverview.co.uk   email: info@littleriverview.co.uk

Horning (Norfolk Broads) map 1/35
Riverside Rentals

Any thatched cottage in Norfolk will be sought-after by self-caterers. Put it right by the water in the Norfolk Broads, and people will go into raptures. *Box End* (**sleeps 6 'plus 2'**) and *Willow Fen* (**sleeps 6 'plus 2'**) are two thatched beauties (Box End is pretty enough to feature on our cover!) within a quartet of properties in the same ownership; the other two are *Willow Lodge* (**sleeps 8 'plus 2'**) and *Little Wiluna*, which is a

Delightfully, all the properties enjoy substantial riverside frontages...

smaller property within the grounds of Wiluna, a fine, imposing riverside property. Add to all their considerable charms the fact that the three principal properties have substantial river frontages, moorings – day boats can easily be hired locally – and gardens, and that they all have light, bright airy rooms, and you have places 'worth the detour'. Also, pets are welcome by arrangement in the three biggest properties, and each has bath *and* shower.

Linen is included. TV and DVD. Cost: about £215 to £1450. Details from Grebe Island Leisure, Wiluna, Ferry Cott Lane, Horning, Norfolk NR12 8PP. Telephone/fax 01692 631549.

www.riverside-rentals.co.uk
email: riverside@riverside-rentals.co.uk

Clippesby (Norfolk Broads National Park)
Clippesby Holiday Cottages

With country views and a wheelchair ramp to the sun deck (**sleep 6**), there are three excellent *Pinelodges* in a woodland setting. We also like the quiet bungalows that overlook fields (two **sleep 4,** two **sleep 6**), and have admired two larger cottages (each **sleeps 8**) along with the two-storeyed *Clocktower Apartments* (**sleeping 4**) with first-floor sundecks looking on to well tended gardens. There's a heated

In the country but not far from the sea...

open air pool, grass tennis courts, a family bar/restaurant serving evening meals, play areas, a small shop and coffee shop and an 18-hole mini-golf course. TVs, central heating and bed-linen; some have open fires too. (Tucked away among trees in a different landscaped area is a **'Visit Britain' Four Star** touring park, with the David Bellamy Gold Award for Conservation.) **'Visit Britain' Four Stars**. Cost: from £235 to £949, including bed-linen, electricity and heating oil. Colour brochure: the Lindsay family, Clippesby Hall, Clippesby, Norfolk NR29 3BL. Telephone 01493 367800; fax 367809.

www.clippesby.com or **www.discoverthebroads.com**
email: holidays@clippesby.com

Stanhoe, near Burnham Market   map 1/31
Post Office Cottage

From Docking, they said, look out for the cottage on the left just after the duck pond. Some duck pond! It's huge, a real eye-opener. But so is Post Office Cottage (Ref CSL) – a real gem in fact. It was originally three cottages, which always makes for an interesting interior. End-on to the road, therefore nice and quiet, with a garden and enclosed parking, we thought it a family house of great

An increasingly rare example of a 'traditional cottage', and super inside.

character. We liked the original paintings, the very comfortable sitting room, with open fire, that looks out on to the garden, and the charming kitchen-diner, with woodburner – not 'last word', but all the more attractive for that. Very usefully, there's a double room (zip-link six-foot wide bed: excellent), at ground floor level plus a bunk bedded room. Upstairs there are two very cosy double bedrooms, one of which charmingly has its own staircase from the ground floor, and a twin. **Sleeps 8 'plus 2'** in total.

Details from English Country Cottages, Stoney Bank Road, Earby, Barnoldswick BB94 0AA. For bookings and brochures, telephone 0870 197 6890.

www.english-country-cottages.co.uk

Norfolk Coast
Sowerbys Holiday Cottages*

Readers have consistently spoken well of this medium-sized agency of about 90 properties, based in sought-after Burnham Market. During 2006 we called to look at a handful of places that had caught our eye, including the irresistible *Coastguards' Cottage* in Thornham (**sleeps 10**). It's in an idyllic position on the village green *and* overlooks the marshes and the sea! At Holme-next-the-Sea we thought *Hope Cottage*, **sleeping 2**,

We absolutely fell for Coastguards! It's in an enviable spot, and most inviting.

and also near the water, an exquisite recent conversion. It's at the end of a tiny lane but is still within the village. In so-chic Burnham Market itself we were much impressed by brand new *Orchard House*, **sleeping 10**, in a leafy enclave on the edge of the village, and, just off the main street but very quiet, a superb 'hideaway' used from time to time by the owners themselves (which our readers like) called *Aviaries Barn*, **sleeping 2.** Details from Sowerby's Holiday Cottages, Market Place, Burnham Market, Norfolk PE31 8HD. Telephone 01328 730880, fax 730522.

www.sowerbysholidaycottages.co.uk
email info@sowerbysholidaycottages.co.uk

Wiveton, near Blakeney
Bones Cottage map 1/38

During a 2005 visit to the north Norfolk coast we made sure to revisit this charming place, **just for 2 people**. In a blissfully quiet and peaceful setting, it is only about ten minutes' very pleasant walk from the hauntingly beautiful saltmarshes at Cley and twenty minutes from the quay at exquisite Blakeney. There is also a good pub just a short walk away. The owners' home (bed and breakfast also available) is adjacent,

Private, inexpensive, close to one of the best parts of the coast. One reader called it 'a little piece of old England'...

but the cottage feels very private. There is a neat, rather cosy kitchen/diner, a shower-room and, in short, a charming atmosphere. Among other details we liked the big window that seems to light up the whole cottage. It looks on to the front garden and gets the sun all day long. Note too that the cottage has its own driveway. Altogether, we thought *Bones* would make an excellent base from which to enjoy the coast, and it is notably inexpensive. Bed-linen is provided.

Small TV. Not suitable for dogs. Cost: about £230 to £300. Further details from Mrs Stocks, Bones Cottage, Hall Lane, Wiveton, Holt, Norfolk NR25 7TG. Telephone 01263 740840.

Holt
No 6 Carpenters Cottages

In this guide for 25 years, with never a complaint! Conveniently situated, this most attractive flint and pantiled terraced cottage lies close to the centre of Holt, a small Georgian town of character. There are good pubs and restaurants, two department stores, antique shops and two fishmongers – good for local crabs! Best

A cosy, very convenient town house that is only twenty minutes from the exceptional North Norfolk coast.

of all is the easy access to the coast (delightful Blakeney is only about ten minutes away) and to such attractions as Felbrigg, Blickling and Holkham Hall. There's a well-equipped kitchen and a bright sitting/dining room, informal, comfortable and altogether inviting, opening on to a secluded walled garden area. The cottage is often used by the owners themselves, and its good standards reflect this fact. We spotted well chosen local pictures, books, including a number about Norfolk, board games and puzzles. The cottage **sleeps 3** in a good-sized twin room and a smallish single.

Cost: about £165 to £345. Small, well behaved dogs are welcome. Further details are available from Mrs Sally Beament, 36 Avranches Avenue, Crediton, Devon EX17 2HB. Telephone 01363 773789.

email: sallybeament@hotmail.com

Holt   map 1/41
Sunnyside Cottage

Also in Holt, just a fifteen minute drive from the North Norfolk coast, this quite excellent and reasonably priced cottage is pleasantly tucked away in a quiet mews. Dating from the 1880s, it's light, bright and spacious, furnished to a high standard in Victorian style but with modern comforts. We endorse the enthusiastic comments sent in by some of our readers: 'Beautifully furnished and equipped'...'immaculate and spotless'...'excellent colour schemes' ...'beds made up with excellent linen – better than I have at home!'...'gorgeous, polished

A very special place indeed, with the rare advantage of being in an inland town with easy access to the coast.

wood floors'. The owners have spent much time working to make Sunnyside Cottage the welcoming haven it is.

Sleeps 5 in a double and two other bedrooms. TV, video, radio, CD player, books and games. Heating, electricity and bedlinen included, but bring your own towels. Stay for as short or long a period as you wish. Cost: reasonable, from under £200 to £380 per week. Not suitable for pets. Details from Michael Drake, Broadland House, Station New Road, Brundall, Norwich, Norfolk NR13 5PQ. Telephone/fax 01603 712524.

email: michael.drake@ukgateway.net

Hunstanton
Northernhay/Highland House

Northernhay is one of our own all-time seaside favourites, a super family house in the 'traditional' resort of Hunstanton: amusement arcades, fish and chips, children running free on a super sandy beach. Parts of the town are quite chic, with good golf, cosy pubs and fine family houses that have easy access to the sands. A

Northernhay is one of the handsomest houses in what is known affectionately as 'Sunny Hunny' – see website details...

spacious and sunny Edwardian villa within a cliff-top conservation area, Northernhay has lots of original features, a conservatory and some bedrooms from which you can see the sea. Most usefully **sleeping 10** in four double bedrooms and a children's double-bunk room, it has a neat garden and secure parking for two cars. *Highland House*, with gardens front and back, is equally full of character and style. Also **sleeping 10** (in six bedrooms: two doubles, two twins and two singles) it combines a number of original features with modern comforts, such as a part-'island' kitchen with glass-fronted cupboard doors and two sumptuous family bathrooms. Linen and bath towels are included. Not suitable for pets. Cost: £375 to £875. Details from Nicky and Angus Runciman, 8 Luard Road, Cambridge CB2 2PJ. Telephone 01223 246382.
www.sunnyhunny.com   email: angusrunciman@hotmail.com

Thornham, near Brancaster   map 1/46
Linzel Cottage

A feather in the cap of the outstanding cottage letting agency Norfolk Holiday Homes, this is a delight. We have stayed here – an autumn break – and remember so many good things about it: the cosy double-aspect 'Smallbone' kitchen/diner, the small but charming dining room, the comfortable sitting room, with a woodburner. There are three

A warm and welcoming family cottage.

bedrooms: a double, a twin and pair of bunk beds. There's a small, enclosed sun-trap garden, a garage and plenty of parking outside the cottage in the lane. (Thornham gets a fair bit of through-traffic on the very scenic A149, but Linzel lies quietly up a little lane off that road.) The village-proper effectively starts about a hundred yards away, and via that one comes to the delightful old village green, from which there is footpath access to the marshes and, beyond, the sea. 'Visit Britain' **Four Stars**.
* We can recommend the nearby Orange Tree restaurant (a converted pub).
Norfolk Holiday Homes, 62 Westgate, Hunstanton, Norfolk PE36 5EL. Telephone 01485 534267/fax 535230.

**www.norfolkholidayhomes-birds.co.uk
email: shohol@birdsnorfolkholidayhomes.co.uk**

Norfolk – countywide
Countryside Cottages*

Is this the best of both worlds? This family-run business takes in both the glorious North and West Norfolk coast as well as the tranquil interior of the county. It has on its books some of the most eye-catching properties in this miraculously unspoilt and uncrowded corner of England. It includes snug and romantic retreats and quiet hideaways such as the *Old*

Owl Cottage is a North Norfolk classic, fitting so well into its surroundings.

Bakehouse at Bale, **sleeping 4**, and beach-side houses such as *Smugglers* at Thornham, which commands breathtaking views and **sleeps up to 10**. Also at Thornham, *Admiral's Lodge* **sleeps up to 9**. A good proportion have open fires or woodburning stoves, and notable views. Some accept dogs. Staying in any of the personally selected, exceptionally stylish cottages is such a civilised way to plan visits to Norfolk's historic houses, market towns, salt marshes, pine fringed sandy beaches and idyllic rural villages.

For further information contact: Countryside Cottages, 5 Old Stable Yard, Holt, Norfolk NR25 6BN. Telephone 01263 713133. Fax 711877.

www.countryside-cottages.com email: ccottages@dialstart.net

Wells next the Sea
Chantry   map 1/47

With easy access to some of the most beautiful parts of the North Norfolk coast, 'Wells' is a small family resort with real character and lots to do. In the heart of the town, but tucked well away from sight and much bigger inside than one would imagine, as well as more imposing from the outside, we thought this delightful: not a show-house, but a practical and welcoming family home on three storeys. It has bags of character, and has been most sympathetically renovated and upgraded by the owners. We liked so many things: the small enclosed 'courtyard' garden, with many flowers and shrubs, the sense of history (it dates in part from the 17th century), the impressive amount of space – a lovely big landing, bathroom and

Notably quiet, though it's in the heart of the little town...

dining room, for example – the original details, such as a rare brass *single* bed in one room, plus some old pine.

Duvets or blankets available. **Sleeps up to 7**. Not suitable for pets. Linen and towels by arrangement. Cost: approximately £200 to £500. Details from Mrs V Jackson, 3a Brickendon Lane, Brickendon, near Hertford, Hertfordshire SG13 8NU. Telephone/fax 01992 511303.

Norwich
Dowager's Cottage (The Old Rectory Hotel)

Just two and a half miles from Norwich, but seemingly out in the country...

Within the mature garden of this highly regarded country house style hotel, this inviting cottage looks directly on to the heated outdoor pool (summer months), enjoys the advantages of self-contained living and immediate access to the hotel and its award-winning restaurant. Just for 2 (double bedroom), we thought it particularly cosy, with a combined sitting room/dining room, compact but fully fitted kitchen, bathroom with bath (shower over) and downstairs cloakroom. Most usefully, there's a direct dial link to the hotel; you can also use the wireless broadband connection. **Sleeps 2**. Weekly bookings: Saturday to Saturday. Non-smoking. No children (under 18) or pets. Cost: about £255 to £350. Gas central heating (included). English breakfast and dinner can be booked in the hotel. Shorts breaks available October to March. Details from Chris Entwistle, The Old Rectory, 103 Yarmouth Road, Thorpe St Andrew, Norwich NR7 0HF. Telephone 01603 700772. Fax 01603 300772.

www.dowagerscottage.co.uk
email: enquiries@oldrectorynorwich.com

Norwich   map 1/48
The Moorings

We visited in 2006, but didn't get as far as testing the cabin cruiser!

Norwich is a visitor-friendly city, and the Norfolk Broads are a must-see for people holidaying in the county. So the idea of a detached riverside holiday cottage just five miles by road from the city centre and a leisurely 50 minutes via the River Yare is something of note. For a four-berth cabin cruiser – a first for us – *comes with the property*. The cottage, which we saw in 2006, only became available in the autumn of 2005, and, being used from time by the owners (always a good indicator) is especially comfortable. For example, the master bedroom has a king-sized bed, there is an open fire in the sitting room and a pool/snooker table in the games room. There are fine landscaped gardens, with a barbecue terrace overlooking the River Yare and secluded rear garden complete with open air hot tub. Plus – of course – the joy of that easy-to-handle cabin cruiser.

Sleeps up to 10. Not suitable for pets. Linen/towels included. Widescreen TV/VCR/DVD/Sky. Also Playstation 2.

www.bythebroads.com   email: ask@bythebroads.com

Cambridgeshire/Lincolnshire/ Nottinghamshire

In our opinion these three counties represent one of eastern and middle England's best kept secrets. We're fond of Cambridgeshire (that exquisite 'city within a university', the vast skies above the Fens, the stark beauty of Ely cathedral), Lincolnshire (the endless sandy beaches, its own great cathedral at Lincoln, the usually deserted Wolds) and Nottinghamshire (deep, dark Sherwood forest, grand stately homes, memories of perhaps our finest novelist, D H Lawrence). Indeed, one of Lawrence's childhood homes is, against all the odds, available as a holiday home. In this corner of England, very soon after you leave main roads you are surrounded by quiet, rural, low key landscapes dotted with small market towns and sleepy villages. We think of Stamford, and marvellous Burghley House on its outskirts; of the genteel but not stuffy little town of Woodhall Spa, of climbing to the top of Boston Stump for marvellous panoramic views. On the coast, 'bracing' Skegness has a certain chic, and the RSPB reserve at nearby Gibraltar Point has an unforgettable atmosphere.

Denton, near Stilton (Cambridgeshire)
Orchard Cottage map 1/49

People who appreciate the classic picture-book country cottage will find this idyllic. Full of character and style (it's well out of earshot of any main roads, but easy to get to), it combines a powerful sense of the past with lots of comfort and warmth. It's like something from an idealised landscape painting by artists of 'the Norwich School'. In a historic part of 'the Shires' (peaceful stone villages, pubs with log fires,

Well away from main roads but actually quite accessible and not remote, this is one of our all-time favourite finds...

perhaps the ghostly echo of a hunting horn), Orchard is a rare example of a sympathetically converted 18th century cottage. In a half acre garden (with croquet), opposite a farm, with fields on three sides and farmland views, it is used from time to time by the owner herself, and is well planned, very comfortable and, in brief, a highly desirable holiday base. Much of the furniture is antique, and even the large bathroom has Victorian fittings; there is an open fireplace in the sitting room and a well appointed kitchen of character which leads into a conservatory. With a deep pond in the garden, this is unsuitable for small children. Dogs accepted by arrangement with the owner. **Sleeps 6**.

Linen and towels are included. Also a plentiful supply of wood and coal. Cost: about £450 to £950. Further details from Jenny Higgo, 22 Stocks Hill, Manton, Oakham, Rutland. Telephone 01572 737420.

www.higgo.com/orchard
email: orchard@higgo.com

Welton-le-Wold, near Louth
Stubbs Cottages

We've stayed in one of the Stubbs properties, namely *Foreman's Cottage*, and it has become a real favourite. **Sleeping 7**, it is located on a high lying part of the family farm, and has fine views. It's spacious and warm, and although it's a not a traditional roses-round-the-door place, it's really 'nice to come home to'. All the Stubbs cottages, in this guide without a break for over 20 years, have a lasting reputation for being

Foreman's Cottage, deep in the Lincolnshire Wolds, is warm, comfy and surprisingly spacious. And as with all the Stubbs cottages, it is reasonably priced.

clean, nicely situated and *very reasonably priced*. They are located in the hilly, wooded Lincolnshire Wolds (where good self-catering accommodation is rather thin on the ground). Among other properties there is, in the nearby off-the-beaten-track village of Welton-le-Wold, *The Old Schoolhouse*, **sleeping 6** and dating from the 19th century. Dogs are welcome. Cost: (approximately) £250 to £395. A useful sketch map of Lincolnshire (so you don't miss the best beaches and resorts) is incorporated in the details, available from Margaret Stubbs, C V Stubbs and Sons, Manor Warren Farm, Welton-le-Wold, near Louth, Lincolnshire LN11 0QX. Telephone/fax 01507 604207.

Fulstow, near Louth
Bramble and Hawthorn

We revisited in 2005 and appreciated, as we have for many years, the 'tender loving care' these charming single storeyed cottages exude. This part of Lincolnshire is a place of vast skies and near-empty roads, and there's easy access to the green and rolling Wolds. These (**map 1/58**) are

Deep in the country but handy for the sea.

just 20 minutes from the sea, and there's a water-sports centre a mile away. Both *Bramble* and *Hawthorn* overlook a paved, gravelled 'courtyard'. There are good-sized open plan sitting rooms with cosy coal-effect fires, spacious bathrooms, and well designed bedrooms (each has a double and twin, though Hawthorn can take 2 extra on a double sofa-bed, therefore **sleeping up to 6**). You'll find fresh flowers, a welcome tray and chilled wine. The 'Information Centre' stocks maps, books and guides, with a video library. Linen and towels included. Non smoking. Children over ten welcome. Not suitable for dogs. Cost: from about £160 for a three-night break to £370 per week, high season. Details: Cheryl and Paul Tinker, Waingrove Country Cottages, Fulstow, near Louth, Lincolnshire LN11 0XQ. Telephone: 01507 363704.

www.lincolnshirecottages.com   email: ptinker.tinkernet@virgin.net

Louth
'All Seasons'

Louth is a special place, a fine English market town, its history and character intact. It's a great base for exploring the underrated county of Lincolnshire. So it's appropriate that these centrally situated apartments, already rejoicing in their 'Visit Britain' **Five Star** status, should have *won the 2006-2007 Gold Award for*

Sumptuously comfortable interiors within a fine Grade II listed property...

the Self Catering Holiday of the Year in the East Midlands. We ourselves visited in 2006, admiring the neat and tidy yard into which guests drive, the well planned interiors of the four stylish, even rather elegant apartments. Within the original pair of Grade II listed Georgian terrace houses, each apartment offers top notch accommodation for **2 to 4 people.** All have superb up to date kitchens with dishwasher, microwave, fridge and freezer, bathrooms with bath *and* shower or shower attachment, co-ordinated bed-linen and soft furnishings, all with elegant *original* Victorian or Georgian fireplaces; CD player, VCR/DVD and widescreen TV. Cost: about £295 to £595. Shorter stays available. Not suitable for pets. Details from Amanda and Adrian Budd, All Seasons Holidays, 140-142 Eastgate. Louth, Lincolnshire LN11 9AA. Telephone 01507 604470. Fax 602026. **www.allseasonsuk.com   email: enquiries@allseasonsuk.com**

Langwith, near Mansfield   map 1/60
Blue Barn Cottage

This delightful family house on a mixed 450-acre farm near historic Sherwood Forest is a favourite of ours. (It has featured in this guide for many years.) It's close to the farm-house at the end of a mile-long track from the village, yet very accessible, being only 15 minutes' drive from the M1 (junction 30). A cosy sitting room – all is very quiet here – with TV leads on to the dining room.

This quiet and spacious house is one of our personal long-term favourites...

Upstairs there is a double bedroom, a family room with a double and two singles, a twin room with cot and a small twin room, all opening off the landing. **'Visit Britain' Three Stars.** There is a large garden and barbe-cue. Cost: from a very reasonable £450, which includes all linen, towels, central heating and a 'welcome pack' of provisions. There is a big kitchen/breakfast room with Rayburn, electric cooker, microwave, fridge, and an extra downstairs toilet/shower. Not suitable for dogs. Further details, together with a colour leaflet, from June Ibbotson, Blue Barn Farm, Langwith, Nottinghamshire NG20 9JD. Telephone/fax 01623 742248.

email: bluebarnfarm@supanet.com

Yorkshire and The Peak District

It says a lot about the many charms of Yorkshire that of all the English counties, this is apparently the one whose inhabitants are most likely to holiday within their own county boundaries. The county's pride in its history and its landscapes is quite touching. There's ancient York itself, and comparatively unsung East Yorkshire, embracing such little known places as the quiet village of Lund and elegant Beverley. There are the renovated mills and industrial museums of West Yorkshire – whose rugged countryside has a charm of its own. And there are of course the better-known Yorkshire Dales and the North York Moors, as well as the North Yorkshire coast.

From the North York Moors, narrow roads lead to secret seaside resorts such as Robin Hood's Bay and Staithes. Nearby Whitby and Scarborough have their own character, but the real pleasure is seeking out little-known sandy coves and silent valleys among the dales and moors.

The best of Derbyshire and Staffordshire is contained within yet another National Park: the Peak District National Park is the longest-established in Britain, and attracts more visitors than any other, but on the whole this region's gritty but picturesque villages and great houses are little known among southerners.

York   map 3/69
York Lakeside Lodges

You'd think you were in the depths of the country rather than two miles from York.

It's great to be just two miles here from the historic heart of ancient York but seemingly in the country. It's a well planned, tranquil place, in which fourteen Scandinavian timber lodges stand (with lots of privacy) on the fringes of a large lake jumping with coarse fish. The fishing is one of the charms of the place: another is its location, with coaches going to the York centre every ten minutes, and a nearby 24-hour Tesco's. Four lodges are **'Visit Britain' Five Stars** (very private, with fine views): two with one bedroom, one with two bedrooms and one with three bedrooms; the others are **Four Stars**. Winner of a Yorkshire White Rose Award for tourism, and equipped to high standards, all are well insulated and double glazed: good for autumn and winter breaks. Options include one, two and three bedroom detached lodges, one bedroom semi-detached lodges, and one and three bedroom cottages at the rear of the owners' house. **Sleep 2 to 7**. Cost: £205 to £710 (and an admirable £98 for a two-night break in winter). Dogs welcome. Brochure from Mr Manasir, York Lakeside Lodges, Moor Lane, York YO24 2QU. Telephone 01904 702346. Fax 701631.

www.yorklakesidelodges.co.uk email: neil@yorklakesidelodges.co.uk

Sawdon, near Scarborough
Sawdon Country Cottages

We love driving via winding country lanes from, say, Pickering or Brompton towards the North York Moors. Without needing to be really remote, you are quickly away from bumper-to-bumper holiday traffic and in deepest rural North Yorkshire. One of our all-time favourite villages is Sawdon,: comfortably hilly, a nice mixture of old cottages in varying

In a quiet village, this is lovely stuff, plus a shared garden with wide-ranging views.

styles, a sense of community, a good pub. Right at the centre of the village (but quiet) are four absolutely charming, very comfortable cottages: we noticed inviting deep sofas, lots of books, well chosen pictures. Two cottages (*Sheila's* and *Middle House*) back on to the village street, and face a pleasant courtyard; the other two (*The Owlery* and *Ivy*) are at right angles to the others, and also look out on to the courtyard. A nice arrangement.

'Visit Britain' **Four Stars**. **Sleep from 2 to 5**. Dogs are possible by arrangement. Cost: about £205 to £510. Short breaks. Details from Jenny Worsley, Kirkgate Lodge, Sawdon, near Scarborough, North Yorkshire YO13 9DU. Telephone 01723 859794. Fax 01723 859144.

www.sawdoncottages.co.uk   email:jenny@sawdoncottages.co.uk

Brompton-by-Sawdon, nr Scarborough
Headon Farm Cottages

We get a buzz from following the no-through-road up to this group of cottages. Skilfully converted from 19th century farm buildings, Headon Farm Cottages (**map 3/76**) are handy for Scarborough and the Moors. *Byre* for example has a kitchen/diner and lounge/diner with plush sofa and chairs, from which open stairs lead up to a double and a twin bedroom with cot. *Barn* is similar, also with

Quiet but not remote, private without being out of touch with people: lovely!

patio doors to the courtyard from the kitchen. *Stables* has space, a beamed lounge, an open staircase off the hall leading to a light landing, a double overlooking the courtyard, a large beamed twin. *Farm House Cottages* have beamed lounge/diner/kitchen (open fire if desired), a double, a twin and a bathroom. All **sleep 4**, plus Z-bed on request in Byre and Stables. Well-behaved dogs welcome: two per cottage. Short breaks from £80. TV/video. Linen and towels provided. Cost: about £190 to £400. Details: Clive and Denise Proctor, Headon Farm Cottages, Wydale, Brompton-by-Sawdon, North Yorkshire YO13 9DG. Telephone 01723 859019.

www.headonholidaycottages.co.uk email: headonfarm@supanet.com

Wrelton, near Pickering
Beech Farm Cottages

The quality of these properties is reflected in the fact that they have won both the (then) English Tourism Council's prestigious 'England for Excellence' award and, in 2002, *for the fourth time*, the Yorkshire Tourist Board's 'Self-Catering Holiday of the Year' award.

In a quiet village on the edge of the North York Moors, the cottages are ideally situated for the many attractions of North Yorkshire – moors, dales, forests, coastal walks, abbeys, castles, historic buildings, seaside resorts, steam railway across moors, historic York, market towns and small villages.

The cottages are in a peaceful and pretty courtyard opening on to fields. This is effectively a hamlet in its own right in which every house is a haven of comfort.

There is a good range of accommodation to choose from. The six larger cottages are rated **Five Stars** by **'Visit Britain'**, the highest quality rating possible. *Beech Royd* and *Tanglewood* both **sleep 4**. *Columbine* and *Bracken Brow* **sleep 6**. For larger groups *The Farmhouse* (a listed building) and *Shepherd's Lodge* both **sleep 10**. They are well equipped, including dishwashers, videos and digital TV. There are also two charming little detached **Four Star** cottages, *Fat Hen* and *Dove Tree,* that **sleep 2 or 3**.

There is an excellent indoor pool and sauna. Children love the play area, the animals (including two 'lovable' llamas) and the paddock. Included are

Effectively a hamlet in its own right, in which every house is a haven of comfort.

The accommodation is great, and the indoor swimming pool is a huge bonus.

electricity, gas (the cottages have gas central heating and double glazing and are cosy for winter), linen, towels, and the use of the swimming pool.

Guests can be certain of a warm welcome, and appreciate personal touches, such as fresh flowers and a home-made cake on arrival. We've met the owners, who take pride in ensuring everything is just right.

Open all year, with short breaks outside the school holidays. Details from Pat and Rooney Massara, Beech Farm, Wrelton, Pickering, North Yorkshire YO18 8PG. Telephone 01751 476612, fax 475032.

www.beechfarm.com   email: holiday@beechfarm.com

Glaisdale Head, near Whitby
Wheelhouse

We've seen some places in our time, but this one really stays in the memory. What an exquisite location! After a leisurely tea on the terrace, we could hardly tear ourselves away. Within a small hamlet in the lee of Glaisdale Moor and Egton High Moor, this charming cottage has stunning views across the head of the valley and to the escarpments of the moors above. But it's not remote: Whitby is just 12 miles away,

This is a marvellously well situated cottage, with exceptionally kind and welcoming owners living next door...

Pickering 15. Close by is a station on the ultra-scenic railway line which runs to Whitby. Within the North York Moors National Park, the cottage has its spacious sitting room and kitchen upstairs (microwave and washing machine) to take advantage of those views. There is a multi-fuel stove in the sitting room. Downstairs are a double bedroom and a twin, plus a large bathroom. There is a terraced patio garden and parking for two cars. **Sleeps 5**. Small dogs are welcome by arrangement. Heating, linen and towels included. Cost: about £250 to £375. Special rates for couples. Details from Colin or Mary Douglass, The Wheelhouse, Glaisdale, Whitby YO21 2QA. Telephone 01947 897450.

Whitby and Sleights map 3/98
White Rose Holiday Cottages

Though we ourselves know 'White Rose' best for the cottages inland at Sleights, there is also accommodation in Whitby. This consists of *The Garden Studio*, a firm favourite with many regulars. Less than three miles from there, Sleights is ideally situated for 'coast and country'. Within the village – one of our own favourites in this part of Yorkshire – 'White Rose' have three cottages in a courtyard known as Garbutts Yard; there are two bungalows and (it was new for 2006)

All three courtyard cottages are nicely maintained and very comfortable...the owners really do 'aim to please'.

a smart dormer bungalow. Very conveniently, the owners themselves live in the village. All the properties are maintained to a high standard, and are **'Visit Britain' Three/Four Stars.** They **sleep from 2 to 10.** TVs, videos, DVDs. Linen and towels included. Cost: about £250 to £1250. Weekend breaks on application. Brochures from June and Ian Roberts, Greenacres, 5 Brook Park, Sleights, near Whitby YO21 1RT. Telephone 01947 810763. ('Please phone if possible: we like to deal with people personally')

www.whiterosecottages.co.uk
email: enquiries@whiterosecottages.co.uk

Beadlam, nr Helmsley
Townend Cottage

During its (yes!) *22 years* in our guide, this charmer of a cottage has been consistently popular with readers. A wing of the owner's 18th century farmhouse, conveniently just off the main road that runs through the village, it stands on the edge of the North York Moors and is less than an hour from Scarborough and York. *A much-loved cottage from which to explore the North York Moors and beyond.* The cottage is comfortable and full of character, and with its Baxi open fire, notably cosy in winter or during those worthwhile autumn breaks. There are good beds, a fine kitchen and bathroom, and all is tastefully decorated and furnished, with double glazing, and gas fired central heating. Some internal stone walls are a feature, and there are oak beams to add character. We like the wide staircase and the big main bedroom.

'Visit Britain' Four Stars. TV/Video/DVD/CD. **Sleeps 4**. Cost: about £190 to £350. Dogs and other pets are welcome. Details from Mrs Margaret Begg, Townend Farmhouse, Beadlam, Nawton, York YO62 7SY. Telephone 01439 770103.

www.visityorkshire.com   email: margaret.begg@ukgateway.net

'In Brief'...

Kirk Cottage, in Staithes, near Whitby (Ref 17016) is at the heart of that famous village, where good quality self catering cottages are at a premium. Grade II listed, it is memorably only 75 yards from the harbour, the beach and – which will inspire many a serious walker – the Cleveland Way. **Sleeps 3**. With steep steps up to the front door it is unsuitable for small children or people of limited mobility. There's an open fire.

Also right on the Cleveland Way in Staithes – not that it actually passes through the sitting room – *Cliff Cottage* (Ref 4635) is a charming former fisherman's property at the top of a cobbled street that climbs up from the harbour. It's just 100 yards from the beach and a pub, with views of the cottage garden and a secluded valley. (And there's great cliff-top walking almost from the front door.) Here too there's an open fire, and it's also unsuitable for small children or people of limited mobility. **Sleeps 4.**

Details from Blakes Country Cottages, Spring Mill, Earby, Barnoldswick BB94 0AA. Brochures and bookings: 0870 197 6896.

Live search and book: www.blakes-cottages.co.uk

Ebberston (near Scarborough)
Cliff House

We are full of admiration for the immense energy and style with which Simon Morris has turned Cliff House's properties into some of *the very best in Yorkshire*. The four acres of land, with the walled garden, an amazing pyramid-shaped treehouse, the secret wooded gardens and the trout pool, are a source of fascination. (Youngsters love the toddlers' play area and the animals.) There is a covered, heated pool with a jacuzzi, a hard tennis court and a big games room with table tennis, pool, and darts.

Cliff House stands conveniently on the A170 – though in several cottages you'd hardly know the road is there – and is only about ten miles inland from Scarborough, with the North York Moors on the doorstep.

Lilac **sleeps 4** in a downstairs twin with en-suite toilet and handbasin, and a first floor double room. There's a downstairs kitchen/diner with open fire, upstairs lounge with garden views, and bathroom. *Maple* with its own small courtyard, **sleeping 6** and suitable for people of limited mobility, has a downstairs en-suite twin, as well as two first floor bedrooms and bathroom. *Beech* (**sleeping 5**) has a downstairs twin room and bathroom, kitchen/diner and lounge with big picture windows enjoying excellent views, a single and a double room upstairs. *Pine* and *Willow* (**sleep 4**) are

A fine arrangement of houses, handy for the moors and the seaside.

There's a high standard of furnishing, comfort, and attention to detail.

'upside down' cottages with bathroom, toilet and two bedrooms on the ground floor; beamed lounge/diner/kitchen (with open fire) taking advantage of first floor views. *Holly* **sleeps 6** in a double and two twins, and is quietly situated near the gardens. Its lounge has an open fire and picture windows; there is a dishwasher. *Apple* (**sleeps 2**) is converted from the laundry and apple store of Cliff House and has a beamed lounge and kitchen/diner, with double bedroom – overlooking gardens and apple trees – and bathroom upstairs. *Pear* also **sleeps 2 (plus 1** in a pulldown bed) and we found it altogether individual and charming, light and interesting. A beamed kitchen/diner leads to the lounge and on into a beamed double bedroom with high sloping ceiling, overlooking the gardens.

'Visit Britain' Four Stars. TVs and videos. Dishwashers in Holly, Beach, Maple and Lilac. Linen, towels, heating included. 'Sorry, no pets.' Cost: £215 to £975. Brochure from Simon Morris, Cliff House, Ebberston, near Scarborough, North Yorkshire YO13 9PA. Tel 01723 859440. Fax 850005.

email: cliffhouseebberston@btinternet.com
www.cliffhouse-cottageholidays.co.uk

Scarborough/Scalby
Wrea Head Country Cottages

These skilfully converted farmhouses have proved a real favourite among readers of this guide for many years, *and we have never had a complaint.*

At the end of a quiet lane, only a short drive from Scarborough (you can see its ruined castle on the headland), the cottages are exceptionally well placed for enjoying both seaside and countryside.

The mainly south-facing, well cared-for properties have been national winners of the then ETC's "England for Excellence" Award for Self-Catering Holiday of the Year. They were also *three time* winners of the 'White Rose Award' as the Yorkshire Tourist Board's Self-Catering Cottages of the Year.

There are nine in all, of differing sizes, with well-tended gardens. Most have sea views. On the edge of the North York Moors National Park, only an hour from York, this is an ideal location to explore villages and market towns, the Heritage Coast and neighbouring forest drives. There's a sauna and an indoor heated pool with a jacuzzi at one end. This sends small waves down the pool to the delight of young children, who also have their

Children love to stay here and to get to know the horses and the teddy bears!

The super swimming pool, the sauna and the jacuzzi add 'that extra something' here.

own Teddy Bears Cottage, a two-storey wooden playhouse complete with Father Bear, Mother Bear and Baby Bear upstairs in bed and its own fenced garden and picnic area. Older children will enjoy the unusually well-equipped adventure playground.

Hay Barn Cottage (**sleeps 8**) impressed us with its clever design whereby sitting room, dining room and kitchen are separate but linked. There are well-chosen fabrics throughout (bedrooms in particular with their pretty duvets, curtains and table lamps are charming). Kitchens are modern, mostly with dishwashers, and overhead beams add character. All have TVs and DVDs, gas central heating and **Four 'Visit Britain' Stars**. Ample parking, laundry room, library (DVDs, books and games); telephone and barbecues are available. No pets, no smoking. Open all year. Cost: from £275 to £1495 (includes indoor pool, gas and electricity, linen and towels). Good value special breaks during the off-season.

Further details from Steve and Sue Marshall, Wrea Head House, Barmoor Lane, Scalby, Scarborough, North Yorkshire YO13 0PG. Telephone Scarborough 01723 375844. Fax 352743.

www.wreahead.co.uk email: ghcg@wreahead.co.uk

Robin Hood's Bay
Farsyde Farm Cottages

Very well positioned on Yorkshire's spectacular 'Heritage Coast', these cottages are close to the fine old fishing village of Robin Hood's Bay, one of the most attractive places in North Yorkshire. (Whitby's just six miles away.) You can walk to the village and beach in a few minutes. The beach is partly sand, with rock pools. *Mistal Cottage*, where we've stayed,

There are marvellous views, and the ambiance is appreciated by readers.

is outstanding, and deserves its **Four 'Visit Britain' Stars**. **Sleeping 4** (non-smokers, please), it has a large living room with marvellous views. The small indoor swimming pool (in a log cabin) is for the private use of Mistal occupants, and Farsyde's fine horses are for guests to ride. The four smaller, **Three Star** Mews cottages look over shared gardens towards the moors. There's a skilful use of space. Gardens have patios, and lawns with garden furniture. This is a farm with *real animals (*large and small*)*, including Paddington, the Newfoundland. Short breaks available October to June. Cost: about £170 to £620. Details/brochure from Victor and Angela Green, Farsyde House, Robin Hood's Bay, Whitby, North Yorkshire YO22 4UG. Telephone 01947 880249. Fax 880877.

www.farsydefarmcottages.co.uk   email: farsydestud@talk21.com

---

Draughton, near Skipton   map 3/93
Grange Farm Cottages

These attractive cottages, which we looked at in detail in 2005, seem to have struck a chord with readers. In quiet but not remote Draughton, they were created from a former farmhouse, and are rare examples of 'traditional cottages': cosy, more 'old world charm' than designer-converted. They have beautiful views across the valley to Bolton Abbey,

Large groups can rent all the cottages...

with its ruined priory and woodland walks. *Delph House* has a stone-flagged kitchen floor, many exposed beams, a woodburner and a four poster bed. **Sleeps 10** in three doubles and two twins. *Garden Cottage* **sleeps 4** in two bedrooms, one with a four poster and one twin. *Grange Farm House* **sleeps 6** in two doubles and a twin; it, like both the others, enjoys original features such as beams and a stone-flagged floor.

Refs B5065/ND52/ND51. Further details from Blakes Country Cottages, Spring Mill, Earby, Barnoldswick BB94 0AA. Brochures and bookings: 0870 197 6896.

Live search and book: www.blakes-cottages.co.uk

Harrogate, The Dales and around
Harrogate Holiday Cottages*

From very comfortable apartments in the town centre to cosy cottages in the heart of the Yorkshire Dales, this agency – which we have known and featured for many years – makes genuine efforts to 'match the client with the property'.

We get excellent feedback from readers. During 2006, for example, about *The Granary*, at Bishop Monkton. It is one of three impressive conversions around a classic, picture postcard farmyard. The Granary **sleeps 6**: all three properties together will, most usefully, **sleep 15**.

Among other places readers have recommended or we have seen are *Crimple Head Mews*, in the country village of Beckwithshaw but just a five minute drive from Harrogate, with a four poster bed and the use of a hard tennis court (**sleeps 5**).

In the town centre of Harrogate there are swish apartments with iron bedsteads and stainless steel kitchens ideal for the businessman and holidaymaker alike, as well as more traditional properties and some handsome Edwardian houses.

The company also operates beyond Harrogate, in and near such places as historic Knaresborough – known for its castle and Mother Shipton's Cave – in which several properties are offered overlooking the lovely River Nidd and Gorge. There are also places at Bedale and Ripon and in surrounding pretty villages such as Bishop Monkton.

There are several properties in Nidderdale, an 'Area of Outstanding Natural Beauty', and in the pretty Dales village of Darley, one of Yorkshire's 'best kept' villages.

About half the properties on the organisation's books accept pets, and several encourage short breaks.

Further details of any of these and an extremely stylish brochure are available from Harrogate Holiday Cottages, Crimple Head House, Beckwithshaw, Harrogate, North Yorkshire HG3 1QU. Telephone 01423 523333. Fax 526683.

www.harrogateholidays.co.uk

email: bookings@harrogateholidays.co.uk

This handsome family house, just ten minutes' drive from Harrogate, welcomes pets, and sleeps up to seven people...

The original milkmaids would not recognise this one-time milking parlour, sleeping just two people...

Kettlewell
Fold Farm Cottages

Kettlewell is one of the most sought-after villages in Yorkshire, and at its heart, superbly well situated, this is a quartet of traditional, quiet, thick-stone-walled, warm and comfortable cottages next to the friendly and hospitable owners' farm. We revisited in 2005, and found everything 'just right'. Not surprisingly the level of

Right in the heart of the village, with the big advantage of private off-road parking.

repeat visitors is exceptionally high. We have met several, revelling in the well cared for interiors, the deep carpets, the good quality lined curtains, the books, the table lamps, the antique or 'country' furniture. Beds are excellent, and original features have been retained. The location is super for exploring the Yorkshire Dales National Park, with Malham Cove and Tarn and Great Whernside nearby. **Sleep 2 to 4**. **'Visit Britain' Four Stars**. TV. Linen and towels provided. Dishwashers in all but *Buttercup*.

Small dogs are welcome by arrangement, but one cottage is totally pet and smoking free, and smoking is discouraged in all the others. Private off-road parking. Cost: approximately £180 to £440. Details from Mrs B Lambert, Fold Farm, Kettlewell, near Skipton, North Yorkshire BD23 5RH. Telephone 01756 760886.
www.foldfarm.co.uk   email: info@foldfarm.co.uk

Burnt Yates (Nidderdale), near Harrogate
Dinmore Cottages map 3/74

We have stayed in the smallest of these three cottages, tucked away close to the owners' house at the end of a neatly maintained private lane. Each (even that smallest one) is spacious and well-cared-for, with many excellent details such as wood burning stoves, tidy flower borders, attractive pictures and old prints, and always-useful Ordnance Survey maps.

A delightful enclave of cottages, well away from the main road, handy for touring.

Plus peace, quiet and privacy without isolation. Converted from 17th century farm buildings in the landscaped grounds of the owners' fine country house, they are handy for exploring the whole of North Yorkshire and its historic towns, houses, gardens, and abbeys.

Sleep 2 to 5. **'Visit Britain' Four Stars**. One is popular with disabled visitors. Linen included. TVs, videos, microwaves. Not suitable for dogs. Cost: about £250 to £600; short breaks from £175. Major credit cards accepted. Details from Alan Bottomley, Dinmore House, Burnt Yates, Harrogate, North Yorkshire HG3 3ET. Telephone/fax 01423 770860.
www.dinmore-cottages.co.uk
email: aib@dinmore-cottages.freeserve.co.uk

71

Buckden, near Skipton
Dalegarth and The Ghyll Cottages

One of our longest-serving inspectors chose to spend a family holiday at *The Ghyll* in 2005 – an accolade in itself. She was delighted by the place, and especially by one of its most-loved features. For at the rear of the trio of cottages, dropping down at a steep angle, is as pretty a bubbling beck as you'll ever see in the Yorkshire Dales. Because of the way the land lies and the situation of the cottages, this feels almost like a private enclave.

Featured by us *without a break since 1983*, both the Dalegarth and The Ghyll properties have **Four 'Visit Britain' Stars**, the latter Disabled Category 2. Better yet, we weren't surprised that owners Susan and David Lusted were runners up in 2004 in the Yorkshire Tourist Board's White Rose Award for 'Outstanding Customer Service'. This tribute came from a reader a couple of years ago: '(It is)...the best self catering we have

A neat cluster of purpose-built traditionally styled houses with superb facilities. The warm, covered pool, and the adjacent solarium, are irresistible, and the whole place is surrounded by the unspoilt beauty of Upper Wharfedale.

rented by far...a high standard of fittings and furnishings, extremely well maintained by the owner on site, for whom nothing is too much trouble...We are visiting in October for the sixth time...'

Lonely roads that go deep into wild country are pleasant enough for the tourist, but when such roads combine scenic beauty with ease of access it is twice as nice! The B6160, which runs from near Skipton, through Upper Wharfedale, to the heart of the Dales, is one of those roads.

A few yards off it, on the south side of the small village of Buckden, in what was once the kitchen garden of a great house nearby, *Dalegarth* consists of a neat cluster of eleven purpose built, traditionally styled stone houses grouped around a dog-leg cul-de-sac. They are modern, neat and tidy, and fit very attractively into the landscape.

During a recent visit we met regular visitors relaxing in their spacious sitting rooms (all are on the first floor) and enjoying woodland and hill views – this is fine walking and touring country. Serious walkers used to aching limbs should note that seven of the cottages (there are two types) have small sauna rooms.

The cottages, which are **ideal for 4 but can sleep 6** (each has two bedrooms, plus a bed-settee in lounge), have excellent bathrooms, state-of-the-art kitchens and large, comfortable lounges with TV/video/DVD players and natural stone fireplaces. They are classified as 'type A' and 'type B' and are identical except that 'type A' have a sauna in the bathroom.

You'll find a breakfast bar in the kitchen, patio-style windows leading out on to a balcony from the lounge and an en suite shower, toilet and vanity unit in the master bedroom.

Dalegarth has an impressive indoor swimming pool, plus a solarium and games/exercise room and an exceptionally attractive terrace to sit on after your swim and admire the scenery. Also, there is a full linen service, a well-equipped laundry room, and all the cottages have a freezer.

David and Susan Lusted live in one of the houses and keep these warmly carpeted, superbly-equipped properties clean and efficiently run.

The three *Ghyll Cottages* were designed specifically for those with mobility problems. Built in natural stone, set in secluded landscaped grounds to the rear of the village of Buckden, in a quiet, sunny location, they share the leisure amenities of Dalegarth, less than two hundred yards away.

Each of the cottages has a covered loggia leading to an entrance porch which opens into a large lounge/dining room, off which is a fully-fitted and extremely well-equipped kitchen, including microwave, dishwasher etc. A double bedroom, thoughtfully provided with versatile 'zip link' beds, a spacious ensuite bathroom with spa bath, walk-in shower, etc, completes the downstairs, with another double bedroom and bathroom upstairs (one cottage has two upstairs bedrooms). The south-facing lounges offer direct access to sunny patios and every property has remote control TV and audio centre, DVD player, video and video library, central heating and a full linen service. Main bedrooms have TV and radio. Wheelchair-bound people staying there have told us that The Ghyll has it 'just right' and could not be faulted for the facilities.

The Lusteds have a policy of welcoming inspection during changeover periods. No dogs at The Ghyll (except guide dogs) but a small dog at Dalegarth is possible by arrangement. All cottages are 'non-smoking'.

Cost: about £372 to £687. Special winter mini-breaks. Details and colour leaflet from Mr and Mrs D Lusted, 2 Dalegarth, Buckden, near Skipton, North Yorkshire BD23 5JU. Telephone/fax 01756 760877.

Disabled readers should note that some while ago The Ghyll Cottages were chosen as national winners by the Holiday Care Service, at the World Travel Exhibition in Earls Court, London.

www.dalegarth.co.uk
email: info@dalegarth.co.uk

The Ghyll represents a considerable investment that has really hit-the-spot...

It is marvellously well situated, with fabulous walking right from the door.

Reeth and Healaugh
Swaledale Cottages

Featured every year in this guide since it was first published in 1983, these cottages make a splendid base from which to explore the still miraculously unspoilt Yorkshire Dales. They are just a 20 minute drive from one of our favourite towns in the north of England – Richmond.

Two properties – *Thiernswood Cottage* and *The Bothy* – are within the wooded grounds of Thiernswood Hall, which is, delightfully, approached by a tree-lined drive a third of a mile long. With an open fire in the sitting room, Thiernswood Cottage is a really inviting place 'to come home to' after, say, walking in the Dales. It is deceptively spacious, with a well equipped kitchen, dining room and cosy sitting room with open fire, two charmingly co-ordinated bedrooms – one double, the other twin bedded, both with en-suite bathroom. **Sleeps 4**. Cost: about £240 to £507.

The Bothy is tucked away, and is **ideal for 2** – indeed, for honeymooners! It is a charming conversion of tack rooms above the old stone stable block of Thiernswood Hall, and, being out of sight of the big house, especially private. There are splendid rural views from the sitting room. Cost: £175 to £353.

Linen and towels are included in Thiernswood Cottage and The Bothy; with heating included in Thiernswood Cottage during the autumn and winter seasons.

In the village of Healaugh is a spacious four bedroomed listed cottage called *Swale View*. This has long been one of our personal Yorkshire favourites. Once the village inn, with many old features retained, it has an open fire in the sitting room, a new kitchen with barrelled dining area ceil-

Swale View used to be the village pub, and retains several original features, including – our favourite! – an open fire.

Thiernswood Cottage is 'deceptively spacious' and also has an open fire. It fits prettily into its wooded surroundings.

ing and also a formal dining room. The main bedroom has a four poster double bed and ensuite bathroom. **Sleeps 6**. Cost: about £295 to £650.

Short breaks in all cottages, £140 to £230. A dog is welcome in Swale View. All have gardens, off-road parking and great views. **'Visit Britain' Four Stars**. Details from Mrs J T Hughes, Thiernswood Hall, Healaugh, Richmond, North Yorkshire DL11 6UJ. Telephone 01748 884526.

www.swaledale-cottages.co.uk

email: thiernswood@talk21.com

Sedbusk, Bainbridge, Hawes, West Burton
Clematis, Well, Shepherd's and Fell View Cottages

Our readers have really taken to *Shepherd's Cottage*, **sleeping 6**, a feather in the cap of Anne Fawcett, whose old stone built cottages are all in picture-postcard locations. We've had so many compliments over the years, especially about this spacious Grade II listed stone cottage, about a mile from Hawes. Built in 1633, it's notable for its original mullioned windows and cosy farmhouse kitchen. There are three character bedrooms – two doubles and a twin. *Clematis*,

Clematis has inspiring views, and is a house of great character and history.

perched on a bank in the sleepy hamlet of Sedbusk, enjoys spectacular views. It has big rooms – notably the welcoming sitting room. **Sleeps up to 6**. In West Burton, 17th century *Well Cottage* sleeps 4 (a twin and a double), with a pretty walled garden. Overlooking the green in attractive Bainbridge, *Fell View* **sleeps up to 5** in two doubles and a single. It has an open fire and an Aga. Each cottage is **'Visit Britain' Four Stars**. Linen/towels for hire. Central heating/electricity included. Dogs welcome. Cost: about £175 to £675. Details: Anne Fawcett, Mile House Farm, Hawes in Wensleydale, North Yorkshire DL8 3PT. Telephone/fax 01969 667481.

www.wensleydale.uk.com

email: milehousefarm@hotmail.com

Snape, near Bedale   map 3/105
The Undercroft (Snape Castle)

You'd hardly believe you're just 20 minutes' drive from the busy A1 as you approach the tranquil parkland which adjoins the village of Snape. The most imposing building by far is Grade I listed Snape Castle (*re*-built between 1420 and 1450!), whose most famous one-time resident, Catherine Parr, was to become Henry VIII's last wife. Providing a rare chance to stay (in 21st century comfort!) surrounded by so much history,

Cleverly combining history and comfort.

The Undercroft is a beauty: spacious, thoughtfully lit, lovingly restored, warm (there's a wood stove, plus underfloor heating) and altogether inviting. We especially liked the deep sofas, the super, separate big shower and the neat stone stairway up to the small twin room, and noted that the good-sized downstairs double makes the property accessible to people with limited mobility. **Sleeps 4**. No smoking, no pets.

For contact details, see the Stately Holiday Homes feature on Pages 22-23.

Stanbury, near Keighley
Sarah's Cottage

This was a real find for us: modestly priced, very comfortable, located in a most interesting and attractive part of West Yorkshire – a really worthwhile find on a bright, breezy day. It has easy access to invigorating country walks, and among much else the Keighley and Worth Valley (Steam) Railway, the Brontë Parsonage at Haworth. There is a well planned small garden, with a bird feeder that

Very modestly priced and lovingly cared-for by the owner – who lives next door.

attracts 'all sorts' and a garden seat from which to enjoy the view, an exceptionally comfortable deep-carpeted ambience, absolute cleanliness. We especially liked the table lamps, the main bedroom with its picture windows, the neat kitchen/diner. There is a small second bedroom with adult-sized bunks and an upstairs bathroom with a power-shower over the bath. There is also a garage. **'Visit Britain' Three Stars**. One well behaved dog is possible. Television and video. Linen and towels included. Cost: about £140 to £280. Further details from Brian Fuller, Emmanuel Farm, 101 Stanbury, Keighley, West Yorkshire BD22 0HA. Telephone 01535 643015.

email: brian.fuller2@btinternet.com

Luddenden Foot, near Hebden Bridge
Haworth   map 3/101/108

It was a reader who had attended a wedding locally who first recom-mended these to us. Semi-detached *Greystones Farm Cottage* is at Luddenden Foot, near Hebden Bridge. Adjoining the owner's house, it is just half a mile from a pub, has good views, a wood-burning stove, and a bathroom with a bath *and* a separate shower. **Sleeps 4.** Ref

Greystones Farm Cottage is a good base from which to explore West Yorkshire.

13082. *Weavers Cottage*, part of a Grade II listed building dating from the 1780s, will appeal to steam rail-way fans, as it overlooks the Keighley and Worth Valley steam railway. Close to Haworth's main street, it's something of a historic rarity, and pri-vate and quiet to boot. **Sleeps 4 'plus 1'.** Ref 17976.

Details from Country Holidays, Spring Mill, Earby, Barnoldswick, Lancashire BB94 0AA. For bookings, and brochures: 0870 197 6895.

Live search and book: www.country-holidays.co.uk

Derbyshire
Peak Cottages*

One of our readers has accused us of featuring mainly big houses, though he did as it happens stay most recently in quite a substantial property on the books of this very good agency, which has been highly instrumental in introducing hundreds of self caterers to the pleasures of 'the Peaks'.

Our reader booked *Harrow Cottage*, Great Longstone, near Bakewell. **Sleeping 6**, it is a typical, spacious barn conversion, with a number of original features and a woodburning stove. Next spring (partly with him in mind!) we'll look at the 'delightful' one-bedroom properties in rural surroundings at Biggin Grange (on the edge of Wolfescote Dale): *Cheese Press Cottage*, *The Old Farrowings* and *Courtyard Creamery*.

Ashford Barns are, for example, in an ideal location in the heart of the Peak District National Park, in a rural spot but in walking distance of three popular villages (Ashford in the Water, Little and Great Longstone). A short walk takes one into Monsal Dale, where fishing permits are available. This is a high-quality two and three bedroom conversion with en suite bathrooms and internal links for when both properties are taken together. A further barn here provides accommodation all on one level.

Hurdlow Grange is a remarkable property – The Grange itself sleeps fourteen.

Impressive Crucked Barn is a historic 'must see' in its own right.

There are about 210 cottages altogether, ranging from converted barns to spacious country houses. Such as *Reuben's Roost*, *Bremen's Barn*, *Hopes Hideaway* and *Purdy's Place*, which have top-quality accommodation. You can also enjoy rural tranquillity at *Rewlach Chapel*, Reepsmoor, near Longnor. In addition, *Taddington Barns* have recently been completed to provide character accommodation in rural surroundings, with the added advantage of a heated indoor swimming pool. Cost: about £135 to £2200.

At Hurdlow Grange, *Cruck'd Barn* and *Bats Belfry* are superior conversions of character, with cruck beams and king post trusses exposed and featured. Ideal for groups, **up to 44 people** can be accommodated in three-, four- and seven-bedroomed properties within delightful rural surroundings.

Details/brochures: Colin MacQueen, Peak Cottages, Strawberry Lee Lane, Totley Bents, Sheffield S17 3BA. Tel 0114 262 0777. Fax 0114 262 0666. For information about on-line booking, a range of photos and details of the availability of the agency's 210 or so properties:

www. peakcottages.com   email: enquiries@peakcottages.com

Great Hucklow, near Castleton
The Hayloft

Getting there is half the fun. You'll drive through countryside criss-crossed by dry stone walls and set off by cloud-scudding skies, then (usually) turn off the A623 towards an attractive stone-built farm. The first floor conversion provides comfortable accommodation (on one side, it overlooks the tidy farmyard and the valley beyond, on the other, higher and wilder country: every room here has a good view). There is a pleasant, good sized sitting room with open fire, well chosen rugs on a polished wood floor, a comfortable deep sofa, a grandfather clock and other antique pieces. The kitchen/diner is well appointed, the bathroom

At the end of a no-through-road, walkers will love this.

is spacious and warm, and there are two twin rooms. The owners' pretty and safely enclosed garden is freely available to guests.

TV. **Sleeps 4**. **Four 'Visit Britain' Stars**. Linen and towels. Dogs welcome. Cost: £215 to £350. (Friday to Friday) Weekend breaks by arrangement. Details from Mrs M Darley, Stanley House Farm, Great Hucklow, Derbyshire SK17 8RL. Telephone 01298 871044.

email: margot.darley1@btinternet.com

Hartington map 3/122
Hartington Cottages

The village of Hartington is one of the most sought-after in the Peak District: pubs, tea-shops, antique shops, excellent walking from the village centre. Also at its heart are three outstanding cottages. One, the inspiring *Knowl Cottage*, overlooks the village and is reckoned to be

Knowl Cottage – a Peak District gem...

between 500 and 700 years old. It has that magical combination – lots of original features (such as a part of the original cruck beams) and a powerful sense of history, plus masses of 21st century comfort. Combining both elements is an open fire in a handsome inglenook fireplace. Not surprisingly, the cottage (**sleeping 6**, with three ensuites) has **Five 'Visit Britain' Stars**. The other two cottages here, *Manifold* and *Dove*, side by side, are tucked away in a private little enclave just behind Knowl. Expensively converted from an old barn, they each have **Four Stars**. Dove **sleeps 2**, Manifold **2 'plus 1'**.

Details from Patrick and Frances Skemp, Cotterill Farm, Liffs Road, Biggin-by-Hartington, Buxton SK17 0DJ. Telephone 01298 84447.

www.hartingtoncottages.co.uk
email: patrick@hartingtoncottages.co.uk

Cressbrook, near Bakewell
Cressbrook Hall Cottages

On a bright recent autumn day we travelled through dramatic and craggy scenery close to the very heart of the Peak District National Park to revisit Cressbrook Hall, half hidden away in glorious parkland. Here, *Hall Cottage* and *Garden Cottage* (each **sleeps 4 'plus 1'**, with the option of a reserve twin room) are private and self contained. We have always liked the cottages 200

We really like the comparatively little known location, a very good touring base.

yards away – especially the spectacular view of the Wye Valley enjoyed by *Lower Lodge, Rubicon Retreat* and the adjacent *Hidesaway*. **Sleeping 6**, this is suitable for wheelchairs. *Carriage Cottage* **sleeps 8/9**. Two bathrooms. Wheelchair-user-friendly. Well behaved dogs are welcome. Recently added are *High Spy* and *Top Spot*, adjacent, **sleeping 11** in five ensuite doubles and an ensuite single, all on the ground floor.

B and B available in The Hall. TVs. Linen included. Cost: £115 to £895. Details: Mrs Hull-Bailey, Cressbrook Hall, Cressbrook, near Buxton. Telephone 01298 871289; fax 871845. Freephone 0800 358 3003.
www.cressbrookhall.co.uk   email: stay@cressbrookhall.co.uk

Offcote, near Ashbourne
Offcote Grange Cottage Holidays   map 3/121

Here are two quite exceptional properties. Close to the edge of the Peak District National Park, each **sleeps up to 14** (plus two cots). And both have received the huge accolade of **Five Stars** from **'Visit Britain'**. But these are details that don't convey their no-expense-spared style and their huge appeal. *Hillside Croft* is a handsome stone-built Grade II listed country house in six acres. Dating from 1709,

Hillside Croft is an outstanding house.

on three floors, it has two log burners, impressive ancient oak beams, a magnificent kitchen, dining room and sitting room, and wide, shallow stairs that will suit the elderly and children. *Billy's Bothy* is a super brick-built conversion in peaceful pastureland. It has oak floors, underfloor heating in the ensuite bathrooms and brass and cast-iron beds, an exceptional farmhouse kitchen. And late in 2006 it will even boast a sauna and small gym. Not suitable for pets, no smoking. Quality catering can be arranged. Details from Pat and Chris Walker, Offcote Grange, Offcote, Derbyshire DE6 1JQ. Telephone 01335 344795 Fax 348358. Mobile 0870 8899493.
www.offcotegrange.com
email: enquiries@offcotegrange.com

79

Darwin Lake, near Matlock
Darwin Lake Cottages

Only about ten minutes' drive from Matlock, in a secluded location by a lake and within a peaceful forest setting, this is a group of extremely comfortable, spacious properties of permanent home standard. We have recently met readers who'd enjoyed a family reunion here, for Darwin Lake lends itself very well to large-group bookings. But there is flexibil-

We have stayed in one of these spacious, expensively appointed properties.

ity too, and along with the large three bedroomed detached cottages there is also a terrace of two-bedroomed cottages. Most bedrooms in each of the cottages are ensuite, decor is pristine, kitchen-diners 'have everything'. Pedestrian walkways allow for a good degree of contact with the lake, of which the holiday cottages have superb views. Videos/TVs/CD-players. Linen, towels and electricity are included. Dogs are accepted in two of the cottages. **'Visit Britain' Four Stars**. Cost: about £270 to £995; short breaks usually available. Open all year. Details/brochures from Nikki Manning, Darwin Lake, The Lodge, Jaggers Lane, Darley Moor, near Matlock, Derbyshire DE4 5LH. Telephone/fax 01629 735859.

www.darwinlake.co.uk
email: enquiries@darwinlake.co.uk

Bamford (Hope Valley, near Bakewell)
Shatton Hall Farm Cottages   map 3/128

It's over 20 years ago, since we first saw the Shatton Hall Farm properties. They struck us then, as now, as a haven of tranquillity. A mile from the main road, up a well surfaced lane, it is memorable for way-marked walks through woodland. *Orchard Cottage* and *The Hayloft*, recent barn conversions, are next door to each other, have beamed living rooms furnished in old pine, and cosy coal-effect gas fires. *Paddock Cottage*, down the

In this guide for many years, and lots of very enthusiastic reports from readers...

yard and with a wood burning stove, is the perfect winter retreat, for a short break or longer. A well behaved dog is allowed there, as there is a fenced car park to this cottage. All the cottages **sleep 4** in two double bedrooms (one is a twin room) plus sofa-beds in Orchard and Hayloft. Recently renewed kitchens and bathrooms helped these thoughtfully planned cottages to achieve a **'Visit Britain' Four Star** rating. Cost: £280 to £475. Open all year. Details: Mrs Angela Kellie, Shatton Hall Farm, Bamford, Hope Valley S33 0BG. Telephone 01433 620635. Fax 620689.

www.peakfarmholidays.co.uk
email: ahk@peakfarmholidays.co.uk

Knockerdown (Carsington), near Ashbourne
Knockerdown Farm Cottages

We've featured this very family-friendly group of cottages for many years, with lots of praise from readers for the welcoming atmosphere and the facilities, as well as the flexible accommodation. We like the way for example that two units (*Bruns* and *Sabinhay*) interconnect to provide an extra-large property.

Families and smaller parties will both appreciate the new on-site Brackendale restaurant, open to the public, and the new Brackendale Spa, which offers among much else 'luxurious massage and facials'.

During one recent revisit to Knockerdown we stayed in *Farwell*, usefully **sleeping 6 'plus 2'** – the 2 in a comfortable and private ground floor bedroom. It is spacious, uncluttered, expensively fitted out: well recommended. And we've stayed in *Middleton*, a neat two storeyed cottage with a twin and a double bedroom and a good use of the available space.

Our main purpose was to visit nearby Chatsworth House and Haddon Hall, but we discovered what a useful touring base Knockerdown makes for other places, with the Dales on the doorstep. Carsington Water (all kinds of water sports, and cycle trails) is a few minutes away on foot.

We have stayed here ourselves, and appreciated the tidy, unfussy interiors...   *...as well as the excellent swimming pool: it was very warm on a chilly autumn day.*

Guests appreciate the excellent indoor, warm pool and leisure centre. It's a pleasant place to make new friends, but also quiet and private. There is an exceptional adventure playground, and three acres for children to romp in.

All the cottages, from one that **sleeps 2** to two that **sleep 10**, with fourteen others in between, **sleeping 4** plus cot **and 6** plus cot, are quite private. We noticed plain white walls, oak beams, pine fittings, good quality carpets, some exposed interior stone walls. Nearly all the cottages have an open plan arrangement of sitting room, dining room and kitchen. We applaud the 'instant heat' convector heater/storage radiators.

Videos, TVs. Video library. All linen and towels are included. No dogs. **'Visit Britain' Three/Four Stars**. Cost (including electricity): about £269 to £2042 weekly, with short breaks usually available (open all year) from about £179.

Details/brochure from Tina Lomas, Knockerdown Farm, near Ashbourne, Derbyshire DE6 1NQ. Telephone/fax 01629 540525.

www.derbyshireholidaycottages.co.uk
email: info@derbyshireholidaycottages.co.uk

Eyam/Hope
Dalehead Court

Here are excellent properties (in two separate locations) including, at Hope, a rather special small property available only since the late spring of 2005. **Sleeping just 2** in a 'super king size' double that's convertible to twins, it has been done to **Five Star** specifications, and, usefully for people with limited mobility, is all on one level. Also at Hope are *Stables,* **sleeping 2**, and *Granary* and *The Lime Loft*. Each **sleeping 4**, they are by a tumbling river, with a good degree of spaciousness. Dogs are welcome in Granary and Stables.

Derbyshire has great appeal, and all these superbly maintained cottages make a fine base.

A private courtyard in the heart of Eyam, one of the most historic Derbyshire villages, with ample private parking, is the location of one of the two cottage-groups in the same ownership. All three at Eyam are finished expensively, with style. *Pinfold Barn*, **sleeping 6,** is an 'upside-down' house with an inviting first floor sitting room, three cosy bedrooms, a stunning 'undersea' bathroom, a separate shower and the main bedroom en-suite. *The Captain's House*, **sleeping '4 plus 1'**, is a Victorian beauty, with a big sitting room, surround-sound cinema TV and a twin and a king-sized double bedroom. Attractive, stylish *Pinner Cottage* **sleeps 2**, also in a king-sized bed. **'Visit Britain' Four and Five Stars**. Dogs welcome in Pinner.

Cost: about £195 to £500. Linen and towels available (free for two-week stays); winter short breaks. Details from Mr and Mrs D Neary, Laneside Farm, Hope, Derbyshire S33 6RR. Telephone 01433 620214.

www.peakdistrictholidaycottages.com email: laneside@lineone.net

Biggin-by-Hartington
Cotterill Farm Holiday Cottages map 3/134

This is a focal point in the Derbyshire Dales, the most impressive part of the Peak District, and it is always a pleasure to turn off a road, well away from traffic, on to the drive up to the cottages to see these three skilful conversions. *Dale View* is an 'upside down' cottage to take advantage of the views (it has a shower, not a bath), This and *Liff's Cottage* each **sleeps 4** in a double and a twin. *The Dairy* is a **2-person** property of great charm, its one (double) bedroom within a gallery overlooking a big living room. A wood-burner is a feature, and there is a spacious bathroom. (The views from the patio of The Dairy and also from the shared spacious gardens are amazing.) *The Milking Parlour*, a recent barn conversion, **sleeps 3**, and is on the ground floor, without steps. All are **'Visit Britain' Four Stars**. Linen, electricity and heating are included. Non-smoking. 'Sorry, no pets'. Cost: about £230 to £460, depending on which cottage and when. Details from Frances Skemp, Cotterill Farm, Biggin-by-Hartington, Buxton SK17 0DJ. Telephone 01298 84447.

www.cotterillfarm.co.uk email: enquiries@cotterillfarm.co.uk

Chinley, near Buxton
Cherry Tree Cottage/The Old House

Twenty-five years in this guide, and never anything but wholehearted praise from readers both for owners Pam and Nic Broadhurst and their properties. It's a marvellous record.

Their two cottages are full of comfort and character, with great attention to detail. *Cherry Tree Cottage* **sleeps 6**. It overlooks the children's picturebook farmyard (little ones can feed the ducks and hens, and older ones are welcome to play more or less at will on the farm). We remember Cherry Tree's big dining room, and readers have written to say: 'The cottage was perfect – we felt at home and relaxed the moment we stepped through the door' and 'so sad to be leaving such great accommodation'.

There's an open fire (plus central heating throughout), fresh flowers, rugs, comfy armchairs and sofas, oak beams, antiques, lots of nooks and crannies, good paintings, excellent views, children's games and toys, comfortable bedrooms. The kitchen (with most attractive tiling) has a dishwasher and microwave. These are probably the best equipped farm-based cottages we know, with shaver points, electric blankets, rotary whisks, coffee filter machines, barbecues.

The more recent property is a historic and intriguing cottage dating from abut 1560, **sleeping 2** and appropriately called *The Old House*. You descend most cosily from a bedroom with a five foot double bed and inspiring views of the Blackbrook Valley, into a lower-level sitting room with antique oak furniture and inglenook fireplace with log burner.

Cherry Tree (on the right) quickly became a firm favourite among our readers, being extremely well equipped, cosy and comfortable.

The Old House is full of history, a most unusual property for just 2 people, who'll love (as we did) the antique oak and the inglenook fireplace with its log burner.

Situated as they are in the Peak District National Park (but only a mile from the village), the cottages make a fine base from which to explore the area. It is, by the way, easy to get here by train.

Both are **'Visit Britain' Four Stars**. Cost: about £230 to £630. Dogs are welcome. TVs/videos.

Further details from Mrs Broadhurst, Cote Bank Farm, Buxworth, via Whaley Bridge, High Peak, Derbyshire SK23 7NP. Telephone 01663 750566.

www.cotebank.co.uk email: cotebank@btinternet.com

Northumberland and Durham

The A1 trunk road is not known for the views it offers, but in Northumberland at least it presents tantalising glimpses of that county's fabulous coast, with an occasional distant sight of possibly the best beaches in England. This most northerly of all the English counties embraces a wide variety of countryside, much of it impressively 'wild and woolly' and some world-class castles: Alnwick, Warkworth, Lindisfarne, Dunstanburgh and Bamburgh. And if you venture into the Cheviot Hills, which beautifully straddle the English-Scottish border, you can be virtually alone except for curlews and skylarks even on an August Bank Holiday. Much further south, we are especially fond of the Tyne Valleys (North and South), and the Roman Wall country. That is well trodden, but little known are the beautiful windswept moors that characterise the three-way border between Northumberland and Durham and Northumberland and Cumbria. County Durham is in fact one of 'England's best kept secrets', not just for its deep, dark green river valleys, its stone villages set off so effectively by flowers, but its great castles (Barnard Castle is very impressive, as is the nearby Bowes Museum) and the historic city of Durham – a castle and a great, sombre cathedral. And one of the best family days out in the north of England is the Beamish Open Air Museum – full of nostalgia for mums and dads, full of things to amuse and educate children.

Greenhead (Hadrian's Wall)
Holmhead Cottage   map 3/136

In the summer of 2006 we revisited this superbly well situated property. It's handy for the main Newcastle to Carlisle road but blissfully quiet, and you'll hardly find anywhere closer to the Roman Wall. Adjoining the owners' home-cum-guest house, the single-storeyed Holmhead Cottage has an open plan sitting room/kitchen/dining room, a twin and a double bedroom, all on the ground floor. There's central heating from the adjacent house (adjusted as required), electricity

Ideally placed for exploring 'the Wall', and very comfortable in its own right.

inclusive, hi-fi and CD player, washing machine, dishwasher, microwave, TV, video. All linen and towels. Private walled garden. Shops, swimming, tennis, riding just three miles away; a pub, a bus stop and a cafe are just half a mile away in the village. Golf is just 500 yards away. Short breaks. Non-smokers only. Not suitable for dogs. Payphone. Note: the Roman Wall visitor centres are open all year: the cottage owner is an expert on the subject. Cost: about £220 to £398. Details from Pauline Staff, Holmhead Guest House, on Thirlwall Castle Farm, Hadrian's Wall, Greenhead-in-Northumberland, via Brampton CA8 7HY. Telephone/fax 016977 47402.

www.holmhead.com
email: via website

Wycliffe, near Barnard Castle
Boot and Shoe Cottage

An especially warm, inviting sitting room, and a delightful location...

We like this very much. With the dark waters of the Tees flowing just feet from the cottage (trout fishing by arrangement), and access via a private lane along the river, the cottage – once used by a cobbler – is idyllic. With the considerate owners living next door, you won't feel isolated, but can unwind in privacy. Among features we approve of: deep sofas, an open fire, old beams, some antique furniture. There is a safely enclosed front garden, and French windows lead out to the back garden and a barbecue area, with steps down to the river bank. TV. Not suitable for dogs (but kennels on site). Linen, towels, coal, logs provided. Welcome hamper, frozen meals to order. **'Visit Britain' Four Stars**. **Sleeps 4** (but, with one 2'6" bed, just three adults), plus an optional double **for an extra 2**. Cost: £190 to £380. Short breaks from £190. Details/brochure from Rachel Peat, Waterside Cottage, Wycliffe, Barnard Castle, Co Durham DL12 9TR. Telephone 01833 627200.

www.bootandshoecottage.co.uk email: info@bootandshoecottage.co.uk

Ray Desmesne, near Kirkwhelpington
Sweethope Crofts 1 and 2   map 3/141

Though we know Northumberland well, and have often travelled the roads – based in at least one case on an original Roman road – that link the River Tyne at Corbridge with the wild moorland and the forests that mark the nearness of the Scottish border, we'd never seen the lovely lough on Viscount Devonport's 'Ray Desmene' estate.

Our excuse to go there, in the summer of 2006, was to see two very appealing holiday houses, *1 and 2 Sweethope Crofts*. They were recommended to us by readers who'd stayed in other Stately Holiday Homes places featured by us in previous editions of this guide. Encouragingly, we arrived at the end of a delightful detour from Corbridge just as they were being spruced up for incoming guests.

The pair of traditional Northumbrian stone cottages at the very edge of Sweethope Lough each sleeps 4 in a double and a bunk-bedded room, with the huge advantage that they can linked to make a single property for a larger family or a group of friends. Among other good things they offer some of the finest lake fishing in the North of England: cottage guests are offered a very generous four free fishing sessions during say, one week's stay). Changeover is on a Friday. One dog is welcome in cottage No 2. Each has a washing machine and No 2 has a dishwasher too.

Details from Stately Holiday Homes: Page 22–23.

Akeld, near Wooler
Akeld Manor and Cottages

On a quiet Saturday afternoon in 2006 we were much encouraged to see how inviting this exceptionally well cared for arrangement of cottages has remained over many years (we have featured it for fifteen years). All was being spruced up for the arrival of new holiday tenants.

One of our readers wrote to say she'd not expected to find a place quite so comfortable and with such extensive facilities on the edge of the 'wild and woolly' Cheviot Hills, with some of the finest and least-crowded beaches in Britain little more than half an hour's drive away.

The 'great comfort' involves interiors five-star hotels would be proud of, with deep carpets, subtle lighting that can add so much to the ambiance of holiday cottages, solid, handsome beds (five-feet wide in some cases), expensive fabrics, excellent insulation, last-word kitchens.

These are eight very sympathetic conversions of one-time farm buildings within 36 acres of the Northumbria National Park, and each one feels private and self contained. They range from a one bedroomed cottage **sleeping just 2, plus baby**, to four cottages that **sleep 4** and three that **sleep 6** (one of those actually **4 'plus 2'**). All have baths, and almost all have shower too. There's an indoor leisure centre, a warm and inviting pool, an antique full-sized snooker table (which might also have side-tracked us), a gym, solarium and games room.

Very sympathetic conversions, with sumptuously comfortable interiors... ...*plus an up to the minute indoor leisure centre that is a huge attraction in itself.*

To complement the excellent accommodation and leisure facilities, there is a tremendous selection of home made meals for guests who occasionally tire of self catering. Quality and prices are exceptional.

There is huge demand among readers of this guide for larger properties, and the splendid *Akeld Manor* can certainly oblige. For the main house of the original estate, **sleeping up to 15**, is a real showpiece. We have too little space to detail all its charms, but there is for example a games room with pool table, a five-foot four poster in one bedroom, a private walled garden, two open fires. Not suitable for pets. Resident on-site staff. Linen included but not towels. Cost: about £313 to £1175. Akeld Manor about £1232 to £2866 per week. Short breaks also available. Details from Pat and Sian Allan, Shoreston Hall, Shoreston, Seahouses, Northumberland NE68 7SX. Telephone 01665 721035. Fax 720951.

www.borderrose-holidays.co.uk email: allan.group@virgin.net.co.uk

Harehope Hall, near Alnwick
Cresswell Wing/Sawmill

Deep in rolling farmland, with views of the Cheviot Hills, Harehope Hall is an imposing mansion, and guests in *The Cresswell Wing* (it is on three floors) have a substantial part of it to themselves, so anyone who appreciates high ceilings, big windows and easy-going, traditional comfort will love it. We like the spacious drawing room with its deep sofas, the open fire

Pleasant accommodation, a fine estate...

(lit when we last called), the big bedrooms – including two atticky ones that would suit children – the 'country antiques'. **Sleeps 8** in two twins and two doubles. (Extra beds available, if needed, plus cot.) Central heating. Most recently available is *Riverview*, **sleeping 6**, adjacent to *Sawmill Cottage*, on a corner of the estate. **Sleeps 4**. These are splendid: better yet, they can be booked together by large groups. They are indeed next to a working sawmill. Linen/towels included. Dogs *and horses* welcome. Note: a speciality here are carriage driving/riding holidays, using the lanes of the estate (but bring your own horses/carriages!). TV. Cost: about £200 to £550. More details from Alison Wrangham, Harehope Hall, Harehope, near Alnwick, Northumberland NE66 2DP. Telephone 01668 217329.

email: john@wrangham.co.uk

Seahouses
Farne House map 3/142

On a bright and breezy day in much-loved Seahouses (a nice mixture of family resort and working fishing port) we visited these quite spectacularly located apartments. Five out of the seven overlook the harbour – always 'something going on' – with views out to sea, and even those that don't reflect the same very high stan-

A spectacular location: comfortable too.

dards of comfort. In the same ownership as Akeld (see previous page) the style of the apartments is plush but rather understated, and definitely uncluttered. Fabrics, furnishings, beds and bedding and kitchens are to a high specification. There's a reliably warm indoor swimming pool and sauna (open 24 hours a day, all year round) with sun lounge. And although you are on the coast, there's easy access to much of the county: Bamburgh for example is a delightful three mile walk along the water's edge. Linen included but not towels. Cost: about £371 to £1031 per week. Short breaks available: you do not have to book a complete week.

Details from Pat and Sian Allan, Shoreston Hall, Shoreston, Seahouses, Northumberland NE68 7SX. Telephone 01665 721035. Fax 720951.

www.borderrose-holidays.co.uk email: allan.group@virgin.net.co.uk

Alnmouth, Bamburgh and around
Northumbria Coast and Country Properties*

A number of regional cottage agencies seem to inspire confidence and even affection among our readers. This is one: we know from our correspondence that it has introduced many people to the magic that is Northumberland.

Sandpiper is at the heart of the little known but most appealing seaside village of Low-Newton-by-the-Sea, close to a charming and unpretentious pub, and just yards from the water's edge. **Sleeping 6**, it is a listed 18th century, one-time fisherman's cottage of character, with a log-burning stove. Dogs are welcome.

At High-Newton-by-the-Sea, *Snook Point* is an extremely comfortable single-storeyed house with sea views. Among others by the coast, there are several properties in famous Bamburgh (best known for its castle and its sandy beach), all of whose sitting room windows face the North Sea. There are cottages of great character in Seahouses, Beadnell, Craster and Embleton, where readers have raved about the fabulous, romantic outlook from *Dunstanburgh View*.

This hugely respected agency covers one of the most scenically impressive corners of England, and is based in Alnmouth. We know three or four of the cottages in the village itself: all a delight! If you should book either of the two old 'smugglers' cottages' in Victoria Place (one is almost *on* the beach) or tucked away *Estuary View* (on three floors), you are in for a treat.

We like the atmosphere of old railways and especially old railway stations, and the agency has a real winner on its books. This is – yes – *The Old Station House*, at Low Akeld, near Wooler. It has been superbly preserved and restored and **sleeps 8/9**.

The brochure for the agency's 200-or-so properties carries a colour photo of each. As well as such highly rural but not remote cottages mentioned above, they include town properties in famous and handsome Alnwick and several in Warkworth (as with Alnwick, the town embraces one of northern England's most famous castles). Another example is the *Old Lifeboat Cottage*, **sleeping just 2**, right on the waterfront and shoreline of the River Tweed estuary at Berwick-upon-Tweed. An amazing location.

Details from Northumbria Coast and Country Cottages, Carpenters Court, Riverbank Road, Alnmouth, near Alnwick, Northumberland. Telephone Alnmouth 01665 830783/830902. Fax 830071.

www.northumbria-cottages.co.uk email: cottages@nccc.demon.co.uk

Glebe House, Bamburgh (not featured) is part of a handsome old vicarage. Sleeps 8.

Estuary View – and yes, the view from the house is as good as you'd hope!

Bamburgh, near Belford/Holy Island
Outchester and Ross Farm Cottages

These stylish and comfortable holiday homes, from which it's a delight to explore Northumberland's spectacular coast, have **Four 'Visit Britain' Stars** apiece. At *Outchester Manor* there are eight superb properties, recent winners in the 'Pride of Northumbria' awards. **Sleep from 2 to 6**. At Ross, there are cottages both in the peaceful hamlet and down the lane to the sea. Spacious *Sandpiper*

Everything is stylish and full of character.

and *Oystercatcher* have charming sitting rooms. Each **sleeps 4 to 6,** but can combine to **sleep 12**. Newly available next door is *Skylark*. Also **sleeps 4 to 6**. Along the sea lane, *West Coastguard Cottage* has a cosy, smallish sitting room, a separate dining room, great upstairs views. *East Coastguard Cottage* is similar (each **sleeps 2 to 4**). *Coastguard Lodge,* **sleeping 2 to 5**, is a gem: a neat garden, a fine sitting room, an expensive kitchen. Outchester cottages cost about £247 to £737, the Ross cottages about £286 to £737. Not suitable for pets, no smoking. Linen and towels are included. Details/brochure: from Mrs J B Sutherland, Ross Farm, Belford, Northumberland NE70 7EN. Telephone 01668 213336. Fax 219385.

www.rosscottages.co.uk email: enquiry@rosscottages.co.uk

Rothbury map 3/140
The Pele Tower

High above Rothbury, though on account of trees out of sight of the town, this is a two-storeyed cottage of great character (some cottage – it is a 19th century extension to the original tower), lovingly cared for by owner David Malia, who lives in 'the big house' next door. Full of history

This is a Five Star beauty, which we re-visited in 2006 – always a pleasure!

and 21st century comfort, the Grade II* listed, 14th century pele tower really is 'something special'. There are stone flags in the excellent modern kitchen, every labour saving device imaginable, video and digital satellite TV. CD/tape hi-fi, 'Play Station 2' entertainment system, a woodstove, extra TVs in bedrooms, teasmade, whirlpool bath and shower, mountain bikes and more. Unsurprisingly it has been shortlisted in the 'England for Excellence' awards and is a former 'Winner of the Lionheart Award: Most Popular Self Catering Accommodation'.

Sleeps 4 in a double room and a twin room. **'Visit Britain' Five Stars**. Unsuitable for pets or smokers. Cost: about £250 to £640. Details from David Malia, The Pele Tower, Whitton, Rothbury, Northumberland NE65 7RL. Telephone 01669 620410. Fax 621006.

www.thepeletower.com email: info@thepeletower.com

89

Bowsden, near Bamburgh/Holy Island
The Old Smithy

Warm and very well planned.

We revisited in 2006, rather enjoying the fact that the cottage is quite hard to find! Though it is indeed in a peaceful rural location, it's only five miles from the Northumberland coast (don't miss Holy Island). When we first called at the detached cottage conversion we met a couple happy to stay put: the woodburner was warming the cottage, and they were comfortably ensconced in the kitchen/diner. Adjacent to that is a cosy sitting room (a former smithy) with a deep sofa/armchairs, attractive stripped pine, rugs, books, well chosen pictures, and other stylish things. This room overlooks the south facing walled garden and the Cheviots. We liked the skilful conversion, with two bedrooms downstairs and one upstairs, the bathroom with shower, a loo on each floor, the central heating that's complemented by the woodburner. This is a traditional farm: natural calf rearing, summer-grass-fed lambs, free range chickens. **Sleeps 6**, plus cot. TV. Dogs welcome. Cost: £240 to £600. Details from John and Mary Barber, Brackenside, Bowsden, Berwick-on-Tweed, Northumberland TD15 2TQ. Telephone 01289 388293.

www.brackenside.co.uk
email: john.barber@virgin.net

Mindrum, near Cornhill-on-Tweed map 3/150
Briar Cottage

Consistently popular with our readers...

So close to Scotland (though actually just insde Northumberland) that you can almost hear bagpipes and see mating haggis, this is a well-cared-for cottage in very pleasant country-side. We've stayed, and remember such details as a log and coal fire lit ahead of our arrival. There are good-sized rooms: from the front window of one we watched cattle on the hills. Used from time to time by the owners, and thus with all the essentials, the cottage has a twin and a double, a good sized bathroom with shower. Small front garden. Large enclosed lawned gardens to side and rear, including a paddock with picnic bench. Private parking. The area is good for touring, with Scotland and the Cheviots so close, and the coast is just half an hour away. Dogs are welcome. TV/video/DVD. Linen, fuel, oil central heating, electricity included. Cost: £210 to £425.

Details from Northumbria Coast and Country Cottages, Carpenters Court, Riverbank Road, Alnmouth, Northumberland NE66 2RH. Telephone 01665 830783/830902. Fax 830071.

www.northumbria-cottages.co.uk email: cottages@nccc.demon.co.uk

Beal, near Holy Island
West Lodge/The Stables/The Coach House/Bee Cottage

The location of *Bee Cottage* (**sleeping 4**) is amazing: it has a memorable panoramic view from most rooms of Holy Island, accessible via the causeway at low tide. Close to newly available *Bee Hill House*, a detached beauty sleeping 10 people, which we'll see in 2007, it has a nicely lit sitting room with a log stove, a modern kitchen, a smart bathroom, a double and a twin. On a grander scale, *West Lodge, Stables* and *The Coach*

Everything here is aimed at the highest standards. See Colour section A, Page 2.

House (**sleeping respectively up to 8, 6 and 9 people**), are recent additions to the Nesbitts' 'family' of cottages. They are beauties: masses of space, grand sitting rooms, sumptuous bedrooms, super ultra-modern kitchens. You'll not get lost, as West Lodge, Stables and Coachhouse are in fairly close proximity to the A1. TVs. Dogs welcome. **'Visit Britain' Four/Five Stars**. Linen/towels provided. Cost: £270 to £1200. Details from Jackie Nesbitt, Springbank, Castle Terrace, Berwick-on-Tweed, Northumberland TD15 1NZ. Telephone 01289 303425. Fax 307902.

www.beehill.co.uk   email: info@beehill.co.uk

Belford, near Holy Island   map 3/156
Bluebell Farm Cottages

In 2006 we revisited to see the considerable upgrading that has been carried out in this most appealing, quiet and competitively priced group of cottages. Tucked away off one of the roads leading out of the historic village of Belford, once a stage-coach stop between York and Edinburgh, they are five stone and pantiled farm-building conversions. Neatly within what is effectively a hamlet in its own

We really liked these unpretentious cottages, and their convenient location.

right, and **sleeping from 2 to 6**, each is *admirably spacious*, with big windows, lots of light and a good degree of privacy. We noted deep sofas and armchairs, patios with picnic-benches and access to barbecues, in the case of *Chillingham, Farne, Lindisfarne* and *St Abbs*, backing on to a little burn. (There is a caravan park in the same ownership, but it is out of sight of the cottages.)

TVs and DVD players. Linen, towels, gas central heating and electricity included. Towels for a small extra charge. Short breaks available. Pets by prior arrangement. Cost: about £210 to £530. Details from Phyl Carruthers, Bluebell Farm Cottages, Belford, Northumberland NE70 7QE. Telephone 01668 213362 or 0770 333 5430.

email: phyl.carruthers@virgin.net

91

Scotland

If we go more than six months without going to Scotland we start to get a bit tetchy. We need a shot in the arm: nothing illicit, just the changing colours of the Cuillin Hills on Skye, absolute peace and quiet on half inhabited islands, an old-fashioned courtesy and integrity among most people one meets. Readers of this guide have described idyllic cottages from where they have explored lochs, glens and burns, mountains, forests and off-shore islands. The north-east of the country has one of the greatest collections of castles in the world, and you can follow a 'whisky trail' to some well-known distilleries. World-famous too are some of the golf courses, such as the Open Championship course at Carnoustie, and the course at St Andrews. For skiers, Glenshee and Aviemore are Scotland's main resorts, but we would say the mountains and hills are even more impressive in spring, summer and autumn. We are keen on the strange 'lunar landscapes' of the wild country to the north of Lochinver, on the Trossachs, and the rolling brown moors of the Border country that is thick with ancient castles and abbeys.

Duns   map 4/154
Duns Castle Cottages

A reader from Reading who stayed here told us said 'It was magical!' And certainly, the idea of staying within or in the grounds of castles appeals greatly. Each property here has its own character, is very private but benefits greatly from the situation – either close to the grand Gothic-fantasy of a castle or on a slightly more distant corner of the estate. We remember the charming *Pavilion Lodge,* a 'folly' gatehouse, a cosy nest **for 2**, with a romantic

A super base for exploring the Borders, interesting in itself, and only – for example – about an hour from Edinburgh.

turretted bedroom reached via a winding stair, and an open fire (the only one that has an open fire, though some others have coal-effect gas fires). *St Mary's* is a rambling family house **sleeping 11** that may be joined to *Coach House* (**sleeps 3**) behind. *The White House,* **sleeping 6**, is private and comfy, *Azalea Cottage* is elegantly furnished and is located above the lake. *Carriage Mews,* **sleeping 5**, forms one wing of the attractive courtyard. Note: the seaside is only 20 minutes away, Edinburgh about 40 – an easy drive in both cases.

TVs. Linen included, towels available (extra charge). Cost: about £195 to £1180. Details from Natalie Scheff, Duns Castle, Duns, Berwickshire TD11 3NW. Telephone 01361 883211; fax 882015.

www.dunscastle.co.uk
email: info@dunscastle.co.uk

The National Trust for Scotland
Holiday Accommodation Programme

We could happily devote a month to visiting some of the most mouth-watering of The National Trust for Scotland's holiday properties.

We are hoping to see a particular rarity on the glorious Isle of Skye. This is *Beaton's Croft*, a traditional croft house, internally reconstructed for the sake of comfort but with the original ambience retained. **Sleeping 2** (with – of course! – a peat fire) it is at Bornesketaig, and has fabulous views across to the Outer Hebrides.

Consider fabulously situated *Mar Lodge*, on Royal Deeside. We know the place and if we had to choose one great estate – there are over 77000 acres of it – that encapsulates the romance and beauty of mainland Scotland, this might be it. All five of the elegant apartments are graded **Four Stars** by '**Visit Britain**', and three of them have the advantage of access via the impressive main entrance. One of them, *Bynack* is notably roomy, and **can sleep up to 15** (though it is available to smaller groups).

Most recently, during a journey through the east of Scotland, we saw the first floor apartment (**sleeping 4**) at *St Andrew's House*, built in the 17th century as an overflow for courtiers attending royal visitors to the Falkland Palace next door. It is in the heart of the attractive little town.

And between Perth and St Andrews, we found two attractive little bungalows (**sleeping 4 and 5**) in the extensive grounds of the *Hill of Tarvit* mansion, built in 1904. A spacious, elegantly furnished apartment (**sleeping 4**) with views over farmland is also available on the second floor.

We also visited Culzean Castle (pronounced 'Cullane'), a magnificent building on the Ayrshire coast, and were impressed by the spacious, high-ceilinged *Brewhouse Flat*, in the west wing, and by *Royal Artillery Cottage*, that forms part of the courtyard next to the castle. Being on the cliff edge, it has impressive sea views. Each **sleeps 4**.

One of the 'attractive little bungalows' in the grounds of the Hill of Tarvit mansion. *This is Steading Cottage, in the grounds of (and facing) Craigievar Castle.*

One can also stay in the most attractive detached cottages in the grounds of picturesque Craigievar Castle. Both **sleeping 4**, *Kennels Cottage* and *Steading Cottage* are only about a hundred yards from the fabulous castle. For a copy of the irresistible brochure contact Holidays Department, The National Trust for Scotland, Wemyss House, 28 Charlotte Square, Edinburgh EH2 4ET. Telephone 0131 243 9331. Fax 0131 243 9594.

www.nts.org.uk email: holidays@nts.org.uk

Gattonside, near Melrose
Drumblair

It was a reader who first told us of this 'outstandingly good' cottage, and we saw it for ourselves on a warm summer Saturday in 2006. It's a delight, with kind and considerate owners to boot. A detached bungalow in a quiet residential road in a village near Melrose, Drumblair has a pleasant, well tended garden and an absolutely pristine interior. Specifically, it **sleeps 4** in a bedroom (king size bed) with ensuite spa bathroom and an ensuite (shower) twin room. There's double glazing and full gas central heating. The spacious sitting room/dining room has views of the Eildon Hills. The utility room houses a washing machine and tumble drier, and there's a store for bicycles or for drying outdoor gear.

A convenient, beautifully cared-for base from which to explore the Scottish borders.

Well behaved dogs by arrangement. Bedlinen, towels, gas, electricity included. **'Visit Britain' Four Stars**. Cost: about £285 to £410. Details from Mrs J Stevenson, Camberley, Abbotsford Road, Darnick, Melrose, Roxburghshire TD6 9AJ. Telephone 01896 823648.

www.drumblairontweed.co.uk
email: jacky.stevenson@drumblair.freeserve.co.uk

Auchengray map 4/181
Muirhall Holiday Cottages

In rural Lanarkshire, *under forty minutes from both Edinburgh and Glasgow*, these four cottages (**sleeping 4, 4, 4 and 2**) have been quite beautifully renovated. Visitors have admired uncluttered, pristine interiors, nicely understated white walls, superb joinery, deep leather sofas, the last word in expensive fabrics, linen and towels, top notch kitchens.

Muirhall fills a gap geographically, but its Five Stars help make it a destination in its own right. We'll see it in 2007...

There's underfloor heating, log and coal fires, remote control Velux roof windows, en-suite bathrooms. Unsurprisingly, they have **Five Stars** from 'Visit Britain'. Facilities includes satellite TV, a sauna, an international standard putting green, mountain bikes, a barbecue, internet access, mobile phones provided, a DVD library. Daily dishwashing is available, a laundry service, a gourmet chef [by arrangement], a welcome basket, a car and driver [by arrangement]. Cost: about £560 to £790. Suitable for pets. Contact Chris and Gabi Walker, Muirhall Holiday Cottages, Muirhall Farm, Auchengray, Lanark ML11 8LL. Telephone/fax 01501 785 114.

www.muirhallholidaycottages.co.uk
email: info@muirhallholidaycottages.co.uk

Straiton, near Maybole
Blairquhan

On a golden summer day in 2006 we turned off a country road to the beautiful Blairquhan estate, to revisit some of the most inviting Scottish cottages we know. They're easily accessible (about half an hour from Prestwick airport, say) and have been featured by us for over 20 years.

McDowall is one of several charmers on this lovely estate. Note that the upstairs twin room has views of the gardens. Note also: there's a downstairs double bedroom.

Cuninghame is a fairly recent conversion, with masses of character. Stay here and you'll experience the fabulous walled garden!

We know all seven properties. *Cuninghame*, converted in 1995 from the original potting shed and bothy and situated on the wall of the glorious walled garden which was a riot of colour when we visited, has a living/dining room/kitchen with woodburner, French windows and a huge arch-to-floor window; downstairs are two twin bedrooms and bathroom; upstairs a further twin room and a spacious playroom. *McDowall*, also a former bothy and on the garden wall, has a kitchen/living room with sofa bed and a double bedroom downstairs; upstairs is a twin room overlooking the gardens. *Kennedy Cottage* forms one side of a courtyard which is part of Blairquhan Castle and has stone carvings dating to 1575. *McIntyre, Farrer* and *Wauchope* are apartments in the former coachman's house and stables; we especially liked the former, **sleeping 6**, with a large upstairs kitchen/living/dining room that has glorious views.

During 2004 Wauchope was greatly enlarged. Downstairs, it has a large living room, an adjoining dining room and kitchen, and a bathroom. (There are two divan beds in the living room.) Upstairs, there are four bedrooms with twin beds, and a second bathroom.

Bishopland Lodge, tucked away on its own, has exceptional views towards the castle and of the Girvan Valley. Throughout we noted excellent carpets and rugs, pretty drapes and duvets, attractive pictures and posters, useful bedside and standard lamps.

All have oil central heating. Prices are from around £221 in winter to £880 in summer. Details from the Blairquhan Estate Office, Straiton, Maybole KA19 7LZ. Telephone 01655 770239, fax 770278.

www.blairquhan.co.uk
email: enquiries@blairquhan.co.uk

Blairgowrie, near Pitlochry
Ardblair Castle Cottages

We've seen some pretty places in our years on *The Good Holiday Cottage Guide*, but the scene at Ardblair really is a delight. In the lea of a picture-book castle, with ginger-haired Highland cattle grazing in the grounds, the two cottages are as 'Scottish' as you will get. They are easily accessible, not remote, and we've had many enthusiastic reader responses over the years.

The location is one of the best possible Scottish touring bases, three minutes' drive from the 'gateway-to-the-Highlands' town of Blairgowrie, but in fine (rolling and wooded rather than bleak) rural surroundings.

The 19th century white timbered coach house and stables that stand in the grounds of the castle have been converted by Mr and Mrs Blair Oliphant into two very well-equipped, extremely comfortable, painstakingly cared-for self-catering units. The open plan kitchen/living room, the tidy looks

An unusual example of Scottish weather-boarding, behind which is an extremely comfortable and informal base from which to explore central Scotland.

A typical sitting room at Ardblair: neat, easy-to-look-after, unfussy and yet perfectly comfortable. 'Nice to come home to' after a day's touring...

of the units, with their fitted neutral carpets (tiles in the bathrooms and kitchens) and simple pine furnishings, all lend a certain stamp of quality. *We have never, in eighteen years, had a reader-complaint*, and we know of many repeat visits.

Among the things people remember are good books to read, a particularly attractive set of carved dining chairs in the *Coach House* and a delightful arrangement of dining table and benches in *The Stable*. The Stable has two bathrooms and **sleeps 9** in twin and triple-bedded attic rooms with sloping ceilings and Velux windows, plus four wee ones in an adult-sized bunk-bedded ground floor room. Though if all nine were in residence space might be tight. The Coach House **sleeps 5** in a double and triple-bedded room.

Guests can enjoy the family's 800 acre farmlands, whose livestock includes the beautiful Highland cattle, geese and occasional visits from a local herd of deer. Not suitable for dogs. Open all year (night storage heating, TV, double glazing). Cost: a *very reasonable* £230 to £395. Linen provided.

Details from Mr Blair Oliphant, Ardblair Castle, Blairgowrie, Perthshire PH10 6SA. Telephone/fax 01250 873155.

Scotland-wide
Scottish Country Cottages*

A 2006 journey through much of Scotland was memorable for the good sprinkling of 'SCC' properties we saw. These included one that offers a rare chance to stay on the island of Lismore, off Port Appin (*Tigh An Uillt*, **sleeps 2**, Ref UPW). Also a substantial modern conversion (though in keeping with its surroundings) near Ballater, on 'Royal Deeside' (*Braehead Steading*, **sleeps 18**, Ref USY). And in Glenisla, near Blairgowrie, we were delighted by the cottages on the *Brewlands Estate* (**sleep from 4 to 12**, Refs UUN, SYH, UNH, SDDB).

Of all the glossy annual brochures that cross our desk, this is one of three or four that immediately grabs our attention.

For example, in a part of Scotland most outsiders don't know – the Ayrshire coast – *High Mains Cottage*, at Ballantrae, is an attractive tradi-

Dalvanie Mill, Glenisla, near Blairgowrie (not featured) sleeps up to six. Ref S33.

Wester Brewlands, on the Brewlands Estate, is prettily situated, and sleeps 12.

tional cottage, well modernised (but still with an open fire) with panoramic views. **Sleeping up to 6**, it has a big garden and is quietly located. A sand-and-shingle beach and a pub serving food are just a mile. Ref UPC.

Another part of the country that's best known by Scots is 'The Trossachs'. Just 200 yards from the focal point that is Loch Katrine, *The Old Smiddy* is a fine property with loch views and a woodburner. **Sleeps 6**. Ref UYA.

A couple of years ago we heard from Buckinghamshire-based readers who stayed in *Macinnisfree Cottage*, on the Isle of Skye. **Sleeping 7**, this looks on to an extraordinary panorama that takes in some of western Scotland's most-loved coastal landmarks and seascapes. Ref SBC.

Any of the cottages on the Ardmaddy Estate, about twelve miles south of Oban, brings together history and fabulous views. There are four extremely well converted cottages, the biggest of which (in terms of accommodation) is *The Stables*, **sleeping 8 'plus 2'**. Ref SBZ.

One of our favourite parts of Scotland is the Kintyre peninsula, and we are very pleased to single out three extraordinary cottages, **each for 2**, once used by lighthouse keepers of the now-automated lighthouse on Davaar Island, near Campbeltown. (Refs SEE/SED/UMG.)

Details and brochures from Scottish Country Cottages, Stoney Bank, Earby, Colne, Lancashire BB94 0AA.

Brochures and bookings: 0870 197 6892.

www.scottish-country-cottages.co.uk

Balquhidder
Rhuveag

Overlooking Loch Voil, near the tiny village of Balquhidder, this well situated house is almost surrounded by a mass of trees, azaleas and rhododendrons. We have seen it, and would class it as 'one in a thousand'. In fact, it's on our list of places we'd like to stay in ourselves some time. Used frequently by the owners them-

One of our all-time favourites in Scotland, both for character and location.

selves, it is warm and very comfortable, with log fires, a Rayburn in the kitchen, and a clothes drying room, as well as central heating. Though rural and 'traditional', there is nothing primitive about the house: in a splendid kitchen it has a dishwasher, washing machine, ceramic hob and more. It **sleeps 8**, and has three reception rooms. The house gets water from a burn which flows through its six acres; there is splendid walking, and tenants may use the 'house rowing boat'. They can sail, windsurf and water-ski on Loch Earn, at the end of the glen. There's an award-winning restaurant half a mile up the road – 'very good, but expensive'.

Dogs are welcome, but this is sheep country, and they must be well controlled. Linen and towels are not available. TV. Cost: about £350 to £475. Details from John and Vanda Pelly, Spring Hill, East Malling, Kent ME19 6JW. Telephone 01732 842204, fax 873506.

Kirkmichael, near Pitlochry   map 4/166
Balnakilly Highland Cottages/Log Cabins

Perthshire – so much more accessible than, say, the western Highlands, is hilly, green and beautiful. These cottages (unpretentious, comfy, quiet and full of character: **Colour section A, Page 3**) are on a 1500-acre estate. You could be 'miles from anywhere', but you're not in fact remote. There are four properties, one of them the traditional stone *Loch Cottage*, two of them Norwegian log cabins, the fourth a two storeyed timber building, finished to a good standard, called

Interior of Rowan, a substantial two-storey timber building that offers traditional 'cottagey comfort'...

Rowan Lodge. We have always especially liked Loch Cottage, newly refurbished in 2005, which all but opens right on to the water.

Sleeps 4, 5 or 6. There's ski-ing in the area in season, and good walking, shooting and fishing are all readily available – on the estate and elsewhere. Dogs are welcome. Linen is provided, towels are available for hire. TV. Cost: £190 to £400. Details from Mr and Mrs Reid, Balnakilly Estates, Kirkmichael, Perthshire PH10 7NB. Telephone or fax 01250 881356.

www.balnakillyestate.co.uk   email: balnakilly@hotmail.com

Ecosse Unique*

We have never, in 25 years, had a whisper of a complaint about this agency, which has about 300 properties spread all over Scotland, from the beautiful Border country to Orkney. In a sense, the organisation was a 'founder member' of *The Good Holiday Cottage Guide*!

Being based in the Borders the agency has been effective in promoting this often overlooked and much underrated region. And during a 2006 visit we saw two absolute delights near Selkirk. These were *The Steading*, on the Whitmuir Estate, and *Knowpark Cottage*, both amid quiet, idyllic country-side, well away from through-traffic. They **sleep 4/5 and 5** respectively.

*Among the many beautifully situated properties on the agency's books is Achduart, **sleeping 6** and overlooking the tranquil Summer Isles. Just an amazing fifty yards from the sea and only four miles from Achiltibuie, it lies at the end of a single-track road and is completely secluded. With its own private garden, and access to a further five acres of wooded garden, it faces south and has spectacular sea and mountain views.*

Most properties, such as *Old Hyndhope*, **sleeping 6**, splendidly situated on a Selkirkshire hilltop, are in peaceful rural or coastal locations. Or, for stimulating city breaks, where apartments often have the edge over hotels, you could consider 17th century *Peffermill House* (**sleeping 6/7**) in Edinburgh, or one of the agency's rather elegant properties in Glasgow.

There are idyllic cottages in Highland Perthshire, such as *Balvarran Mill* (**sleeping 4**) near Pitlochry, near Loch Tay, and, in the hills of a private country estate near Dunkeld, the spectacularly positioned *Keeper's House* (**sleeping 6/7**).

There are also a number of excellent cottages round Loch Ness, such as *Bunloit Farmhouse* (**sleeping 5**), where the view is simply jaw-dropping.

On the ever-romantic islands of Skye, Mull and (just off the mainland near Kinlochmoidart) the privately owned Eilean Shona, there are excellent shoreline cottages (of all sizes) in locations to die for, while on the mainland there are many traditional Highland cottages set amid equally stunning scenery. Check out, for example *Bunallt Eachain* (**sleeping 6**) and *Achleek* (**sleeping 5/6**) on the shores of Loch Sunart, or *Achduart* (**sleeping 6**) which overlooks the lovely Summer Isles, off the west coast.

Do request their brochure: Ecosse Unique Ltd, Lilliesleaf, Melrose, Roxburghshire TD6 9JD. Telephone: 01835 822277. Fax 870417.

Or check their web sites:

www.unique-cottages.co.uk and **www.uniquescotland.com**
email: reservations@uniquescotland.com

Dunning, near Perth
Duncrub Holidays

Chapel House incorporates original features (as does The Tower House)...

In a superb location for people wanting to explore 'the heart of Scotland' and, say, the Trossachs, sometimes called Scotland-in-a-nutshell, there are two much-admired 19th century chapel apartments, a ten minute walk from the conservation village of Dunning (it's easy to locate: only just south of the A9 trunk road). *The Tower House* (**'Visit Scotland' Five Stars**), the ultimate romantic hideaway **for 2**, has an open plan kitchen/dining/sitting room on the ground floor and, via a narrow stone spiral staircase, an upper floor double bedroom (five foot bed) and bathroom. *Chapel House* (**Four Stars**) in part is modern, incorporating parts of the original chapel. It **sleeps 4** in an ensuite twin (or double) and upper floor double bedroom and bathroom. Visitors can enjoy a game of badminton and table tennis in the nave of the chapel. Linen and towels are included. TVs, videos, central heating, washer/dryers. Well behaved dogs are welcome in Chapel House. No smoking. Cost: about £320 to £550. Switch/Solo/Access/Visa/Mastercard. Further details from Wilma Marshall, Duncrub Holidays Ltd, Dalreoch, Perth PH2 0QJ. Telephone 01764 684100. Fax 684633.

www.duncrub-holidays.com   email: ghc@duncrub-holidays.com

Abade Self Catering is a hand-picked group of quality cottages, lodges and unusual places to stay in the glorious county of Perthshire. Owners with Abade (an old Scots word for abode, or home) aim to give their visitors a really good holiday experience, by not only providing excellent high quality self-catering accommodation in beautiful locations, but also applying that attention to detail that makes all the difference between 'a good time' and a really memorable holiday.

Perthshire is perfect for sightseeing, with everything to offer from a *ceilidh* to a classical concert, gardens to grand castles, golf courses, whisky distilleries, restaurants and much, much more.

You can choose an apartment in a castle, a 19th century chapel tower, a converted mill by a lochside, a charming garden flat in an old clock tower, and others. Most are just an hour's drive from Edinburgh and Glasgow airports. The central part of Scotland is packed with alternatives, from St Andrews, 'home of golf', to a remote highland glen with dramatic scenery, and wildlife the only company.

For that luxury holiday break, a romantic getaway, a really comfortable home from home, or just for your holiday, choose an Abade holiday. (Visit our website to make your choice.)

Details from Wilma Marshall, Abade, Dalreoch, Dunning, Perth PH2 0QJ Telephone 01764 684100. **www.abade.co.uk   email: ghc@abade.co.uk**

Advertisement feature

Tomich, near Cannich
Tomich Holidays

One of our favourite short journeys in the north of Scotland is westwards from Beauly, near Inverness, via quiet country roads bordered by trees, towards sleepy, little known Cannich, and then to end-of-the-road Tomich, a beautiful stone-built place, preserved as a conservation

Even in Highland terms the location is outstanding, and the properties excellent.

village. What we go to see is a delightful arrangement of stone and slate courtyard cottages. There's a snug and cosy Victorian dairy and six two-storeyed timber chalets. The cottages have memorable panoramic views and are highly graded by **'Visit Scotland'**. The Victorian dairy is a stone-built cottage, part of a Grade II listed building. A short stroll away, among trees, are the timber chalets, private but not remote, within 100 yards of another. Each is roomy, simple and 'practical', but comfortable, with balconies for wildlife spotting, birch trees and grassy banks. Most are booked by guests returning for 'endless walks', the cycling, the wildlife, the quiet, and the lovely indoor pool. Dogs welcome. TVs/videos/DVDs. **Sleep 4 to 6**. Cost: £230 to £590. Details from Tomich Holidays, Guisachan Farm, Tomich, By Beauly, Inverness-shire IV4 7LY. Telephone 01456 415332 or fax 415499.

www.tomich-holidays.co.uk   email: admin@tomich-holidays.co.uk

Lochaline (Morvern)
Shore Cottage   map 4/183

The location is stunning even in Highland terms. Even better: one of our favourite short ferry crossings in the whole of Scotland operates from close to this charming substantial property that was originally an inn (built 1846). The ferry is however infrequent, and doesn't operate particularly early or late, so disturbance should be minimal. This is one of

An enviable location on the Morvern shoreline, with inspiring views...

our favourite corners of the whole country, and we suggest that if you are visiting the Isle of Mull you contrive to take the 'long route' from Oban on one leg of the journey and this less well known five minute crossing on the other. The walking (and strolling!) is marvellous, traffic a rarity.

Specifically, the house **sleeps 6**, has a bathroom with bath and shower, an open fire and a large enclosed garden. In living here you will no longer be required to provide refreshments for passing travellers, but you will find a pub 600 yards away. Ref 16444.

Details from Country Holidays, Spring Mill, Barnoldswick, Lancashire BB94 0AA. Bookings/brochures: 0870 197 6895.

Live search and book: www.country-holidays.co.uk

Scotland-wide
Large Holiday Houses*

In early 2006 we visited the people behind this extraordinary organisation and looked at – more or less at random – a couple of the sort of properties on their books that we know appeal to readers of this guide.

We drove via quiet roads towards Portmahomack, and the very imposing but nevertheless privately situated, early 19th century country mansion called *Pitcalzean House*. We don't have the space here to do justice to this fabulous property, but we remember elegant rooms, fine furniture and paintings, as well as a warm and welcoming atmosphere. It **sleeps up to 23 people, plus 4** in a separate cottage.

There are over a hundred impressive properties (**sleeping from 7 to 37**) spread widely over Scotland that are on the books of Large Holiday Houses, run by Wynne Bentley, who founded it in 1997. Her own base, *Poyntzfield House*, a Grade A listed Georgian mansion (**sleeping 16 plus 4 under-10s**) near Inverness, is among them. She offers a compelling combination: the romance of great houses and castles, marvellous locations and the huge appeal of properties where extended families or groups of friends can stay together. Several are historically important, such as the 11th-century *Dairsie Castle* (**sleeping 8/13**) in Fife, close to St Andrews, and cliff-top *Craighall Castle* (**sleeping 10**) in Perthshire.

Calgary Castle, which enjoys one of the best views on Mull, facing sandy Calgary Bay beyond meadows framed by woods, is more modern, having been built in the 18th century as a laird's house. Despite its tower and mock battlements, it has a comfortable, lived-in atmosphere.

We had a delightful stay, ten miles south of Oban, at the secluded *Bragleen House* (**sleeping 7/8**) at the end of a five-mile lane beside Loch Scammadale. The owner, who built it in 1996, ready for his retirement, has combined luxury with comfort – spacious rooms, deep sofas, double-glazing and a fitted kitchen complete with bread-maker. After a walk up the glen at the back, we strolled later in the day down to the loch: perfect!

Details and a copy of the brochure (one of the best we've seen) from Wynne Bentley, Large Holiday Houses Ltd, Poyntzfield House, Poyntzfield, Dingwall, Ross-shire IV7 8LX. Telephone 01381 610496. (She also has a number of large properties in France: see Page 270.)

www.LHHScotland.com   email: LHHS@LHHScotland.com

Lickleyhead Castle, Aberdeenshire. Family owned, never a ruin, it retains much of its original medieval atmosphere. Sleeps 14.

Drumrunie House, Braemar. A great 'good four star' family house, with super gardens and stunning views. Sleeps 12.

Scotland-wide
Little Holiday Houses*

As you might expect from the people behind Large Holiday Houses (see previous page) this is a very judiciously chosen selection of properties.

From a 2006 visit we especially remember a very special, historically fascinating, quite lovingly restored thatched cottage right by the harbour at Avoch, a fishing village on the Moray Firth. It is a joy: a great rarity, an uncompromising tribute to the devotion of the owner to complete authenticity. **Sleeping 4,** it's called *Fisherman's Cottage*. Dogs welcome.

If you appreciate fine period houses for themselves you will probably like *Lochnagarry*, at Golspie in Sutherland. **Sleeping up to 10**, it is notable for elegant, high ceilinged rooms. There is a Rayburn and an open fire.

Almost any rural property on the stunningly beautiful west coast will appeal to readers of this guide. For example, *Clachan Garden*, near Ullapool, is a top notch property in a fabulous setting, located within one of our favourite features – a walled garden.

Culkein, equally memorable and pristine, is perched on the shores of Eddrachillis Bay, north of Lochinver, and underneath magnificent and famously photogenic Suilven mountain. It has an especially inviting and stylish sitting room, with an open fire. This and Clachan Garden **sleep 9** and **7 'plus 1'** respectively.

Too often overlooked by visitors to Scotland, the peaceful, fertile Black Isle (the original of the 'black' has nothing to do with colour) is also a useful jumping-off point for seeing much of the far north. **Sleeping 6**, the *West Wing* of Poyntzfield House – see also the opposite page – is a part of the fine Georgian mansion that is normally rented out as a whole by large groups but at quieter times of the year gives smaller parties the chance to experience the splendid ambience.

There's a super farmhouse kitchen, a snooker room with a *full size table,* a large grassy area for outdoor games.

Details and a copy of the brochure (one of the best we've seen) from Wynne Bentley, Little Holiday Houses Ltd, Poyntzfield House, Poyntzfield, Dingwall, Ross-shire IV7 8LX. Telephone 01381 610496.

www.LittleHolidayHouses.com
email: LHH@LHHScotland.com

Smartly on parade: handsome Clachan Garden is on the shores of Eddrachillis Bay, beneath Suilven mountain...

The School House, Glenfinnan, is on 'the 'Road to the Isles'. With a cosy woodburner, it's rather romantic. Sleeps 8.

Glen Strathfarrar, Struy, near Beauly
Culligran Cottages

We have enjoyed a short stay in one of the four Scandinavian chalets here, long a favourite with readers. They are quite spacious, very warm, have picture windows, and **sleep up to 7**. On a Nature Reserve, but not remote, and close to a salmon-rich river on a sporting estate, Frank and Juliet Spencer-Nairn have five properties, the other a characteristic, traditional *This is one of the best places in Scotland to observe wildlife in its natural habitat.* cottage with a blend of 'antiquey', solid and modern furniture – plus a stag's head! Three chalets have two bedrooms, the fourth three, as has the cottage. All have a good fitted kitchen, the larger properties having a shower as well as a bath. We enjoyed the 15 miles of metalled but private road leading up Glen Strathfarrar, surely one of the Highlands' best kept secrets, 'similar to Glen Affric but more intimate'. Ideal for biking: bikes for hire. No TV. Trout and salmon fishing. Guided tours of Frank's deer farm. Dogs welcome. Cost: about £179 to £479. Open mid-March to mid-November. Details from Frank and Juliet Spencer-Nairn, Culligran Cottages, Glen Strathfarrar, Struy, near Beauly, Inverness-shire IV4 7JX. Telephone/fax: 01463 761285.

www.culligrancottages.co.uk and **www.farmstay-highlands.co.uk/culligran**
email: info@culligrancottages.co.uk

Dalcross, East Inverness
Easter Dalziel   map 4/189

This neat and tidy, notably well cared for trio of traditional, stone built cottages makes an exceptionally good base from which to explore the whole of the north, east and west of Scotland. Unpretentious but comfortably furnished, they are surrounded by a large grassy area, with a pretty heather garden to the front and *Always a warm and friendly welcome,* panoramic views of the surrounding *and unfussily comfortable cottages...* countryside. On a working farm with beef cattle, sheep and grain, the jewel in this particular Scottish crown is *Birch*, at one end of the three adjoining properties. It is thickly carpeted, comfortably furnished, its pale green soft furnishings and deep-pile carpets easy on the eye. There's an appealing separate dining alcove. **Sleeps 6**. *Rowan* and *Pine* (**sleeping 4 and 6**) are a little more old fashioned but comfortable, warm and cottagey. They are reasonably priced, and open all year. **'Visit Scotland' Three/Four Stars**. TV. Dogs welcome. Linen and towels included. Cost: about £160 to £510. Details from Mr and Mrs Pottie, Easter Dalziel Farm, Dalcross, Inverness IV2 7JL. Telephone and fax 01667 462213.

www.easterdalzielfarm.co.uk email: ghcg@easterdalzielfarm.co.uk

Rural Retreats*
Dumfries/Newtonmore/Plockton

We are fond of the little-known country north of Dumfries where Rural Retreats (see also Page 246) have four properties on the superb green, rolling 3300 acre Crofts Estate. We visited in the summer of 2006, and saw *Marwhirn Cottage*, **sleeping 4**, and *Marwhirn House*. Close together but still private, both are beautifully located half a mile down a private drive. We met holiday tenants installing themelves in Marwhirn House, and loving it.

Among several superbly well situated properties is *Borenich*, near Pitlochry, very close to (though not quite in sight of) Loch Tummel. **Sleeping 6**, with a zip-link double bed in the main bedroom, it has an open fire and stands within an acre and a half of its own grounds. Also in Perthshire, *Gushat* is an extended semi-detached cottage converted from the village shop. **Sleeping 6**, it's right opposite a nine-hole golf course!

Sitting room of Borenich, a super, detached, recently refurbished property near the popular town of Pitlochry.

Lochenkit, near Dumfries, lies on a private estate, and sleeps up to eight people in comfort and style...

In the Highland village of Newtonmore, situated in the new Cairngorm National Park and thus well placed for walking, is stone-built, detached, 100-year-old *Woodlands Cottage*, **sleeping 5/6**. This charming cottage has a woodburner in the especially handsome sitting room; there's a private enclosed garden, and the River Spey is an easy ten minute stroll away.

And just two miles from Plockton, one of the prettiest and most visited villages in the Highlands, *Achnandaroch Lodge* is a Swiss-chalet style property, **sleeping 9**. Just five miles from Kyle of Lochalsh and the now-free bridge to Skye, it means that that fabulous island is within the scope of, say, a summer evening excursion.

Lochenkit is a 19th century farmhouse on a private estate. Refurbished to high standards, it **sleeps 8** in great comfort. It is on the edge of the moors, with delightful walks. There's a large farmhouse kitchen with an Aga, a sitting room with a log fire, one king-size bedroom with ensuite bathroom, one double and two twin rooms.

Details and a copy of the organisation's impressive brochure from Rural Retreats, Draycott Business Park, Draycott, Gloucestershire GL56 9JY. Telephone 01386 701177, fax 701178.

www.ruralretreats.co.uk

email: info@ruralretreats.co.uk

Kinlochlaggan, near Newtonmore
Ardverikie Estate Cottages

In the summer of 2006 it was a pleasure, not just a duty, to revisit the holiday properties here. For they are surely among the most beautifully situated in the whole of Scotland – which is to rate them very highly!

We met tenants staying in *Gallowvie Farmhouse* and admired spacious rooms, high ceilings, deep sofas, lots of comfort. With, for example, a five-oven Aga, and accommodation for **up to 13**, it has lots of atmosphere. Also, there's an enclosed mature garden. We also revisited *Inverpattack Lodge*, standing on its own on a hillside overlooking the road with good views, **sleeping up to 12**. It has a good sized sitting room, a big dining room and farmhouse kitchen. We have always liked this a lot: a real, rather nostalgic 'family house'.

The estate, rising above and around Loch Laggan, is a kind of microcosm of the extraordinary Highlands. It even embraces a substantial sandy beach that is just one bonus for city dwellers escaping to one of the characterful cottages tucked away in the heart of, or on the edge of, the Estate.

It's well away from any town, a real tonic for people wanting to get away from city cares, but it's not actually in the back of beyond.

There's a good range of sizes and different degrees of seclusion as well as different styles of interior. If you prefer family furniture to MFI and care more about seeing a deer, a hare or a pine marten while you are doing the washing up than about dishwashers and deep-pile carpets, these could be for you. All the houses except *Pinewood*, incidentally, have open fires with free firewood.

Most recently available is *Rowan Brae*, **sleeping 6** and quietly situated close to the water and good walking. We admired the special character of *Ardverikie Gate Lodge* – a listed building this, by a road, best suited to a couple plus, say, one friend or relative. The spiral stair is excellent and fine prints and a particularly good bedroom enhance its appeal further. Pinewood has an especially cosy dining room, gets lots of sun and is indeed among the trees. Not a luxury item but, we thought, welcoming and comfortable. **Sleeps 4**.

Gate Lodge absolutely sets the mood as you approach this memorable place...

Inverpattack sleeps twelve, with masses of space and even more 'character'.

Cost: about £393 to £1450: not expensive if you consider how many the larger properties sleep. Details from Desiree Bruce, The Estate Office, Kinlochlaggan, Inverness-shire PH20 1BX. Telephone 01528 544322.

www.ardverikie.com   email: bookings@ardverikie.com

Attadale, near Lochcarron

We revisited Attadale on a glorious summer day in 2006. The fabulous gardens that are just one reason for booking a holiday in one of the charming, bright and spacious cottages on the estate were surely at their best.

On a previous and memorable occasion we had taken a train from Kyle of Lochalsh to Inverness, getting off at the tiny station halt ('by request only') that serves the Attadale estate. The line and its surroundings got us reaching for our index of superlatives: 'unforgettable scenery'..'a blissful escape from the everyday world'...'exceptional even in Highland terms'.

By road, the A890 must surely be one of the most scenic routes in the Highlands, especially where it veers westwards from the Ullapool/ Inverness road, and then arrives at Kyle of Lochalsh, across the water from Skye. With panoramic views at every turn, it surely underlines one's belief that Scotland is one of the most beautiful countries in the world.

Across the loch from the elongated, pretty, white-painted village of Lochcarron you take a private drive; with the single track railway and the loch behind us, we reached the owners' impressive mansion, and from there drove out into the estate, passing the beautiful gardens that are open to the public, and finally reached the cottages.

Guests have complete access to the estate, famous for its wildlife and its natural beauty, except from 15th August to 15th October when they are asked to keep to the paths while deer are being culled. Loch fishing up in the hills is available, and following a seven year restocking programme, sea trout and salmon have returned to the River Carron: day tickets are available.

In the cottages we noticed open fires or wood stoves, good beds, lots of lamps, many very attractive pictures (some by the owners' daughter, who is a painter). Here was a delightfully lit alcove, there a congenial juxtaposition of dining room and kitchen.

Such a romantic, 'away from it all' location, with comfy estate cottages...

...in complete harmony with their beautiful and unspoilt surroundings.

Sleep 4 to 8. Well behaved, sheep-respecting dogs welcome. Linen and towels provided. No TV reception. Cost: from £275 to £490. Details and colour brochure from Frances Mackenzie, Attadale, Strathcarron, Wester Ross IV54 8YX. Telephone/fax 01520 722862.

www.attadale.com   email: cottages@attadale.com

Glen Coe
Glen Coe Cottages

On a quiet Saturday morning in 2006 we took 'the old road' up towards Glencoe to revisit one of our all-time favourite Scottish holiday cottage set-ups: *24 years in the guide*, and never a complaint. So close to the mysterious and famous glen, to get to these three neat, tucked away pebbledash bungalows in their leafy enclave overlooking the River Coe you cross a cattle grid and pause beside the mirror-like Torren lochan (featured in the latest Harry Potter adventure, 'The Prisoner of Azkaban' – filmed in Glencoe). After this you continue along a track to the three cottages, which combine mod cons with just a hint of the outdoor life – the setting is beautiful and not remote and you do not have to have climbing boots to enjoy it. Fishing is available in the owners' two trout lochs and in the river that flows prettily past the doorstep.

A high standard of comfort is achieved despite the comparatively small size and open plan nature of the single-storey buildings. All the cottages have underfloor heating, fired by an eco-friendly woodchip boiler, and dishwasher, and a shared laundry room for those damper days – for this is

The river and the dramatic glen are near: one is memorably 'close to nature'.

The cottages are 'compact', but well planned and notably warm all year round.

'outward-bound country'. There's a large drying room in the laundry building, a TV/video in each cottage, a payphone and internet access.

All three cottages have a good degree of privacy, because they separately face the river through big picture windows and do not look directly at each other. The River Coe is very well fenced off from the properties and there is no danger to little ones. There is a lot of pinewood, well fitted kitchens and sitting-cum-dining rooms.

This is an excellent base from which to tour not only the wild landscape of Glen Coe and Rannoch Moor but, being close to the Corran Ferry, it is quickly accessible to the Morvern and Ardnamurchan peninsulas and, beyond them, the Isle of Mull. Fort William is half an hour to the north.

Sleep 6 to 8, or the whole place can be taken over by a group of **up to 24**. **'Visit Scotland'** Gold Award for Environmental Management; member of ASSC. **Three 'Visit Scotland' Stars**. Dogs welcome, 'wi-fi' is installed (no charge). Discount for couples-only, children under two free, cots and highchairs included free. Cost: up to a maximum of £795, weekend booking at £98 per night. Details from Victoria Sutherland, Torren, Glencoe, Argyll PH49 4HX. Telephone 01855 811207. Fax 811338.

www.glencoe-cottages.com email: victoria@glencoe-cottages.com

Arisaig, near Mallaig
Arisaig House Cottages

We stayed here in 2005. Better yet, we went by train, and loved the fact that we needed to ask the driver to stop especially for us at what is all but Arisaig House's own little railway station.

It's very special in all sorts of ways, both for itself and for its location. Built as a grand private house in 1864, rebuilt after a fire in 1937, used by the SOE during the Second World War and later opened as a luxury hotel by the Smither family, Arisaig House is a solid stone building occupying a marvellous hillside setting with views to the sea. When the Smithers decided to retire they moved into the main part themselves, leaving four attractive houses on the estate available for holiday lets (**two sleeping 8, one 6 and one 3**), together with two apartments (**sleeping 4 and 2**). All have been decorated and furnished to the same rigorously high standard that won the hotel many accolades. A first for us was to see that the three principal houses each have a computer giving internet access.

Largest of the houses is *The Bothy,* which has two double bedrooms, two twins, two bathrooms and a piano. We particularly admired the terrace outside the lounge, as it runs all along one side overlooking the gardens

The setting (on the magical 'Road to the Isles') is wooded and utterly peaceful...

...and every one of the properties is reliably stylish and very comfortable.

with the sea beyond. *The Courtyard Apartment*, the smallest property (**sleeping 2**), has a lovely mountain view.

The legendary 'Road to the Isles' north to Mallaig (nine miles) passes the main entrance, so guests can easily take a boat trip to Skye or the smaller islands. To the east a fast scenic road leads through the mountains to Fort William (35 miles), and the top-class nine-hole Traigh golf course is only six miles away. On the estate itself, a new all-weather tennis court has been built in the walled garden, and there is a games room with table-tennis, pool table and exercise machine. Mountain bikes are available for hire, and a ten-minute walk takes you direct to a small, sandy beach.

The Arisaig website shows up-to-the-minute availability and all the accommodation can be booked on line (5% discount).

Details from Andrew Smither, Beasdale, Arisaig, Inverness-shire PH39 4NR. Open all year. Some short-breaks are available. No pets. Linen and towels included. Cot and highchair available. **'Visit Scotland' Three/Four Stars**. Telephone 01438 869489.

Aultbea, near Gairloch
Shore Croft

This **Five Star** house is in a beautiful part of Scotland, on a peninsula overlooking Loch Ewe, only yards from a pebble beach, and just 20 minutes' drive from charming Gairloch. The fine architect-designed house has the further advantage of memorable views. **Sleeping up to 8** in great comfort, Shore Croft has accommodation on two floors.

The house is quite an attraction in itself, and the location sets it off beautifully...

Downstairs there's a very large kitchen/dining room with dishwasher, range cooker, a large American fridge freezer and microwave. There is a dining table seating eight and French doors opening on to decking with garden furniture and a barbecue, a large sitting room with open fire, satellite TV, DVD and music system, plus a cloakroom. Upstairs, the master bedroom has an en-suite shower room and separate dressing room; there are three further twin bedded rooms and a family bathroom.

Open all year. Cost: about £495 to £1050 per week (Christmas and New Year prices on application). Dogs welcome. No smoking. Contact Hilary Cowan. Telephone 0151 494 1488.

www.shorecroft.co.uk
email: hilary.cowan3@btinternet.com

Achnamara, near Lochgilphead
The Bothy map 4/206

Many of our readers love properties without mains electricity (mostly for nostalgic reasons), along with seclusion in a beautiful and private place; *The Bothy*, **sleeping 4**, might suit them. On its own in 45 acres of mixed woodland, it's adjacent to over a mile of coastline, with a private jetty, slip and boathouse suitable for small boats. There are woodland walks and

The owners' house: Millstone on the right.

stunning views. Boat trips can be arranged. This well built log cabin (**'Visit Scotland' Four Stars**) is warm and cosy, with a woodburning stove that heats the water, so a hot bath is easy. There are two bedrooms: one double (large), the other bunk bedded (small). Bedlinen and towels provided. The sitting room and kitchen are open plan and have double-glazed windows.

NB A second property, *Millstone Cottage* (**sleeping 4**, attached to the owners' house – see photo) is also available.

Details from The Cottage Collection, 17-23 Ber Street, Norwich NR1 3EU. Telephone 01603 724809.

www.the-cottage-collection.co.uk
email: bookings@the-cottage-collection.co.uk

Strontian, by Acharacle
Seaview Grazings

For about twenty years now, this harmonious, easy-on-the-eye arrangement of Scandinavian log cabins has proved to be the makings of a delightful getting-to-know-the-Highlands experience for cottage guide readers. And many of these have become regulars at Seaview Grazings: 70% of bookings are repeats, with many weeks sold out months in advance. When we last visited, the Hanna family who run it were awaiting the arrival of a family who have been coming here for a fortnight's holiday *three times a year for seventeen years*.

The eleven-acre site has five cabins (**sleeping 4 or 5**) on a lightly wooded hillside facing the loch. Built of real pine-logs, they are available throughout the year, being of permanent-home standard with double-glazing, modern kitchens and full bathrooms, all now with over-bath shower. Each feels private, but many guests like the fact that there are neighbours (and the owners) near at hand. Shops and pubs are only a mile away.

All the cabins, which are regularly refurbished, have large windows to make the most of the lovely views, yet they have a really warm atmosphere inside, with full central heating. The fully-fitted kitchens have four-ring electric cookers, washing machines, fridge/freezers, microwaves and roomy cupboards.

Boat-hire can easily be arranged locally, as can loch fishing – for beginners as well as more experienced anglers – up in the hills. The area is also excellent for all grades of walking. 'Wild glens, peaceful woodlands, beautiful coastal walks and mountain challenges – at the end of a week we'd experienced only a fraction of what was on offer', wrote one reader.

Yet another extraordinary location on the west coast of Scotland! Quite amazing... *Each of the log houses feels private and self contained, but there's no isolation.*

Motoring from Strontian is a joy too. We ourselves arrived after a visit to Mull via the 19-mile drive from the pretty ferry crossing at Lochaline.

Blankets/duvets, linen, towels, electricity included. Children's cots and highchairs available free of charge. Three cabins have two bedrooms (double and twin), the others have three (double, twin and single). Cost: from about £260 to £610. Some short breaks available. Details from John Hanna, Seaview Grazings Holidays, Strontian, by Acharacle, Argyll PH36 4HZ. Telephone 01967 402409.

www.seaviewgrazings.co.uk
email: gareth@seaviewgrazings.co.uk

Elgol/Staffin

Over the years we've visited a good clutch of properties on Skye in the hands of the ever more interesting and go-ahead Welcome Cottages organisation. Here are two that retain a lot of their original character and are in scenically impressive locations. In the exceptionally quiet and attractive village of Elgol, near Broadford, a cottage **sleeping 6** (Ref W41104), with an open fire, has the huge advantage for any but the most confirmed lounge lizards of being

At Elgol, near Broadford, this is 'one to remember'. At the end of a beautiful country road, it has spectacular views and an open fire. Sleeps up to six people.

just five minutes from the Cuillin Hills. Further north, at Staffin (Staffin Island is famous for its birdlife) is a handsome, traditional crofthouse (Ref W4138) that makes a comfortable holiday base. **Sleeping 4**, it has panoramic views, a woodburning stove and is handy for visiting impressive Dunvegan Castle.

For availability and bookings, contact Welcome Cottages, Spring Mill, Earby, Barnoldswick, Lancashire BB94 0AA. Brochures/bookings: 0870 197 6957. Properties in France are also available: see Page 271.

www.welcomecottages.com

Stein (Isle of Skye)
The Captain's House

We appreciate almost every corner of Skye, but we especially like the more out-of-the-way places. One such is the quiet, pretty, waterside village of Stein **(map 4/203)**, where nothing is out of place within its row of white houses. They incorporate one of the best pubs and one of the best seafood restaurants on the island. The handsomest house of all,

The Captain's House is an excellent property, a great place from which to explore the whole of Skye...

known for its ground floor art gallery and craft shop, is The Captain's House. The first and second floors of this make up a spacious holiday house (self-contained, private and quiet). We liked the big sitting room, the deep sofa and armchairs and the Victorian tiled open fire. The large kitchen/breakfast room overlooks the loch, as do all but one of the rooms in this appealing property; off it there's a separate dining room. There are two large bedrooms, one double and one twin. **'Visit Britain' Three Stars**. **Sleeps up to 4** (cot available). Non-smoking. Linen, not towels, included. Dogs by arrangement. Cost: about £225 to £390. Details from Mrs Cathy Myhill, The Captain's House, Stein, Waternish, Isle of Skye IV55 8GA. Telephone 01470 592223/592218.

www.the-captains-house.co.uk   email: cathy@the-captains-house.co.uk

Dervaig (Isle of Mull)
Penmore Mill

Even during its first year in the guide we had happy reader reports about this. An old watermill (**sleeping 8/9 people**) just outside the village of Dervaig – famous for the tiny Mull Little Theatre – was imaginatively converted by Pat and Iain Morrison, who live in the house behind. We guessed Pat is an artist: the bathroom is a pale turquoise, and each bed-

Mull is 'a different world', and this is a superb base from which to explore it...

room, two doubles (one downstairs), a twin and one with bunks, features its own colour scheme set off by pine floors. A long pine table is the centrepiece of the fitted kitchen – fridge-freezer, washing-machine, dishwasher, microwave, double-electric oven – which has a terracotta tiled floor with cosy underfloor heating and a farmhouse atmosphere. It leads into the sitting room with its log-effect stove and deep sofas. A sheltered patio-deck makes a pleasant sitting/eating area. Iain runs the island's Turus Mara boat trips, so most guests go to see Fingal's Cave on Staffa and to the Treshnish Isles, home to a colony of puffins. Cost: about £500 to £850. Details from Pat Morrison, Penmore Mill, Dervaig, Isle of Mull PA75 6QS. Telephone/fax 01688 400242.
email: info@turusmara.com   www.mull-self-catering.co.uk

Isle of Mull (Carsaig)   map 4/200
Pier Cottage/The Library

This is an unusual and most appealing holiday property. A few yards above the rocky shore on the island's south coast, these two remote cottages convey something of an 'end of the world' feeling as you approach them. Access is along a four-mile narrow wooded lane off the single-track 'main' road, which is one of the most scenic we've ever driven. The single-storey stone *Pier*

Marvellous, we thought, for autumn and winter breaks. Weekends may be available. (This is Pier Cottage.)

Cottage has a verandah where we found two happy visitors watching out for otters and seals over a late breakfast. None appeared while we there but as a consolation they gave us bunches of delicious grapes from the prolific vine that covered the ceiling. Wood-panelling inside Pier Cottage (**sleeping 3/4**) gives it a cosy feel and there are masses of books. *The Library* – built originally to house more of the owner's books – is a roomy, open-plan log-cabin (**sleeping 4/6**) up the terraced garden. An unusual feature is a small plunge-pool in the shared rock-garden. Cost: £295 to £495. Details from David McLean, The Oasis, 181 Lyham Rd, Brixton, London SW2 5PY. Telephone 020 8671 6663. Mobile (part-time) 07738 816469.
email: dhmclean@tiscali.co.uk

113

Isle of Carna
Isle of Carna Cottage

Having featured this cottage in our guide for two years we actually stayed in it in 2006 – an idyllic short break. You almost have the whole of the little island to yourself: there are just two other cottages, only one of those for holiday letting (see below):

This cottage really is one in a thousand!

hard by the landing stage for the 16-foot boat, with outboard, that comes with your booking. 'Isle of Carna' cottage is two hundred metres along the pretty foreshore from there. For many visitors its appeal is not just the closeness to nature but the fact that there is no electricity. Cooking is by means of a bottled-gas stove, lighting by gas or candle, plentiful heating/water by a Parkray Anthracite stove – we tested it – an open fire and closed stove. There's a Calor gas fridge.

The beautiful 600-acre traffic-free island lies in the middle of Loch Sunart, between the peninsula of Ardnamurchan to the north and the remote hills of Morvern to the south. The 550 ft rocky peak offers spectacular views (we did the climb!) and there are many rocky inlets and beaches ideal for watching wildlife: seals, herons, cormorants, eagles, buzzards, porpoises, otters, foxes and red deer live here. Originally a shepherd's bothy, the cottage is a cosy, well equipped, tranquil base for trips on or off the island. Caretakers contactable by radio at any time. Cost (including boat): about £525 to £800. Dogs welcome. Linen supplied, but not towels. **Sleeps up to 8,** with two adult sized bunk beds. Details from Timothy and Sue Milward, Pine House, Gaddesby, Leicestershire LE7 4XE. Telephone 01664 840213. Fax 840660. **www.isleofcarna.co.uk email: timothy@timmilward.wanadoo.co.uk**

Isle of Carna
Carna Farmhouse

You'll probably initially be transported to your holiday accommodation on Carna by one of the Jackson family, who run boat charters and look after both of the letting properties. The second of the two, Carna Farmhouse, is owned by them. Closer to the landing stage than Isle

Looking towards Carna Farmhouse, from beside Isle of Carna Cottage.

of Carna Cottage, it's a comfy bungalow, **sleeping 4 plus 2**. Here, there's electric light (only) from a generator. Linen and towels included.

Also available on the mainland: a fine, spacious apartment at Glenborrodale, overlooking Carna (accessed from very steep stairs).

Details from Allison and Andy Jackson, Bruach na Fearna, Laga Bay, Acharacle, Ardnamurchan, Argyll PH36 4JW. Telephone 01972 500 208. Fax 500222. Mobile: 07799 608199.
www.west-scotland-marine.com email:ardcharters@aol.com

Three Mile Water (Fort William)
Druimarbin Farmhouse

Revisited by us in the summer of 2006, this fine, pleasantly rambling family house – just three miles south of Fort William – has marvellous views of Loch Linnhe. We appreciate the home comforts, the character and the location: excellent for touring. Reached via its own drive, and on the edge of woodland, it **sleeps up to 7/8** (in comfortable beds) – though the handsome dining table

This is a warm and comfortable base for a family holiday in the Highlands, with many gratifying reader reports...

will actually seat 12. There is an open fire (logs are supplied) in the drawing room, which is graced by fine paintings, antique furniture, comfortable sofas, old fashioned armchairs. There are lots of good books, the odd bit of tartanry to remind you you're in the Highlands, a very well equipped kitchen, a payphone, Ordnance Survey maps.

TV, video and DVD. Bedlinen included. Walk-in drying room. Dogs possible by arrangement. Cost: £700 to £800 per week. Further details are available from Mrs Anthony German-Ribon, 57 Napier Avenue, London SW6 3PS. Telephone/fax 020-7736 4684.

www.coruanan.co.uk   email: germanribon@googlemail.com

By Fort William   map 4/209
Coruanan Farmhouse

A memorable visit of our 2006 visit to the Highlands was to a house amid lovely, partly wooded country high above the Fort William-Corran road, at the end of a private lane. In the same ownership as Druimarbin (see above) and quite close to that, Coruanan has a partial view of Loch Linnhe and a superb view of Ben Nevis. **Sleeping 6**, it has an intriguing

One of the happiest discoveries of our summer 2006 visit to the Highlands.

history: in 1745, the site was the home of the standard bearer to Lochiel (Clan Cameron Chieftain) during Bonnie Prince Charlie's Jacobite Rebellion. The standard was found at the turn of the century in one of the old buildings here where it had lain since the rebels' defeat at Culloden. It is now at Achnacarry Castle, home of the present Lochiel.

A sitting room with an open log fire, a cosy kitchen/diner, central heating and double glazing, a drying cupboard (for outdoor clothing), telephone, colour TV, DVD and CD players, a dishwasher, washing machine, tumble drier, microwave and fridge freezer make this a truly comfortable house.

Cost: about £500-£800 per week. Long weekend breaks (winter only) £350. Dogs possible by arrangement.

Details as for Druimarbin, above.

115

Achahoish, near Lochgilphead
Ellary Estate Cottages

Over the years, one of our greatest pleasures in putting this guide together has been driving westwards and then further westwards on the Scottish mainland. And then, if we're lucky with our itinerary, catching a Caledonian MacBrayne ferry to one or more of the Hebridean islands.

While still on the mainland, the journey to the Ellary estate, via ever narrower country roads, and with ever more impressive panoramic views at nearly every turn, is one of the most memorable for us. It's 25 years since we first came here (*the Ellary cottages have appeared in every edition since our first*) and it seemed appropriate to make one of our occasional revisits in the summer of 2006.

Ellary stands out as a haven of quiet and calm, an antidote to stress. It is one of those places that *guarantees* 'peace, perfect peace'. (Even the nearest shop is 20 minutes' drive!)

The 15,000 acres on the sumptuous promontory between Lochs Sween and Caolisport, in Argyll, belong to the Ellary estate, an ancient family property that is partly farmed (predominantly sheep) yet mostly left wild

Ellary Cottage is a favourite of ours. Sleeping 4, it's the oldest of the cottages.

Location, location, location...it's a pleasure to sit and drink in the scenery.

for recreation purposes. Guests are welcome to wander where they will.

No-one can guarantee that you'll see otter, deer, eagles, peregrines, wildcats or any other estate residents, but they will certainly tell you where and when to look. There are several lovely beaches of white sand, and fishing – trout from the lochs and salmon and sea trout in Lochead Burn. Four of the self-catering units are ranch-type chalets, simply-built wooden structures with wide verandahs overlooking the loch. The cottages, recently much upgraded and without exception havens of comfort and warmth are mostly of stone. *The Lodge* is a particular joy: we loved the spiral staircase! There is an open fire as well as night storage heaters, a double room and two twin rooms. We also admired *Gardener's Cottage* and looked in again to one of our all-time favourites, *Ellary Cottage*.

All this adds up to a peaceful retreat that is also suitable for energetic families, to which many of our readers return year after year.

Sleep 4 to 8. Cost: about £215 to £550. Pets usually possible by arrangement. Details from The Estate Office, Ellary, Lochgilphead, Argyll PA31 8PA. Telephone 01880 770232 or 770209. Fax 770386.

www.ellary.com   email: info@ellary.com

Scotland-wide
Blakes Country Cottages (Scotland)*

While asking for directions in a rural general store to a nearby hamlet during a visit to the Ullapool area we got talking to people staying in a Blakes cottage nearby, called *Caberfeidh* (**sleeping 6,** Ref 1809). We were asked to tea – and, of course, to admire the cottage, a converted croft. We *especially* admired the fabulous views, the open fire, the seven acres of orchard, the private path to the lochside, and much more. We found ourselves rather envying our hosts and proud tenants.

Though they don't have a separate brochure for Scotland, Blakes offer some very fine Scottish properties, many of which have featured on the organisation's books for years.

We've long known and liked the Ormsary Lodges (Refs SH8201-8203). Not featured.

Four Winds: you could spend a week or longer just gazing out of the window.

We've heard from two readers who like the look of a superbly located property at Glenelg, which is easily accessible to the short ferry crossing to the Isle of Skye. **Sleeping 4**, *Rams Cottage* is a recent conversion that combines comfort *and* character, and is well situated for memorable walking – plus the chance of seeing otters. Ref 14464.

A reader who stayed at *Four Winds*, at St Monans, overlooking the Firth of Forth ('fabulous views from every room, including the loo!') recommends it highly. **Sleeping 4**, it is a traditional end-terrace fisherman's cottage renovated to 21st century standards. Ref B5743.

Most usefully there are three very comfortable (**Four Stars**) apartments superbly located in Oban, a vital jumping off point for the Hebridean islands and some ferry trips that are a delight in themselves. **Sleeping 2, 4 and 6**, these *Esplanade Court Apartments* overlook Oban Bay: such a lot going on! Refs B5888, B5890, B5892.

More rural are the *Dalhousie Estates Holiday Cottages*, three detached estate cottages nestling in the scenic and unspoilt Glenesk area. One of the cottages is spectacularly located in a remote part of Glen Mark: *Glenmark Cottage* (Ref SM16) is a 'back to basics' property dating from 1870 – no electricity, but there is gas and an open fire.

Further details are available from Blakes, Stoney Bank Road, Earby, Barnoldswick BB94 0AA. Bookings/brochures 0870 197 6896.

Live search and book: www.blakes-cottages.co.uk

Arduaine, near Kilmelford
Arduaine Cottages

We'd not seen these two beauties since a new owner took over. A very skilful upgrading, plus masses of 'TLC', have made both *The Chalet* and *The Post House Cottage* among the most desirable holiday properties on the west coast. We visited in 2006, and although there are so many good things to single out we especially remember harmonious light, colour

On Scotland's beautiful west coast, with stunning panoramic seascape views.

schemes, one of the most charming and beautifully lit kitchen-diners (in Post House) we have seen, top quality beds and fabrics, expensive and well chosen floorings, lighting and mirrors. The Chalet **sleeps 2 'plus 2'**, with an open plan sitting room/kitchen, double sofa bed and a dining table by a picture window to take advantage of the view of Loch Melfort. The separate bedroom has twin beds. The Post House Cottage has a large kitchen/diner, plus picture-windowed sitting room, and **sleeps up to 5** in two bedrooms, one with a king sized double, the other with a double and a single. TVs, DVDs, videos, stereos. Pets welcome. Linen and towels included. Cost: from about £240. Details from Julie Rowden, Arduaine Cottages, Arduaine, Argyll PA34 4XQ. Telephone 01852 200216.

www.arduainecottages.com   email: arduainecottages@aol.com

Machrie, near Port Ellen/Bowmore   map 4/215
Machrie Hotel Lodges

Islay is one of our all-time favourite Hebridean islands, and the *Machrie Lodges* are superbly positioned near the Machrie Golf Course and the Machrie Hotel. The hotel has a reputation for providing the best food on Islay: a huge bonus for self caterers, and there's an ongoing programme of improvements to its lodges. We visited two of three that have been

You don't have to be a golfer...

upgraded – though they are all acceptable for a holiday base. We found these two delightful: closest of the group of fifteen to the golf links, and with superb views of Laggan Bay (though every property has panoramic views). We admired a spacious triple aspect sitting room/diner/kitchen, cosy bedrooms – two twins, one en suite – an excellent sense of colour co-ordination: we liked the deep-cushioned cane sofa and armchairs in dark green and tartan, the big reading lamps, the plain walls. **Sleep up to 6** (with sofa bed). TV. Dogs welcome in the 'standard' lodges. Linen/towels included. Cost: £180 to £750. Details: the Machrie Hotel, Port Ellen, Isle of Islay, Argyll PA42 7AN. Telephone 01496 302310. Fax 302404.

www.machrie.com   email: machrie@machrie.com

Carradale, Kintyre
Torrisdale Castle Cottages and Apartments

In the summer of 2006 we revelled in a long overdue revisit to a handful of properties that for us encapsulate the charms of one of the most delightful parts of Scotland. For within Torrisdale Castle itself (well down the leafy, rather secret, eastern side of the Kintyre peninsula, just a few minutes' drive from Campbeltown) and on its fine, wooded estate there are respectively spacious, very private, comfortable apartments and individual houses of character and long lasting appeal. *All have featured in this guide for 25 years without a break.*

We revisited most of them. We noted, in the castle, high ceilings, large rooms, comfortable sofas, well equipped kitchens or kitchenettes, and just enough individual little details (like secret alcoves that actually form part of the turrets) to add a touch of character and individuality to each one. The flats **sleep between 4 and 6**, with lots of space for an extra bed, and are **'Visit Scotland' Three Stars**.

The cottages are on a leafy and exceptionally quiet estate, and are all well away from each other. They are not show-houses, but are 'practical' and notably inexpensive. *South Lodge*, which **sleeps 2**, is on the 'B' road that runs the length of the peninsula, but it is mainly used by local and holiday traffic. It has the advantage of overlooking a pretty and sandy bay which is, of course, readily available to all guests here. We actually stayed here when we visited last year: comfy, quiet, nicely self contained. We particularly liked *Lephinbeag Cottage*, at the end of its own rough drive, overhung with tall trees and with a babbling burn rippling beside it. It is quite small (two bedrooms, **sleeping 4**) but one of those places that, with a peat or log fire burning, after a day tramping through the hills, has lots of charm.

Lephincorrach Farmhouse, with its spacious kitchen and dining room, **sleeps 10** in five bedrooms. *Garden Cottage*, **sleeping 4** in two bedrooms – a downstairs double and, intriguingly, an attic room reached by ladder – is beautifully, peacefully situated among trees. *Glen House* is a converted croft house, **sleeping 7** in three bedrooms.

Televisions. Dogs are welcome. Cost: about £150 to £490. Further details are available from Mr and Mrs Macalister Hall, Torrisdale Castle, Carradale, Kintyre, Argyll PA28 6QT. Telephone/fax 01583 431233.

www.torrisdalecastle.com
email: machall@torrisdalecastle.com

Spacious Lephincorrach Farmhouse sleeps 10 in five bedrooms.

The castle, looking out to sea, contains several impressively roomy apartments.

Brechin (for the Glens of Angus)
Parker's Retreat

Here is a rare chance to explore, from a sumptuously comfortable base, a comparatively little-known corner of Scotland (but golfers should note that it's becoming known as 'Carnoustie Country'). It comes in the form of newly restored redundant cowsheds and a milking parlour, and has **Five Stars** from **'Visit Britain'**. We know and like the region, and would enthusiastically 'wave the flag' for it: there's easy access for example to the more south easterly of the beautiful Glens of Angus, and yet you're only

Not yet seen by us (to be remedied in 2007!) this is a Five Star treasure...Nearby Brechin is close to the Cairngorm National Park and, for serious fishing, the River South Esk is easily accessible.

about ten miles from sandy beaches. Among places to visit is Glamis Castle (about twelve miles). Specifically, the lovingly restored property has its own secluded orchard – an idyllic place, with apple, pear and plum trees – panoramic views across undulating countryside and access to about 1000 acres of arable land and forest rich in wildlife But it's not 'back of beyond': there are for example pubs serving food within about three miles.

The spacious and elegant accommodation includes a large farmhouse kitchen, a utility room and two sitting rooms. The house **sleeps 6** in three double bedrooms, all en suite. Much more detail on the exceptionally good website.

Not suitable for pets; no smokers. Cost: about £350 to £725 for most holiday weeks. Short breaks possible. Details from Alexis Litton, Greenden Farmhouse, Farnell, Brechin DD9 6TS. Telephone 07831 333333.

www.parkersgreenden.co.uk email: enquiriesparkers@btinternet.com

---

Some do's and don'ts (for readers)

Do ask whether short breaks are available in cottages that appeal, even when owners don't make a lot of this in their promotion.

Don't arrive before you are expected: if possible let owners know in advance what time you expect to arrive, and stick to it.

Do check that 'suitable for the disabled' means just that, and not simply that you will find a couple of wide doors and a low sink.

Do own up to breakages. Don't be embarrassed. Unreported objects missing or broken can be infuriating for all concerned.

Don't bottle up complaints and problems. Tell owners or agents about your worries on the evening of your arrival, if possible.

Discover Scotland

On a perfect early-summer day in 2006, near Gatehouse of Fleet, we turned off the busy Dumfries to Stranraer road into the peaceful backwater of Mossyard, getting closer and closer to a picture-perfect stretch of coastline. Firstly, we looked at a most exquisitely located chalet, with marvellous views of inviting white sandy beaches. Secondly at restored stone late19th century farmworkers' cottages and updated cottages from the 1960s.

It was just a snapshot of an organisation which has an impressive geographical spread that takes in the whole of Scotland. We already know many of the cottages. There is an exceptionally attractive colour brochure and a detailed website with online booking.

The agency has introduced many of our readers to Dumfries and Galloway. Among places 'worth a detour' are the Rhinns of Galloway, the south west extremity of Scotland that terminates in 200 feet high cliffs. From several high points, Ireland seems almost near enough to touch.

Outstanding places include the marvellously well situated *Fonthill*, **sleeping 6**, in Kippford, known for its sailing centre and, in Rockcliffe,

Colleagues have stayed in The Auld Schoolhouse, just a short walk to a beach.

A Highland classic: Baile na Creige, not featured, is just eight miles from Inverness.

with a magnificent sea view, *Colbeine*, a family house of character. This also **sleeps 6**. Colleagues have also enjoyed a summer holiday in *Auld Schoolhouse*, Skyreburn, **sleeping 7**. They loved its quiet position, the burn running through the well kept garden.

We know several of the agency's properties on the Isle of Skye. One, *Willowbank*, is in the village of Broadford, on the main route from the mainland (via the bridge) to Portree. Outwardly pretty, inside it is a delight, with big rooms and views of the water. The big first floor sitting room is a particular joy. **Sleeps 8**.

Past the hamlet of Elgol itself, in an exquisite location with amazing views of the Cuillin Hills over Cuillin Sound, *Port Elgol Cottage* is also memorable for its cosy interior. Having visited it ourselves and met the owners, we can believe what they say about visitors spending 'most of their time looking out of the windows'! **Sleeps 4**.

Details of these and much more, and a good brochure, from Discover Scotland Ltd, 27 King Street, Castle Douglas DG7 1AB. Telephone 01556 504030. Fax 503277.

www.discoverscotland.net

email: discover.scotland@virgin.net

121

Cumbria and the Lake District

Of all the regions of Britain, with one exception, it's the Lake District that comes closest to hanging up the 'house full' sign all year round. (The exception is the Cotswolds.) Readers of this guide, and other holiday tenants, seem to be as content in a tucked-away Lakeland cottage during an icy February as during a hot August (we are too, though we insist on a log fire or a glass-fronted woodburner – the best kind). So don't take it for granted that the cottage that has a waiting list in high summer is available in winter. Especially among those idyllic places that are perched above or right beside famous lakes such as Windermere, Coniston, Derwentwater and Ullswater. After a recent visit, we know how they get those so-perfect photographs of looking glass lakes reflecting a cloudless blue sky and the awe-inspiring hills! Seen from above, unforgettable. But we are fond of less well known lakes such as Thirlmere, Bassenthwaite and Esthwaite, and of holiday cottages on the fringe of the Lakes-proper, such as the sleepy Eden Valley, still one of 'England's best-kept-secrets', There is something special about striking off into the empty hills on one of those windswept, bright and showery days of early spring when clouds are scudding across the ever-changing sky, or walking through the grounds of one of the region's great country houses when winter closes in.

Kirkland, near Penrith map 8/220
Kirkland Hall Cottages

Beck is a perennial favourite, and very cosy for just two people...

One of our most enjoyable cottage revisits of 2005 was to this delightfully situated group of cottages: one of our long-term favourites in all of Cumbria. On a bright, chilly early autumn day open fires and log burners were warming the cottages, and we envied the mainly regular visitors their cosy hideaways. We strolled round the gardens, which are great fun for energetic youngsters – and admired the rural views. At the foot of the Pennines, in an Area of Outstanding Natural Beauty, you're well placed both for visiting 'The Lakes' and the Northumberland-Durham border country. The four cottages have hand-built farmhouse kitchens with dishwashers. Woodburners back up the central heating, fuel included. *The Haybarn* (**sleeps 6/7**) has a huge sit-in fireplace, a conservatory, two bathrooms and a minstrels' gallery. *Beck Cottage* is single-storeyed, in its own grounds. **Sleeps 2**. *Stables Cottage* has a really welcoming interior and a south facing patio. **Sleeps 4**. *Shearers Cottage* (**sleeps 4**) has its own private garden. One dog by arrangement in Shearers. **'Visit Britain' Four Stars**. Cost: from £195 to £650; short breaks in low season. Details: Lesley and Ian Howes, Kirkland Hall, Kirkland, Penrith, Cumbria CA10 1RN. Telephone/fax 01768 88295.

www.kirkland-hall-cottages.co.uk
email: kirklandhallcottages@hotmail.com

Ambleside and Central Lakeland
Cottage Life and Heart of the Lakes*

This important agency, featured by us for more than 20 years, handles some real gems, several of which we have stayed in. Of course, we only have room to mention a handful of the 330 or so on the organisation's books – this year, for example, we've had excellent reader reports of a charming, authentic 17th century cottage called *High Beckside*, near Patterdale (**sleeps 7**), and – we've stayed there too – of *Acorn Cottage* *(***sleeps 5***)*, within walking distance of Coniston.

Some properties are in quite famous places, and they don't come much more famous than Far Sawrey, one-time home of Beatrix Potter. There, *Rowan Cottage*, **sleeping 5**, has lots going for it, such as a multi-fuel stove, views of fields and trees from the back and a pub a short walk away.

Big family party? Consider Hart Head Barn, sleeping up to ten and superbly located in famous Rydal...

Lion and Lamb cottages are in the heart of Grasmere: you will be the envy of the people who throng to the village...

Lion and *Lamb* cottages, for example, are two charming properties that date back to the 18th century and are in the heart of Grasmere village, probably one of the Lake District's half dozen most sought-after holiday bases. Now renovated and comfortably furnished, both cottages make an excellent base. Both **sleep 6**.

Hart Head Barn was converted from an old Lakeland stone barn and as you might imagine now offers very substantial accommodation. With wonderful views, in a peaceful location, this outstanding property is situated in the hamlet of Rydal, between Grasmere and Ambleside. **Sleeps 10**.

A ten minute drive from Keswick, in the village of Mungrisdale, *Elind Cottage* is part of a Grade II listed barn, with a wealth of beams and evidence of a flair for interior design. It is full of character, and makes a very comfortable holiday home. **Sleeps 4**.

Just a couple of minutes' walk from the centre of Ambleside is *Wren Cottage*. Newly renovated and upgraded, while retaining many authentic features, this **sleeps 2** and will appeal to couples looking for a village (or perhaps small town) 'pied-à-terre'.

The properties range from **'Visit Britain' Two to Five Stars**, and all include free leisure club membership. Further details of all these and of course many more are available from 'Heart of the Lakes'/'Cottage Life', Fisherbeck Mill, Old Lake Road, Ambleside, Cumbria LA22 0DH. Telephone 015394 32321. Fax 33251.
www.heartofthelakes.co.uk   email: info@heartofthelakes.co.uk

123

Kirkoswald, near Penrith
Howscales

Half hidden away, very quiet and peaceful, Cumbria's Eden Valley is a 'best-kept secret' that also offers easy access to The Lakes. These five properties make a fine introduction to this corner of Cumbria. Extensive, beautifully kept gardens (runners up in the 'Cumbria In Bloom', self catering section, in 2004 and 2005) surround the property, with quiet sit-

Very comfortable, very well situated for touring. a super Eden Valley base...

ting-out places for guests to relax in and enjoy the marvellous open views of the surrounding countryside. The cottages are most lovingly cared-for, grouped appealingly round a cobbled courtyard. We've stayed here, in one of the three two-storeyed properties that have their open plan sitting room/dining-room and kitchen areas on the first floor to make the most of the splendid views. The other two are single-storeyed, one of them (*Hazelrigg*) a former milking parlour that is suitable for wheelchair-bound guests. This **sleeps 2** in a zip-link double. Our favourite is roomy *Inglewood* (**sleeping 4**), stylish and inviting, with superb views. TVs. No smoking. Dogs possible. Details from Liz Webster, Kirkoswald, Penrith, Cumbria CA10 1JG. Telephone 01768 898666. Fax 898710.

www.howscales.co.uk   email: liz@howscales.co.uk

Watermillock, near Ullswater
Land Ends   map 8/236

As you approach these cottages along little-used country lanes, you feel 'a hundred miles from anywhere', but in fact you're just a mile or so from Lake Ullswater. The four log cabins are in 25 peaceful acres of gardens and natural woodland, with streams and exceptional birdlife, on the slopes of Little Mell Fell. Opposite the cabins is "guests' own" lake, with ducks

Bed and breakfast is also available here.

and moorhens and areas of mown grass with seating for walking or relaxing. (Look out for red squirrels, tawny owls and woodpeckers.) Dogs are 'very welcome', and can get plenty of exercise. There is a second lake further down the grounds, and an 18-acre field for strolling in. You are surrounded by dramatic scenery, many attractions and superb hillwalking. The nearest village (Pooley Bridge) is three miles away, but there is a pub serving good food just a mile down the road. Dogs, by the way, are welcome.

Sleep 2 to 5. TVs. **'Visit Britain' Three Stars**. Linen is included, but not towels. Cost: about £270 to £540. Open all year. Details/brochures from Land Ends, Watermillock, Cumbria CA11 0NB. Telephone 017684 86438.

www.landends.co.uk email: infolandends@btinternet.com

Talkin, near Brampton
Long Byres

Among so many things readers have (over 25 years!) loved about Long Byres is the fact the owners say 'Do bring your children and dogs...'! Better yet, owner Harriet Sykes (who runs the place and lives adjacent) says 'the more boisterous the better, and as many of each as you like.' She goes on to say, 'the cottages are child- and dog-proof. We are what we are, we know our market and we don't overcharge.' The formula seems to work: there are many repeat visitors. As well as enjoying forays to such famous places as Windermere, Keswick and Ullswater, guests tend to be people who appreciate this 'serenely wild' corner of the Cumbria/Northumberland border country.

We revisited one recent early autumn, and found that the character of the seven former farm buildings still comes over. The two larger cottages have enjoyed a complete refurbishment, and have been extended to provide three bedrooms, one ensuite, plus a family bathroom. The kitchen/living rooms in both cottages have been redesigned and updated, and look out on to their own gardens and across the farm towards the Lake District. They will be available for booking after Easter 2007. Please check the website for further information and pictures.

With their easy access to the Lakes, the Roman Wall country and the Scottish border, these are unpretentious and inexpensive, and have always brought a good response from our readers...

Interiors are unfussy and practical, and we've checked out the ongoing programme of upgrading...

All the cottages enjoy splendid views. A charming beck ripples along within 50 yards of the property. Talkin Tarn, as pretty as several of the Lakes-proper, is within walking distance; Talkin village, which is half a mile away, offers the choice of two excellent pubs. Brampton, three miles away, is the nearest town. It has a railway station, and the Sykes are happy to meet people from the train.

Dogs are welcome, and children will enjoy the pets' corner, the dogs, the cats, the horses and the newly acquired alpacas. Cost: about £163 to £450, including electricity, hot water, heating, linen and towels. Details from Harriet Sykes at Long Byres, Talkin Head, near Brampton, Cumbria CA8 1LT. Telephone 016977 3435.

www.longbyres.co.uk
email: stay@longbyres.co.uk

Loweswater, near Cockermouth
Loweswater Cottages at Scale Hill

Featured in this guide for *twenty-five years without a break*, these cottages have never brought anything but whole-hearted praise from our readers, with never any kind of complaint.

Michael Thompson once owned and ran one of the best known hotels in the region, but some years ago this was transformed into highly regarded self catering cottages, now looked after by daughter Heather.

All of the cottages are very comfortable, attractively lit, and altogether welcoming. Each one has memorable views from the windows which, considering the location, is a huge bonus.

Sheila's, at the far end of the building, is open plan, with a triple aspect sitting room and French windows on to a private garden. When we last called, a cheerful fire was burning in the grate. **Sleeps 4** in two bedrooms, each with private bathroom. *Barty's,* in the middle of the original inn, and with access from the cobbled courtyard, has the great advantage of a sitting room across the whole of the building and is thus – something we like a lot – 'double aspect'. It **sleeps 2** in a four poster.

Opposite the former hotel is the converted Coach House, which contains four cottages. Low key in decor, and tasteful, they are kept up to a high standard of decoration with good quality wallpaper and carpets common to all. They are *Lanthwaite, Shell (*recently enlarged, and now with a four poster*), Brackenthwaite* and *Howe.* A detailed colour brochure provides a good impression of all the properties.

Dogs are welcome. There are televisions and central heating throughout. Cots, highchairs and all heating, lighting and linen are included in the rates. Cost: approximately £270 to £770 per cottage, depending – as always – on which cottage you choose and when you go.

Scale Hill (arrowed): how is this for a cottage location? It is quite outstanding even compared with other parts of the Lake District, and our readers have come to love it.

For further details and a copy of that exceptional loose-leaf brochure, contact Heather Thompson, Scale Hill, Loweswater, near Cockermouth, Cumbria CA13 9UX. Telephone 01900 85232. Fax 85321.

www.loweswaterholidaycottages.co.uk
email: thompson@scalehillloweswater.co.uk

Windermere, Ambleside and beyond
Lakelovers*

Over the years this much admired, very personally run Lake District agency has become something of a 'cottage guide' fixture, and we regularly get feedback from readers. During 2006 this included enthusiastic reports on *Craigside* (**sleeping 8**), a fine modern property near Bowness, almost on the shores of Lake Windermere, and *Orchard Cottage* (**sleeping 4**), near Troutbeck, and superbly well situated for walkers.

We know a good proportion of the properties on the agency's books, and have stayed in several. Most recently in *Fell Cottage*, at Troutbeck, a semi-detached but still private house with impressive views (and a ten minute walk from *fabulous* views). **Sleeps up to 4**. Also *Rigges Wood*, virtually on the shores of Esthwaite Water, with partial views of that, and just two minutes' drive from the fascinating and historic village of Hawkshead. It's a warm and comfortable family house, **sleeping 6** in a double and two twins, with a most efficient coal-effect gas fire, a pleasant family dining room, lots of irresistible books and a good-sized back garden.

Roger Ground is an exceptional property, combining history and modern comforts.

Valentine Cottage (not featured) makes a rather special and romantic retreat.

Also a few minutes' walk from Hawkshead and Esthwaite Water, *Roger Ground House* is a Grade II listed delight. **Sleeping up to 14** – one bedroom has a six foot wide bed – with, among so much else, two fine oak staircases, mullioned windows, stone-flagged floors, comfortable furnishings and decor, this property really is 'something special'.

On the shores of Lake Windermere, *Beech Howe,* **sleeping 6**, is very sought after. On a steep bank, separated from Windermere only by lush tree-filled gardens, with no less than 200 yards of private lake frontage, there are views of England's biggest lake from virtually every window.

Among so many outstanding properties we like (and have stayed in) is *Curdle Dub*, at Coniston, a listed building in a pretty row within walking distance of the village and the lake. If you stay here, don't miss a trip on the famous restored steam-driven gondola. There is an open fire. **Sleeps 4**.

For a copy of an outstandingly well written and seductive brochure contact Lakelovers, Belmont House, Lake Road, Bowness-on-Windermere LA23 3BJ. Telephone 015394 88855. Fax 88857. Brochures: 88858.

www.lakelovers.co.uk
email: bookings@lakelovers.co.uk

Elterwater, near Ambleside
Meadowbank/Garden Cottage

We try to be even handed, but have
to admit this is one of our favourite
three or four properties in the whole
of 'the lakes'. In the heart of a
sought-after village, with a good pub
close, it's of permanent-home standard, with a stylish, spacious, uncluttered interior (we loved the red carpeting and the tartan covers in the

main sitting room: see **Colour sec-**   *This must be one of the finest holiday*
tion A, Page 4), an impressive, tra-   *houses in the Lakes: grab it when you can!*
ditional pine kitchen, a medium
sized, well tended and enclosed garden that gives on to open fields. (We
also admired the view from the main bedroom.) **Sleeps 8/10.** Within the
garden, but unobtrusively, *The Garden Cottage*, **sleeping just 2** in a double, can be taken separately, or is an excellent addition to Meadowbank
for a large family party. Three TVs/videos/Sky film/sports channels.

Bed-linen included. Pets not allowed. Cost: (Cottage) £200 to £360,
(House) £490 to £2200. See the website for full details of price, availability and special offers.

www.langdale-cottages.co.uk email: patricia.locke@btinternet.com

Graythwaite, near Lake Windermere
Graythwaite Farm   map 8/244

We appreciate Lake Windermere
even more since the headache-induc-
ing waterskiers have been given the
heave-ho. It's the sometimes overlooked western side we go for most,
(which you should get to if possible
via the charming ferry route from   *In one of our favourite corners of the*
near Bowness, and where you'll   *Lake District, these are half hidden away.*
bump into people looking for Beatrix

Potter's house at Far Sawrey.) Considering there are ten units available at
Graythwaite Farm, within four acres of woodland, they are hidden away
from the country road that snakes from Newby Bridge to Hawkshead. Most
of the skilful and harmonious conversions have an open fire or a woodburner,
and they **sleep from a cosy 2 to a convivial 10**. It's a pleasant mile-long
walk to the shores of Windermere, and there's a two-and-a-half-acre stocked
trout pool, as well as access to Graythwaite's exceptional gardens, which are
open to the public. Refs (of a sample three of the ten properties, respectively
Greenhowes Cottage, Bibby Lot and *Eel House*) are LMX, LMY and LMR.

Details from English Country Cottages, Stoney Bank Road, Earby,
Barnoldswick BB94 0AA. Bookings and brochures: 0870 197 6890.

www.english-country-cottages.co.uk

Applethwaite, near Keswick
Croftside/Croft Corner/Upper House/Lower House at Croft House Holidays

Only just over a mile from Keswick are five properties, all in peaceful, rural settings, with stunning views to Skiddaw, Borrowdale and the north-western fells. *Croftside*, **sleeping 4**, and *Croft Corner*, a ground-floor apartment **sleeping 2**, are located at Croft House – a handsome Victorian country house. A Croftside visitor said: 'After 25 years of Lakeland holidays this is the best accommodation *Croft House: an exceptional location and super views, a mile or so from Keswick.*

we've stayed in.' Said another, of Croft Corner, 'Thanks for the little touches that made us feel so much at home'. A colleague stayed in *Lower House*, **sleeping 4**. She described great views, and 'everything light and open plan'. A visitor to *Upper House,* **sleeping 6**, said: 'Wonderfully equipped, fantastic view'. At *Croft Head Farm*, **sleeping 8** (it's a detached barn conversion with a snooker room) a visitor highlighted 'the serene and picturesque location'. **'Visit Britain' Four Stars**. TVs/videos/DVDs. 'Sorry, no pets'. Linen, towels, heating, electricity, cot/high chair included. Open all year. Cost: £270 to £975. Short breaks from £162. Details: Mrs J L Boniface, Croft House, Applethwaite, Keswick, Cumbria CA12 4PN. Telephone: 017687 73693.

www.crofthouselakes.co.uk   email: holidays@crofthouselakes.co.uk

Cockermouth and Ravenglass

Only about five miles from one of our own favourite lakes (Buttermere) and just three miles from historic Cockermouth, a fine barn conversion **sleeps 4** in a double and a twin **(map 8/254)**. Ref W8258. Looking west, we happen to think the Cumbrian coast is one of the north country's best-kept-secrets. One of our all-time favourite places is Ravenglass. Just a mile and a half from there, in a high-lying situation with panoramic views of the Irish Sea and, if you're lucky,

This detached barn conversion, near Cockermouth, will suit keen walkers.

sunset over the Isle of Man, another detached barn conversion **(map 8/253)** combines masses of character with 21st century comforts. **Sleeping 6**, it makes a good base for a short break, and is near a pub. Ref W4359.

For availability and bookings, contact Welcome Cottages, Spring Mill, Earby, Barnoldswick, Lancashire BB94 0AA. Telephone 0870 197 6957. A number of properties in France are also available.

www.welcomecottages.com

Borrowdale, Keswick and around
Lakeland Cottage Holidays*

Reader reports over many years have indicated that the precise geographical coverage of this long established agency of 60 or so properties is a great selling point: almost everything is within a ten mile radius of Keswick.

The majority of properties are managed (bookings, cleaning, spring cleaning and maintenance) by the agency, and those that aren't have owners close by to maintain standards. The brochure is full of practical advice and, interestingly, understated cottage descriptions – the superlatives are saved for the landscape! If you want more illustrations, see the agency's website for galleries of digital photos, or take their 360 degree 'virtual tours' of selected properties.

During our most recent (autumn) visit to the Lakes we picked out a good handful of properties we'd not seen before: big houses with fine views, stone cottages, white-walled cottages, farmhouses and town-house terraces. And next time round we'll want to see a cottage recently recommended by readers, which is one of two on a traditional 17th century farmstead at Penrudduck, near Ullswater, that **sleep 3 and 5** respectively.

Candlemas (not featured) is a newer property sleeping 4. Just ten minutes from Keswick centre, it has memorable views...

High Ground, below Catbells, is a rarity. Sleeping 8, it was built in 1910 by an Austrian Christmas card manufacturer!

Serious walkers would love *Townhead Barn*, **sleeping 6/8**. Situated in the quiet village of Threlkeld, it is off the beaten tourist track yet, amazingly, less than five miles from Keswick.

In the tiny hamlet of Seatoller, in the Borrowdale Valley (most of the surrounding countryside is National Trust owned), is a former quarryman's cottage called *Bell Crags*, where we really liked the open fire in the sitting room and the patio by the stream plunging down from Honister Pass, with views across to the magnificent old High Stile oakwood. **Sleeps 5/6**. The agency has several properties in Keswick itself, and we were impressed by *Underne*, a comfortable, surprisingly spacious terraced cottage in a peaceful corner of this important centre. **Sleeps 4/5**.

Further details and a copy of an informative brochure are available from Lakeland Cottage Holidays, Melbecks, Bassenthwaite, near Keswick, CA12 4QX. Telephone 017687 76065. Fax: 76869.

www.lakelandcottages.co.uk

info@lakelandcottages.co.uk

Elterwater, near Ambleside
Wheelwrights Lake District Holiday Cottages

We've heard from a good number of readers who first discovered the delights of the Lake District after booking a cottage through Wheelwrights Lake District Holiday Cottages.

The company, which has been letting cottages in the heart of Lakeland for nearly 30 years, making it one of the first in its field in the whole country, handles 76 properties, and because it is one of the smaller letting agencies, the staff are familiar with every property and can advise on the best match for clients' particular requirements.

Wheelwrights' properties are set amongst some of the most stunning scenery in the Lake District – which is saying something! Many are in the Langdale Valleys (Great and Little), which are dominated by the magnificent Langdale Pikes. Others are in the picturesque villages of Grasmere, Hawkshead, Outgate, Coniston and Ambleside. They lie within a ten mile radius of Elterwater, where Wheelwrights' office is based, and all provide ideal points from which to explore the whole of the fabulous Lake District National Park.

The range of properties is wide. Some are converted barns or farmhouses, others are Lakeland-stone cottages and village houses, and there are some modern houses and apartments. They are all equipped to a very high standard with **'Visit Britain'** gradings from **Three** to **Five** stars. The smallest properties **sleep 2** and the largest **sleeps 15**. Most accept pets.

Prices per week range from £285 (low season) to £2000 (peak season). All the properties can be seen on the website – **www.wheelwrights.com** – on which you may also check the layout of each cottage by clicking on the floorplans button. (Not to scale.)

Contact the Wheelwrights office for any further information you may require about any of the cottages found on their website or to request a colour brochure:

Wheelwrights Lake District Holiday Cottages, Elterwater, Ambleside, Cumbria LA22 9HS. Telephone 015394 37635.

www.wheelwrights.com
email: enquiries@wheelwrights.com

Most Wheelwrights properties allow almost immediate access to some of the most romantic landscapes in the country.

The majority of the cottages and houses on offer are places of character. We know several, and will see more during 2007.

Bassenthwaite
Bassenthwaite Lakeside Lodges

There can be a degree of one-upmanship when people say 'We holidayed on Bassenthwaite'. For access to this, one of Lakeland's most beautiful but least-known lakes, is famously quite difficult. These fine lodges, however, border the lake's shore, with easy and immediate access to the water.

Tucked away down a leafy lane among mature trees, and run with great professionalism, the community of about 60 log cabins/lodges, fifteen of them for holiday let, have been much praised by readers for about fifteen years. Standards are high.

We especially admire the most recent properties, **sleeping up to 6,** in a private location on the edge of the development, with the most impressive lake views of all, but were very pleased to spend time in one of our long time favourites, *Overwater* (right by the lake) – and also to see *Broadwater*. This is especially geared to 'wedding day' and honeymoon couples, and we were very impressed by the walk-in closet that's big enough to take a wedding dress in all its glory.

While not for those who want to be lonely as a cloud, this remains the sort of location where visiting children – and adults – will enjoy making new friends, though they can be private too. We noted the care taken in choosing top-notch kitchen and bathroom ranges, likewise comfy sofas more usually associated with up-market traditional holiday houses.

As well as generous balconies with gas barbecues and outdoor furniture, the lodges have picture windows, TVs and videos. There is a free video,

Right by the shore of one of Cumbria's least known but pleasantest lakes.

Interiors are sumptuous, and we were not surprised by all the repeat bookings.

books and games library. Nearby you can hire mountain bikes, play tennis and golf, and go horse-riding. Keswick is just ten minutes' drive.

Dogs are permitted only in the category of the smaller Parkland, Lakeside and Woodland Lodges. Linen and towels are, as you would expect here, included.

Cost: about £360 to £1010, depending on which property and when. Short breaks are available. Details available from Bassenthwaite Lakeside Lodges, Scarness, Bassenthwaite, near Keswick, Cumbria CA12 4QZ. Telephone 0845 4565276. Also: 017687 76641. Fax 76919.

www.bll.ac
email: enquiries@bll.ac

Sebergham, near Caldbeck
Monkhouse Hill Cottages

In this guide for over twenty years, with a huge following among readers, these lovingly cared-for cottages are well located in the quieter, more northerly part of 'the Lakes'. Keswick (via lovely Mungrisdale), Bassenthwaite Lake, Cockermouth, the coast, the Eden Valley and the Northumberland border are all within a pleasant drive. Set back from a not especially busy B-road, they are easy to find but completely rural.

After regular upgrading, the cottages are among the best properties in Cumbria – *indicated by the fact they have previously won the Silver Award in Excellence in England*. They form a most attractive, exceptionally neat, clean and tidy enclave round a former farmyard, with impressive panoramic views, and they are run with understandable pride and great professionalism by the resident owners, who have three young children and are therefore tuned in to the needs of families on holiday.

We were keen to see the latest addition, which is *Great Calva*. Most usefully **sleeping 12 'plus 2'** in seven bedrooms, it has the always-desirable feature of an upstairs sitting room, a sauna and spa, and a '**Visit Britain**' grading of **Five Stars**. We met an extended family staying, coming to the end of their holiday and not wanting to leave.

Also recently on the scene, also with **Five Stars**, is *Cloven Stone*, designed for two couples. This too has an upstairs sitting room, which we loved, to make the most of the views, and two downstairs doubles – one of which can be reorganised as a twin. There are seven other cottages, each with its own particular endearing features. There are three which **sleep 2**, two **sleeping 4**, one **sleeping 6**, and one **sleeping 8**. Most will take at least one cot.

An award winning, absolutely pristine, neat and tidy arrangement of cottages....   *...with comfortable interiors, a food ordering service and children's playground.*

Cost: about £340 to £2280 (inc electricity, linen and towels). Also available is an on-line ordering service for, for example, three-course suppers, celebratory buffets, home cooked freezer meals, grocery hampers, freshly baked bread, papers, wine and beer, and more. Dogs are welcome in most cottages. Free use of hotel leisure club with indoor pool. TV/video/DVD, CD/radio. There's a laundry room, a games room, a children's playground.

Colour brochure from Jennifer Collard, Monkhouse Hill, Sebergham, near Caldbeck CA5 7HW. Telephone/fax 016974 76254.

www.monkhousehill.co.uk   email: cottages@monkhousehill.co.uk

Buttermere
Bowderbeck

It's not hard to see why this place is so sought-after. For the character of the picture-book cottage, a classic of its kind, has been well preserved: it has even doubled up as 'Dove Cottage' in a film about Wordsworth. But it now incorporates 21st century comforts, with for example a timber

Lake District cottages don't come much more authentic or well located than this.

extension at the end of the whitewashed-stone 17th century cottage of a kind Wordsworth would not have known; he'd have appreciated its view of Buttermere, which for many visitors is the most romantic and beautiful lake of all. The lake shore is only half a mile away, and children will love the little beck that runs alongside the cottage. (This makes Bowderbeck unsuitable for children under five.) Specifically, there are rugs on slate floors and a handsome (and original) stone staircase up to a roomy first floor, where there is a spacious main bedroom, a roomy twin, a single, a separate wc, shower and bathroom, plus WC. **Sleeps 7 'plus 1'**. Not suitable for pets. No smoking. Payphone. Linen supplied, not towels. Cost: about £420 to £625. No TV reception. Details from Michael and Anne Bell, New House, Colby, Appleby-in-Westmorland, Cumbria CA16 6BD. Telephone 017683 53548.

www.bowderbeck.co.uk   email: info@bowderbeck.co.uk

Burton-in-Kendal, near Kendal   map 8/268
4 Green Cross Cottages

The cosy 'traditional' cottage, well supplied with 21st century comforts without the loss of its character, is a rarity. More so when it's loved and occasionally used by its owners. This one fits the bill! Dating from 1637, with old beams, it's an ideal base for the Lakes, South Cumbria and the Yorkshire Dales. In a short terrace of cottages, with the rear on the main street, it has a charming living room

Comfortable and welcoming (and rather good value), in a village setting. We revisited in 2005...

with a dining alcove and limestone fireplace. We admired the 'cottagey' interior with its matching fabrics and the well equipped kitchen. There's a wide, easy staircase to the first floor, two bedrooms and a bathroom with large airing/drying cupboard. Parking for one car, courtyard garden; payphone, TV/video. The village is a charming 'mix,' with period houses, two shops, and pubs with restaurants. **Sleeps 4**. Cost: £160 to £350, including gas central heating. Short breaks from just £100. No smoking, pets possible by arrangement. Linen included. Maps, videos, books and games. We'd give it **Four Stars**! Details from Mrs Frances Roberts, 32 Sevenoaks Avenue, Heaton Moor, Stockport, Cheshire SK4 4AW. Telephone 0161 432 3408. **email: ft.roberts@btinternet.com**

Windermere and Ullswater
Matson Ground Estate Cottages

Although it's just a mile from ever-popular Windermere and its lake, Helm Farm is a top-quality conversion of traditional farm buildings in a remarkably peaceful situation. The locations and the cottages themselves are memorable. **Sleeping 2 to 5** in four units, each enjoys privacy and has been designed to a high standard. *Helm Lune* **sleeps 5** in a double and a triple (three single beds, two of which can form a second double). The Habitat style (lots of pine) is set off by a high ceiling, beams in the spacious living room, and an open fire.

Helm Eden **sleeps 4** in a double and two full size bunks, *Kent* **sleeps 4** in a double, with **2** in children's bunks. *Helm Mint*, **sleeping 2**, is on the ground floor only, and has a cosy L-shaped living room/kitchen. It is the only one without a fireplace. (Helm Mint is available at a reduced rate if taken with Lune, Eden or Kent.) All include linen, towels, TV/DVD, plus microwaves. Washer/driers in all except Mint. Lune includes a dishwasher. Outside payphone, barbecue, shared garden with furniture. Fuel for open fires and night storage heating is included. Cost: £125 to £575; short breaks available. Not suitable for dogs. Footpath walks from the door. **'Visit Britain' Three Stars**.

In the beautiful Grisedale Valley, close to Helvellyn and many other mountains, we found the spacious, modernised 17th century farmhouse called *Elm How* and the smaller, quaintly beamed *Cruck Barn* – adjoining properties **sleeping 10 and 2** respectively. There's a degree of remoteness, among stunning mountain scenery, in these 'away from it all' places. No TV reception due to the hills, but DVD and CD players are available.

Linen/towels provided. Dishwasher in Elm How. Microwaves, washer/driers. Woodburner (fuel provided) in Elm How. Electric storage heating

We're especially fond of Elm How, which is in a really appealing location...

Cruck Barn: history, original features and mod cons rolled into one...

included. Barbecues. Not suitable for dogs. **'Visit Britain' Three/Four Stars**. Popular *Eagle Cottage* perches above Glenridding village and **sleeps 4**, with views all round, including the lake. Steep approach track. TV/DVD and CD player. Linen, dishwasher, microwave, open fire, storage heating. Cost: £225 to £1150. Not suitable for pets. **'Visit Britain' Three Stars**.

Colour brochure from Matson Ground Estate Company, Estate Office, Matson Ground, Windermere, Cumbria LA23 2NH. Telephone 015394 45756. Fax 47892.

www.matsonground.co.uk   email: info@matsonground.co.uk

Patton, near Kendal
Shaw End Mansion

Just three miles north of Kendal, this is a secluded rural setting, with good views of the Howgill Fells, and popular lakes such as Grasmere and Windermere about half an hour's drive. Up on the hill, Shaw End is a most impressive major restoration of a Georgian mansion. It has a lot of history, with the advantages of what

Shaw End Mansion: a degree of grandeur, with great views from each apartment.

is effectively a new building. There are four high ceilinged apartments, all accessed via the impressive main entrance, two on the ground floor, two – reached via a fine, sweeping pine staircase – on the first floor, all with superb interiors, including large sitting rooms with open fires, and exquisite views of the River Mint, in which children love to play. Guests have the run of the 200 acre estate. Three apartments **sleep 4**, one **sleeps 6** meaning that **a total of 18 people** can stay here for, say, a wedding or a family get-together. Trout and salmon fishing (one rod) is available. TV, washing machine, telephone, microwave, linen included, towels available for a small extra charge. Cost: about £220 to £410. Details from Mr and Mrs E D Robinson, Haveriggs Farm, Whinfell, near Kendal, Cumbria LA8 9EF. Telephone 01539 824220, fax 824464.

www.fieldendholidays.co.uk email: robinson@fieldendholidays.co.uk

Bailey, near Newcastleton
map 8/222
Bailey Mill Inn

We've featured these courtyard apartments, only just inside the English border, for many years. All five are in an arrangement of single and two-storeyed buildings in the converted 18th century grain mill, one of them, *The Folly*, **sleeping up to 8**: a bargain for larger groups. Most **sleep 2 to 6**. A ground floor apartment called *The Store* houses the original arch-

Scotland is just a caber's toss away...

way, dated 1767. There's a jacuzzi, a sauna, a toning table, and a meals service in the licensed bar. Dogs welcome. Baby sitting. TVs; microwaves. Looking in on the Copelands' handsome horses, riding (and learning to ride) is very much a part of Bailey Mill, and full-day stable management courses are available 10am to 4pm (£30 per day), also full board riding holidays. **'Visit Britain' Two and Three Stars.** Cost: about £178 to £598. Short breaks – out of season – from £108 per cottage for two nights. Further details from Pamela Copeland, Bailey Mill, Newcastleton, Roxburghshire TD9 0TR. Telephone 016977 48617.

www.baileycottages/riding/racing.com

email: pam@baileymill.fsnet.co.uk

Crosby Garrett, near Kirkby Stephen
Mossgill Loft/Mossgill Chapel

Crosby Garrett is a delightful, well spaced out, blissfully quiet village in the Upper Eden Valley, distinguished by a viaduct on the Settle to Carlisle railway, with the fells only a few yards beyond. In the heart of the village, in striking distance of the Lake District, on the eastern edge of Cumbria, these lovingly cared for properties are among our absolute favourites in the north of England.

The location is excellent for walking both long and short distances, being only two miles from the Coast to Coast route and near the Pennine Way. The Cumbria Cycleway is just a mile away, and the Smardale Nature Reserve is half an hour's walk. The market town of Kirkby Stephen has pubs, restaurants and antique shops. A nine hole golf course is nearby.

A Victorian Baptist chapel conversion has created two attractive self-contained holiday lets, furnished to a high standard and with many original features. There's central heating throughout, log fires, off road parking and private sitting out areas. Fuel, electricity and linen are all included. A cot and high chair are available. Dogs welcome, at a cost of £10 per dog per week.

Mossgill Chapel, which we visited for the first time two years ago, has a large tiled kitchen with an oil-fired Rayburn, electric hob, microwave and fridge/freezer. A warm utility room houses a washing machine and tumble dryer and provides plenty of space for drying walking clothes. An upstairs sitting room has an open fire, beams, comfortable furniture and TV/DVD. There are two bedrooms, one twin with en-suite bathroom and one downstairs double with a bathroom next door, including a shower.

Fitting harmoniously into the village scene.   *Lovingly planned and cared-for interiors.*

Stained glass windows are an attractive feature on the staircase. All is light and bright, with a stylish sense of colour and design. Cost: from about £290 to £375. Short breaks at a bargain £65 per night. **Sleeps 4 plus cot.**

Mossgill Loft is approached by a short flight of stone steps. There is a large living/kitchen area, a double bedroom and bathroom. There are lattice windows, beams, an open fire and rugs on wooden floors. Plus an electric cooker, microwave, washing machine, fridge and TV/DVD. The two properties can be taken together – the makings of a memorable family holiday. The owners' tennis court is available on request. Cost: from £185 to £250 per week. Short breaks at £50 per night. **Sleeps 2.**

Furrher details from Clare Hallam, Mossgill House, Crosby Garrett, Kirkby Stephen, Cumbria CA17 4PW. Telephone 017683 71149. **email: clarehallamuk@yahoo.co.uk**

137

Wales

Almost as soon as you're over the border into Wales (say via Ross on Wye, or Ludlow) the magic, the sense of the past and the scenic beauty are all-enveloping. Wales feels bigger than many first time visitors expect. Every few miles, every turn in the road seems to promise new things to see, more history to reach out and touch. The survival of the language, the terrain and the vast supply of 'tangible' history means the place is packed with interest and visitor-appeal.

A good number of readers have taken to the Pembrokeshire Coast and, for example, the Llyn Peninsula, in the north. In Pembrokeshire, Tenby is much-loved, while people who discover resorts such as Broad Haven and Newport tend to rave about here. There are lofty peaks and magnificent beaches, and although the most dramatic scenery is around Snowdonia, almost every corner of the Principality is holiday country. There are the rolling, lightly wooded English-Welsh borders, the brown moors of the Brecon Beacons National Park, our own favourite coastline around Barmouth, the rather proud, rather self contained town of Dolgellau and nearby Portmeirion, the architectural fantasy that's like a cross between Portofino and Munchkin-land. (We don't quite buy the 'Italianate' tag – we've never seen anywhere like it in Italy!) There are castles to storm, ponies to trek with, salmon and trout to catch, steam trains to travel on.

Or consider the scenic British Rail line that runs from Shrewsbury across to Welshpool, goes over the Mawddach estuary and then via Barmouth up to Harlech Castle and beyond. And there's the Isle of Anglesey: one of our favourite towns in the whole of Britain is Beaumaris, just over the Menai Straits, and the hinterland is as Welsh as anywhere we know.

St David's map 5/276
Beth Ruach

We remember these as among the best we've located in west Wales. *Beth Ruach* is on a grand scale, up a private drive, spacious (and pleasantly cool on the hot day of our visit) with a particularly comfortable sitting room. It has a skilful layout of bedrooms and **sleeps (yes!) up to 16 people**. This also has sea and country views from upstairs: but, of course,

Beth Ruach is a very stylish, comfortable and spacious family house...

you would want to explore this fabulous part of Wales, not just look at it! Linen and towels included. TVs. Payphone. Cost: about £395 to £2395. Not yet seen by us (to be remedied in 2007) are *Hendre Loan*, in a fine, high situation in the St David's conservation area **(sleeping 6)** and *Whitesands* **(sleeping 12)**, a colonial-style bungalow with fabulous sea views.

Details, with an excellent brochure, available from Thelma Hardman, 'High View', Catherine Street, St David's, Pembrokeshire SA62 6RJ. Telephone 01437 720616.

www.stnbc.co.uk   email: enquiries@stnbc.co.uk

Saundersfoot, near Tenby
Blackmoor Farm Holiday Cottages

Superbly well situated, just two miles from the glorious Pembrokeshire coast, and only a short drive from Saundersfoot's glorious sands and Tenby, these excellent cottages have been enjoyed by our readers for over twenty years. Though not 'remote', they are nicely tucked away via winding country lanes. Better yet: Blackmoor Farm is surrounded by its own 36 acres of pastureland, accessible only by a private drive.

Families with children have always praised these cottages: indeed, as we arrived on our last visit, young children were playing happily among the trees near these beautifully cared for cottages. They also appeal to people who appreciate purpose-built accommodation in an attractive courtyard location. Resident owners Len and Eve Cornthwaite try to ensure that families enjoy a warm, friendly atmosphere. Blackmoor Farm has cattle grazing peacefully, and the old stables in the spacious gravelled farmyard contain a resident donkey called Dusty: children can enjoy rides on Dusty outdoors most days. (Be warned: more than one adventurous child has asked if next time the family can book one of the well appointed, discreetly situated mobile homes!)

There are just three cottages, south facing, side by side in a courtyard setting. Accommodation is two-tiered. Downstairs there are two bedrooms (each with full size twin beds, which can convert to bunk beds) and a well fitted out bathroom with bath *and* shower. Upstairs there is a large open-plan room containing the kitchen/dining section and comfortable living area leading on to a small patio balcony. A sofa bed allows the cottage to **sleep a maximum of 6**. The single-storeyed *Stable Cottage*, a converted farm building, **sleeps 2**, and has an appealing triple aspect living room. The decor and furniture are modern, comfortable, simple but attractive. Each cottage is well equipped, heated by storage heaters and, with double glazing and good insulation, cosy in the early and late seasons.

Cost: about £280 to £508 (less than this for Stable Cottage). TVs. Linen is provided, towels available for a charge. Laundry facilities. Games room. Not suitable for dogs and other pets. More details from Len and Eve Cornthwaite, Blackmoor Farm, Amroth Road, Ludchurch, near Saundersfoot, Pembrokeshire SA67 8JH. Telephone/fax 01834 831242.

www.infozone.com.hk/blackmoorfarm
email: ltecornth@aol.com

South-facing balconies, each with a table and two chairs for alfresco meals.

Stable Cottage – just right for 2, and a modestly-priced introduction to Wales.

139

Walwyn's Castle, near Little Haven
Rosemoor

Twenty-five years can't be wrong! Tucked neatly away in the Pembrokeshire Coast National Park, well away from any main roads, the quiet and attractively situated Rosemoor cottages have featured in this guide since it first appeared in 1983.

The sandy beaches of Little Haven and Broad Haven, which has a handy supermarket, are within three miles' drive and Haverfordwest, the old county town, is about six miles away. And Walwyn's Castle? It's the remains of a Norman castle superimposed on an Iron Age fort.

The cottages, all annually graded by **'Visit Wales'**, were created from the red sandstone outbuildings of the large Victorian house in which the Dutch owners live. Each cottage is described in detail, complete with floor-plans, in Rosemoor's attractive and informative brochure, illustrated by neat pen-and-ink drawings. The estate extends for 34 acres, of which 20 have been officially designated as a nature reserve. Walking trails lead through woodland and around the picturesque five-acre lake. For naturalists and bird-watchers, it's all a delight.

Each time we've visited, most recently last autumn, we've been impressed by their variety as well as their very high standards. Six are grouped round a large three-sided open courtyard which has a central lawn; at the back they look on to wooded countryside. These include the spacious combination, with internal connection, of *Peace* (**sleeping 4**) and *Apple* (**sleeping 6**). Apple has three bedrooms and two bathrooms, one of which is en-suite to a ground floor bedroom, professionally designed for disabled use. *The Coach House*, nearby (**sleeps 5**), is capped by a small belfry and has a patio on to a walled garden, while *Holly Tree* (**sleeps 3**) has a view of the lake.

The three-bedroomed Coach House is distinctively capped by a small belfry. It is of course just one of Rosemoor's several 'characterful' properties here in rural West Wales. It is handy for beaches and lovely countryside, but not remote.

Most of the cottages have dark slate floors topped by attractive rugs, with underfloor heating. We also admired the polished dark grey Welsh slate working surfaces in the fitted kitchens and liked the smart modern bathrooms tiled in black and white. Cost: about £150 to £1440. Dogs welcome. Home-cooked meals available. Linen supplied. Laundry facilities. Four cottages have woodburners. Games room and playground. Brochure from John M and Jacqui Janssen, Rosemoor, Walwyn's Castle, Haverfordwest, Pembrokeshire SA62 3ED. Telephone 01437 781326. Fax 781080.

www.rosemoor.co.uk   email: rosemoor@walwynscastle.com

Llanfallteg, near Whitland
Gwarmacwydd Farm Cottages

At the centre of a working farm that
children will love (lambs, calves,
rabbits to meet, and ancient woodlands to explore), this is a particularly quiet and spacious arrangement
of cottages. It has featured in this
guide for many years, with lots of
enthusiastic reader responses. The
focal point here is the owners' handsome Georgian home. Adjacent to
the main house are *The Coach House*
(**sleeps 4/6**) and *Butler's Cottage*

*A reliably warm welcome at this very
quiet, spacious and comfortable place.*

(**sleeps 2/3**), which can be linked to make one bigger property. Across
grassy open ground, but still part of the original farm, stand *The Old Barn*
and *Tower Cottage*, **sleeping 6** and **2/3** respectively, and also combinable.
Our favourite has always been the roomy, stylish Coach House, with a
triple-aspect sitting room/diner and central heating. **'Visit Britain' Four
Stars**. No smoking. TV. Well behaved dogs by arrangement. Linen (not
towels) and heating included. Cost: £125 to £450. Details and brochure
from Angela Colledge, Gwarmacwydd Farm, Llanfallteg, Whitland,
Carmarthenshire. Telephone 01437 563260; fax 563839.

www.a-farm-holiday.org email: ghg@gwarmacwydd.co.uk

Newgale, near St David's   map 5/284
Bryn-y-Mor

The location is amazing! Observed by
grazing cows, we drove along the side
of a couple of fields to reach this
1930s bungalow. It stands alone in a
quarter of an acre of grassed ground,
high on the cliff-top above Newgale
Sands, seven miles from St David's.
From it a gate leads straight on to the
Pembrokeshire Coast Path along the
cliffs or down to the sandy beach. The

*Idyllically situated on cliffs overlooking
St Brides Bay and sandy beaches.*

cottage is simply furnished (though fully heated) and has four bedrooms
(**sleeping 9**). These are all off the sitting-room, which also leads on to a
long covered-in verandah facing the sea, recently modernised to provide
panoramic dining and sitting areas. This can be a wonderful sun-trap or a
great spot for simply enjoying the view. There's a good stock of jigsaws and
books but no TV, though an aerial is available for anyone who brings their
own. Personally we much preferred watching the waves and birdlife! Dogs
welcome. Linen and towels not included. Cost: about £300 to £750. Details
from Simon and Susie Arbuthnott, Belgate House, Shobdon, Leominster,
Herefordshire HR6 9NJ. Telephone 01568 708038. Fax 708106.

email: buthers@zoom.co.uk

Coastal Wales
Quality Cottages Cerbid*

In an idyllic, quiet backwater of deeply rural Pembrokeshire and, better yet, down a sleepy lane, Leonard Rees's Cerbid Cottages *have featured in this guide every year since it first appeared in 1983*. We revisited them a couple of summers ago, and rediscovered their distinctive charms.

The high standards here tend to be reflected by the quality of Leonard Rees's agency properties, ninety per cent of which are within five miles of the sea – a huge selling point.

For example, just a few minutes from Newgale beach, which consists of over a mile of golden sands, is *The Red Hen House*. A superb barn conversion with sweet-smelling honeysuckle over the door, it is idyllically set in a secret valley conservation area complete with a private south-facing garden and a nearby trout lake. The feature stone fireplace makes it a good bet for the shoulder season.

If you want a dramatic coastal location, you will be impressed, as we were, by *Craig Yr Awel*, on Whitesands Bay, just a few yards above the beach. We could enjoy a week here just watching the ever-changing sea

The Cerbid cottages effectively form a hamlet of their own – utterly peaceful, each cottage with a high degree of privacy, everything beautifully cared-for.

The Red Hen House is an admirable barn conversion, and is marvellously well situated. It has 'honeysuckle round the door', and an open fireplace...

below. During a most enjoyable visit we noticed lots of books to read, comfortable leather armchairs. There's an open fire which is an absolute delight when the sea mist comes down or autumn nights close in, and a glazed patio with, as you would imagine, spectacular views. **Sleeps 10**. Dogs are welcome here.

In the beautiful lush and wooded Gwaun Valley between Fishguard and Newport, *Pontfaen* is a most impressive Victorian country house which **sleeps 11**.

A handsome full colour brochure, which also contains details of the Cerbid properties, can be obtained from Leonard Rees, Cerbid (GHCG), Solva, Pembrokeshire. Telephone 01348 837871. Freephone 0800 169 2256.

www.qualitycottages.co.uk

email: info@qualitycottages.co.uk

Boncath
Fron Fawr

Though we have featured them since 1985, we recently revisited to check out these three established cottages (deceptively spacious and as clean as the proverbial whistle), and a new property. This **sleeps 8** and is double glazed and centrally heated, with a large wood-beamed lounge and a wood-burning stove. All the cottages

A short drive from good beaches that are one of West Wales's 'best-kept secrets'.

are equipped, as one of our readers put it, with 'virtually everything': TV, hairdryer, microwave, dishwasher and enough kitchen equipment to keep any cook happy. Fron Fawr is a short drive from some delightful seaside places (good beaches, views and never any crowds). You will find a rolling lawn with swings where children can play, and enticing paths into woodlands inhabited by badgers, rabbits and a resident pair of buzzards.

Cost: approximately £210 to £1200 per week. Linen, towels, gas, electricity and wood are provided. The cottages have three or four bedrooms, and **sleep between 5 and 8**. Details and brochures from Jackie Tayler, Fron Fawr, Boncath, Pembrokeshire SA37 0HS. Telephone 01239 841285. Fax 841545.

www.fronfawr.co.uk   email: ghcg.cottages@fronfawr.co.uk

Cenarth Falls, near Cardigan Bay   map 5/289
Penwern Fach Cottages

Not yet seen by us (to be remedied in 2007) Penwern Fach Cottages come recommended for all sorts of good reasons, including the fact that they are situated in ten acres of beautiful countryside, with glorious views across the rolling landscape of the Teifi Valley and Preseli Hills. The five cosy cottages, converted from traditional stone farm buildings, still with exposed beams, are ideal (at any

Very comfortable, deeply rural, each with its own distinctive character and charm.

time of the year) for romantic breaks **for 2** or for family holidays. Each cottage has all the home comforts you'd expect, plus wood-burning stoves. There are spacious gardens, a children's games room, a football field and a 250-yard golf practice area. The cottages also have their own patio areas. Discounted rates are available at a nearby indoor pool and leisure club. Just six miles away are the beautiful beaches of Cardigan Bay, along with spectacular cliff-top walks and lots of outdoor activities for all the family.

Contact Yvonne Davies, Cenarth Falls Holiday Park, Cenarth, Newcastle Emlyn, Ceredigion SA38 9JS. Telephone 01239 710345. Fax 710344.

www.penwernfach.co.uk   email: enquiries@cenarth-holipark.co.uk

Penrallt, near Boncath
Clydey Country Cottages

A reader from Shrewsbury wrote to us in 2006 about Clydey's 'extraordinary location' and its 'clever marriage of what appeals to children and adults alike'.

There are nine cottages, all beautifully converted from original outbuildings. Dewi and Jacqui Davies took over the 20-acre estate in 2003, giving up high-powered jobs in the City of London, because they wanted to enjoy bringing up their young family in a much more pleasant environment, particularly as Dewi comes from Wales. They have certainly found a lovely spot, on high ground deep in the Pembrokeshire countryside and boasting glorious views.

There's a luxurious indoor heated swimming pool with a sheltered sun terrace from which there are stunning views, plus sauna, gym and games room to complement the existing outdoor hot tub. And for further relaxation, beauty treatments are now on offer in the comfort of your own cottage.

The decor and furnishings of the cottages (**sleeping 2 to 6**) have been chosen to complement the age and style of the buildings. They retain their wooden beams and stone inglenooks and now feature farmhouse-style kitchens and fireplaces with multi-fuel stoves. Most have four-posters and/or king or 'super king' sized beds and dishwashers. All have DVD players and satellite TV.

A nature trail leads down into woods and there's a playground area which

This is indeed 'a haven of outstanding natural beauty, peace and tranquillity'...

...in twenty acres of grounds, with a heated swimming pool, and much more.

includes a Wendyhouse, rope swing and sandpit. There are two resident ponies, a small flock of sheep and numerous chickens and ducks. The nearest shop is a couple of miles away and there's a pub and micro-brewery, the Nag's Head, which is 'child-friendly and highly rated for its food'.

Welcome pack provided of tea, coffee and milk, together with fresh flowers, local home-made preserves and basket of logs. Shared laundry room. Highchairs and cots available. Portable barbecues. Sorry, no pets. Cost: approximately £300 to £900. Details from Dewi and Jacqui Davies, Clydey Country Cottages, Penrallt, Lancych, Boncath, Pembrokeshire SA37 0LW. Telephone 01239 698619; fax 698417.

www.clydeycottages.co.uk   email: info@clydeycottages.co.uk

Rhyd-Yr-Eirin, near Harlech

For more than twenty years we've had a special fondness for this cottage. We love its character and its unforgettable location. When we say it's isolated, we mean *isolated*! It's full of atmosphere. You are 900-feet up, sheltered by hills to the north and east, in an oak-beamed, three-bedroomed, 17th century farmhouse with an unusual stone staircase, original sitting-room window, antique fur-

Splendid isolation, lots of atmosphere.

niture and a wide-ranging Welsh-holiday library. There is an open fire in the inglenook (coal/wood provided) and each room has a storage or wall heater. The all-electric kitchen, bathroom and shower-room are up to a very high standard. Harlech and the glorious, sandy beaches are only fifteen minutes away by car, allowing for gate-opening! There's a concealed TV/DVD player, radio/CD player, telephone, double-oven cooker, microwave, fridge-freezer, dishwasher, washing machine, spin-dryer.

Sleeps up to 7. Cost: £150 to £550 (discounts for two-week bookings). Well-trained dogs welcome. Details with map and plans of the house and garden (including the bog-garden) from Mr Chris Ledger, 7 Chelmer Road, London E9 6AY. Telephone 020 8985 1853.

www.rhydyreirin.com   email: info@rhydyreirin.com

Llanbedr, near Harlech
Nantcol   map 5/313

Another extraordinary location. From this 14th century stone built Welsh longhouse, five miles from Llanbedr village up a narrow valley road, you can walk straight up into the hills. It is perfection for walkers, bird watchers and lovers of the countryside: a spectacular location, spectacular views. In other words – it's one in a hundred! You can explore Snowdonia, relax on sandy beaches or play

What should we show – the house itself or the fabulous view? We revisited two summers ago – a pleasure, not just duty.

golf at Royal St David's, Harlech, a championship course. As we walked in, it was a joy to see real log fires burning at both ends of the living room. This oak beamed cottage is filled with many interesting pieces of old Welsh furniture. The spacious farmhouse kitchen was just as welcoming, with a large oak table and, yes, an oil-fired Rayburn stove. Another bonus: no TV! **Sleeps 7** plus cot. Linen not provided. Open all year. Short breaks possible. Pets by arrangement (small charge). Cost: from about £400. Details from Stephanie and John Grant, Bollingham House, Eardisley, Herefordshire HR5 3LE. Telephone 01544 327326.

www.north-wales-accommodation.co.uk
email: grant@bollinghamhouse.com

Aberdovey
Aberdovey Hillside Village

On a sunny south-facing hillside overlooking the Dovey estuary in the Snowdonia National Park, this 'village' of 20 smart pebble-dash cottages and apartments, most **sleeping 4**, was designed and developed in the 1960s and '70s by John Madin, the noted Birmingham architect.

He built the first, *Eastward*, for his own family holidays and gradually added more along landscaped terraces. Now his family has grown to include nine grandchildren, but they still come to stay every year.

Each time we walk around the 'village' (most recently last autumn) we are impressed by the way the accommodation has been fitted so neatly into the hillside, surrounded by gardens and linked by terraces and paths.

All the properties make the most of the wonderful estuary view with a terrace or balcony big enough for eating *al fresco*. Several have a split-level design, such as Eastward and *Westward*. **Sleeping 8**, these both have four bedrooms (one ensuite) on the lower level, with spacious pine-clad sitting room and dining areas upstairs with tall picture windows and high ceilings. Guests can enjoy the view from the comfort of high quality leather suites or on the long balconies, with their garden tables and chairs.

Dolphin and *Porpoise*, both **sleeping 6**, have magnificent panoramic views and an unusual sleeping balcony within a double-height living-room. Via a bulkhead ladder, the balconies are furnished with twin beds. Porpoise is suitable for people with restricted mobility, as it has no steps.

Featured in this guide for almost 25 years, with lots of repeat bookings.

Not that we're surprised: the quality of the cottages and the location are notable.

From the 'village', a narrow street twists down into the small seaside town of Aberdovey, which has a good sandy beach, tennis courts, bowling green and a links golf course. It's also on the Machynlleth-Pwllheli coastal railway line, one of the most scenic in Britain.

Outdoor playground, games room with table tennis and pool, and toddlers' playroom. Laundry. Dogs welcome. Cost from £190 to £840, including electricity, heating, bedlinen and complimentary membership of Machynlleth leisure centre (seven miles away). Short breaks available. Details/brochures from Aberdovey Hillside Village, Aberdovey, Gwynedd LL35 0ND. Telephone 01654 767522. Fax 767069.

www.hillsidevillage.co.uk
email: info@hillsidevillage.co.uk

Uwchmynydd, near Aberdaron
Talcen Foel

It would be hard to find a more away-from-it-all spot than this old Welsh farmstead cottage. It is in the hamlet of Uwchmynydd, below the summit of Mount Anelog, at the western tip of the Lleyn Peninsula. After a scenic drive along seventeen miles of country lanes from Pwllheli, we eventually found it up a gated track which climbed around a hillside bordered by heather and gorse before ending along the edge of a field.

In ten acres of pasture, it's a fine comfortable cottage (**sleeping 2 to 4**) with wonderful sea and mountain views. On a clear day the Irish coast and Wicklow Hills beyond are clearly visible and also the mid-Wales coast. Inside, the interior has been sympathetically rebuilt and modernised while retaining its original character. To make the most of the views, the spacious lounge – originally a cowshed – has windows on three sides, but is kept cosy in cooler weather by a woodburner in an attractive fireplace. Up a couple of steps you reach the kitchen-dining room which has a flag-stone floor and large inglenook with an oil-fired range. The fully-fitted galley kitchen area includes a microwave and washing machine. Both bedrooms, a double and a twin, are at the front and the double offers sea views from the comfort of its bed. Above the kitchen-dining room, an open 'crog loft den' on a balcony reached by a wooden ladder provides huge fun for children to hide away and play in.

When we called there, two Hertfordshire teachers were enjoying a mid-

A super addition to the 'cottage guide' family, with fabulous views...

It is comfortable but not 'prissy', combining modern needs and history.

morning coffee on the patio. 'We've been coming regularly ever since it was converted in 2001', they told us. 'It's just what we need as a com-plete break from our classrooms'.

The cottage is on the Pilgrims' Way coastal path, two miles from the sea-side village of Aberdaron (shops, pub and beach) and one from the excel-lent seafood restaurant at Penbryn Bach, mid-way between Sanctuary Cottage and Penbryn Bach Cottage (see opposite page).

Available July/August, first week of September, Christmas and New Year. Ideal for honeymooners, 'stressed out' couples, walkers and birdwatchers. 'Sorry, no pets'. TV, video. Linen not provided. Friday to Friday book-ings. Cost: from about £450 inclusive of electric and storage heaters (win-ter) with reductions on fortnightly bookings.

Details: Roger Jones, Roger's Retreats, The Old Granary, Tremadog, Gwynedd LL49 9RH. Telephone 01766 513555.

Tal-y-Bont, near Conwy
Pant Farm

We like turning away from the main road and going along a private, gated track to get to this fine property. The main part of the farmhouse dates back to the 16th century, but restoration includes just about every 21st century creature comfort. It has a good-sized 'farmhouse' kitchen/ breakfast room with a dishwasher, a microwave and pine furniture. There's a utility room with washing

In ten acres of pastureland, this property has long been one of our readers' favourites in North Wales.

machine, a dining room with massive inglenook fireplace and a sitting room featuring inglenook, bread oven and TV/video, sympathetically extended with French windows to the garden. Upstairs there's an elegant master bedroom (king sized bed), a twin-bedded room with washbasin and a third bedroom with two single beds. The bathroom has a bidet, and a second bathroom comprises shower, toilet and washbasin. (There's also a downstairs loo/washroom.) The house has double glazing, gas fired programmed central heating during winter lets, a woodburner. Not suitable for dogs. **Sleeps 6**. Cost: £295 to £550. Available all year. Linen not provided. Details: Roger Jones, Roger's Retreats, The Old Granary, Tremadog, Gwynedd LL49 9RH. Telephone 01766 513555.

Tal-y-Bont, near Conwy
Robyn's Nest map 5/331

Across the drive from Pant Farm, though self contained, *Robyn's Nest* shares a remarkable situation in ten acres of land, overlooking the River Conwy and positioned perfectly for the coast (ten miles) and the heart of Snowdonia (Betws-y-Coed's just six miles). Although it can be used to augment the Pant Farm accommodation for larger groups by 2/4, it can be rented separately. The house

It's just across the drive from Pant Farm, and enjoys the same remarkable location.

offers split level accommodation with a king sized bed in the main (ensuite) bedroom and a dining area and big sitting room on the first floor, overlooking the valley. Better yet, there is a woodburning stove, as well as programmed central heating available at an extra charge. The ground floor contains a modern fitted kitchen, separate bathroom and toilet and a twin bedroom. There's an old stable door out on to a private paved patio area.

TV/video. **Sleeps 4**. Not suitable for dogs. Cost: £450. Available main season/bank holiday weeks only. Linen not provided. Details: Roger Jones, Roger's Retreats, The Old Granary, Tremadog, Gwynedd LL49 9RH. Telephone 01766 513555.

Aberdaron
Sanctuary Cottage (Bryn Du Farm)

Tucked away along narrow lanes on the Llyn Peninsula, this has sandy beaches within a mile and a half and a network of footpaths leading to the sea. The large lounge has an inglenook fireplace with multi-fuel stove, an old dresser with Willow Pattern plates, TV/video and dining table. Open stairs lead to the first floor, with one double bedroom, one twin bedded room and a third bedroom with bunk beds. All the rooms are small and cottagey, with rural views.

Good views, an open fire, peace and quiet. Having a restaurant next door is a bonus, not a disadvantage.

The bathroom has an electric shower over the bath. There's a well-modernised kitchen/diner with cooker and microwave. A utility room off the kitchen houses the fridge/freezer, washing machine/dryer, and dishwasher. Fronting the length of the cottage is a large conservatory with cane furniture and dining table and chairs – well recommended by guests! Windows are double-glazed. **Sleeps 6**. Cost: £295 to £550. Available all year. Not suitable for dogs. Linen not provided. Details from Roger Jones, Roger's Retreats, The Old Granary, Tremadog, Gwynedd LL49 9RH. Telephone 01766 513555.

Pwllheli   map 5/314
Gwynfryn Farm Holidays

This impressive 100-acre organic farm on the Lleyn Peninsula is looked after at every stage by the owners themselves, including the dozen WTB **Four and Five Star** cottages created here from original barns. They **sleep from 2 to 8**. Prices

Very family orientated, a great location.

include the use of an indoor pool, a gym, tennis court and playroom, family bikes and more, and electricity, towels, bedding and heating are also 'all-in'. There are 'no hidden charges'. And children will love the pigs and chickens to feed, and the cows to watch being milked. There are wood-burning stoves, dogs are welcome, home-cooked meals are available. The newest properties are *Glaslyn* and *Crafnant*, both graded **Five Stars**. They have tiled floors, leather furniture and two bathrooms. B&B is available in the farmhouse. Pwllheli and the sea are just a mile away, part of a stretch of 'heritage' coast noted for its sandy bays and rocky headlands. Cost: about £250 to £975. Details are available from Alwyn and Sharon Ellis, Gwynfryn Farm, Pwllheli, Gwynedd LL53 5UF. Telephone 01758 612536.

www.northwales-countryholidays.com
email: frank@gwynfryn.freeserve.co.uk

North and Mid Wales
Snowdonia Tourist Services*

You 'know where you are' with this long-established agency: all their properties are in the Snowdonia National Park, or on the Llyn Peninsula, or the Isle of Anglesey, or the North Wales Coast. This well established holiday letting agency has about 145 properties, from traditional country cottages, farmhouses and bungalows to town houses and holiday chalets. All are graded by **'Visit Britain'**.

During a recent 'cottage guide' revisit we saw a good handful of properties. These included *The Coach House* and *Granary* at Llangristiolus, on the Isle of Anglesey. Both are listed buildings, ideal for families. In eight acres of woodland and attractive gardens, just three miles from a sandy beach, The Coach House **sleeps 5**, the Granary **sleeps 4**. Pets welcome. At *Fox's Lair*, a large conservatory is an excellent vantage point for panoramic views of the sea, Caernarfon Castle and the Menai Straits. There's an open-style kitchen/dining area and sitting room with a large open (feature) fireplace. A pretty garden leads to woodland. One pet is welcome. **Sleeps 6.**

Among our long-term favourites is *Bryn Heulog*, a detached villa with uninterrupted views of the spectacular estuary and the mountains. Open

Amid eight acres of woodland and gardens, The Granary is on Anglesey.

Bryn Heulog has an open fire, and spectacular estuary and mountain views.

fire. **Sleeps up to 8**. No pets. Central heating throughout. *The Captain's Beach House*, in a private location on Aberdesach beach, is surrounded by dramatic sea and mountain scenery. **Sleeps 6**. One dog welcome.

And driving down towards the harbour at Porthmadog we came across one of a number of townhouses (*South Snowdon Wharf*), overlooking the estuary, with panoramic views of the Snowdonia Mountains. In some cases the sitting room is on the first floor to take advantage of the views.

Short breaks are available in many properties, and most are available all year round. Details and brochures can be obtained from Snowdonia Tourist Services, High Street, Porthmadog, Gwynedd. Telephone 01766 513829. Fax 513837.

You can visit the easy-to-use website for virtual tours of cottage rooms, see photos of most rooms and check availability:

www.snowdoniatourist.com

email: all@sts-holidays.com

Portmeirion, near Porthmadog
Portmeirion Cottages

In 2005 we stayed (one night: all too brief) in this enchanting hillside village created by the distinguished architect Sir Clough Williams-Ellis. Begun in the 1920s, its higgledy-piggledy pastel-coloured buildings make staying there a real experience. We strolled on the lovely sandy beach at the foot of the village and bought some of its famous pottery. **Sleeping from 2 to 8**, there are fourteen cottages, each one a picturesque gem

An extraordinary 'village', with a very special place in our readers' affections.

(some have small gardens). The cottages are cosy, 'lived-in', deceptively spacious. We spotted antiques, good beds, well-equipped kitchens and often superb views from upper windows. Newspapers, bread and milk are available from a shop and guests have free use of the Portmeirion Hotel's heated pool by the sea from May to September. You can also eat there – in style – or in the hotel by the village entrance. Cost from £602 to £1381; three/four night winter breaks from £281 to £649. Satellite TV, heating, towels and linen. Details from Portmeirion Cottages, Portmeirion, near Porthmadog, Gwynedd LL48 6ET. Telephone 01766 770000.

www.portmeirion-village.com   email: hotel@portmeirion-village.com

---

Llanrug, nr Llanberis
Bryn Bras Castle   map 5/326

Wales is indeed 'a land of castles', and one of the most memorable is a castle in which self-caterers can actually stay. As indeed have many readers during the 25 years in which we have featured Bryn Bras. Within the castle is a selection of beautifully appointed, spacious, warm and comfortable apartments, each

In this guide for 25 happy years!

with a suite of rooms of distinctively individual character, set off with antiques. The Regency castle (Grade II* Listed) lies among the Snowdonian foothills, in 32 quiet acres, with landscaped gardens, woodlands and its own panoramic hill-walk overlooking the sea and Snowdon. Centrally situated for exploring the charms of North Wales and Anglesey, with excellent restaurants and pubs nearby, Bryn Bras is a much loved home and guests appreciate the historic surroundings, peaceful grounds and degree of care in the castle apartments (sleeping 2 to 4). Flexible start/departure days. **'Visit Wales' Five Stars**. Dogs are not allowed, nor are children. Short breaks all year round. Fully inclusive cost: £500 to £900; short breaks from £195 (two people two nights).

Details from Mrs Gray-Parry, Bryn Bras Castle, Llanrug, near Caernarfon, North Wales LL55 4RE. Telephone/fax 01286 870210.

www.brynbrascastle.co.uk   email: holidays@brynbrascastle.co.uk

151

Maesycrugiau and Tregarron

In a super location in the valley of the River Teifi the first of these properties (Ref W8409) is actually the wing of a larger house. It has a woodburning stove and **sleeps 6**. There is a four poster bedroom and an attic bedroom that our own children would have loved when small. You're only about five miles from the Brechfa Forest, where there are mountain bike trails, and a pub/-restaurant is only a mile away. Also

This attractive farmhouse is well placed for walkers, whose dogs are welcome.

close to the Teifi, a farmhouse in over 70 acres of land (Ref W40696) and just two and a half miles from the pleasant small town of Tregarron enjoys impressive views of the Cambrian Mountains. Among many good things there's a pool table, a woodburning stove, a king sized bed in one bedroom and two TVs – one with satellite. And there are even facilities, with plenty of paddock space, for guests to bring their own horses for a holiday. **Sleeps 7.**

For availability and bookings, contact Welcome Cottages, Spring Mill, Earby, Barnoldswick, Lancashire BB94 0AA. Telephone 0870 197 6957. Properties in France available too.

www.welcomecottages.com

The Gower Peninsula map 5/345
Crwys Farm/Tankey Lake Livery

A quartet of quite notable properties, rejoicing in **Five Stars** from **'Visit Britain'** and **sleeping 8. 8, 4 and 4** respectively, make a fine base from which to explore the much-loved 'Gower'. A good number of original features at Crwys Farm have been preserved, blending in sympathetically with 21st century comforts. Refs ONQ, ONR, ONT and ONS. At Tankey Lake Livery, Llangennith, nestling in 31 acres of the owner's

Oak Barn is one of the larger properties at Crwys Farm: a super family house.

small working farm, are two single-storeyed cottages called *Bluebell* and *Buttercup*, conversions from a 16th century barn. One **sleeps 2**, the other **sleeps 4**, and both are suitable for wheelchair access. Refs JYW/JAM. Outdoor pursuits include surfing, windsurfing, canoeing, pony trekking, bird-watching, fishing, golf, hang-gliding and caving.

Further details available from English Country Cottages, Stoney Bank Road, Earby, Barnoldswick BB94 0AA. For bookings and brochures, telephone 0870 197 6890.

www.english-country-cottages.co.uk

Brecon Beacons and around
Brecon Beacons Holiday Cottages*

Here's another of our '25 years in the guide' people. Liz Daniel's much admired agency is a remarkable organisation, with over 270 cottages and farmhouses in and around the Brecon Beacons National Park. We're not surprised that it recently won the accolade of 'Best Small Business in Wales', and that Liz herself has figured in the finals of 'Welshwoman of the Year'. The properties range from a tiny cottage such as *Blaentrothy*, providing a very high level of comfort **for 2** people in a lovely setting, to spacious, rambling farmhouses **sleeping – yes! – up to 50** that are ideal for families and reunions.

We have visited and revisited over the years, and most recently we saw two of the larger properties. Firstly, the remotely-situated (but by no means bleakly lonely) *Crofftau*, whose long, beautifully-furnished sitting-room/dining room upstairs has a steep beamed ceiling, wood burning stove and spectacular mountain views on both sides. It is hard to believe that it was once a barn. **Sleeps 8**. Cost: £820. We don't have enough space to do justice to it but, for example, we were much impressed by the panoramic views, the space, the antiques, the pictures, the huge first floor living room and its rare and extraordinary 1950s Wurlitzer juke-box.

Dovecote Cottage, with a hard tennis court and three miles of fishing on the River Usk, is in a most beautiful location, with views of the Listed

Crofftau is one our favourite houses in the whole of Wales. Not least because there's a Wurlitzer juke-box!

Duffryn Beusych is a cosy charmer, and the owner will prepare a meal for guests on arrival 'at cost'.

octagonal 18th century dovecote and ancient stone bridge over the river. The impressive sitting room has heavy oak beams, having once been the old laundry, a large wood-burning stove in an inglenook fireplace and comfortable sofas and chairs. **Sleeps 8**. Cost £690.

Neat and pretty *Duffryn Beusych* is beautifully situated, with memorable views of The Sugar Loaf and the Black Mountains. Better yet (as far as we are concerned!) the approach to it is via a steepish farm drive and over two fords. It **sleeps 3/4**, and has a woodburning stove.

Details from Elizabeth Daniel, Brecon Beacons Holiday Cottages and Farm Houses, Brynoyre, Talybont-on-Usk, Brecon, Powys LD3 7YS. Telephone 01874 676446. Fax 676416.

www.breconcottages.com   email: enquiries@breconcottages.com

153

Sennybridge, near Brecon
Cnewr Estate

We can hardly think of a better spot from which to enjoy the Brecon Beacons National Park than the holiday houses on the Cnewr Estate. You can choose between a big 1890 farmhouse and a shepherd's cottage, both of them on the 12,000-acre estate (owned and farmed by the same family since 1856), and all much praised by readers over the years.

We sometimes happen on houses or cottages that fit perfectly into their surroundings and give immediate access to much treasured corners of the country: we would include these.

The whole area is ideal for walking, and you could spend a day on the mountains without leaving the estate. There is fly-fishing on the estate's Cray Reservoir, *one of only four in Wales with wild trout*, as well as the hill streams.

Cnewr Farmhouse, which **sleeps 12** in five twins and one double, has a long dining table big enough to seat everyone comfortably in the huge well-equipped kitchen. The main sitting room has unspoilt views down the valley and there is also a TV-lounge/children's room, two bathrooms and shower room. The owner's private dining room is available by arrangement for special occasions. There's lots of warmth and a good number of 'country antiques'.

The other property is beside the Sennybridge to Ystradgynlais road but the windows facing it are double-glazed, though there is little traffic. *Fan Cottage* overlooks Cray Reservoir, having been built as a shepherd's cottage to replace a house lost when the reservoir was built. It has one double and two twin bedrooms, bathroom, sitting room, dining room and large kitchen. It **sleeps 5/6**.

Each property has an open fire (logs provided free), payphone and TV. Well-behaved dogs welcome. Linen and towels provided. Cost, including heating and electricity, from about £200 to about £750. Short-breaks are available at less busy times of the year.

Detailed brochures are available from the Cnewr Estate Ltd, Sennybridge, Brecon, Powys LD3 8SP. Telephone 01874 636207. Fax 638061.

www.cnewrestate.co.uk
email: cottages@cnewrestate.co.uk

Cnewr Farmhouse can accommodate twelve people. It's a comfortable, rambling place of great character...

Fan Cottage, where we have stayed briefly, overlooks peaceful Cray Reservoir, amid fine scenery...

Abergwesyn
Trallwm Forest Cottages

Located most unusually at the heart of a working forest, in a deeply rural part of mid Wales, this is a clutch of cottages converted from former farm buildings. All are **'Visit Wales' Four Stars**. *Siskin*, a detached stone cottage, is **for a couple** (non-smokers). *Nant-Garreg* is full of character, has oak beams, an inglenook fireplace and **sleeps 4**. Two cottages,

Peace, perfect peace, deep in the forest. There are mountain bike trails and a Mountain Bike Centre: details on www.coedtrallwm.co.uk

Kestrel and *Red Kite,* are two-bedroomed and very comfortable. *Trallwm Farmhouse* **sleeps 7**, has a large lounge/diner and a blend of rustic and modern, with one of the three bedrooms downstairs. *Magpie* is a cosy cottage for a non smoking couple. *Trawsgyrch,* a large, traditional Welsh stone farmhouse overlooking hayfields, is well equipped for the **9/10 it sleeps**. Cost: from about £237, fully inclusive, for 2 people. One well-behaved dog is welcome by arrangement (in Nant-Garreg, Siskin and Trawsgyrch). TVs throughout and phone in Nant-Garreg, Siskin and Trawsgyrch only, plus payphone for general use. Details from George and Christine Johnson, Trallwm Forest Lodge, Abergwesyn, Llanwrtyd Wells, Powys LD5 4TS. Telephone/fax 01591 610229.

www.forestcottages.co.uk   email: trallwm@aol.com

We go out of our way to locate cottages that offer peace and quiet.

The West Country

John Betjeman was one of Cornwall's best-loved advocates ('Safe Cornish holidays by the sea'...), and it seems that every corner of the West Country has lots going for it – the proximity of child-friendly beaches, the wild moors, the two national parks, great stately homes. We remember marvellous sunsets, luscious crabs, clotted cream and Cornish pasties, coastal footpaths, ancient castles. On the eastern side of the River Tamar from Cornwall is Devon, with dramatic tors and moorlands fringed by charming villages. Notably, and uniquely in England, it has two separate (unlinked) coasts – a north and south. On the borders of Devon and Somerset, Exmoor is pony trekking and walking country, where wild ponies and deer roam freely. Exmoor has a stretch of coast it can almost call its own, and some spectacular views. In Somerset, Cheddar Gorge and Wookey Hole are memorable. Over the border in Dorset, it is easy to find country houses off the tourist beat and holiday resorts full of history and charm (Lyme Regis is a delight.) And the best of Wiltshire is the essence of rural England, unchanged for hundreds of years. It is dotted with ancient pubs, and half its holiday cottages seem to be thatched!

Botelet, near Herodsfoot
Manor Cottage   map 6/348

With its origins mentioned in the Domesday Book, oak beams, flagstone floors and open fireplaces, this 17th century listed longhouse is – not surprisingly – a real favourite among cottage guide readers. The dining room doors open on to a private walled garden created from earlier ruins, and the kitchen features a covered floodlit well (a first for us!).

A spacious traditional farmhouse, suitable for family groups and couples.

Coupled with this is a flair for design for which Richard Tamblyn has been featured in Elle Decoration. The cottage has been furnished to a standard that makes guests instantly feel at ease: they often choose to stay twice a year. Brass beds are made up with antique linen, the fire is lit and the table laid; with 300 acres, with a neolithic hill-fort, fields, lanes and a woodland walk, there is plenty to explore. The Tamblyn family have been on the farm since 1860 and the present generation live in the Georgian farmhouse across the cobbled courtyard.

Sleeps 5 in three bedrooms (double, twin, single); one bathroom, one shower room. Linen is supplied. Dishwasher, fridge/freezer, washing machine, dryer, microwave, TV, video, CD/tuner. Woodburning stove. Babysitting. Dogs by arrangement. Cost: £270 to £970. Please note that a further cottage (*Cowslip*, not yet seen by us) is available. Further details from Julie Tamblyn, Botelet, Herodsfoot, Liskeard, Cornwall PL14 4RD. Telephone/fax 01503 220225; fax 220909.

www.botelet.co.uk
email: stay@botelet.co.uk

Treworgey Manor, Liskeard
Coach House Cottages

It was one of our readers who first brought the manor, in the same family for over 500 years before coming under the stewardship of Jeremy and Jane Hall, to our attention. She said 'It's a fabulous conversion, beautifully and imaginatively done.' Equally enthusiastically, one of our inspectors says that Treworgey Manor and its cottages have 'the happy knack of maintaining a high degree of comfort without losing the character of the place'.

Even the large heated outdoor pool looks no more out of place than the ancient clock tower, the symbol of this architecturally pleasing group of 16th century courtyard cottages. An all-weather tennis court, games room and boules pit complete the outdoor attractions.

Discovering this beautifully cared for Cornish oasis of comfort and style on a warm summer afternoon raised our morale considerably!

You could even hold a small dance in *The Coach House* which, **sleeping 8**, has a half size snooker table in the sitting room. There is one double bedroom with en suite bathroom, a further double bedroom, one twin-bedded room, a bunk-bedded one, a bathroom and a separate shower room, making it ideal for two families, or for those bringing grandparents. *Paddock View* and *Deer Park* both **sleep 6**, but vary in the distribution of bedrooms and also in decor, each being delightfully distinctive, with good use made of original beams, paintings, ornaments and objects of interest from the old manor buildings.

Middle Barn **sleeps 4** in a double bedroom and a twin, and has an upstairs bathroom. Pets are accepted in this property. Dogs will certainly appreciate the walks, the Manor being tucked into 100 acres of pasture and woodland. Children will also have fun exploring the nooks and crannies around the courtyard, not least the mysterious priest's hole.

With a roaring log fire for company there is every temptation to stay put in your own little world. Which is where short breaks, weekend parties – renting all four cottages – come into their own. Each garden has a table and chairs, plus barbecue.

Electricity and calor gas are included, and also an initial basket of logs (each property has an open log fire); linen is supplied, except beach towels; there is a laundry room, payphone and TVs with DVD players. Cost: about £160 (three night short break) to £1180. Details are available from Jeremy or Jane Hall, Coach House Cottages, Treworgey Manor, Liskeard, Cornwall PL14 6RN. Telephone 01579 347755. Fax 345441.

www.treworgey.co.uk   email: info@treworgey.co.uk

Duloe, near Looe
Trefanny Hill

The cottages here, each one with its own special character and each, we've noticed over 25 years of featuring 'Trefanny', with its own following, are very special. One couple told us they booked a cottage here with the aim of making it their touring base for a week. 'But', they said, 'we never left "the village", as we came to know it. It is such a retreat from everyday cares, so peaceful and nostalgic.'

It's hard to believe that over 40 years ago, when the Slaughter family first discovered Trefanny Hill, it was a desolate ruin. Nestling above a tributary of the West Looe River, this ancient farming settlement was at one time a thriving, medieval smugglers' hamlet which in the last century was granted its own school, smithy and chapel. Even today, Trefanny Hill retains a village atmosphere. The cottages are lovely, their stone or white-

There is a village atmosphere at Trefanny Hill. The cottages are well spread out and enjoy a feeling of independence.

Each cottage has its own individual character. They range in size from those for 6 to mini cottages just for couples.

painted walls draped with ivy, roses and other climbers and looking just like everybody's idea of what a country cottage should be. Each has bags of character, and reveals the Slaughters' amazing eye for detail. There are seventeen cottages in all—well spread out, each with its own garden.

There are five different sizes of cottage, appropriate to the size of your family, ranging from a cosy cottage just for 2 (either with an antique brass double bed or four poster, or king-size/twin beds) to a three-bedroom for 6 (7 with a cot). Among the little extras you will find are plenty of books (including a set of coffee table items on wild flowers, trees, birds). There are video recorders, hairdryers, electric blankets, hot water bottles, alarm clocks. The kitchens are fully equipped with filter coffee makers, spice jars, wine coolers, microwaves, dishwashers and extras galore. All the cottages for 3 or more also have a washing machine/tumble dryer installed, while the smaller ones without this have access to washing machines and dryers in a traditional Cornish building nearby.

Each garden has chairs, a table, a parasol and a good barbecue so you can enjoy fine weather to the full. Standing in 75 acres, Trefanny Hill is surrounded by rolling greenery and commands a wide panorama over the Looe Valley. Among the permanent residents are the ducks on their pond, the chickens, doves, cats, Jacob's sheep and shire horses. The wild flowers in springtime are particularly magical. There are no half-hidden eyesores that detract from the peaceful atmosphere. The interiors of the cottages are like private homes. The furniture is good, old and varied. Each cottage is different; some have Laura Ashley and Sanderson wallpaper and fabrics, most have oak beams up to 400 years old, and log fires.

Perhaps the most memorable part of our most recent visit was strolling downhill past the heated outdoor pool that is accessible to all Trefanny's guests – it is amazingly scenically situated, and always warm – and then through fields towards a wooded stream where we discovered *Tregarrick Millhouse*, another of those substantial family houses that make these journeys so worthwhile. We do not have the space to convey all its delights, but noted most appealing reds and greens in the decor and, outside, large grounds with a stream and a mill pond. **Sleeps 6**.

A tea and coffee tray greets every arriving guest, and all linen – crispy white, generous in size – is provided. Shared amenities include that beautiful heated swimming pool, a children's play area, a grass lawn with badminton net, a golf net for driving practice and more. There is an attractive lake with wildlife, a full size tennis court, and an enchanting bluebell wood.

Most unusually, cottage guests at Trefanny Hill have their own cosy little inn, which is much enjoyed for drinks, snacks and full meals.

In this attractive setting, people staying at Trefanny Hill have ready access to one of the most impressively situated outdoor pools in Cornwall!

The tiny inn within the hamlet is also a popular feature, where you can relax in a cosy, informal atmosphere for drinks or candlelit dinners. Dishes are cooked to order using fresh local produce (freshly caught local fish and organic steaks being the specialities of the house), or alternatively you can eat in the privacy of your own cottage by choosing from the full and varied menu offered by a home cooked meals service.

More fishing (lake, river and sea), windsurfing, including hire and instruction, riding, golf, sailing and many more activities are all available in the area. Each cottage has an information folder and relevant Ordnance Survey maps. We wish this was universal!

A typical comment culled from the visitors' books in the cottages reads 'For a long time we have looked for a holiday that offers top class hotel accommodation with the freedom of self-catering – at last we have found it'. Said one Lancashire visitor, 'it's the most honest brochure I have seen in many years'. And a Surrey couple have been to stay – yes! – 41 times!

Cost: about £150 to £1945. Children and well behaved pets are welcome. Details from John and Suzanne Slaughter, Trefanny Hill, Duloe, near Liskeard, Cornwall PL14 4QF. Telephone 01503 220622.

www.trefanny.co.uk
enq@trefanny.co.uk

Pelynt, near Looe
Tremaine Green

Effectively making up a hamlet in its own right, the cottages at Tremaine Green convey a charming sense of belonging, and there are usually opportunities for children to make new friends. As one reader wrote: 'This really is a place for 'a memorable holiday'.

In this group of traditional craftsmen's cottages, the whole family will appreciate the games room with table-tennis, pool, darts and other games. They'll also appreciate the lovingly kept, award-winning gardens. Good beaches and restaurants are a short drive away, as is 'quintessential' Polperro. Also, there's a hard tennis court, putting green, swing-ball, pigmy goats, ducks, miniature ponies etc to feed. Hamlet, the owners' blue Great Dane, completes the picture.

Every building is named after its original use, such as *Blacksmith's*, *Carpenter's* and *Miller's*, and each is decorated inside with interesting pictures and artefacts, particularly antique tools. Leather hobnail boots and saddlery are interesting reminders of *Ploughman's* history, while *Cobbler's* boasts authentic relics from a shoemaker's.

We love the fact that Tremaine Green's cottages are private and self-contained...

...but are at the same time part of a tucked away hamlet, 'part of a whole'.

There are eleven cottages altogether (**sleeping 2 to 6**), each with its own individual charm. Most have exposed stonework and many have an antique four-poster or half-tester bed at least in the main bedroom. Cots and occasional single beds are available in most cottages. The kitchens in cottages **sleeping 4** or more have dishwashers and fridge-freezers. We liked the comfortable settee/deep armchairs in Ploughman's and the inglenook fireplace with the original cloam (bread) oven, also *Dairymaid's* antique half-tester bed, the pretty fabrics and the open fire. *Tinner's*, which has a bunk bedroom and shower downstairs, plus two doubles upstairs, is popular with families, as children sleeping in the bunks can feel independent.

The double glazing and the oil-fired central heating make all this cosy in winter. (Four cottages have real fires as well.) Videos and DVDs are available for rent. Tickets for the Eden Project (14 miles away) are for sale to avoid queuing at the ticket office there. Dogs and other pets welcome. Linen provided. TVs, videos and DVDs for rent. Cost: about £180 to £946. An excellent brochure is available from Justin and Penny Spreckley, Tremaine Green Country Cottages, Pelynt, near Looe, Cornwall PL13 2LT. Telephone 01503 220333; fax 220633.

www.tremainegreen.co.uk   email: stay@tremainegreen.co.uk

Duloe, near Looe
Treworgey Cottages

For all its usefulness, the **'Visit Britain'** grading scheme doesn't accord cottages special credit for being in idyllic locations. So in our book (literally) these are **Five Star**-plus, with all the comfort and style that implies *and* a memorable situation.

High above the River Looe, with spectacular south-facing views over patchwork fields and the river itself, they are outstanding. Better yet, owners Lynda and Bevis Wright have landscaped the prettiest of individual private gardens for each cottage, with masses of flowers.

Each cottage exudes good taste and is individually styled, mostly with family antique furniture, original paintings, wool carpets, oriental rugs, plenty of lamps and books. Bedrooms have exceptionally attractive four posters or beautiful brass beds with really comfortable mattresses, antiques, lace and fresh flowers.

Add to this a delivered candlelit dinner (from Treworgey's mouthwatering menu) by your roaring log fire, a good video from the Wrights' comprehensive library and you'll think you have died and gone to heaven! (Don't worry about the washing up – the dishwasher will do it!)

There is plenty to do here too (the Eden Project, for example, is only half an hour away), and the landscaped outdoor pool is stunning. Readers are full of praise about that: 'really warm...open and steaming as late as October, when the weather allows'... There is excellent riding available on site, an all-weather tennis court, indoor and outdoor playground with wendy house and more, and a delightful collection of animals: the goats

Unusually for this sort of set-up, every property has its own cottagey garden...

Such a lot of style and attention to detail has gone into every one of the interiors...

and Bramble the pony spend most of their time befriending guests.

Short breaks are welcome out of season. With log fires and ample central heating, Treworgey is very popular in winter and for Christmas and New Year. (By the way Treworgey is easy to get to by train – there's even a tiny toy station down the lane at Sandplace.)

Cost: from about £275 per week to £2071, according to cottage size and season. **Sleep from 2 'plus baby' to 8**. Children are welcome. Telephone 01503 262730. Fax 263757.

www.cornishdreamcottages.co.uk
email: treworgey@enterprise.net

Looe Valley
Badham Farm Holiday Cottages

There are not many 'deeply rural' properties you can still reach by train. But this is one, via Causeland Halt on the scenic Looe Valley Line – a most charming feature that Jan and Pauline Scroczynski plan to make more of as they continue to upgrade these popular cottages. Newly built is the ground floor two bedroom timber frame *Oak Cottage*, with block and render facing, **sleeping 4,** and *Ash Cottage*, similarly built, accessible to the disabled, and **sleeping 5**. Likewise the three bedroom *Larch Cottage*, **Five Star** rated and **sleeping 6**. Again wheelchair friendly, it's in two acres of landscaped garden, close to a pine forest.

Both 'deeply rural' and near the sea – a powerful combination in holiday houses.

All neatly complement the other six cottages, **sleeping between 2 and 10** (in the *Farmhouse*). Bonuses include an animal and bird paddock, a coarse fishing lake and tennis court, along with a convivial bar and a large games room.

Dogs at £20 a week. Cost from about £200 to £1000 including heating; also short breaks. Contact Jan and Pauline Scroczynski, Badham Farm Holidays, St Keyne, Liskeard, Cornwall PL14 4RW. Telephone/fax 01579 343572.
www.badhamfarm.co.uk email: badhamfarm@yahoo.co.uk

Coverack, near Helston
Trevarrow Cottage map 6/360

The quaint Cornish fishing village of Coverack, very well located on a south easterly corner of the Lizard peninsula, is the kind of place that photographers drool over. And this idyllic looking cottage looks as good as any you might see on chocolate box lids or jigsaws. Also, Trevarrow would surely win the prettiest-cottage-in-the-village award on account of its pastel-pink walls and thatched roof. Better yet, it was once a smugglers' hideaway. Though it has been properly modernised, it still has its original shipwreck beams and inglenook fireplace. It has an excellent and well-equipped kitchen with, microwave, washing machine/tumble dryer. Short breaks at an advantageous price are available off peak. Electricity is included, as is

Trevarrow is one of the prettiest houses in one of Cornwall's most sought-after coastal villages.

linen (though not towels). Friday to Friday bookings. No smoking. **Sleeps 6**. Cost: about £395 to £825. Further details from Amanda Wiseman, Shenstone Court, Court Drive, Shenstone, Lichfield, Staffordshire WS14 0JQ. Telephone 07980 370373 or fax 01543 481272.

email: wisemanaj@googlemail.com

Praa Sands
Sea Meads Holiday Homes

It's one thing to be 'by the sea', but at Sea Meads you can not only see and hear the waves, you can almost touch them. The location itself is impressive: a mile-long sandy beach, facing due south into the broad sweep of Mounts Bay, a nine-hole golf centre, riding stables within easy reach. And of course there's the charm of the properties themselves.

On a recent revisit we were delighted to rediscover the properties on a private road almost hidden from the little cluster of buildings above the beach. Sea Meads is a group of five detached houses, each with its own private garden facing the sea, spacious lounges with large sliding patio windows through which to enjoy those views, dining areas with serving hatch from modern kitchens equipped with dishwashers, fridge-freezers, cookers with extractor hoods, microwaves, washing machines, clothes driers, bathrooms with heated towel rails and wall heaters – everything to permanent-home standards.

*Solmer, Sunwave, Sea Horse*s and *Sunraker* are all similar. On the ground floor there is a twin-bedded room with en-suite bathroom and toilet, and a small room with double bunk beds. Upstairs are two large bedrooms (one double, one twin) – each has a small balcony with magnificent sea views, and a second bathroom with shower unit. The ambience is one of brightness and light, with comfortable furniture and charming domestic touches. There is plenty of space, a private garage to each house, room in the garden for ball games, all-in-all a recipe for the most exacting family who just want to laze about or go in for strenuous activity. **Sleep up to 8**.

The fifth house, *Four Winds*, **sleeping 5**, is lower lying and separate from the others. We loved the big, comfortable sitting room and the linked sun

This is a typical bedroom-balcony view! *Semi-tropical gardens, superb interiors.*

lounge on to the sea side; we also liked the different-level dining area and the ensuite bedroom with impressive sea views.

Cost: approximately £295 to £1145, depending on which property and when you go. TVs/videos. Dogs are welcome. Linen is included, towels available on request. There is a games room, with table tennis, pool and darts.

Details from Best Leisure, Old House Farm, Fulmer Road, Fulmer, Buckinghamshire SL3 6HU. Telephone 01753 664336. Fax 663740.

www.bestleisure.co.uk

St Austell
Bosinver Cottages

We were not surprised that 'Bosinver' won the accolade of 'Self Catering Establishment of the Year' in the Cornwall Tourism Awards for 2005 *and* 2006, and the Silver Trophy in the self catering catering section of the South West Excellence Awards. For the place is outstanding.

Among the nineteen cottages owned and run by the astonishingly energetic Pat and David Smith, people have been completely bowled over by *Coliza*, a lovely thatched two-storey cottage (**sleeping 4** plus cot). It looks and feels old, yet it's only been completed during the last couple of years.

The variety of sizes of property here offers something for everyone. The old thatched farmhouse **sleeps 12**, *Laburnum* and *Jacks Barn* both **sleep 8**, and the combinations possible make it easy for groups wanting to celebrate special occasions. Most are totally private and overlook meadows teeming with wildlife and friendly farm animals.

The cottages are scattered among trees, gardens and meadows around the 30-acre estate, just three miles from the sea and a five-minute stroll from Polgooth's village shop and pub. Pat furnishes each one individually, with antiques, local materials and traditional crafts.

Bosinver has received a Green Tourism Award for safeguarding the environment, but also provides plenty to do. One family told us they had problems getting their children away from the adventure playground with its trampoline, slides, playhouse, rope bridge and climb-on tractor. They will appreciate the new play barn being built. In a glorious south-facing position, one end of it is glass and oak from floor to ceiling. It will incorporate

A 'Green Tourism' Award and more (see above) from the Cornwall Tourist Board.

...and plaudits from us for a massive upgrading during recent years.

an 'R and R' area with sofas for mums and dads, and a small 'gym area'.

There's also a heated outdoor pool (April to September), sauna, tennis court, coarse fishing and games room with table-tennis, pool, darts and table football. Bikes can be hired.

Cots and highchairs available. Dogs by arrangement. No smoking. Some properties Friday-Friday, some Saturday-Saturday. Short breaks from November to April. Cost: from about £250 to £2000 per week from the smallest, **sleeping 2**, to the largest, **sleeping 12**. Details from Mrs Pat Smith, Bosinver Farm, St Austell, Cornwall PL26 7DT. Telephone/fax 01726 72128.

Fowey
Fowey Harbour Cottages*

Harbour Cottage is right on the waterfront: you can literally step from the garden into your boat...

Specialising in Fowey Harbour, on the south Cornish coast, this long-established agency is run with style. Cottages include *Harbour Cottage*, with direct frontage to the harbour in Fowey (two bedrooms, **sleeping 6**: **'Visit Britain' Three Stars**), *The Penthouse*, in the centre of Fowey, a four-storey town house with parking space and a roof-top terrace from which there is a 360° outlook over the harbour (three bedrooms, **sleeping 6**: **'Visit Britain' Three Stars**), *17a St Fimbarrus Road*, Fowey, an apartment in a tall Victorian terrace house with windows overlooking the whole of the harbour (two bedrooms, **sleeping 4**: **'Visit Britain' Three Stars**) and a selection of stone-built cottages in the village of Polruan on the other side of the harbour, including *Rose Villa*, a pleasant cottage in Polruan, opposite Fowey, with a patio garden. It **sleeps 5** in three bedrooms. **'Visit Britain' Two Stars**. Most **sleep 4 to 6**. Dogs welcome in most, all have TV. Linen for hire. Cost from £175 to £1200. Short breaks at certain times. Details from David Hill, 3 Fore Street, Fowey, Cornwall PL23 1AH. Telephone 01726 832211. Fax 832901.

www.foweyharbourcottages.co.uk   email: hillandson@talk21.com

---

Looe   map 6/366
Wringworthy Cottages

Family orientated, rural but near the sea.

Only about ten minutes' drive from Looe, one of the most sought-after Cornish resorts, but in a blissful rural location, the eight cottages that were once part of the stone farmstead at Wringworthy have been lovingly converted to retain many original features. All are well-equipped to offer the sort of 'home from home' cottage enthusiasts so appreciate, and make an outstandingly good touring base for the delights of Cornwall – National Trust houses and gardens, moors, the Eden Project and more. Each with **Four Stars** from **'Visit Britain'**, the cottages (which hold a 'Green Acorn' Award for sustainable tourism) **sleep from 2 to 8**, and have the big advantage (often referred to by readers of this guide) of resident owners. There's a notably warm heated pool, safe play areas, outdoor games, barbecues and more. There are tame farm animals, and a games barn, and one cottage is wheelchair-adapted. Cost: about £146-269 to £399-1065 per week. Short out of season breaks. Linen and towels included. No smoking. Pets welcome.

Details from Michael and Kim Spencer, Wringworthy Cottages, Morval, Looe, Cornwall PL13 1PR. Telephone 01503 240685, fax 240830.

www.wringworthy.co.uk   email: holidays@wringworthy.co.uk

Polperro
Marigold and Penny

Modestly priced considering their much sought-after location, these two former fishermen's terraced cottages are tucked away down one of the narrow streets of this picturesque fishing village. Each has a small, square, low-ceilinged room on each of the three floors – a kitchen/dining-area at the bottom, sitting room with

Cosy, unpretentious, very reasonably priced for such a famous location...

TV on the first floor and a bedroom at the top with a four poster bed. They have been comfortably adapted **for 2 to 4** people each. *Penny* is one terrace back from the harbour in 'The Warren' at the most desirable end of Polperro, and close to the smuggling museum. *Marigold* is a couple of streets back, but still has a view of the busy little harbour. At Penny you'll be tempted to spend time in the bedroom, as it has a harbour view. At Marigold, where the rooms are slightly bigger, steep steps outside the back door lead up to a sloping garden and seat to enjoy the view over the village rooftops. Cost: about £175 to £385. Fully equipped. Heating *and parking* included. Linen provided but not towels. Details and photos from Martin Friend, The Maltings, Malting Green Road, Layer de la Haye, Essex CO2 0JJ. Telephone/fax 01206 734555.

email:martinfriend6018@aol.com and/or **teresa@tesco.com**

Portscatho   map 6/355
Pollaughan Cottages

It's no surprise that these fine cottages (**Colour section A, Page 5**) have received a string of awards. Such as a Green Tourism Gold Award, and first place in the 2006 'Sustainable Tourism Cornwall' awards and The Accessible Holiday of the Year' scheme. The latter is important: Pollaughan is suitable at the highest

See Page 11 for more information about Pollaughan's approach to Green Tourism and to high accessibility standards.

level for people with disability. (Said one wheelchair-bound guest we met in *Owl Cottage*, **sleeping 2**, 'It's wonderful here. I trust it won't be our last visit'.) Like *Willow Barn*, which **sleeps 6**, it is geared for accessibility, though as with *Farm House*, a Victorian charmer, **sleeping 5**, with antique pine furniture, and *Swallows Barn*, **sleeping 2**, the main thrust is in providing a home from home The latest addition is *Meadows*, a detached property **sleeping 6**, with jacuzzi and woodburner. Typical of the caring approach of the owners are the provision of a welcoming cream tea and a basket of toys for children. Unsuitable for dogs. Linen and towels included. Short breaks. Cost: about £300 to £1030. Valerie Penny, Pollaughan Cottages, Portscatho, Truro, Cornwall TR2 5EH. Telephone 01872 580150.

www.pollaughan.co.uk   **email: info@pollaughan.co.uk**

The Roseland Peninsula
Roseland Holiday Cottages*

Based in Portscatho, this medium-sized agency is notable for its variety. There are 66 cottages, dotted around the idyllic semi-tropical Roseland Peninsula whose southerly point is postcard-pretty St Mawes. Most are by, or very near, the sea. All are described in detail in its stylish brochure – a real armchair 'voyage of discovery'. On our most recent visit we noted two that were

Martha's Cottage is thatched, Grade II listed, and near a super family beach!

totally different: *Martha's Cottage* (**sleeping 4**), an old Grade II listed thatched house at Treworthal, four minutes' drive from Pendower Beach, and *3 Tregarth Cottages* (**sleeping 6**), one of three smart new terrace houses on the hillside above St Mawes, five minutes' walk away. Its lounge (upstairs) opens on to a balcony with lovely sea and river views. At Gerrans, the old village chapel near the harbour has been divided into two imaginatively designed houses: *Sunday House East* (**sleeping 8/10**) and *Sunday House West* (**sleeping 6**).

Details/brochure from Roseland Holiday Cottages, Crab Apple Cottage, Portscatho, Truro, Cornwall TR2 5ET. Telephone/fax: 01872 580480.
www.roselandholidaycottages.co.uk
email: enquiries@roselandholidaycottages.co.uk

Portscatho, near Truro
Pettigrew Cottage   map 6/370

Quite simply, being in one of the most sought-after coastal villages in Cornwall, this is much in demand. It is just the sort of seaside hideaway artists and writers dream of – yet it equally well suits a small family. Rich in history, tucked away only 150 yards from the harbour, it was once the home of sailmaker Edward Peters, great-great-grandfather of the present owner, Hilary Thompson, who has written a book about him. It still feels like a family home, which is much of its charm: the kitchen/diner is equipped with electric cooker, microwave and more. **Sleeps 4**, in a first floor

A lucky find in sought-after Portscatho.

front double bedroom, with sea view, and a back twin bedroom with a view over the small back garden with a cobbled yard and barbecue area. The living-room has an open fireplace of local stone, handy for early or late holidays. Linen on request; cot on request; TV. Car parking (one vehicle). Dogs by request. Cost: from £200 to £475. Details from Hilary and Philip Thompson, Chenoweth, 1 The Quay, Portscatho, Truro, Cornwall TR2 5HF. Telephone 01872 580573.

web: members.aol.com/hilnphil/index   email: philnhil@tiscali.co.uk

167

Helford River and Falmouth
Cornish Holiday Cottages*

This agency is one of the best of its size that we know, in Cornwall or elsewhere. There are just 40 or so genuinely 'hand-picked' properties, and we know for a fact that owners (we've heard from them) compete to get on the organisation's books.

Tregullow, in Maenporth, is a modern bungalow **sleeping 4**. It occupies a wonderful clifftop position overlooking Falmouth Bay. The sumptuously comfortable L-shaped lounge, with French windows and an open fireplace of Cornish slate, makes the most of the view. An archway leads from the neat dining room with pine dresser into the kitchen, fitted with oak cupboards, electric oven, hob, microwave and dishwasher.

In a leafy residential area is *Helford Point*, a property of high quality **sleeping up to 8**. It is a four-bedroomed bungalow in a large garden, with stunning views of the mouth of the Helford River and Falmouth Bay.

Closer to Falmouth – in fact, just two minutes' walk from the High Street – *6 Jane's Court*, **sleeping 4/6**, is in Packet Quays, with views from the two bedroomed apartments over Falmouth Harbour. Built in 1985, it is part of an architect's award winning complex. So expect high standards.

Helford Point has fabulous views out to sea, and lies in an Area of Outstanding Natural Beauty. It sleeps 8.

Though close to Falmouth town centre, 6 Jane's Court is quiet. It too has amazing views.

Different in character is *Sail Loft* (**sleeps 5** plus cot), part of the group of holiday cottages at Calamansac, in the wooded western headland of Port Navas Creek overlooking the Helford River. Designed to maximise the views of the river, the first floor living accommodation is entered via a bridge and balcony from private car parking.

We also loved the *Rose Cottages*, in the so-picturesque waterside village of Durgan. They are three charming old fishermen's cottages – modernised but retaining all the original features – just a stone's throw from the beach. Each **sleeps 4**.

Cost: from about £160 to £1575. Dogs and young children welcome. Further details available from Emily Boriosi, Cornish Holiday Cottages, Killibrae, Maenporth, Falmouth, Cornwall TR11 5HP. Telephone/fax 01326 250339.

www.cornishholidaycottages.net

email: Info@cornishholidaycottages.net

Cornwall – countywide
Forgotten Houses

Even in terms of the often remarkable properties we see on our travels, some of these are extraordinary. It would take many weeks to visit all of what the brochure (full of historic and architectural details) calls 'these unusual holiday homes' – largely in Cornwall – a modest way of saying that they all benefit hugely from their location, architecture or history. Which as Stephen Tyrrell, the brains, and occasional renovator behind this extraordinary concept says, means most are listed, and many have been carefully modernised. This also means that some, by necessity, 'do not meet the modern standards of use or convenience'.

Nor will he budge from this formula, telling us during a recent visit that his strict criteria meant turning down some properties rather than create a suburban version of the countryside. Instead, most properties – about 35 in all – are built of stone, with walls two feet thick under slate roofs. Nearly all have fireplaces or stoves with wood supplied as part of the rent – as well as television and washing machines, books and games.

The approach is perhaps best summed up by the most famous house, *Mellinzeath*, close to the Helford River. Thought to have been rebuilt after a fire in 1665, it **sleeps 4/5**, with a Land Rover ride for guests and their luggage to the house – a 600 metre walk from your car! 'Return to the roots and get back to basics,' urges one guest. 'A beautifully restored cottage, and a fireplace that takes six-foot logs has been burning continuously for six and a half days.'

Most have two, three or four bedrooms, but there are also a few larger properties – such as *Manorbier Castle*, Pembrokeshire, **sleeping 12** plus cot. Fascinating, but with walls and towers you should keep a careful eye on the children.

Last year we took a fresh look at *Lower Bosvarren*, one of six houses in the hamlet of Bosvarren, up a tree lined drive just ten minutes' drive from Falmouth. A listed Elizabethan farmhouse, redecorated in 2002 and 2004 and fun for families, it retains original features, including the roof of small 'scantle' slates and two granite bread ovens. It **sleeps 8** in four double bedrooms, plus cot, and is oil fired centrally heated.

Previously we saw *Bosbenna*, a spacious house with three big bedrooms and a 'Heidi' attic up a ladder. *Badgers* (Helston), **sleeps 4/6**, and likewise has a gallery loft with two beds reached by ladder for two adventurous children. 'Having been to Cornwall many times we can honestly say Badgers is the loveliest cottage we have stayed in,' wrote one guest.

Bosvathick Lodge, near Falmouth, **sleeping 4**, though the smallest of all the properties, has its own little drive, lawn and large garden. Like most others it accepts dogs, and, again like so many others, it seems, is close to a prize-winning pub.

For a copy of a functional, not glossy but detailed brochure, with floor plans, contact Forgotten Houses, Bosvathick, Constantine, Falmouth, Cornwall TR11 5RD. Telephone 01326 340153. Fax 340426.
email: Info@Forgottenhouses.co.uk
Or see the well regarded website: www.forgottenhouses.co.uk

South West Cornwall
St Aubyn Estates

We have much enjoyed our travels to the four separate and highly desirable coastal locations in the south and 'the far west' of Cornwall where James and Mary St Aubyn offer really high quality holiday properties in stunning coastal locations.

One of them is near the historic town of Marazion (near Penzance) and six are near the dream-holiday picture-postcard village of Porthgwarra.

At *Venton Farmhouse*, Marazion, for example, we love the space, the quiet, the upgrading to an extremely high standard with no loss of character. Among many good things is the view across the water to St Michael's Mount, the spacious walled garden (unusual for a seaside location) and a private path to the rocky beach below. We admired excellent local pictures, six foot double beds in several instances, a superb dining table, a top notch kitchen, stylish and understated colours. With **Five 'Visit Britain' Stars** (no surprise), it **sleeps 10**, and is not overpriced from £665 to £1945.

Within a few minutes' drive of Land's End, via narrow high hedged lanes towards the sea at Porthgwarra, we located picturesque *Corner Cottage* and *Cove Cottage*. Literally yards from the cove, each was occupied by people delighted by their find. In Cove we admired a well planned combined kitchen/dining room/sitting room, and an unusual basement with a

Venton Farmhouse is a superb property, overlooking St Michael's Mount...

We looked at two fine properties in picture-postcard Porthgwarra Cove...

glassed-over stream below. **Sleeps 4** in a double (ensuite) and a twin. In Corner we liked the double brass bedstead, the expensive pine floor. **Sleeps 2**. Each has central heating.

Also at Porthgwarra, *Higher Roskestal* is a fabulous conversion of a detached farmhouse with stunning sea views. It **sleeps 6** in three bedrooms, all ensuite (**'Visit Britain' Five Stars**). *Three Chimneys* is a complete renovation of two hill-top cottages, **sleeping 8,** and is the latest addition to the portfolio. More remote is *Faraway Cottage* at Nanjizal, **sleeping 4**. Also at Nanjizal, *Bosistow Farmhouse* **sleeps 7**.

Details and brochure from Clare Sandry, St Aubyn Estates, Manor Office, Marazion, Cornwall TR17 0EF. Telephone: 01736 710507. Fax 719930.

www.staubynestates.co.uk

email: godolphin@manor-office.co.uk

St Martin, near Helston
Mudgeon Vean Farm Holiday Cottages

On her glorious newly produced brochure – some memorable photos – owner Sarah Trewhella neatly conveys the charms of Mudgeon Vean, so prettily situated near the Helford River. The two cottages, *Swallow* and *Swift*, are identical, **sleeping 2 to 4**, plus cot/zed-bed. Nicely converted from the former dairy, they have a cosy open-plan sitting room/dining room/kitchen around an open fire. The third, *Badger*, **sleeping 2/6** plus cot, is attached to the

There's an outdoor play area, a table tennis room, and a private woodland walk.

farmhouse. The small arable/orchard farm has inspiring valley views and produces apple juice and cider. The farm, with **Three Stars** from Southwest Tourism, is bordered by a beautiful National Trust walk to the Helford River, and the coves of the Lizard and the beaches of North Cornwall are in easy driving distance. Cost: about £150 to £425. Dogs by arrangement (£10 pw). Linen included. Details from Mr and Mrs J Trewhella, Mudgeon Vean, St Martin, near Helston, Cornwall TR12 6DB. Telephone 01326 231341.

www.mudgeonvean.co.uk
email: mudgeonvean@aol.com

St Tudy, near Wadebridge
Chapel Cottages   map 6/385

Twenty years in this guide, many enthusiastic reader reports (including lots of return visitors). Original stable front doors, beamed ceilings, polished slate floors, window seats and (in three) large granite fireplaces with cloam ovens amount to 'masses of character'! *Chapel Cottages,* which we revisited recently, are a group of four listed stone-built cottages on the edge of the quiet village of St Tudy (a

Twenty years with us, a visitor-friendly base from which to explore Cornwall.

shop and an inn are a short walk away). Each cottage has a character of its own, with good bedrooms – one with a double and a single bed, the other with twin beds – and everything on hand. The pine kitchens are attractive, with individual washing machines. In easy reach are Bodmin Moor, the Eden Project, the Camel Trail to Padstow, and the beaches of Trebarwith, Polzeath and Daymer Bay. Cost: about £150 to £410 per week. TV. Linen, cots and high chairs are included. Private parking. Not suitable for pets. Details from Clifford and Margaret Pestell, 'Hockadays', Tregenna, near Blisland, Cornwall PL30 4QJ. Telephone/fax 01208 850146.

www.hockadays.co.uk   email: chapelcottages@aol.com

171

Port Gaverne, near Wadebridge
Gullrock

The location is superb: close to the sea, but not buffetted by it, in a charming little seaside village that has somehow remained self contained and is never overrun by visitors. Better yet, these cottages, just two minutes' stroll from a sandy beach, are rich in local history.

Half-hidden away nicely down a narrow lane the cottages are on three sides of a grassy courtyard with flower borders. The building was originally constructed about 200 years ago to cure and store the fish catches landed in the cove, and was used for this until the turn of the century.

The cottages are sensibly priced (particularly good value outside the main season), 'unpretentious and practical' units in what can sometimes be an expensive corner of the West Country. We particularly liked the bigger, *Seaways*, which **sleeps 6** in three double or twin rooms, with a spacious sitting room and a pleasant outlook on to the courtyard at the front and trees at the rear. The charming and cosy flat called *Creekside*, looking in part over the courtyard, is cleverly arranged to **sleep 6** in four bedrooms.

Each unit has a dishwasher, microwave, fridge-freezer, TV and video, CD/radio cassette and full central heating. An outbuilding houses washing/drying machines, a payphone and an assortment of garden furniture. The grounds include not only the courtyard, but an outer garden with barbecue and picnic area, and there is a parking space for each cottage. The

Even by coastal Cornish standards, this is an exquisite little place.

And the cottages themselves are in a pretty and rather historic courtyard.

beach, just 75 yards from Gullrock, is very sheltered, providing safe bathing and fascinating rock pools. The coastal path crosses the head of the beach, leading over the westward headland to the village of Port Isaac, and east along wild and remote clifflands to Trebarwith.

Visitors' pets are welcome, and Gullrock's resident pets are all friendly. Sample prices, which include electricity and heating, are: £200 February, £390 May, £720 August. Discounts are available to parties of three people or fewer from April to October, except in the summer school holidays.

Full details from Malcolm Lee, Gullrock, Port Gaverne, Port Isaac, Cornwall PL29 3SQ. Telephone 01208 880106.

www.goodcottageguide.com/self_catering_accommodation/gullrock.html
email: gullrock@ukonline.co.uk

Crackington Haven
The Old School Cottages

Tucked into the hillside immediately below the beautiful Norman church of St Genny's in the tiny hamlet of Churchtown is the Old School. Closed as a school in the 1960s, the sturdy stone building has been cleverly converted into holiday cottages. It makes an ideal base for holidaymakers of all ages as this part of the North Cornish coast, an Area of Outstanding Natural Beauty owned by the National Trust, offers unrivalled swimming, surfing and walking.

The building has superb sea views and is a short walk from Crackington Haven beach, across the headland and down the coast path to the beach. Just behind the beach are a pub and two cafes. One of the cafes, The Cabin, barbecues meat from its own farm in the evenings. In the other direction, the path leads to secluded beaches offering perfect solitude.

All the cottages are equipped to a high standard, with slate flagged or varnished wooden floors strewn with rugs, central heating, open fireplace or cast-iron stove for burning coal or logs, TV, electric stove, dishwasher, microwave, picnic tables, patios and individual gardens.

The School House (**sleeping 6/7**) has a large sitting room, kitchen/diner, double (with sea view) and twin bedrooms on the first floor and a twin with extra futon on the second floor (also sea view).

Lanes (**sleeping 4**) is at the front of the building, south facing, so the sun streams into its kitchen/diner and large sitting room all day long. There is a bathroom downstairs with one double bedroom and one twin upstairs.

Bloomers and *Francis* (both **sleeping 5**) enjoy superb sea views from all rooms, with accommodation on three floors. They have a large living/dining room each with picture windows and door on to a terrace, a spacious double bedroom and bathroom on the first floor and twin and single rooms on the second floor.

Cost about £275 to £770, including linen. Laundry room with payphone. Dogs welcome except in The School House. Details from Martin Smith, 1 Lower Kelly, Calstock, Cornwall PL18 9RX. Telephone 01840 230771.

www.stgennys.co.uk

email: oldschool@stgennys.co.uk

Even for coastal Cornwall, these cottages are superbly located.

Happily, the accommodation more than matches the geographical situation.

Crackington Haven
Mineshop Cottages

A holiday here brings you to within a short walk of some of the most dramatic coastal scenery in Cornwall. And as you go from one tiny, hidden lane into another (shortly after you turn west off the A39 Camelford-Bude road and come, finally, to leafy Mineshop) you feel a million miles from the workaday world.

On our last summer revisit, Mineshop's wandering ducks were being fed by guests sitting contentedly on the verandah of *The Old Shippon* in the cool of the evening. They (the guests, not the ducks, although the latter may have tried to accompany them!) planned to walk down the green and tranquil footpath to the beach at Crackington Haven (where there is an excellent pub and coffee shop). In one of the lodges, in the same green and generally sunny location, a couple were brewing up and simply enjoying the view of the garden.

Mineshop has a strong following among people, including readers of this guide, who like getting 'away from it all' without feeling isolated: the owners of the Mineshop cottages live in the centre of what is effectively a private hamlet. More than half of each year's visitors have been here before, and one family has been 30 times!

Effectively under the same ownership, but elsewhere in this dramatically striking corner of North Cornwall, is a quite excellent cottage, beautifully located high on a headland, and very private. This, *Cancleave*, has dramatic views of the famous bay. There are comfortable sofas and lots of pine. Outside, there is a big lawn adjacent to the coastal footpath. **Sleeps 8** in four bedrooms.

Cost: approximately £150 to £768 per week, according, as usual, to size and season. Short breaks from £100. Bedlinen is supplied in all the cottages. (Cots provided.) TVs, laundry room. Obedient dogs are allowed.

For further details please contact Mr and Mrs Tippett, Ref: GH, Mineshop, Crackington Haven, Bude, Cornwall EX23 0NR. Telephone 01840 230338.

www.mineshop.co.uk
email: info@mineshop.co.uk

The exceptional Crackington Haven beach, notable even for North Cornwall, is just a short walk from the cottages...

...one of which is the spacious and private Old Shippon – where on one visit we met guests feeding the ducks.

174

Blisland
Hockadays Cottages

For people who want to slow their pace of life, yet still be within fifteen minutes' drive of the spectacular coast, about 25 minutes from the Eden Project and handy for the Camel Trail to Padstow, these two charming cottages could be 'just the job'. In deeply rural North Cornwall,

Such a lot of care and attention goes into these 'two-plus-baby' cottages...

approached delightfully via leafy lanes, *Demelza* and *Rowella* are looked after by caring and conscientious owners. Each is within a converted 17th century barn that feels very private, and each is a wonderful hideaway **for 2** plus a baby. Among the details are white painted walls setting off oak beams, wall lamps, some original features such as wooden lintels, small paned windows, and cottage doors. Each has a living room, a separate well equipped kitchen, double bedroom and bathroom. One is an 'upside down' house, with the bedroom downstairs. There is a big garden, parking and excellent views. The nearby Blisland Inn is a 'Campaign for Real Ale' award winner. TV. Linen is included. Regrettably, they are not suitable for pets. Cost: about £140 to £310. Details from Margaret Pestell, 'Hockadays', Tregenna, near Blisland, Cornwall PL30 4QJ. Telephone/fax 01208 850146.

www.hockadays.co.uk   email: tregennacottages@aol.com

St Issey, near Padstow
Trevorrick Farm Cottages

map 6/405

We love the caring atmosphere owners Melanie and Mike Benwell have created here. There are ducks to feed, a well equipped outdoor play area, a games room and a heated pool: all appeal greatly to families and couples. The six barn conversions, refurbished in recent years, are in an Area of Outstanding Natural Beauty, close to beaches and the Eden Project, and

Easy access to some of North Cornwall's many sandy beaches is a bonus here...

within walking distance of Padstow. *Lily Pad Cottage* (with four-poster), and the popular *Old Round House* (with garden) are cosy hideaways **sleeping 2**. Single-storeyed *Serendipity* (**sleeps 2 to 4**) is suitable for people with limited mobility. *Owl's Roost* and *Curlew Cottage* are two storeyed; *Badger's Way* is the largest of all and has a garden. These **sleep 4**. TV plus video and DVD. Log burners/open fires. **Four Stars**. Cost: £225 to £950. Out of season short breaks. Dogs welcome in some cottages, linen included; baby-sitting and B & B available.

Details from Melanie and Mike Benwell, Trevorrick Farm Cottages, St Issey, Wadebridge, Cornwall PL27 7QH. Telephone 01841 540574.

www.trevorrick.co.uk   email: info@trevorrick.co.uk

The West Country
Classic Cottages*

Featured as they have been in this guide *without a break for 25 years*, readers may have noticed that we have a special fondness for 'Classic'. But there's more to it than that, for this is an absolutely outstanding family-run organisation. Based in Helston, Classic accepts fewer than half the properties that are offered, and even then invariably insist on various improvements being made. So it's not surprising that the organisation is known for its uncompromisingly high standards. Altogether, the agency has nearly 600 properties to choose from, so everyone can be sure of finding somewhere to suit their needs.

Most properties are in Cornwall but there's a good selection in Devon and a handful in both Dorset and Somerset. Each one is illustrated with at

Thatched and 'beamy', The Hermitage is one of several cottages in Crantock, 'across the estuary' from Newquay.

Forge Cottage is another: most attractive from the outside, its interior is light and bright, and there's a multi-fuel stove.

least two colour photos in Classic's detailed and attractive 320-plus page brochure.

'Classic Cottages is ferociously proud of the West Country,' it says. 'We scour every cliff, cove and cranny for just the right properties with just the right owners. The climate helps, as do the views.'

Guests are always welcomed with fresh flowers and a tea tray. Then, once they have settled in, a comprehensive 'Minimum Inventory' ensures that they have everything on the premises that they could possibly need 'to bake a cake or cook a roast'.

During our most recent visit (we'll visit another cross-section of properties in the summer of 2007) we met several families delighted with their accommodation. Some were staying in the quiet village of Crantock, where Classic has nine properties, just across the estuary from Newquay. It's a popular place for people who want the thrill of Atlantic surf on a sandy beach but find Newquay itself rather too 'lively' for their liking. It has the advantage of a post office/store, antique and crafts shops, and a good pub. The properties include *Forge Cottage*, a Grade II stone building (**sleeping 4**), a short walk from the beach, *The Hermitage*, a thatched white cottage (**sleeping 4**), and *Rosemaddon Cottage* (**sleeping 6**), whose large sitting-room is bordered on two sides by a minstrels' gallery.

On the other side of Newquay, *Anneth Lowen* (**sleeping 4**) is a beautifully appointed little detached house in the hamlet of Bosoughan. It has its own enclosed terraced garden, a cosy kitchen/breakfast-room with a Rayburn and microwave, and a spacious sitting/dining-room with gorgeous fabrics and a wood-burner.

In a narrow street leading down to Boscastle harbour we saw *Lowen Cottage*, a snug end of terrace cottage (**sleeping 3**). It has Cornish slate

Trewane Cottage has great charm, with a very fine and spacious drawing room.

And Trewane Mill is both spacious and cosy. A bonus is its enclosed garden.

floors, a multi-burner stove, and a small Shaker-style kitchen overlooking the garden. There are two upstairs bedrooms, one with an attractive brass bed. This is an idyllic retreat, a few minutes up the road from the village centre, but is not suitable for children from one to twelve, nor for pets.

Seventeenth-century *Trewane Cottage* (**sleeping 6**) near Padstow, close to the wide sandy beaches of Rock and Polzeath, with spectacular walking and cycling all around, is packed full of comfort and character. Also available is *Trewane Mill* (**sleeping 6**). This former flour mill is notable for its large country kitchen with an Aga and for its own enclosed garden.

Among Classic's locations outside Cornwall, one of the most distinctive is the village of Corfe Castle in Dorset. At the entrance to the village, *Brook Cottage* is a picture-book, semi-detached Grade II building, **sleeping 6**. Its sitting/dining-room is especially appealing, with heated Purbeck stone floors, a coal-effect gas stove, exposed beams and a substantial pine

Visitors to famous Corfe Castle tend to gaze admiringly at Brook Cottage.

Anneth Lowen is a beautifully appointed detached house sleeping just four people.

dining table. Delightfully, a stretch of the famous Swanage Steam Railway passes the cottage's enclosed garden.

For further information and a copy of their impressive brochure, contact Classic Cottages, Leslie House, Lady Street, Helston, Cornwall TR13 8NA. Telephone 01326 555 555. Fax 555 544.

www.classic.co.uk   email: enquiries@classic.co.uk

Cornwall – countywide
Cornish Traditional Cottages*

Who'd have thought it? The business that began after the original Cornish Traditional Cottages directors bought and renovated a derelict cottage in Padstow for family use and then found that other people wanted them to let their properties developed into one of the most highly regarded in Britain: it's the longest-established cottage letting agency in Cornwall.

Since its beginnings the agency has prided itself on its personal service. You can speak to 'a real person' (not a machine) between 9 am and 9 pm seven days a week. Then there is the 'smiles' system of rating properties – generated entirely by customers from the grading the company asks them to give a cottage's fittings, furnishings and equipment.

We certainly smiled last autumn when we came across two cosy charmers in a cobbled street close to the National Trust harbour of Boscastle. Here

Carveth is yet another of the agency's properties that enjoys a superb location.

Bridge Cottage, sleeping 6, is in the highly sought-after village of Boscastle.

the agency offers two character cottages, each sporting three smiles. *Bridge Cottage* (**sleeps 6**), though completely renovated, retains its period charm, with a view overlooking the river leading to the harbour mouth from the king size double bedroom, one of three upstairs.

Likewise, *Millstream Cottage* offers a double fronted cottage whose front door opens on to a small sitting room with beamed ceilings, windows to the lane and looking to the headland at the harbour mouth. **Sleeps 4**.

Superbly well located, at the head of a tidal creek on the River Fowey (from the comfort of your cottage you can watch the ebb and flow of the tide, probably putting the cottage into the 'we hardly left the place for a week' category so beloved of cottage guide readers) *Pont Quay Cottage* **sleeps 4/6** – including a double-bunk room suitable for children.

It's just a mile by car and car/pedestrian ferry to Fowey or – even more appealingly – half a mile by boat on the Pont Pill creek. (Guests can make arrangements to bring their own boats.)

Enjoying remarkable views, *Titania* is a spacious detached bungalow, **sleeping 6**, in two twins and a double, in a quiet residential cul-de-sac just a mile from St Ives and about a fifteen minute walk to the beach. At the rear, a gently sloping path leads up to a raised terrace with patio furniture and a beautiful garden with a large lawn, apple tree and flower borders.

On the approach road to Mousehole (remember to pronounce it 'Mousel'), *Carveth*, **sleeping 4**, is the upper part of a detached house with good sea views from a double and twin bedroom and, even more notably, with views of the splendid St Michael's Mount – from a bright and sunny sitting room with five big windows. Opposite the cottage there's a footpath to a stony beach and a rockpool and – a first for us – a children's seawater bathing pool, exposed at high tide.

Garden enthusiasts will love the cottages at Tregrehan, which has a famous collection of camellias, rhododendrons and conifers. The walls of the estate's old grain mill enclose a secret garden (guaranteed in our experience to appeal to visiting children) at the entrance to *The Coach House*, which has a bunk room and a king size bedroom, both with an additional single bed. *Sprys Cottage* is tucked away from the main courtyard and **sleeps 2** in a double room. *Gamekeepers Cottage* is the end cottage in the old carriage house and **sleeps 4** in a king size double and a twin room. There is a spacious walled garden. The cottages here are graded 'two-smiles'. The Eden Project and Carlyon Bay's golf course are less than ten minutes' drive away.

Deeply rural Fentondale sleeps 4, and dates in part from the 17th century...

Pentire Cottage, on Pentire Farm, has an open fire and memorable views...

At the end of a rough track – but enjoying spectacular views over the Camel Estuary – is Pentire Farm, with one-smile properties. These include the *Farm Wing* (**sleeps 6 to 8**), with four bedrooms, one with substantial bunk beds, and *Pentire Cottage* (**sleeps 4 to 6**) with a working open fire. Beamed farm-style kitchen. One bunk room downstairs, a double and a room with two pine singles upstairs.

More deeply rural in location, lying opposite farm buildings, is *Fentondale Cottage*, a three-smile renovated and extended detached cottage of 17th century origin. More beams, slate floors and the occasional changes of levels. **Sleeping 4,** it stands alone in the farming hamlet of Fentondale, about five minutes' drive from St Breward, which has a post office/stores, a church and a pub with a small restaurant.

Pets are welcome in about a third of the agency's properties.

For further details and an excellent brochure, with a clear and attractive illustration of each property, contact Cornish Traditional Cottages, Blisland, Bodmin, Cornwall PL30 4HS. Telephone 01208 821666, fax 821766.

www.corncott.com
email: info@corncott.com

Cornwall and beyond
Farm and Cottage Holidays*

We first became aware of this long-established family run agency when a reader praised *Old Holcombe Water Farm*, at Clatworthy, five miles inland from Watchet, in North Somerset. It has three delightfully converted barns (**sleeping 2 to 4**) across lawns, and an orchard across from the 17th century farmhouse. Children delight in helping with collecting eggs and milking, as well as enjoying the farm's clotted cream and

Near Boscastle, in North Cornwall, this lovely house (not featured) sleeps 8.

occasionally ice cream! A regular reader has her eye on *Destiny Cottage*, near Port Isaac, in North Cornwall. On a working farm, **sleeping up to 5**, it is of a high standard and offers excellent walking. But these are just samples of over 750 properties in Cornwall, Devon, Somerset and Dorset, **sleeping from 2 to 22**. Details/brochures from Farm and Cottage Holidays, Victoria House, 12 Fore Street, Northam, Bideford, Devon EX39 1AW. Telephone 01237 479698 for brochures or 479146 for bookings.

www.holidaycottages.co.uk
(up to date availability and secure on-line booking)
email: enquiries@holidaycottages.co.uk

Scorrier, near Truro
The Butler's Cottage   map 6/362

This is very much our readers' kind of place – stylish, sensibly priced, quiet and very comfortable. They also approve of the thoroughbred horses that graze in the park that fronts the elegant main house. Butler's is a comfortable, spacious, recently renovated wing of 'the big house'. We admired the terraced garden at first floor level, the super and well equipped flagstoned kitchen, the antiques, the excellent paintings and prints, the first floor sitting room with beautifully chosen sunflower yellow sofa and armchairs, the long bath in the excellent bathroom. All is stylish and elegant, but not

This is one of our personal favourites in Cornwall – quiet, comfortable, stylish.

uncomfortably so: you can put your feet up here and unwind. All in all, this is a gem: the only thing lacking is the butler to wait on you. With an open fire in the sitting room, central heating, books and board games, we thought this would make a good base in the autumn, winter or spring.

Sleeps 4. TV/video; payphone. Pets possible by arrangement. Linen/ towels included. Breakfast pack. Cost: about £250 to £360. Weekend breaks. Details from Richard and Caroline Williams, Scorrier House, Scorrier, Redruth, Cornwall TR16 5AU. Telephone 01209 820264. Fax 820677. **email: rwill10442@aol.com**

Tintagel
Tregeath

This traditional farmworker's cottage has proved popular with readers ever since we first published in 1983. We revisited last year, and confirmed that in its way it's a real charmer. Quietly situated on a little-used country road, it is 'unpretentious', with a degree of character. There's a small rear patio, ideal for lazing in the summer sun, listening

Not far from Tintagel, this does not claim to be a show-house, but we like it, and have always had good reader reports.

to very little except the sound of sheep from adjoining farmland. About a mile from Tintagel, and one and a half from the surfing beach at Trebarwith Strand, this is no showhouse, more a sensible family home with a very convenient galley-kitchen, a combined sitting/dining room and stairs up to two bedrooms (note that one has a 4'6" wide bed; the other a 4' wide bed). There's a good-sized single room that's adjacent to the sitting room, a washing machine and separate tumble dryer, and a pleasant enclosed and safe garden. **Sleeps up to 5** plus cot. **'Visit Britain' Three Stars.**

Cost: £110 to £410. TV/video in each bedroom. Payphone. Single dogs welcome. Further details from Mrs E M Broad, 'Davina', Trevillett, Tintagel, Cornwall PL34 0HL. Telephone/fax 01840 770217.

Stratton/Pyworthy, near Bude
Lovers Retreat/Hopworthy Farm   map 6/399/400

As far as we're concerned, any comfortable, quiet, warm and well run property near Bude is immediately 'in the frame': it's one of our favourite places in the whole of the West Country. In Stratton, a mile and a half from the resort, three-storeyed 200-year old *Lovers Retreat* has a five foot wide 'sleigh' bed and a woodburning stove. **Sleeps 3, Four Stars**, Ref 17925. In a more rural situation, you can even bring your own

Lovers Retreat, sleeping three, is handy for Bude, and in a historic village...

horses to Hopworthy Farm, a short drive from Bude and in striking distance of Dartmoor. Graded with an admirable **Five Stars** from 'Visit Britain' it offers stabling, livery and the use of an indoor school. Impressively, and in line with much current demand, *Hopworthy Farmhouse* **sleeps up to 18** – Ref 18016.

Details from Blakes Country Cottages, Spring Mill, Earby, Barnoldswick BB94 0AA. Brochures and bookings: 0870 197 6896.

Live search and book: www.blakes-cottages.co.uk

181

Croyde and beyond
Marsdens Cottage Holidays*

Leafing through the new Marsdens brochure is a joy in itself, and a reflection of the company's reputation both for absolute integrity and properties of a very high standard. We have featured them here for 24 years, during which time we have received *nothing other than the most wholehearted praise*.

The staff all have an intimate knowledge of North Devon; all properties are inspected annually and have **'Visit Britain'** star gradings. Around half the 300 or so properties are in and around Croyde, a small charming village of much thatch, with dunes between it and Croyde Bay's wide sandy beach. The rest are scattered across the area from the small sandy resort of Instow around the coastline to Exmoor.

Rose Cottage is a delight. Its large enclosed garden has countryside views.

The Stables has, in turn, views out to sea and along famous Woolacombe Sands.

Rose Cottage, in Muddiford, a small village just outside Barnstaple, is as pretty as its name implies. **Sleeping 6 'plus cot'** in a double, a twin and two singles, it is a semi detached cottage with a large, enclosed garden overlooking rolling countryside. The inglenook, original bread oven and woodburning stove in the living/dining room add warmth and character.

Refurbished for 2007, *The Stables* is an outstanding detached house enjoying views out to sea and along Woolacombe Sands. Stylish and designed to top specifications, this does indeed offer 'something a little bit special'. Light, bright and modern, with tones and textures reflecting the natural coastline, it **sleeps 8** in two doubles and two twins. There is a large, paved terrace from which to enjoy those views and two living rooms (satellite TV DVD, further TV and Play Station 2).

Newly available are two properties on the outskirts of Berrynarbor in the lovely Sterridge Valley. *Derrivale*, a large, detached cottage, provides plenty of space **for 6**, both inside and out. Delightfully, it backs on to its own two-acre private natural woodlands. There is a small patio, a level lawned area and a pretty stream fronted cottage garden to the front. Inside, modern comforts blend well with old fashioned charm and character: flagstone floors, inglenook fireplace, range cooker, bedrooms with vaulted ceilings and beams, alongside TV, DVD, Play Station 2, stereo, 'American style' fridge freezer, dishwasher, microwave, washing machine, tumbler, super-king (zip link) beds in one bedroom, a five foot iron bed and ensuite shower room in the master bedroom.

Jan's Barn – a converted hayloft – **sleeps 2 'plus cot'** in a double room overlooking the garden. Shower room (no bath). The upstairs living room has TV, DVD, stereo and woodburning style stove, with a kitchen area to one end. Quietly situated within the owners' grounds, there is a private sitting out terrace and south facing garden overlooking the valley.

Derrivale has its own two-acre private natural wood, and an inglenook fireplace.

Jan's Barn is a cosy, quietly situated converted hayloft sleeping just two.

In a secluded, tranquil location, *Mully Brook Mill*, at Umberleigh, is indeed a restored mill with retained original mill workings behind glass panels that can be illuminated and seen from the large dining table seating up to ten people – invite friends to this refreshingly unusual cottage steeped in history. The first floor living area contains original features and a woodburning stove. A door leads on to a decked patio which looks over the leat (spot the otters!) and is within earshot of the waterfall. Three bedrooms have original beams and some sloping ceilings: a double with ensuite shower, a twin (can make a six-foot double) and a further double.

At the end of a long woodland track, *Modbury Cottage* is the typical picturesque thatched 'chocolate box cottage'. With a wealth of character features, it is up to the moment with furnishings and a brand new kitchen. At Buckland Filleigh, deep in rural Devon, it has its own secluded gardens. **Sleeps 4** in a double and a twin. It has water supply from its own well.

Mully Brook Mill is a sympathetic conversion of - yes! - the original mill.

Modbury Cottage is a thatched 'chocolate-box' delight, with its own well.

For further details of these and the many others in an outstanding brochure, contact Marsdens, 2 The Square, Braunton, Devon EX33 2JB.

Telephone 01271 813777, fax 813664.

Full on-line availability and booking on the website:

www.marsdens.co.uk   email: holidays@marsdens.co.uk

Langtree, near Great Torrington
Stowford Lodge Holiday Cottages

Well away from any traffic, accessed via narrow, high banked lanes typical of this part of Devon (we had to check our map carefully when we first visited!) these four properties have proved very popular with readers. They **sleep 6, 4, 4** and **4**, and have been converted from farm buildings with style and skill. *Warren* and *Halcyon* are suitable for wheelchairs. A special feature is the indoor heated swimming pool: lovely warm water, curtained windows; wall pic-

Deep in rural Devon: new owners ready to make 'cottage guide' guests welcome.

tures/hangings, underwater lighting. The cottages stand in six acres, surrounded by beautiful, rolling Devon countryside: a peaceful, quiet, relaxing location. There is a well equipped children's play area, with plenty of space for them to burn off excess energy! Dogs are welcome (small charge). Linen provided. **'Visit Britain' Three Stars**. Cost: £220 to £570. Details and brochure from Rich and Diana Jones, Stowford Lodge, Langtree, Torrington, North Devon EX38 8NU. Telephone 01805 601540, fax 601487.

www.stowfordlodge.co.uk   email: enq@stowfordlodge.co.uk

A cardinal sin in any cottage is to arrive too early to claim it, lest you find her ladyship on her hands and knees in the kitchen. Yes, it **has** happened to 'cottage guide' readers...

Countisbury
Kipscombe Farm

Most usefully **sleeping 8** (recommended by two readers during 2006), *Kipscombe Farm* (Ref HTU) is a spacious self contained wing of a fine 17th century farmhouse, with its own secluded garden. There's a woodburning stove in an inglenook in a big, beamed sitting room and – for that touch of rural farmhouse authenticity – an Aga in the spacious modernised kitchen. The location is 'a delight'. Guests (the house **sleeps**

It's a spacious self contained main wing of a beautifully situated farmhouse.

8) have access to 640 acres of National Trust farmland, and there are coastal footpaths direct from the property, with some spectacular views: on a clear day you can see across the Bristol Channel to Wales. The 'twin' coastal villages of Lynton and Lynmouth, possibly our own favourite resorts in the whole of Devon, are under three miles away, and we'd always recommend a boat trip from Ilfracombe to Lundy Island.

Details from English Country Cottages, Stoney Bank Road, Earby, Barnoldswick BB94 0AA. Bookings and brochures: 0870 197 6890.

www.english-country-cottages.co.uk

Hollocombe, near Chulmleigh map 7/445
Horry Mill Cottage

This cottage quickly caught the attention and imagination of readers of this guide who appreciate a remote rural scene as notable today as it is in a faded photo on the wall of the cob-style cottage. **Sleeping 6** in two double rooms and a twin, there is also a child's room, with a cot or a 2ft 6ins bed. The fully equipped bathroom has a free-standing electric shower. We admired the

Absolute peace and quiet: a delight...

huge inglenook fireplace and bread oven in the sitting room, also the small south facing sun parlour with grapevine. There is a well equipped kitchen and dining room seating six and high chair. An open fire, with logs provided free, complements oil fired central heating. The Hodgsons will collect local dishes ordered in Crediton, or elsewhere. Pophams restaurant, with a national reputation, is close by. Linen and towels provided. TV, video and stereo/CD player. One dog by arrangement. Non smokers preferred. Cost: from £260 to £525. Details from Sonia and Simon Hodgson, Horry Mill, Hollocombe, Chulmleigh, Devon EX18 7QH. Telephone 01769 520266.

www.horrymill.com   email: sonia@horrymill.com

Combe Martin, near Ilfracombe
Wheel Farm Country Cottages

Effectively a little hamlet, very well placed for traditional family seaside holidays though comfortably just-inland, this has long been one of the most popular groups of cottages we feature. During one recent revisit we met readers (a young couple with a small baby) staying in one of the cottages and asked what they liked most about Wheel Farm. They said: 'It's private, but we don't feel cut off. It's in the country but near the sea, and we love the gardens.'

Nestling in a sheltered valley close to the picturesque village of Combe

Stable and Linhay: everything is 'just so', and the North Devon location is a delight.

Every cottage has a beautifully planned and reliably comfortable interior.

Martin, near beautiful, wide, sandy beaches such as Woolacombe's (fifteen minutes' drive) and Croyde (twenty minutes), and overlooking Exmoor National Park, Wheel Farm provides an ideal holiday setting for all the family. The eleven acres of grounds have award-winning gardens, patios, millponds (fenced), grassland and wooded copse walks.

Converted from an old water mill (the wheel still remains) and barns, the cottages have exposed stone walls and beams, rustic charm, and yet provide all modern amenities. All have full gas central heating, microwaves, TVs, videos and dishwashers (except those just for 2).

Four of the cottages have four-poster beds; six have wood-burning stoves. They are furnished to a high standard with Victorian farmhouse antique and pine furniture, deep upholstered suites, good quality fitted carpets and drapes. They range from cosy units designed **for 2** to bigger ones that spaciously **accommodate 6**, plus cots. Facilities include an impressive heated indoor swimming pool, sauna, mini fitness room, LTA standard tennis court, children's playground – all free of charge.

Linen and mid week maid service are included, towels available for hire. Laundry room with token-operated washers and dryers. Groceries can be provided for arrival and hand baked pies, pastries and cakes are available. Arrangements can be made for baby sitting, tennis tuition, taxis, riding, golf, cycling. **'Visit Britain' Four Stars**. 'Regret no pets.' TVs. Cost: about £250 to £1150; short breaks low season only. **Closed end of October 2007 to end of March 2008**. Brochure from Mr and Mrs J G Robertson, Wheel Farm Country Cottages, Berry Down 16, Combe Martin, North Devon EX34 0NT. Telephone 01271 882100. Fax 883120.

www.wheelfarmcottages.co.uk email: holidays@wheelfarmcottages.co.uk

Brendon, near Lynmouth
Rockford Lodge

This cottage is one of our all-time favourites, particularly for its location: it's a special pleasure to leave our car in the main part of the hamlet of Rockford (just a pub and a handful of cottages) and walk a few yards over a footbridge across the tumbling River East Lyn to see Rockford Lodge again and, sometimes, to meet the contented people staying in it.

One of the *The Good Holiday Cottage Guide* inspectors, who has compiled a 'top ten' of his favourite cottages, includes Rockford Lodge in it. He – like us – enjoys places that ramble a bit, and have something of a farmhousey character. Tucked away in a secret, wooded valley on the edge of mysterious Exmoor, Rockford has a big kitchen with a cosy Aga, fitted carpets, lots of books, paintings and a very big, carpeted upstairs bathroom. The river that rushes past the garden fence does not do so loudly enough to keep one awake! The footpaths in the beautiful woods outside the conservatory-like 'river room' beckon one for walks. Described over the years by readers as 'a genuine home from home' ... 'wonderfully well equipped' ... 'the setting is marvellous', the cottage is used quite frequently by the owners themselves. **Sleeps 6** plus cot.

Dogs are welcome but not cats. TV. Cost: about £400 to £660. Further details available from Mrs E M Adnitt, 82 The Row, Lane End, High Wycombe, Buckinghamshire HP14 3JU. Telephone 01494 882609.

email: ema.rockford@sagainternet.co.uk

Many years in this guide, Rockford Lodge has a most unusual situation ...

... whereby you park your car and then cross a river via a footbridge. Delightful!

Please note: we cannot vouch for every property on an agency's books, but only those we have seen. Most agents have at least a handful of modest properties that appeal to a specific market (for example, fishermen, walkers and stalkers), or sometimes properties at the extreme edge of the region they deal with that are not typical of what they offer. But in principle the agencies we feature are reliable and conscientious...

Ashwater, near Holsworthy
Braddon Cottages and Forest

Super new additions are the all-weather foot- and cycle paths.

We have long admired these six properties, all separate and detached, with lawns and gardens to boot. Close to the Devon/Cornwall border, and most appealingly at the end of a long drive, they are surrounded by hundreds of acres of meadow and woodland that is part of the owners' imaginative broadleaf planting scheme. All have woodburners and fine views over the well stocked three-acre fishing lake. Fishing is free, reserved for residents.

The Linhaye and *Lake House* are large, purpose-built houses **sleeping 12 plus 2**, each convertible into two self-contained, sound-proofed apartments. Microwave, dishwasher, washing machine, dryer, gas central heating, double glazing, barbecues. There's an all-weather summer house near the lake, an all-weather tennis court and a games room with a full size snooker table. TV/videos, payphones. Linen/towels provided. Well behaved dogs welcome. Open all year. **'Visit Britain' Three Stars**. Cost: £140 to £1250, bargain breaks from £80 2ppn. Details from George and Anne Ridge, Braddon, Ashwater, Beaworthy, Devon EX21 5EP. Telephone 01409 211350.

www.braddoncottages.co.uk email: holidays@braddoncottages.co.uk

Near Brendon/Near Bude   map 7/426

This striking house at Welcombe is exceptionally well situated in terms of things to see and do...

We like the way many North Devon properties offer the chance to explore much of the best of North Cornwall, as well as certain parts of Somerset and Exmoor. In the appealingly named village of Welcombe, a mile from Welcombe Bay and well placed for some of the most spectacular places along the North Devon and the North Cornwall coast, eye-catching *Chapel Cottage* (Ref W40147, **sleeping 7/8**) has the makings of a memorable family holiday. It has a woodburning stove. And only a short walk from Bideford, a substantial detached house on a working farm at the end of a long private drive provides a 'deeply rural' experience without isolation. It **sleeps 9** in five bedrooms, has two woodburning stoves, and welcomes one dog. The famous golden sands at Westward Ho! are just a short drive away. Ref W41242.

Welcome Holidays, Spring Mill, Earby, Barnoldswick, BB94 0AA. Brochures and bookings: 0870 197 6957.

www.welcomecottages.co.uk

Widecombe-in-the-Moor
Wooder Manor

Good self-catering on Dartmoor is rare, but our readers love this neat grouping of properties converted from an old coach-house and stables. And with the Bell family's home close by (a working farm amid 170 acres of woodland, moor and granite tors), guests are guaranteed a personal welcome. Widecombe-in-the-Moor is a mere half mile away. (See

Dartmoor is magical, and these properties, open all year, are at its heart.

Colour section B, Page 2 for the view from Wooder Manor.) *Wooder House* itself **sleeps 12** in five bedrooms; its ambiance comfortable and relaxing. Two cottages **sleep 6**, the others **sleep 4.** Ideal for walking, fishing, canoeing, cycling or riding. Central heating and a laundry room; bed linen by arrangement; microwaves, TV, metered electricity. Cots and highchairs free; log fires in *Honeybags* and Wooder House. **'Visit Britain' Three/Four Stars**. Dogs by arrangement. Cost: from £200 to £500, £280 to £540 or £700 to £1200, **sleeping 4, 6 or 12** respectively. Ample parking. Details from Angela Bell, Wooder Manor, Widecombe-in-the-Moor, Newton Abbot, Devon TQ13 7TR. Telephone/fax 01364 621391.

www.woodermanor.com

Higher Clovelly/Bradworthy
Lundy View/Tamar Lodges   map 7/438/432

We love cottages with good views, and here are two that as well as having lots of other good things going for them, have a notable outlook both over countryside and coast. With memorable views of Bideford Bay and Lundy Island, *Lundy View* (Ref 17431) is one of a number of properties within a converted Grade II listed barn. Unusually, the main bedroom has its own spiral staircase leading to a 'viewing room'. **Sleeps 6**. At Bradworthy, on the Cornish

Very well situated for exploring both North Devon and North Cornwall, located half a mile from a village.

border, two unusual (in cottage terms) Scandinavian-style lodges – Tamar Lodges – have comfortable open plan sitting rooms, pine panelling and exposed beams. They have the further advantage of open plan gardens. Both *Willow* and *Pine* (Refs 50281/50280) **sleep 4** in a double and a twin.

Details from Country Holidays, Spring Mill, Earby, Lancashire BB94 0AA. Brochures and bookings: 0870 197 6895.

To 'look and book': www. country-holidays.co.uk

Devon: coast and country
Toad Hall Cottages*

Featured by us without a break for seventeen years, people seem to like Toad Hall so much because of its romantic retreats, seaside villas and picture-postcard hideaways, all in sought-after locations throughout Devon, Cornwall, Exmoor and now Dorset.

A visit to Thurlestone, South Devon last September confirmed this impression. Dotted along the main village street are archetypal thatched or character cottages with flower-strewn gardens. Among them, close to the village pub and shop, is charming 17th century *Bay Tree Cottage*, which **sleeps 6**. The delightful refurbished *Jasmine Cottage*, **sleeping 8**, provides a charming place to return to after a busy day seeing the delights of the South Hams. Add to these the nearby *Whitegarth*, **sleeping 6**, a sumptuous, spacious detached bungalow with a jacuzzi bath and steam room and the elegant top of the range *Stable Cottage*, **sleeping 6/8**, and you have the measure of the place. The beach is about 15 minutes' walk from all these.

There's also *Higher Furlong*, a spacious detached family house, **sleeping 10**, on the exclusive Yarmer Estate with sweeping views of the bay. Along with *Warren House*, **sleeping 9**, with superb gardens. The splendidly situated *Seamark Cottages*, just 500 yards from Thurlestone beach, have far reaching sea views and an indoor pool. Added to these is *Thorpe Arnold*, **sleeping 8 to 16**, adjacent to the 9th green on the Thurlestone Golf Course.

Idehill Cottages, near Honiton. comprises just three cottages with their own fabulous private 18 hole, 5,377 yard golf course, exclusively for the use of guests. The cottages **sleep between 2 and 6**. *The Old Shippon* at Buckland Brewer, transformed into a quaint and characterful cottage, lies amid the most peaceful and secluded countryside. It **sleeps 4**.

Previously we've praised *Cliff Cottage* at Dittisham, in The Dart Valley, **sleeping 6**. Also *Alice Cottage*, at Start Bay, South Devon. Once owned by Christopher Robin, son of AA Milne, the author of Winnie The Pooh, it is peaceful, private and comfortable. **Sleeps 6** 'plus cot'.

Every cottage on the agency's books is known to at least one member of the Toad Hall staff. About half the properties accept dogs and many have open fires. Details and a comprehensive brochure are available from Toad Hall Cottages, Elliott House, Church Street, Kingsbridge, South Devon TQ7 1BY. Telephone 01548 853089. Fax 853086.

www.toadhallcottages.com email: thc@toadhallcottages.com

There are several gems in pretty Thurlestone. This is Bay Tree Cottage...

...and this is stylish Stable Cottage, handily sleeping up to eight people.

Salcombe, near Kingsbridge
Salcombe Holiday Homes

Closely associated with sailing, fishing and fabulous beaches, this delightful South Hams resort also enjoys a local climate that's especially pleasant even by West Country standards. Owners Tim and Ginny Windibank delight in promoting local properties that match their own expectations: this means exacting standards, with members of staff visiting each property prior to every arrival. (There are 150-plus properties, including many cosy cottages and flats **for 2/4 people** and fifteen properties **sleeping from 10 to 18**).

New to the agency's books, and one of the landmarks of Salcombe, is *The Custom House*. Fronting on to Custom House Quay, this substantial three storey house is next to the lifeboat station and has staggering views over the main anchorage. **Sleeping 10**, the property is a memorable holiday spot for two families who want to be right at the centre of things.

Snapes Loft, **sleeping 7**, is higher up the town but retains the nautical feel in a huge upstairs room with polished wood floors and a vaulted ceiling with ships' mast supports. One end is all glass, allowing panoramic views over the town, and there are views almost as good from the garden.

The Custom House gets our vote. What a beauty, and it sleeps ten people!

We'd happily spend a week just gazing out from the balcony of Wellingtons.

Tucked away up a narrow lane, close to the town's main car and boat parks, is *Gwen's Cottage*. This is an ideal peaceful hideaway for a family (**up to 6 people**) with a dog as, although the property is close to town, the lane leads up to a track skirting the banks of one of the pretty creeks with 360° views over the estuary.

With views as our theme we must mention *Wellingtons*, a beautiful two bedroomed apartment with leafy surroundings situated above the town and looking out to the mouth of the harbour and the sandy beaches at East Portlemouth on the other side of the estuary. The layout and furnishings are of the highest standard. For a colour brochure, contact Salcombe Holiday Homes, Orchard Court, Island Street, Salcombe, Devon TQ8 8QE. Telephone: 01548 843485.

www.salcombe.com email: shh@salcombe.com

See also the sister agency: Dartmouth Holiday Homes, 1a, Lower Street, Dartmouth, Devon TQ6 9AJ. Telephone 01803 833082.

www.dartmouthuk.com email:dhh@dartmouthuk.com

Membury, near Axminster
Cider Room Cottage

We regret the gradual passing of this sort of cottage. 'Traditional', with much of its original character intact, it lies deep in the rolling Devon/ Somerset border country, next to the family-in-residence but with plenty of privacy – we like it very much. The location is rural and peaceful, but not isolated, and the cottage is neat and attractive: it will suit people who prefer an individual cottage to being part of a complex. The views

Very reasonably priced indeed, but certainly worth its Four Stars grading, this cottage is cosy and traditional...

of green, hilly farmland are delightful, and there are ducks, dogs, cats and pet Vietnamese pot-bellied pig to delight small children. The cottage has a spacious, comfortable stone-flagged and carpeted sitting room, two pretty bedrooms, lots of beams, rustic stone walls (there is a shower-room, not bath). We spotted lots of books and fresh flowers.

TV. **'Visit Britain' Four Stars**. Dogs by arrangement. Cost: £175 to £300. Details from Pat and David Steele, Hasland Farm, Membury, Axminster, Devon EX13 7JF. Telephone 01404 881558. Fax 881834. **email: ciderroomcottage@rscontracting.co.uk**

Modbury, Ivybridge
Oldaport Farm Cottages

We like cottages that are 'miles from anywhere', especially if there's a quiet beach a mile and a half away. So do many others, as last year's visit to this property, tucked away in the South Hams, confirmed. One couple have been back ten years running. Cathy Evans runs the four cottages and the 70-acre farm (**map 7/435**) overlooking

Much appreciated by readers, and by us: we will be revisiting during 2007...

the beautiful Erme estuary. Much thought and care has gone into the conversions. Three cottages, **sleeping 2/4, 6** and **6**, were created from the old stone cowshed and dairy. The fourth, *Orchard* – single storeyed and **just for 2** – overlooks the paddock where miniature Shetland ponies graze beside chickens and ducks. Latch doors, pine furniture and comfortable furnishings convey the right mood, and there are games and books. The farm is famous for its championship Lleyn sheep. The South Coastal footpath is nearby, as is Dartmoor. **'Visit Britain' Four Stars**. Laundry room, payphone. TV. Bedlinen included. Cost: £210 to £610. Dogs welcome low/mid season. Short breaks, low season. Details from Miss C M Evans, Oldaport Farm Cottages, Modbury, Ivybridge, Devon PL21 0TG. Telephone 01548 830842. Fax 830998.

www.oldaport.com   email: cathy@oldaport.com

...ins Farm, Suffolk. Impressive rural views, a notable pool and sauna. And the cottages ...lves have been described by more than one reader as 'little showhouses'. Page 32.

...odge, Norfolk. In delightful gardens, with the bonus of an impressive leisure centre, ...re well recommended. It's an uncrowded, 'accessible' part of Norfolk. Pages 46/48.

...rm Cottages, Norfolk. A real tour de ...near the Broads. Page 49.

Clippesby Cottages, Norfolk. Happily, both rural and not far from the sea. Page 53.

...k Holiday Homes. Their many gems include (left) this remarkable property right by the ...at Hunstanton and (right) another seaside property at Heacham. Pages 50/51.

Farsyde Farm Cottages, North Yorkshire. These have so much going for them, such as horses ride and easy access to one of the most sought-after stretches of the Yorkshire coast. Page 69.

Fold Farm Cottages, North Yorkshire. It's the genuine article: a real 'village idyll'. Page 71.

Dalegarth/The Ghyll, North Yorkshire. Cc excellence deep in the Dales. Pages 72.

Peak Cottages, Derbyshire. A much-loved part of England, reliable cottages of character. Page 77.

Cressbrook Cottages, Derbyshire. No ne go to Switzerland: you'll find it here! Pa

Bee Cottage, Northumberland. 'Traditional' or modern, with Holy Island views. Page 91.

Blairquhan, Ayrshire. Properties of gre character, long-term favourites. Page 9

Colour section A, Page 2

...nding even in 'cottage guide' terms, Holiday Houses in Scotland...

...includes for example Auchinroath House (left) and Achinduich (above) Page 102.

...all, Lanarkshire. Superb, Five Star ..., a great touring location. Page 94.

Loch Cottage, Perthshire. Many years in this guide: a quiet, rural Scottish classic. Page 98.

...an Cottages, Inverness-shire. A classic ...nd location, good fishing. Page 104.

Torrisdale, Kintyre. Go down the beautiful peninsula: it's 'a world away'. Page 119.

...oe Cottages, Argyll. One of the most ...g of all cottage locations Page 108.

Parkers Retreat, Angus. A fabulous base from which to explore hidden beauties. Page 120.

Attadale, Wester Ross. Even in terms of the Highlands, this is a fabulous place...

... with (normally) unlimited access to th estate. Just imagine the invigorating wa

...the wildlife you'll see and a memorable escape from 'the real world'. Page 107.

Long Byres, Cumbria. Twenty-three yea with us: a 'serenely wild' spot. Page 12.

Meadowbank, Cumbria. This is definitely one of our Lake District 'top ten'. Page 128.

Monkhouse Hill, Cumbria. One of our s for 23 years: so much 'TLC'. Page 133

Aberdovey Hillside Village, Ceredigion. Fabulous views, properties ideal for families. Page 146.

Rosemoor, West Wales. 'Family-orienta near good beaches, deeply rural. Page

eirion, Gwynedd. A fantasy-world by n, cottages a delight. Page 151.

Clydey, West Wales. Readers have loved these cosy, welcoming cottages. Page 144.

arm, North Wales. Gorgeous: a urner and central heating. Page 148.

Trallwm Forest Cottages, Mid Wales. Quiet, not pricey, 'deeply rural'. Page 155.

Beacons Holiday Cottages, Mid Wales. A most attractive region and a superb io of properties characterise one of the best cottage agencies in Britain. Page 153.

ghan, Cornwall. Surely a contender for p Ten in the UK'. Page 166.

Treworgey Coach House, Cornwall. Comfort, style, lots to do, a hundred acres. Page 157.

Trefanny Hill, Cornwall. Private, well spaced out, lots of individual character. The place is like a hamlet in its own right, and even has its own country inn, serving excellent food. Pages 158-159.

Bosinver, Cornwall. Both very rural and handy for the sea. Energetic, most welcoming owners have turned these properties into some of the best in Cornwall. Page 164.

Sea Meads, Cornwall. Strikingly close to the sea, lots of modern comfort. Page 163.

Gullrock, Cornwall. A little-known sand beach just a short stroll away. Page 17.

Mudgeon Vean, Cornwall Very much geared to families, very informal. Page 171.

Mineshop, Cornwall. Twenty-three year this guide, an amazing location. Page I

Colour section A, Page 6

...nys, Cornwall. Over 20 years in our guide. in one of the most memorable locations in ...all: comfortable, substantial properties, with some sea views. Page 173.

...: Cottages, Cornwall. In – yes! – 25 years we have never, once, had a whisper of a ...int about this extraordinary organisation. It's virtually a household name. Pages 176/177.

...h, Cornwall. Unpretentious, comfy, ...ked by readers. Page 181.

Rural Retreats (nationwide): so many real beauties. Main feature, Pages 242/243.

...ens Holidays, North Devon. An exceptional agency, in a quieter part of the West ...y, and known for its superb brochure. Pages 182/183. See also over page:

Mill Field is among our Devon favourites. The views are great, and the house is private but not remote. It's new to the admirable Marsdens' agency: see the previous page (bottom).

Wooder Manor, Devon. You can hardly get closer to the heart of secret, ancient Dartmoor than one of these fine properties. Your dog (by arrangement) will love it here. Page 189.

Compton Pool, Devon. Close to the sea but completely rural. In new ownership, these well con and most attractive cottages are predictably popular among families with small children. Page

Horry Mill, Devon. A much-liked 'traditional' cottage, a fine wooded location. Page 185.

Fursdon, Devon. Ever fancied life in ar so-English country house? Try this! Pag

The West Country
Helpful Holidays*

Because *The Good Holiday Cottage Guide* celebrated its first quarter-century at the same time as 'Helpful', we inevitably feel a certain bond. But it's a remarkable organisation by any standards, and happily still very much a family concern. It's no exaggeration to say that the agency is known throughout the travel and leisure industry for its uncompromisingly high standards.

The Bowaters famously believe in saying what properties are really like, warts and all, and have an exceptional variety, from boathouses and 'beach houses' to historic country houses and picture-book thatched cottages.

Their properties are spread all over the West Country, from Land's End to Somerset and Dorset – seaside and inland. And a glance at their unconventional brochure, detailing approximately 530 cottages, underlines their 'truth will out' philosophy.

The company was, for instance, closely involved in the design of *Great Cleave* (**sleeping 8**), formerly a threshing barn and one of a group of three located down a long lane, with wonderful Dartmoor views, close to Drewsteignton. The 'upside-down' look, with the upstairs living/dining room rising high to the apex, with fine beams and tresses, works a treat. *Old Orchard*, **sleeping 4**, got our stamp of approval for its freshness and rural charm, as did *Little Cleave,* fractionally smaller but also **sleeping 4**. All share eight acres of pastureland, a fenced pond with ducks and chickens (complimentary free range eggs usually available).

Half a mile from open moorland, and just three from the ancient small town of Chagford, is a beautiful Grade II listed 14th century longhouse, in 30 acres of farm and parkland on the edge of the Teign Valley. *Northill* is a superbly comfortable and sympathetically renovated property, with a fine collection of antique furniture, high quality fittings and soft furnishings in all six bedrooms, four bathrooms, drawing and dining room and modern kitchen – all with good views over the grounds and the moor. **Sleeping up to 10**, the house provides a superb base for a family gathering, walking holiday or just sheer relaxation throughout the year; with large open fires for winter and a perfect *al fresco* area for those balmy summer months.

Five miles from Cullompton, *Halsbeer Farm* incorporates four thatched cottages, three adapted for wheelchair user, that happily retain the distinc-

Northill is a Grade II listed 14th century Devon longhouse in 30 acres. Ref A66.

The charming Music Room is a stunning and harmonious hideaway. Ref C617.

201

tive flagstones and original timbers. *Cider* and *Swallow* both **sleep 6,** while *Haybarn*, which we looked over, has a sturdy Elizabethan style four poster and a galleried landing. **Sleeps 7**. The fourth property, *Apple*, is the farmer's fine thatched farmhouse. **Sleeps 3**. A huge barn, converted into a conservatory, can seat gatherings of up to 25; an indoor swimming pool is complemented by a children's play area.

One delightful journey of discovery led us to *Lower Elsford*, near Lustleigh. It is a classic rural Devonshire enclave, four skilful barn conversions adjacent to the owners' house in 35 acres of garden and farmland, from which at certain points it is possible to see the sea.

Among many good things, we admired deep sofas, woodburners, high ceilings, good quality rugs and table lamps, and many charming personal details. A well heated indoor swimming pool in a converted piggery (we loved the piggy murals!) even has an open fire: a first for us! There are lots of animals for children to make friends with. **Sleep 2 to 5**.

Beside the River Avon, on the South Devon coast, and on an excellent and varied stretch of coast (sandy beaches, coves, cliffs, golf courses, pretty thatched-cottage village centres) is the charming *Music Room*. This stunning retreat **sleeps 2** under its vaulted stucco ceiling, with four massive arched windows running the length of the room. The Music Room was once the home of concerts and recitals, but now has a new life as a superb holiday home for a couple wishing to explore the stunning coastline and countryside.

Helpful is increasingly strong on large houses for large parties. These include a brilliantly converted barn (with an impressive tally of ten bed-

Many Helpful properties are 'amazing'. This beauty is at East Portlemouth, in the 'South Hams'. Ref L213. Sleeps ten.

Close to the western edge of Dartmoor, at Lydford, this fine house sleeps up to six people in comfort. Ref A51.

rooms and ten bathrooms) which has superb views of the River Dart, and a former hotel superbly situated in St Agnes on Cornwall's north coast of sandy surfing beaches.

Extraordinary *Sandridge Barton*, **sleeping 12**, which 'Helpful' describe as 'sensational', is a fabulous Georgian mansion in a secluded location overlooking the Dart Estuary, with a mosaic-lined indoor swimming pool any middle-ranking Roman emperor would have been proud of.

Other supremely well sited, very high quality sea-view houses, **sleeping 10 or more people**, are near Prawle Point, Salcombe, in southernmost Devon, and Port Isaac, in Cornwall.

High on the Exmoor National Park, with stunning views to the sea and across the varied landscape of the moors, is a magnificent sixteen-bedroom, 19th century house. *Porlock Vale*, at the gateway of the great outdoors, is a truly breathtaking holiday home for all the family. It **sleeps up to 32** and there are even stables for guests to bring their horses. Twelve acres of grounds and gardens surround the house, full of mature trees, huge lawns (croquet, play area) and rhododendrons, all managed for maximum wildlife habitat; wistaria cascades from the verandah, with the pebbly beach only two fields away. Inside, the house has a wonderful mixture of comfort, elegance and space, with comfy leather sofas, two sitting rooms and an elegant staircase for grand entrances.

In Somerset, they have cottages, farmhouses and a superb country house on Exmoor and on the slopes of the Quantock Hills. These include a Grade II listed miller's house in the county's lush farming centre, and a converted cider barn from which you can walk to the tops of the Mendips.

There is a detached late-Victorian gem of a house in Bath-stone just a mile and a half from the centre of Bath itself, and in Dorset there are notable cottages in valleys beneath the downs.

Naturally, Helpful have many cottages in and around Chagford, their very popular little 'home town' on Dartmoor's edge, and in its neighbour, Drewsteignton, a village above the dramatic River Teign valley, near amazing Castle Drogo. Here there are four classic thatched cottages. All of these have the considerable attraction of open fires or woodburners.

Euan and Su Bowater are owners themselves. Slumbering under a traditional thatched roof in the Teign Valley below Castle Drogo is their picture-postcard *Gibhouse*, in peaceful gardens by a stream, with superb views of rolling hills.

Weekly prices range from about £144 to £7200. Dogs are welcome in many properties. Details are available from Helpful Holidays, Chagford, Devon TQ13 8AW. Telephone 01647 433593. Fax 433694. Or have a look at their website:

www.helpfulholidays.com
email: help@helpfulholidays.com

Gibhouse is an idyllically located cottage near Castle Drogo, above. Note: it gets booked up early! Ref A14.

Just inland from Torbay, this house (at Stoke Gabriel) sleeps twelve. Ref C618.

Porlock Vale makes a super holiday home for a big family. Sleeps up to 32! Ref F30.

Compton Pool, near Torquay
Compton Pool Farm Cottages

These cottages are in a location that readers (especially families) have raved about: only ten minutes' drive from the centre of Torquay, but entirely rural, with easy access to Torbay, and Dartmoor only a short drive away. They have featured in this guide for 20 years.

Since the spring of 2006 the properties have became even more sought-after. In the hands of new owners, serious upgrading has put them on an entirely different plane.

Hot on the heels of achieving **Five Stars** for all the cottages and the *Gold Award* for the best tourism website in the South West, Compton Pool Farm has achieved yet another top honour: being the first Five Star self-catering establishment in Devon to be awarded the *Green Tourism Award*, relating to energy use, waste management and care for the local environment. In fact it was a key objective for the farm to be a fully sustainable business.

There are far too many good things for us to detail here, but, for example, indications of the exceptional quality of these cottages are in the marble floors to kitchen/dining areas, the well appointed bathrooms and shower rooms with power showers, the hand crafted contemporary furniture produced in the UK.

There are expensive king size beds in all double bedrooms and full size singles in twin rooms (no bunks), the best quality soft furnishings, with all bedding and towels included, flat screen digital TVs, DVD players and Bose HiFi systems (plus extra TVs in all double bedrooms).

There are eight cottages, namely *Ambrook* (**sleeping 8**), *Arch* (**4**), *Bidwell* (**6**), *Bow* (**2**), *Crazy Well* (**6**), *Kester* (**4**), *Redlake* (**4**) and *Wray* (**4**).

Significantly, the numbers of people the cottages originally slept have been reduced, with guests' comfort in mind. There is a super indoor swimming pool to enjoy, and a tennis court on site.

Absolutely top-notch accommodation in the care of new, on-site owners that is winning prestigious awards and also gets the vote of many 'cottage guide' readers...

As regular readers will expect, Compton Pool is high on our agenda for an extended visit in the summer of 2007!

Details from Compton Pool Farm, Compton, Devon TQ13 1TA. Telephone 01803 872241. Fax 874012.

www.comptonpool.co.uk email: info@comptonpool.co.uk

Dartmouth
Dartmouth Holiday Homes

With the sun sparkling on the sea, packed pleasure boats puttering up the river, and cream and brown trains transporting people on the restored Dart Valley Railway, this chic, beautifully cared for resort is rather special.

There are a good number of holiday homes right in the town (some self-contained houses, many apartments), the best of which are looked after by the highly professional and welcoming Ginny and Tim Windibank and their staff. Ginny and Tim also own the successful Salcombe Holiday Homes.

We looked at a cross section of what they have available, most of them with the sort of view that could keep one sitting quietly in a bay window or on a balcony – just gazing at the river and the town – for hours on end.

Sleeping 10, *36 Clarence Street* is a spacious period townhouse close to the heart of the town. It has fabulous views from the feature attic sitting room. From the kitchen is an atrium with glazed roof, terracotta floors and comfortable seating. The property also benefits from garage parking and a pretty terraced, part lawned garden at the rear with views to the harbour.

Properties in Above Town nearly all benefit from views over the river and towards Kingswear. *Bell Cottage* is just such a property. Full of character and decorated to a high standard, this four storey house, **sleeping 4**, has 180 degree panoramic views from all the main rooms, patios and a pretty conservatory. *13 Above Town* is a delightful four storey house **sleeping 6**, which is surprisingly roomy and has a pretty garden with wonderful views. Again the property has a Dartmouth relative rarity: a garage. The cosy *Flat 1* in *Speedwell House* does not have views but is ideal for those who want to be a very short, level walk to the centre of town and close to the Lower Ferry which provides a regular connection with Kingswear.

Numbers 9, 11 and *25 Sandquay Road* **sleep 6, 4 and 4** respectively, and are a short walk up river from the central shops and quays. All are com-

In a quiet location just above the new Dart Marina, 9 Sandquay Road sleeps six.

Bell Cottage (sleeps four) has 180-degree panoramic views from all the main rooms.

fortable, well equipped and in a quiet location just above the smart new Dart Marina with restaurants, bar and river access, close to the Higher Ferry to Kingswear. With coastal and country walks, nearby beaches, sailing, fishing, great shopping and super restaurants. Dartmouth is a great place all year round.

Details and brochures from Dartmouth Holiday Homes, 1a Lower Street, Dartmouth, Devon TQ6 9AJ. Telephone 01803 833082. Fax 835224.

www.dartmouthuk.com email: dhh@dartmouthuk.com

Rattery, near Totnes
Knowle Farm

One family who stayed here in 2005 registered a complaint. They could hardly ever persuade their little ones to go out and about for the day, so content were the children to spend their time with Knowle's collection of chickens, ducks, pigs, rabbits and donkeys. Delightful! Then they had to contend with the outdoor play areas and one of the best indoor playrooms for under fives we have seen, including a ballpool, slide and toys.

There's a genuine attempt to answer children's needs without neglecting adults, who love the the the cottages themselves, converted as they are from stone and slate barns, with the big advantage of woodburning stoves.

Moncks Green **sleeps 6** plus cot, with a double, twin and bunk rooms downstairs, plus bathroom/wc with shower. Upstairs is a large living-room that has a high ceiling and exposed trusses, commanding impressive views, also a dining-room and shower-room/toilet. *Applecross*, **sleeping 4** plus cot, has

In 44 acres, the farm has an exceptional playroom and a whole host of pets...

...as well as swimming for all the family in a most inviting indoor pool.

double and bunk rooms downstairs with bathroom/toilet with shower. Again there are good views from the upstairs living/dining room. *Clematis*, **sleeping 2** plus child or cot, is a cosy single-storey cottage with a wood panelled ceiling in the living/dining room area, full of character like the others. *Woodbine* (**sleeping 8** plus cots) is suited to two families. Downstairs it has a galleried living/dining area with high ceiling, exposed beams and trusses, a double bedroom with en-suite facilities, and a twin room. The first floor gallery sports a gorgeous sitting area, a double and bunk room, plus bathroom/wc with shower. *Foxglove* and *Cow-mumble* both sleep 4 plus cots, with double and twin bedrooms downstairs, along with bathroom/wc and shower. The living/dining and kitchen areas upstairs have lovely views over the countryside.

The farm, in 44 acres, also offers a 34 by 17 foot heated indoor pool, tennis court, and indoor table tennis and pool table. Dartmoor is about five minutes away, the coast about half an hour. Not suitable for pets; electricity and heating by meter; duvets (with linen) supplied. TV. Highchairs, cots and stair gates. Cost: from about £250 to £1565.

Details from Lynn and Richard Micklewright, Knowle Farm, Rattery, near Totnes, Devon TQ10 9JY. Telephone/fax 01364 73914. There's lots more information on the website, including prices and current availability:

www.knowle-farm.co.uk
email: holiday@knowle-farm.co.uk

Fursdon, near Exeter
Fursdon

Astonishingly – and it's exactly the sort of thing that appeals to readers of this guide – the 700-acre estate in the Exe Valley in rural mid-Devon has been the home of the Fursdon family *since 1259*. The present generation, David and Catriona, let out two apartments on the first floor of their handsome manor house whose origins date from the 13th century. *Garden Wing* (**sleeping 3**), which opens on to the walled rear garden, has a large double bedroom, a small single and a cosy sitting-room with the much loved advantage of an open fire (logs supplied) and enough books to keep the most avid reader happy for months.

Park Wing (**sleeping 6**), which enjoys magnificent views over the land-scaped parkland at the front of the house, has a large en-suite double bed-room. Two further (twin) bedrooms are at the back and share a shower room. The spacious lounge, again with masses of books, and the large kitchen both enjoy the front view too. Catriona, who masterminds the decor, chooses furnishings and colours that suit the age of the rooms. Both apartments have good-sized kitchens with dining-tables and are equipped with gas-cooker, dishwasher, fridge-freezer and microwave.

We were not at all surprised to learn that one family has been coming here regularly for seventeen years and another has visited several times from Alaska. Guests can make use of the extensive gardens and woodland. Young visitors particularly enjoy getting to know the three friendly ponies and Catriona's flock of black Welsh Mountain sheep, while tennis players

Not just another holiday booking, but a chance to savour a fine country house...

...in which the advantages of good-quality kitchens are not forgotten.

will be delighted by the well-maintained grass court (bring your own rac-quets). Swings and slides for children. Table-tennis in a barn. Fishing is available on a private stretch of the Exe, two miles away.

TV, DVD, CD player. Washing machine and dryer in courtyard. Linen and logs provided. Cot and highchair available. Bookings Friday-Friday. Cost: about £310 to £750 per week. Short breaks available. Not suitable for dogs. Details from Catriona Fursdon, Fursdon, Cadbury, Exeter EX5 5JS. Telephone 01392 860860. Fax 860126.

www.fursdon.co.uk

email: holidays@fursdon.co.uk

Upottery, near Honiton
Otter Falls

It's hard to credit that you're just three hours from London in this exceptionally peaceful spot. Amid 130 acres, on the edge of the Blackdown Hills – something of a 'best kept secret', and much under-rated – there are cottages converted from what were originally farm buildings (including one-time barns) and Finnish lodges overlooking fish-ing lakes. All the accommodation

Peaceful but not isolated. Unusually, you can choose a cottage or a Finnish 'lodge'.

has either a log fire or a woodburning stove – which always gets our vote, and which, added to the cosy, comfortable, nicely lit interiors, make these properties a good choice for an autumn or winter break. Some have four poster beds.

For details of these and other Devon properties (and other holiday accom-modation throughout England, Scotland and Wales) contact The Cottage Collection, 17-23 Ber Street, Norwich NR1 3EU. Telephone 01603 724809.

www.the-cottage-collection.co.uk
email: bookings@the-cottage-collection.co.uk

The Isle of Wight   map 7/483/484
No 3 Old Coastguard Cottages/Greystones

Good quality self catering properties on the Isle of Wight are at a pre-mium. Planning restrictions are very tight, so cottages tend to have per-manent residents. Close to the beach at Freshwater Bay, *No 3 Old Coastguard Cottages* (Ref W8342) is a gem, a pretty terraced Victorian cottage **sleeping up to 5**. It's located in a quiet lane with a lawned garden, and, delightfully, you can walk from the gate just the short distance to the beach. Among other 'Welcome' properties is an excellent detached

One of the most desirable holiday houses on the Isle of Wight, this former vicarage, Greystones, sleeps up to ten.

house called *Greystones*, on the edge of Freshwater village, close to a sandy beach and most usefully **sleeping 9/10**. Very much a family house, it used to be a vicarage. Ref W8158.

For availability and bookings contact Welcome Cottages, Spring Mill, Earby, Barnoldswick, Lancashire BB94 0AA. Brochures and bookings: 0870 197 6957.

www.welcomecottages.com

Beer
Jean Bartlett Cottage Holidays*

A highly regarded fixture in this guide for many years, concentrating very astutely on a specific and very popular area, this medium-sized agency has been described in glowing terms by many of our readers, *with never a complaint*.

'Jean Bartlett' handles properties from Honiton to the coast of East Devon and West Dorset: some grand, some modest and inexpensive. We have visited about a dozen, most in sight of the sea and one or two right on it.

On our most recent visit we looked at *Hope* and *Creole* cottages, both former fishermen's houses with beautiful gardens, right in the centre of Beer village, at *Chapel Cottage*, a quietly situated thatched beauty just inland, and at *The Belvedere* and *The Look Out,* spacious and most appealing apartments, with sea views, also right at the heart of Beer.

Hope and Creole (**sleeping 5/6**) are furnished to permanent home standards and are much admired by passers-by. They have good sized sitting rooms with deep sofas and chairs, upholstered window seats and an original beamed fireplace. Both have modern kitchens, three bedrooms and a bathroom (Creole has an additional *ensuite* bathroom) plus the benefit of a private parking space.

For guests who are seeking absolute top-of-the-range accommodation, the agency offers several **Five Star** standard properties. For example, there is *Steppes Barn* – a spacious barn conversion near the River Axe, which has plenty of space for guests who wish to take advantage of the location and bring a boat.

Picture-book villages such as Branscombe are a short drive, as are the resorts of Sidmouth and Lyme Regis. Near Branscombe, for example, *Rockenhayne Farmstead* has a delightful stone-built cottage and a stunningly well restored barn that retains its original 16th century oak beams. For people happy with more basic accommodation there is also a static caravan, commanding superb views of the wooded valley.

Costs range from about £160 to £2000. Dogs accepted in about half the properties by arrangement. Details/brochures from Jean Bartlett Holidays, Fore Street, Beer, Devon EX12 3JA. Telephone 01297 23221. Fax 23303.

www.jeanbartlett.com
email: holidays@jeanbartlett.com

Hope and Creole Cottages offer a rare chance to be based in the heart of Beer.

Chapel Cottage is 'a quietly situated thatched beauty just inland'...

Corfe Castle
Scoles Manor

Even by our standards the location is remarkable: the view of Corfe Castle, framed between the Purbeck Hills, has been the inspiration of many a painter. Close to the castle, these three cottages have been imaginatively created within a long barn/ dairy. They have large windows, pine furniture, smart kitchens and such

Many years in this guide, and geared to family holidays: babysitting available.

features as exposed stone walls and oak beams. Owners Peter and Belinda Bell live in the adjoining manor house. The thirty-acre estate, enviably located at the end of a 600-yard farm track, is home to ducks, gamefowl and doves. And the Purbeck Way footpath to Corfe Castle or the sea passes by the property. There are sandy beaches at Studland and Swanage, a short drive, or you can walk to small coves. A cosy pub is just two fields away. All are ETC **Four Stars**. Single-storeyed *Dairy* has four double rooms and two bathrooms, *Great Barn* three double rooms (two bathrooms), *Little Barn* two bedrooms (one with bunk beds). Central heating, bedlinen, payphones, starter pack of groceries, babysitting. Open all year. Cost: £225 to £1030. Short breaks. Details from Peter and Belinda Bell, Scoles Manor, Kingston, Corfe Castle, Dorset BH20 5LG. Telephone 01929 480312. Fax 481237. **www.scoles.co.uk   email: peter@scoles.co.uk**

It's nice to eat out, but a shame not to stay in sometimes to take advantage of the last-word modern kitchens many cottages have.

Coastal Dorset
Dorset Coastal Cottages*

We've long been impressed by the fact that this agency concentrates purely on traditional cottages, most dating from the 17th, 18th or 19th century. To insist that they should also be *within ten miles of England's important World Heritage 'Jurassic Coast'*, between Studland and Lyme Regis (most are within five), is an even greater challenge.

But it has paid off, which says a lot about the charm of this part of the country and the persistence of Charles and Jennie Smith in pursuing their idea of the perfect country cottage. Many are thatched, with open fires.

Our first visit was to Winfrith Newburgh, where the agency is based: we were very taken with *Milton Cottage*, a traditional thatched cottage, **sleeping 4**, with two-feet-thick walls and distinctive 'eyebrow' dormer windows. Similarly, *Jasmine Cottage* **(sleeps 4 plus cot),** is an 18th century mid-terrace cottage in the pretty village of Upwey, with easy access to ridge walks. Weymouth is three miles away.

This, along with *Bow Cottage*, Charmouth, a detached property **sleeping 4/6 plus cot** and close to a sandy beach (ideally placed for fossil hunting) are in accordance with the agency's character-cottage pledge.

There are around a hundred properties in the portfolio. Some can accommodate large groups, such as *The White House,* at Kimmeridge. This not only has direct access to the Coast Path and sea views, but with five bedrooms and five bathrooms, it **sleeps 10 plus cot.**

In the Bridport area, *Medway Farm,* Askerswell, tucked down a private road in a rural setting, has accommodation for **up to 10/12 people**. This is shared between two stone barn conversions, *Coombe Barn* **(sleeping 4 plus cot)** and *Haydon Barn* **(sleeping 6 plus cot)**. Anglers take note: a sloping field leads to a well stocked trout and coarse fishing ponds.

Many cottages take pets; most are available for short breaks. *All include linen and towels, as well as electricity, gas and oil*. Details from Dorset Coastal Cottages, The Manor House, Winfrith Newburgh, Dorchester, Dorset DT2 8JR. Telephone 0800 9804070. Fax 01305 854988.

Note that the agency's cottage-grading is reviewed annually against questionnaires returned by clients...

www.dorsetcoastalcottages.com
email: hols@dorsetcoastalcottages.com

The agency has three properties at Seatown and Golden Cap: memorable!

Milton Cottage, Winfrith Newburgh, has two attractively beamy bedrooms.

211

South and West
Hideaways*

The widely admired family-run agency has some of the best cottages we know in the south and south west of England. Many are picture-book places 'suspended in time': a chance to catch the flavour of some of England's most unspoilt corners.

Based between Salisbury and Shaftesbury, Hideaways is strongly represented where Wiltshire blends lazily with Dorset and Hampshire; it also extends into Cornwall, Devon and Somerset, with a good selection of properties in the Heart of England, and more besides.

A rare instance of a quite excellent cottage in the Forest of Dean, where (in one of England's best-kept-secret places) really good self catering is thin on the ground, *The Old Pumphouse* is outstanding. **Sleeping up to 6**, it is approached by a woodland track and stands on its own in a clearing

With its handsome old beams, and accommodation all on the ground floor, Drovers Barn appeals to us a lot.

Used occasionally by the owners themselves (a good sign), Shedrick slumbers in deeply rural Dorset.

by a trout pond. A real 'hideaway' indeed! Another is tucked away in the New Forest. *The Lodge,* near Fordingbridge, is a sunny three-bedroom thatched cottage which shares the owners' three-acre landscaped woodland garden. With distant views over the Forest from its balcony and terrace, this is another 'hideaway'. **Sleeps 6/7.**

Dorset is true thatched cottage territory, and last autumn we visited *The Owl Box* in the hamlet of Throop, twelve miles from Dorchester. This cosy Grade II, ultra-romantic cottage lies deep in the countryside, where the sound of barn owls provides a suitably soothing accompaniment. Once a thatched brick and cob barn, lovingly converted to a cottage with a spacious, open living-room, original beams and timber cladding, this is heaven-sent for those who dream of the ultimate bolthole. **Sleeps 2.**

On a previous Wiltshire-Dorset visit we were impressed, among others, by *Shedrick,* a 17th-century thatched cottage situated on its own deep in the Dorset countryside near Chard, which lost none of its character (oak beams, low ceilings) when it was modernised. So it has a cosy atmosphere and the convenience of a large fitted kitchen. The three bedrooms (**sleeping 6**) are a double with ensuite shower room/wc, a double with a brass bed, and a twin. The garden has a secluded patio area and barbecue.

Kate's Cottage, Winterbourne Kingston (**sleeps 5**), is over 200 years old and lies along a track on the village edge. It is well placed for visiting some of the most spectacular stretches of coastline in England.

We have also admired *The Old Stable*, **sleeping 4**, a traditional thatched cottage in the meandering village of Rockbourne, on the northern edge of the New Forest. Romantic *Garden Loft* (**sleeping 2**), also in Rockbourne, is a cosy studio flat tucked away beyond a wrought iron gate and up a flight of steps. In a nearby village, *The Coach House*, standing opposite the former village rectory, incorporates a particularly impressive, heavily beamed and timbered bedroom with sloping ceilings. **Sleeps 2 'plus 2'**.

In Somerset, the long climb to Middle Burrow Farm, near Timberscombe, is rewarded by the initial sight of *Upper Barn* (**sleeps 4 plus cot**), a fascinating property, as much for its interior as its exterior. Converted from a former threshing barn, some 300 years old, it is unique in that an archway divides the ground floor where the bedrooms are located – one a twin, the other a double. Staircases from each lead to the first floor and a long beamed sitting-room, sensitively furnished. A bridleway leads to open moor a quarter of a mile away: Dunster is four miles away, the attractive village of Wootton Courtenay under a mile. Well behaved pets welcome.

The Old Stable, in pretty Rockbourne, in Hampshire, is one of our favourites. It has an open fire and several antiques.

The interior combines a strong sense of history with 21st century comforts. It is on the northern edge of the New Forest.

Sleeping 4/6 plus cot, *Drovers Barn*, at Shrewton, makes an ideal base for visiting Wiltshire's best known historic sites, including Stonehenge, Avebury and ever-enigmatic Silbury Hill. The accommodation is all at ground floor level, with oak beams, reclaimed pine floors and a particularly stylish interior decor. The property looks out on to a two-acre garden bordering the River Till.

The Lodge, near West Wittering, West Sussex, with its origins in the 18th century, is an enchanting cottage within the grounds of the owners' Georgian farmhouse. It **sleeps 3, or 2 'plus cot'**.

Details of these and other properties from Hideaways, Chapel House, Luke Street, Berwick St John, Shaftesbury, Dorset SP7 0HQ. Telephone 01747 828000, fax 829090.

www.hideaways.co.uk
email: enq@hideaways.co.uk

Lyme Regis, Charmouth and around
Lyme Bay Holidays*

The considerable success of this agency – featured by us for twelve years – surely lies in the fact that most of its properties are within ten miles of quiet, sandy, slightly old fashioned Charmouth, which we'd call one of Dorset's best kept secrets, and of the genteel seaside resort of Lyme Regis.

Some properties stick in our mind for their real character. One is *Pound House Wing* (**sleeps 4 'plus 1'**), close to Hawkchurch, rich in atmosphere and full of intriguing corners. This is a happy property, geared to the present day but furnished in sympathy with its history as the converted wing of a 14th century farmhouse. It even has its own priest-hole, discovered during renovation. There are exposed beams and flagstone floors.

The property, in twelve acres of grounds with bluebell woods, is a quarter of a mile from the road but accessible along a well maintained track suitable for most family cars. We liked it a lot when we visited last autumn, and it's only fifteen minutes from the coast at Lyme Regis.

We're keen on a picture-postcard thatched cottage tucked prettily away in a secret, miniature valley and called *Sunshine Cottage*, in which on a blustery day a couple were very cosily installed (it sleeps **just 2**). Dating back in part to the 16th century, this charming property has a third of an acre garden. We also liked a spacious detached family house called *Penderel*, **sleeping 7 'plus 1'** plus cot. We appreciated the big rooms, the open fire, the quietness – even though Charmouth's high street is only a matter of yards away. It has now been upgraded to **Four Stars**.

We also admired a row of pastel-coloured properties on Marine Parade, all distinctly different but enjoying unique sea front views. 'An outstanding location' said **'Visit Britain'** of one. Two of the most appealing are *Benwick Cottage*, pictured below, and *Library Cottage,* which features a south-facing terrace that has an unobstructed view of the exceptional bay.

Dogs are welcome in over a third of the 200 to 210 properties. For a copy of the brochure, with good colour line drawings and precise descriptions, write to David Matthews, Lyme Bay Holidays, Wessex House, Uplyme Road, Lyme Regis, Dorset DT7 3LP. Telephone 01297 443363, fax 445576. Freepost RLYG-GZSA-CEYA, Lyme Regis, Dorset DT7 3BF. There's a very comprehensive website, with internal photographs and on-line availability and booking:

www.lymebayholidays.co.uk   email: email@lymebayholidays.co.uk

Pretty Benwick is likely to have been familiar to Jane Austen, who loved Lyme.

This pretty thatched cottage makes a cosy hideaway for two people…

Chew Magna, near Bristol
Chew Hill Farm Cottages

Featured in this guide every year *since its very beginnings in 1983*, these exceptionally neat-and-tidy, scrupulously clean, bright and spacious cottages are situated on a high lying farm from which (including certain rooms in the three holiday houses) there are impressive views over the Mendip Hills and some- times quite memorable sunsets. Visitors are well placed for visiting

Twenty-five years in this guide, and never the suggestion of a complaint...

Bath, Cheddar Gorge, Wookey Hole, and Bristol, with its theatres and shops. In *Bailiff's House*, which **sleeps 6**, we admired the big kitchen with its smart units, washing machine and microwave, the very large triple aspect sitting room and separate dining room. There are private gardens. The pleasantly high-ceilinged *West Lodge* is Victorian and **sleeps 4** in a double and two singles. *East Lodge* **sleeps 6** and has a 22 ft long sitting room.

TVs. Linen provided, towels for hire. Dogs possible by arrangement. Cost: £200 to £600. **'Visit Britain' Three Stars**. Details from Mrs S Lyons, Chew Hill Farm, Chew Magna, Bristol, North Somerset BS40 8QP. Telephone 01275 332496; mobile 07831 117186.

Poole map 7/476
Fisherman's Quay

We've had so many ecstatic reader reports about this house over the years, and sometimes think we could do with a week here ourselves, just gazing at the view! With its uninter- rupted views of Poole Harbour (said to be the second largest natural har- bour in the world), from which car

Take binoculars to make the most of the extraordinary wide-ranging views...

ferries run to the Channel Islands and to France, this three storeyed house is in a spectacular location. Looking down over the impressive Fisherman's Harbour, two balconies offer an extraordinary vantage point from which to watch every type of waterborne activity – not least, the skills of the pilots guiding huge ships to their berths near Poole Quay – itself bustling with smaller craft and pubs, restaurants, galleries, shops and museums. There are two double rooms, one ensuite, and one twin, main bathroom (both bathrooms have showers), a first floor sitting room with those panoramic views, a well fitted kitchen, dining area, a ground-floor cloakroom, patio and barbecue. Not suitable for pets, infirm or very elderly people, or very young children. Non smokers preferred. Parking space and integral garage. Central heating is included. Cost: £350 to £700. Details from Dr D Halliday, 1 Grange Drive, Horsforth, Leeds, West Yorkshire LS18 5EQ. Telephone 0113 2584947.

215

South and South East

We can't deny that it's hard to find real pin-drop silence in the south east of England, though we are constantly surprised at how much of rural Hampshire, Kent, Sussex and Surrey have gone into the 21st century so miraculously well preserved. We associate the best of those counties with the smell of wood-smoke on autumn days, hop fields, 'tile hung' cottages, sleepy red-roofed villages beneath wooded escarpments, manicured topiary gardens. Within easy reach of several of the cottages featured in this section are Winston Churchill's Chartwell, near Westerham, Knole House, at Sevenoaks, Sissinghurst Castle, the celebrated Pantiles, in Tunbridge Wells – perhaps the most elegant 'shopping precinct' in England – the historic Cinque Ports. It's scattered with castles of the toy-fort kind – Bodiam, Hastings, Arundel, Leeds, Hever – and great cathedrals such as Winchester, Chichester and Canterbury (we'd also include Guildford's: 1930s plain-Jane from the outside, exquisite inside). It is also the most fruitful corner of Britain for antique-hunters, with a good sprinkling of old-fashioned tea shops, many in gabled old towns that have defied the depredations of developers. And we have noticed readers now include Paris in their 'interesting days out' list – for it's an easy matter to pick up a train at Ashford and have lunch in Montmartre instead of, say, Midhurst.

Milford-on-Sea
Windmill Cottage map 2/478

A long-term favourite among readers of this guide, this is a neat, tidy, modern, Georgian-style red brick property that's pleasantly in keeping with the rest of Milford-on-Sea, whose village green and 'character shops' maintain a sense of bygone and rather genteel charm. The house is a joy, with good quality carpets, and is pristinely clean and well cared for. The through sitting/dining room has a bow window to the front and

This is a modern, clean and tidy house with everything you could need to give you a virtually chore-free holiday...

French windows to the enclosed back garden. Every electric appliance is to be found in the brand new kitchen, including a washing machine, dishwasher, fridge-freezer, tumble drier and microwave. There are three bedrooms (one double, one twin, one a small single). **Sleeps up to 5**. There is a modern bathroom, and ample parking space plus a garage in a nearby block. The New Forest, Lymington and Bournemouth are all within easy reach. Village shops are a six minute walk, and cliffs, together with a pebbly beach, are three minutes by car.

Cost: about £230 to £545. TV. Dogs are welcome at £10 each. All linen is included, as well as heat and lighting. Incoming telephone. **'Visit Britain' Three Stars**. Further details and brochure from Mrs S M Perham, Danescourt, Kivernell Road, Milford-on-Sea, Lymington, Hampshire SO41 0PQ. Telephone 01590 643516. Fax 641255.

www.windmillcottage.info   email: enquiries@windmillcottage.info

Lymington
New Forest Cottages*

We've noticed from our correspondence over the years that a good number of readers were introduced to the charms of the New Forest courtesy of this organisation, which we have featured in the guide for over two decades.

From their office on a neat, cobbled slope leading down to Lymington's quayside, the staff handle around a hundred carefully vetted properties in and around the region.

On the Solent foreshore, with fabulous views across to the Isle of Wight, is *Sowley Gate House* (**sleeping 10**). This spacious holiday home stands in a large, sunny garden surrounded by open forest and farmland, with direct access to a private shingle beach.

The Bee Garden, in the village of Norley Wood, is – typically for this agency – full of character and charm.

Park Farm Cottage is another thatched gem, of which there are many on the agency's books.

Also in the forest is *Dell Cottage* (**sleeps 7**), tucked away along a lane, yet within five minutes' walk of a country pub and just a short drive from Lyndhurst.

Facing Lymington's Town Quay and the fishing boats, yachts and cabin-cruisers on the river is a stylish second floor flat in *Admiral's Court*. The large sitting room/diner has a picture window and a glazed enclosed balcony. **Sleeps 6**.

Between Lymington and Beaulieu, *Bee Garden* is a spacious thatched bungalow, **sleeping 6**, in the tiny village of Norley Wood: it has a pleasant open plan sitting/dining room and a spacious and well-screened garden. Ponies also graze immediately outside *Badgers Walk*, a cottage (**sleeping 5**) in the forest outside Burley. *Hawthorne Cottage,* on the outskirts of Brockenhurst, is a delightful Victorian cottage (**sleeping 3**) overlooking a sweep of open forest – perfect for a romantic week.

Details and a colour brochure can be obtained from New Forest Cottages, Ridgeway Rents, 4 Quay Hill, Lymington, Hampshire SO41 3AR. Telephone 01590 679655. Fax 670989.

www.newforestcottages.co.uk

Chiddingly, near Hailsham
Pekes

Up a quiet lane bordered by trees, one goes 'back in time'. For the partly-Tudor manor house that is the focal point of the estate and a clutch of extremely characterful holiday houses – was first *renovated* in 1550!

During a recent visit, accompanied by the owners (Mrs Morris is the grand-daughter of the man who bought the estate in 1908), we looked inside three of the five distinctively different properties in and around that fine Tudor house. They enjoy the jacuzzi, a sauna, and an indoor swimming pool. There is a tennis court and lawn badminton.

Mounts View has stunning views from the good sized sitting room, off which there is a dining alcove. It also has a 'barrel sauna' on the terrace. **Sleeps 6 'plus 2'.** The humblest property is cosy, tile-hung *Gate Cottage*. Up the steep staircase are a double and a twin, with space for 2 on a bed-settee.

All the cottages have well equipped kitchens: washing machines, tumble dryers, mixers and dishwashers. *Tudor View* is close to the main house, has an open fire and a smart kitchen/diner. The twin bedroom leads into the double bedroom, with a door on to the patio and garden. **Sleeps 5 'plus 2'.**

We have always liked *The Oast House,* which has its own private 'state of the art' jacuzzi in a cabin in the grounds. Its porticoed entrance leads into a biggish hall and a large, circular dining room. The kitchen has a table big enough for the largest get-together; the sitting room has French windows on to the garden. The green-covered stairs and big landing lead to the master bedroom with an enormous four-poster bed. There is a second large circular family room with a double and two singles, a twin bedroom and a very small single. **Sleeps 7 'plus 5'.** *The Wing* is unusually shaped, with a smart kitchen and several inter-connecting rooms. **Sleeps 5.**

Cost: Oast House £1256 to £1883; Cottages and Wing £385 to £835. Mounts View £818 to £1080. Short breaks: Oast House £825 to £1076. Cottages and Wing £240 to £504. Mounts View £480 to £670. (Different prices apply to Christmas and New Year.) TVs. Children welcome, also dogs, especially in the three cottages. Central heating and open fires or open-front woodburners. Linen for hire. '**Visit Britain' Three/Four Stars**. Details from Eva Morris, 'Pekes', 124 Elm Park Mansions, Park Walk, London SW10 0AR. Telephone 020 7352 8088. Fax 020 7352 8125. Also 01825 872229, Saturday to Monday.

www.pekesmanor.com email: pekes.afa@virgin.net

A fine Tudor manor house, with a non-Tudor swimming pool and tennis court.

We've always liked the Oast House, especially its large, circular family room.

218

Appledore
Ashby Farms Cottages

Rural Kent is a largely unsung corner of England that most outsiders never discover. But Ashby Farms Cottages offer the chance to get to grips with, for example, the Weald of Kent and – within striking distance – the hauntingly beautiful Romney Marsh.

Roughlands, outside Woodchurch, is a conventional detached bungalow, quite roomy and blissfully quiet, with pleasant open views and gardens back and front. Fully fitted modern kitchen and bathroom. There is a twin and double-bedded room, with a bed available for a 5th person.

Only a hundred yards away but completely hidden in woodland, the specially designed and pine built *Fishermen's Lodges* (**sleep 6**) reminded us of Scandinavia, even down to the setting, close to two isolated fishing lakes. The familiar A-shape encompasses a large double bed sleeping area reached by an open rung wooden ladder. On the main level are two twin bedrooms, bathroom and a modern well-fitted, galley-style kitchen. Sliding patio doors open on to a large wooden verandah. There are pinewood walls and furnishings, full carpeting, and the lounge/dining area benefits from the full height of the lodge.

Numbers 2, 3 and 4 Spring Cottages, in the adjacent small village of Kenardington, are within a terrace of brick-built dwellings (a shepherd lives in the other one). Each **sleeps 5** in three bedrooms reached by steepish stairs. They are simply furnished, but bright and attractive, have modern kitchens and bathrooms, fitted carpets and TVs. Fine rural views from the rear. Pretty front gardens.

On the road leading into Appledore is a semi-detached cottage called *65 The Street*, unpretentious but with a good-sized kitchen and a modern bathroom. Modestly furnished, **sleeping up to 5** in three bedrooms, it is well placed for those who like to be close to shops and pubs. There is a neat garden at the back, and attractive rural views.

Cost: about £120 (for a short break) to £450. Dogs welcome. Fishing permits are available at £40 per week for a family of 4 (also by the day), and rough shooting at £12.50 a day. Linen and towels for hire. Further details from Ashby Farms Ltd, Place Farm, Kenardington, Ashford, Kent TN26 2LZ. Telephone 01233 733332. Fax 733326.

www.ashbyfarms.com
email: info@ashbyfarms.com

Fishermen's Lodges: Scandinavian flair, close to two isolated fishing lakes. Easy-to-maintain interiors.

Spring Cottages: No frills, but clean, tidy and bright.

219

Golden Green, near Tonbridge
Goldhill Mill Cottages

Festooned with awards, and featured in this guide for almost 20 years: it's not surprising these have become such firm favourites with our readers. Reader endorsements and awards are impressive: they have won the South East England Tourism Self Catering Holiday of the Year Award *four times* and twice received the Silver Award in the England For Excellence Self Catering 'Oscars' from the English Tourism Council (now 'Visit Britain').

When you see *Figtree Cottage*, it's difficult to imagine the site was once pigsties, for this seemingly small property opens into a spacious high ceilinged, south facing, living-room with a large comfortable sofa that converts to a double bed, an open log burner and dining area. We liked the use of reclaimed bricks, tiles and oak beams. **Sleeps 2** plus child.

Figtree clicks in neatly with its big brothers. We have previously praised *Ciderpress Cottage,* converted from a pair of Tudor barns, **sleeping 4 plus an occasional 2** on a sleeping gallery, for its soft furnishings, good paintings and antiques, also its curtained gallery reached by apple ladder from the living-room. There is a top-notch kitchen, and a master bedroom equipped with en suite bathroom, as is the second bedroom.

Walnut Tree Cottage, likewise converted from the old cowshed in a group of buildings dating back to the Tudor period, rightly enjoys a reputation for its close carpeted comfort, linked with its colour coordinated duvets and curtains, and is congenially lit with wall lamps. Attractive water colours hang on pastel walls. There's a seriously comfortable three piece suite and a free-standing log fire in the living room, a wrought-iron spiral staircase to the upper floor (contained within the roof space, with exposed beams), and a 'last word' kitchen. **Sleeps 6** – each of the three (two five-foot doubles, one twin) bedrooms has an en suite bathroom. Immediately outside is the charming garden by the river, the mill stream, the swans.

All three stand within the 20-acre grounds surrounding Goldhill Mill, mentioned in the Domesday Book. And each carries the **'Visit Britain'** top **Five Stars** grading. Figtree is also rated Mobility Level 2 in the National Accessible Scheme for disabled people, Ciderpress Level 1.

Non smokers please. TV/video. Telephone. Linen/towels provided. Barbecue available. Floodlit tennis court. Cost: £240 to £775. Long-term winter lets possible. Details from Shirley and Vernon Cole, Goldhill Mill, Golden Green, Tonbridge, Kent TN11 0BA. Telephone 01732 851626; fax 851881.
www.goldhillmillcottages.com email:vernon.cole@virgin.net

Walnut Tree is quiet and full of character.

And all the interiors blend old and new.

Eastwell Manor, near Ashford
Eastwell Mews

The nineteen individually styled cottages or courtyard apartments in the grounds of the sumptuous Four Star Eastwell Manor Hotel are quite exceptional. Readers have loved them, and it was a delight for us to revisit in the autumn of 2005.

The hotel, an ivy-clad Jacobean-style stone mansion with turrets, tall chimneys and arched leaded glass windows, lies in 62 acres of parkland and landscaped gardens surrounded by a working estate of 3000 acres.

Everyone staying in the cottages or apartments has use of all the hotel's extensive facilities as if they were a hotel guest. Indeed, the cottages and apartments are sometimes used to provide extra bedrooms when the main building is full, so they are equipped and furnished to the same standard.

With one, two or three bedrooms – each en-suite and with its own TV – they have been cleverly converted from the old Victorian stables. Each apartment or cottage has spacious accommodation with kitchen, dining and living areas. All of them are superbly furnished, with top-quality fabrics and linen. They are a short walk from the hotel and its convivial bars

With the fine hotel (and all its impressive facilities) as a focal point...

...these stylish and comfortable cottages really do offer 'the best of both worlds'.

and award-winning wood-panelled restaurant (AA 'Two Rosettes' and RAC 'Blue Ribbbon').

The hotel's Pavilion leisure complex is even closer. It has a brasserie restaurant, a cocktail bar, a 20-metre heated pool, a 'Dreams' beauty therapy salon and a spa that incorporates steam room, sauna, jacuzzi and hydrotherapy pool. Upstairs is a state-of-the-art gymnasium.

A further advantage is that the Eurostar station at Ashford is only a few minutes' drive away and the Eurotunnel terminal just 20 minutes' drive. So you're well-placed for a day-trip to France.

The cottages and apartments can be rented on a self-catering basis or hotel-bedroom basis. All have satellite TV, video, fax and ISDN. Well-behaved dogs welcome. Costs on a weekly basis from about £440 to £1100. Short breaks also available.

Details and brochure from Eastwell Manor, Eastwell Park, Boughton Lees, Ashford, Kent TN25 4HR. Telephone 01233 213000.

www.eastwellmanor.co.uk

email: enquiries@eastwellmanor.co.uk

221

Cotswolds, Heart of England, Welsh Borders, Home Counties

Sometimes it seems as if the villages, the farmsteads, the silent green churchyards can't quite be real. How can the Cotswolds have survived intact and so all-of-a-piece for so long? About a hunded miles from London, 25 from Birmingham, lies a Munchkinland of old walled gardens, honey-coloured villages snug within rolling green valleys, clear rivers and shallow trout streams and sturdy manor houses. Roughly, the Cotswolds stretch all the way from Gloucester and Herefordshire in the west to Bath in the south, and to Oxford in the east, passing close to the fertile Vale of Evesham. Probably the most popular village is Bourton-on-the-Water; less commercialised are the Slaughters (Upper and Lower), Moreton-in-Marsh, the straggly village of Blockley, imposing Broadway, Winchcombe. Our own favourite is probably Stanton – but not many people know it. There's Cirencester, with its Roman amphitheatre, and Stratford-upon-Avon is closer than you might think. To the west and the north is country known as the 'Heart of England'. You'll see ruined abbeys, castles, half timbered buildings, cider-apple orchards. To the east are the Chilterns, the upper reaches of the Thames, rural Hertfordshire and a range of undiscovered country that is 'so near but so far'.

Richards Castle, near Ludlow
The Barn   map 9/499

We've long considered this to be a very desirable and rather romantic hideaway, **sleeping up to 4**. With panoramic views, at the end of a leafy drive that leads uphill to the owners' house, *The Barn* is indeed a converted barn, timbered throughout, skilfully done. It is a little gem, with a charming sitting room, a 'deck' leading to an orchard and garden, two smallish but cosy bedrooms, which respectively have a double bed and *a four foot double plus a single sleeping platform*. A well equipped kitchen and dining area is incorporated within the living room. We were pleased to note a Clearview woodburning stove – effective and trouble-free (logs included), but with that lovely glow that 'makes' a room – thoughtful lighting, absolute peace and quiet. Organic vegetables and free-range eggs are often available. TV. Electricity, linen and towels included. Not suitable for dogs. Non smokers preferred. **'Visit Britain' Four Stars**. Cost: about £225 to £420. Details from Sue and Peter Plant, Ryecroft, Richards Castle, near Ludlow, Shropshire SY8 4EU. Telephone/fax 01584 831224.

We thought this ideal for a couple wanting a little space. Modest outside, it is a real charmer (and roomy) inside...

www.ludlow.org.uk/ryecroft
email: ryecroftbarn@hotmail.com

Tintern, near Chepstow
Riverside Cottage

Watching the River Wye go by...

Though you can't see the join, this property is technically just inside Wales. It stands (memorably) about as close to the River Wye as you can be without actually getting your feet wet. Detached, stone-built, most attractive to look at (though the best view is from the far side of the river), the house is within easy walking distance, alongside the river, of Tintern Abbey: throbbing with visitors during summer weekends, more 'moody' at other times. And there is much excellent and more serious walking beyond. With stone walls, exposed beams, rugs on a tiled floor, the house **sleeps 4** in a double and a twin; the L-shaped sitting room has an open fire. Ref ODA.

Note: there is a terrace adjacent to the river where after cottage-visiting on a busy summer Saturday we were pleased to lean and put our minds into neutral. But – though there are railings – children should be watched. In fact, the property is 'unsuitable for small children'.

Details from from English Country Cottages, Stoney Bank Road, Earby, Barnoldswick BB94 0AA. Brochures and bookings: 0870 197 6890.

www.english-country-cottages.co.uk

Craven Arms/Lower Dinchope
Coach House/Lower Dinchope Big Barn   map 9/497/498

A super place for a family or a group of friends to get together. Sleeps up to 18.

Craven Arms is a famous focal point in Shropshire, and *The Coach House*, part of which dates from around 1780, is itself a fine rendezvous for **up to 18 people**. Among other good things that you'd associate with a big family house there's an open fire *and* a woodburning stove, as well as a big dining-kitchen ideal for those 'where shall we go tomorrow?' conferences. Ref 15812. Also in this green, hilly and heavily wooded border county, *Lower Dinchope Big Barn* is a spacious, well equipped barn conversion which can **sleep 15** in comfort. With oak beams and half timbered walls, twin stairs to each wing and plenty of space, it will suit larger groups. Just two miles from the Craven Arms, it has large gardens, with meadow and woodland beyond. In addition to the main sitting room – it has a woodburner – there is a children's sitting room. Ref 12348.

Country Holidays, Spring Mill, Earby, Barnoldswick, Lancashire BB94 0AA. Brochures and bookings: 0870 197 6895.

www.country-holidays.co.uk

Stanton Lacy, near Ludlow
Sutton Court Farm Cottages

Grouped congenially around a courtyard, these skilfully converted stone farm buildings have long been a favourite among 'cottage guide' readers. Although this is no longer a working farm, it is surrounded by farming activity. (The lambs in the paddock in springtime are a reliable source of entertainment.) The cottages enjoy peace and quiet in an idyllic situation close to the owners' timbered farmhouse and provide an exceptionally comfortable base for exploring the quiet Shropshire countryside and the historic market town of Ludlow only five miles away. Many varied attractions are within easy reach: ruined castles, black and white villages, gardens, farms, shops and markets.

The six cottages (*Barleycorn, Woodsage, Sweetbriar, Hazelnut, Holly* and *Honeysuckle*, **sleeping 4, 6, 4, 4, 2 and 2** respectively) are comfortably furnished, with wood burners in Barleycorn and Woodsage. Each bathroom has an overbath shower, and there are TVs, videos and CD music systems. There are fitted carpets, night storage heating and electric blankets for the winter months. Holly is all on the ground floor, and has additional features suitable for accompanied wheelchair users. Honeysuckle is a first floor apartment, **cosy for 2**, with chairs outside to enjoy the evening sunshine. They all enjoy **'Visit Britain's'** highly desirable **Four Stars** classification.

There is an information room, payphone, laundry facilities and a children's playroom. Horse riding, cycle hire, trout fishing and golf are nearby. Cream teas and home cooked evening meals may be provided given at least 24 hours' notice. Christmas and New Year are special here, with *real* Christmas trees, decorations and mince pies awaiting visitors, a remarkable number of whom return here time and time again.

This excellent place is comfortably within our and our readers' top twenty in the British Isles, and probably in the top five in the Heart of England/Welsh Border country...

The cottages are open all year round and also offer bed and breakfast and short breaks from two nights. Well behaved pets are welcome in some cottages, at an extra charge. Cot and highchair available. Cost: from £210 to £499 (linen, towels, electricity and logs included). Details from Jane and Alan Cronin, Sutton Court Farm, Little Sutton, Stanton Lacy, Ludlow, Shropshire SY8 2AJ. Telephone 01584 861305, fax 861441.

www.suttoncourtfarm.co.uk

email: enquiries@suttoncourtfarm.co.uk

Cirencester
Cotswold Water Park: Lakeside Lodges

Over the years, while cottage visiting in Gloucestershire, we've spotted
The Cotswold Water Park from a
distance. Its 11,000 acres make a
peaceful and attractive location for a
tranquil holiday break in a rural setting with, among other good things,
picnic and barbecue sites, a beach of
Blue Flag standard, cycle tracks,
windsurfing, sailing and much more.

A different slant on a Cotswold holiday.

Lakeside Lodges provide accommo-
dation within the Park, **sleeping from 6 to 8**, though the configuration of
beds varies. Some have two doubles and a twin room, others may have a
double master bedroom and a children's room with bunk beds. Pets are
welcome. All have an open plan living area cum dining area downstairs,
opening on to a private sun deck. As well as the immediate charms of the
place, the Cotswolds offer a mass of 'places to go and things to see'.

Details from The Cottage Collection, 17-23 Ber Street, Norwich NR1
3EU. Telephone 01603 724809.

www.the-cottage-collection.co.uk
email: bookings@the-cottage-collection.co.uk

How Caple, near Ross-on-Wye
Cider Mill   map 9/514

Private and self contained, *Cider Mill* (**sleeping
4**) is really cosy and nicely lit – we met two
couples comfortably installed – with an inviting, log-burning fire in an inglenook, carpets
and rugs. The well equipped farmhouse-style
kitchen has a stable door on to a terrace and
rose garden. *Gardener's Cottage* (**sleeping up
to 8** in a twin and three doubles, with three
bathrooms) is very spacious: a real family
house, with beams, good carpeting and, again, a
most appealing sitting room with three deep
sofas as well as armchairs, books and an open
fire. There are french windows on to the garden. The separate dining room has a dining
table seating eight – helping to create one of the
most convivial properties we know. (Well-

*A delightful twosome in rural
but not remote Herefordshire,
with the owner at hand.*

behaved dogs welcome in Gardener's.) TVs. Linen/towels included. Cider
Mill cottage is **'Visit Britain' Five Stars**. Gardener's **Four**. No smoking in
Cider Mill. Cost: about £300 to £800.

Further details from Sue Farr, Garraway House, How Caple, Herefordshire
HR1 4SS. Or telephone 01438 869489.

Frampton-on-Severn, near Gloucester
The Orangery

One of our most memorable re-visits of 2006 was, on a glorious late summer day, to this extraordinary Grade II listed 18th century 'garden house'. We have known and loved it for many years, as have dozens of readers, and were agog to see the major upgrading of a number of rooms within the seductively beautiful building.

We took time to re-acquaint ourselves with the exterior, strolling beside the lily-strewn, carp-rich, ornamental canal that sets it off so handsomely. That's part of a Grade I listed garden, but guests have a double bonus in the form of their own private garden too. A note to new arrivals: though the entrance is at the side of the property, they should contrive to see the building from the front before they go in, though as side entrances go, it's a delight, as it gives on to the meadow-like village green.

In a lovely sheltered spot on the east bank of the River Severn, Frampton is known for its traditional rural scene, with summer cricket on the green and the famous Frampton Country Fair in the autumn. For nearly a thousand years the Frampton Court Estate has been at the heart of this ancient settlement, where splendid buildings around the green include the Orangery.

This is a rare delight, a real treat for people blessed with a sense of history.

Every single room is a gem, but this is no museum piece, and is to be 'lived in'.

We used to describe the interior as fascinating and comfortable rather than grand, being much impressed by the tiled fireplaces in the (south-facing) drawing room and dining room, by the spiral staircase, by the fabrics based on the Frampton Flora painted by five sisters in the 1800s. But the careful restoration and decoration of the last couple of years have lifted much of the interior on to a new plane, with the kitchen a special delight, in which the rare, original 18th century limestone walls of the building have been exposed. *All* the rooms are now pristine and beautiful, with antiques set off nicely by well chosen fabrics and, in the drawing room, a charming wall painting.

Cost: about £600 to £1000 per week.

Sleeps 8. Long weekends possible. TV/video/DVD. Central heating. Well-behaved dogs welcome. Details from The Secretary, Frampton Court Estate Office, Frampton-on-Severn, Gloucestershire GL2 7EP. Telephone/fax 01452 740698.

www.framptoncourtestate.co.uk
email: clifford@framptoncourt.wanadoo.co.uk

Goodrich, near Ross-on-Wye
Mainoaks Farm

We can hardly think of a more agreeable place from which to explore the Welsh borders and 'deepest Herefordshire', and it was a pleasure recently rather than a duty to revisit these superbly well situated cottages. 'Superbly well' means close to the shores of the River Wye, which is quite rare for a holiday house and much sought-after.

Turning off a B-road, we followed a farm lane and arrived at this quiet enclave of well converted stone built farm cottages. Each has its own character, ranging from 'bijou' to 'farmhousey and rambling'. Arriving by chance as a team of cleaners was busy preparing the cottages for incoming guests, we took time to look at all the cottages, noting for example the fine views from some windows, exposed beams, a nice spiral staircase.

They vary usefully in size – *Cider Mill*, for example, **sleeps up to 7**. We noted a number of appealing features: a woodburning stove in *Peregrine*, **sleeping 6**, which we also thought had 'a nice family atmosphere' and which was *converted* in 1659! It has a cruck beam in the bedrooms; Cider Mill's big, convivial dining table; the four poster bed in *Huntsham* (**sleeps 4**); the upstairs sitting room in *The Malthouse* (an 'upside-down' house, so designed as to make the most of the view).

The quality of the conversion work is exceptional with fine stone and brickwork and an impressive attention to architectural detail.

Ross-on-Wye and Monmouth are about ten minutes' drive, and Cheltenham Spa and the cathedral cities of Hereford, Worcester and Gloucester are easily accessible. The farm has a mile of frontage to the

A marvellous and unusual location, and very sympathetic conversion work.

Rather 'rustic' and comfortable rooms that reflect the very stylish exteriors.

River Wye, and salmon and course fishing beats can be booked locally. There are several golf courses, pony trekking, mountain bike tracks and inspiring waymarked Forestry Commission walks.

TVs, DVDs, radios/CD players and microwaves in each. Linen and towels included. Dogs by arrangement. Short breaks available. '**Visit Britain' Three/Four Stars**. Open all year. Cost: about £230 to £790.

Details from Patricia Unwin, Hill House, Chase End, Bromesberrow, Ledbury, Herefordshire HR8 1SE. Telephone 01531 650448.

www.mainoaks.co.uk
email: info@mainoaks.co.uk

Owlpen, near Uley
Owlpen Manor Cottages

Readers often ask if and when we've stayed in the cottages we write about. We've stayed twice at Owlpen, which we have a special affection for, as it has featured in this guide since our tentative beginnings in 1983. We stayed most recently during a golden late summer, in light, spacious *Manor Farm*, at the very heart of the estate.

With its softly enfolding hills, its mellow buildings, its woods and pastures, Owlpen is an amazing survivor, a thousand miles from the rat-race, a small corner of England preserved at its most nostalgic and unspoiled.

The nine cottages, and fine Tudor manor house where owners Nicholas and Karin Mander live, complement the idyll. The cottages are scattered throughout the many-acred valley, along a lane here, up a track there, in sight of the main house, or tucked away in the woods. *Grist Mill* (**sleeps 8/9**) – we've stayed in it: a remarkable historic survivor – and *Woodwells* (**sleeps 6**), are favourites. But on a late summer day we also admired *Summerfield* (**sleeps 2**), *Marlings End* (**sleeps 5**), *The Court House* (**sleeps 4**), *Peter's Nest* (**sleeps 2**), *Tithe Barn* (**sleeps 2**), *Manor Farm* (**sleeps 4**) and *Over Court* (**sleeps 5**). The latter two can be let as one large family house **sleeping 9**, with an internal door from one to the other.

We can also recommend the cosy restaurant, where visitors to the manor house rub shoulders with cottage guests. In a converted old cider house,

The Grist Mill is a historic building skilfully adapted to modern use...   *...but it's just one of several properties of great character in an amazing location.*

this feels like a cross between a smart restaurant for an occasion and an upmarket pub. There's an excellent, sophisticated menu, and good wines.

The Manor House and three of the properties are officially 'listed' as buildings of architectural and historic interest, but their intrinsic charm is enhanced by contemporary comfort and cosiness, and an exceptional flair for decor, fabrics and furnishings. There are remote control TVs, videos, radio/alarms, antiques, telephones, hairdryers and food mixers (some have dishwashers, microwaves, freezers, washing machines, log fires and four-posters), and an on-site laundry service. All the cottages have '**Visit Britain' Four Stars**. They have central heating, and are set off by well chosen paintings, deep sofas, good quality fabrics and some king-size beds.

For a copy of the most attractive colour brochure, contact Nicholas and Karin Mander, Owlpen Manor, near Dursley, Gloucestershire GL11 5BZ. Telephone 01453 860261. Fax 860819.

www.owlpen.com   email: sales@owlpen.com

228

Canon Frome, near Ledbury
The Swiss Chalet

On a warm late summer day, needing to check the local map even though we had been here before, it was a pleasure to rediscover this (really!) unique property, recently repainted and 'freshencd up'. By a weir on the River Frome, The Swiss Chalet is a most delightful and amusing holiday cottage. It has the makings of a romantic stay **for 2**. From a comfortable but naturally not large, double

This is one of the most romantic places we know: you can hide yourselves away!

bedroom, on the ground floor, you ascend a 'ship's ladder' to the first floor where you can hide yourselves from the world. From a balcony overlooking the water you will probably see kingfishers, and in late autumn see salmon jumping the weir. There are deep and comfortable sofa/chairs, a kitchenette with dining bar, lots of warmth, a high beamed ceiling: all this adds up to a remarkable holiday retreat.

TV. Dogs by arrangement. Cost: about £194 to £370. Linen provided. Further details from Julian and Lorna Rutherford, Mill Cottage, Canon Frome, Ledbury, Herefordshire HR8 2TD. Telephone 01531 670506 or 07901 667474.

email: julian.rutherford@virgin.net

Fairford/Chedworth
The Mill Cottages/Littlecote   map 9/519/529

The Mill Cottages, at Fairford, are two little gems within a handsome Grade II listed Mill House. Just a short walk from Fairford's peaceful market square, one is bordered by water on three sides and both have open fires. **Sleep 6 'plus 1' and 7 'plus 1'**. Refs NQL and NXE. Also, quite near the fabulous Chedworth Roman Villa (stunning mosaics) pretty, detached *Littlecote* makes a handsome small base for exploring the area. Or you could just stay put and unwind in comfort. (The living

Millstream Cottage (the two gables, above) is one of 'The Mill Cottages'. A reason for its popularity among readers is its proximity to the centre of Fairford.

room, for example, has an open fire and rugs on a flagstone floor.) **Sleeps 3 'plus 1'** in a zip-link twin and a single plus a second single bed. Ref NW6.

Details from from English Country Cottages, Stoney Bank Road, Earby, Barnoldswick BB94 0AA. Brochures and bookings: 0870 197 6890.

www.english-country-cottages.co.uk

Docklow, near Leominster
Docklow Manor

The location is a delight: very quiet, though not isolated, amid peaceful countryside, and with views towards the Black Mountains and Brecon Beacons. Most recently, on a perfect late August morning, we turned off the Bromyard to Leominster road and then along a tree lined private drive to revisit one of the consistently best loved cottage enclaves we know: it has featured in this guide every year *since it was first published in 1983.*

Docklow is in easy reach of Ludlow, one of the handsomest towns in England. There are National Trust mansions and gardens nearby, and the cathedrals at Hereford and Worcester are easily accessible.

We met the fairly new owners for the first time. They, Jane and Brian Viner, have retained and refurbished three of the original seven cottages. We looked in all three, and met very contented guests – in one case, readers of *The Good Holiday Cottage Guide.*

Specifically, *Woodlands Cottage* has three double bedrooms and a well-equipped kitchen, with dishwasher, washing machine and tumble dryer. It has its own front garden, with a barbecue and glorious views. *Yewtree Cottage* has two double bedrooms, a comfortable kitchen/living-room, and a private back garden with access to a secluded orchard. *Manor Cottage* is a romantic hideaway, with a four-poster bed. Like neighbouring Yewtree, it overlooks an ancient stone cider press: a picture-postcard setting.

Staying at Docklow is like being part of a traditional English village.

Cottage interiors are comfortable, warm, quiet and have plenty of character.

Each cottage has a TV, video recorder, and books, videos and games. The more energetic can enjoy the manor house's five acres of formal gardens and woodland, or play table tennis and table football in the Victorian conservatory. Guests are encouraged to feed the free-range bantams, and play with Fergus, the golden retriever. (Note: well behaved dogs are welcome.) Children are welcome: the Viners have three, who deliver occasional treats to the cottages such as home-made ice-cream. The Viners also offer dinner either in their manor house or, pre-prepared, supplied to the cottages.

Cost: from £175 for three nights in Manor Cottage in low-season to £550 for a week in Woodlands in peak season. **'Visit Britain' Three Stars**. Linen included.

Details from Docklow Manor, Docklow, Leominster, Herefordshire HR6 0RX. Telephone 01568 760668. Or you can book through the website:

www.docklow-manor.co.uk   email: enquiries@docklow-manor.co.uk

Little Boynes Holiday Cottages
The Orangery and The Byre

A few minutes' drive along country lanes from quaint old Upton-upon-Severn are two charming properties, both centrally heated and pristinely clean and tidy. The converted *Orangery* **sleeps 4 plus 2** in two bedrooms (a double and a twin), a well-equipped kitchen, an open plan sitting/dining room with a log burner and a sofa bed. The sympathetically converted *Byre* has one bedroom

This was a lucky find last summer...

with a double or twin beds as required, a bathroom with shower-over, and an open plan kitchenette and living room, with futon for 1. Guests in both share the use of the indoor swimming pool (32°C, all year round) the spa and jacuzzi, games room and gardens. Linen and fuel included. Digital TV, DVD, video, music system. Microwave and fridge/freezer. Shared laundry room with washing machine/dryer.

Cost: from about £360 to £630 for the Orangery and from about £180 to £350 for the Byre. No pets, no smoking, no children under seven. Details: Chris and Sheila Martin, Little Boynes, Upper Hook Road, Upton-upon-Severn, Worcestershire WR8 0SB. Telephone/fax 01684 594788.

www.little-boynes.co.uk email: info@little-boynes.co.uk

Sedgeberrow, near Evesham
Hall Farm   map 9/538

We know these properties well, and have stayed several times, always appreciating the tea tray, with scones and jam. Plus wine! The seven cottages are exceptionally sympathetic barn conversions that benefit from their quiet village location (a shop/post office, a good pub) on the edge of the Cotswolds, a few minutes' drive from busy Evesham. Each retains a number of original features.

Reliably comfortable, with easy access to the Cotswolds and Shakespeare country.

The cottages are fully equipped to a high standard, and the rather cosy interiors (good beds!) include a number of antiques. Guests can relax in an acre of gardens, or use the owners' heated outdoor pool, only a five minute walk away. **Sleep 2 to 6.** Cost: about £225 to £750, including linen, towels, heating and electricity. TV, video, DVD in all cottages. Washer/dryer and dishwasher in all the cottages. Pets not accepted.

Details from Rebecca Barclay, Hall Farm Cottages, Sedgeberrow, Evesham, Worcestershire WR11 7UF. Telephone 01386 881243.

www.hallfarmcottages.net
email: enquiries@hallfarmcottages.net

The Cotswolds
Discover the Cotswolds*

This agency gets much of its strong following from its personalised, 'hands on' approach. With just 30 or so cottages on her books, owner Alison Lewis knows every-stick-and-stone, which our readers love.

There's a nice mixture of rural and village or small-town locations. For example, in a little jewel of a village called Condicote, *The Old Chapel* is a romantic hideaway **for 2 people**, plus a 'guest bed' for children over eight. There's a woodburning stove.

A recent arrival on the scene, next door to Barn Cottage (pictured below) is *Rick Cottage*, in Chipping Campden. **Sleeping 6**, it has been designed with seriously disabled guests in mind.

Among places we have yet to see but have had glowing reports of is *Swallow Barn* (**sleeping 6**). Peacefully situated in the hamlet of Duntisbourne Rouse, a fifteen minute drive from Cirencester, it's one of a pair on the owners' farm. Comfortably furnished to a very high standard – it's **'Visit Britain' Five Stars** – amid idyllic countryside, this makes a super retreat. Families will appreciate the bonus of a large grassed area away from the cottage and safely fenced off, especially designed for children's games.

One of our favourite Cotswold villages is Oddington (the two good pubs are a bonus!). There, 'Discover the Cotswolds' has *Rose Cottage*, a little gem quietly located on a back lane. **Sleeping 4**, and incorporating a number of original features, it has an open fire and 'a tiny but south-facing and secluded back garden'.

But lack of space prevents us from doing more than scratch the surface of this admirable organisation: the well organised, easy to use website will reveal all.

Walnut Wing Cottage (on the left) shares the historic character of this classic Cotswold stone beauty...

Barn Cottage (not featured) is 'the real thing' – and is about 400 years old. Better yet, it's near Chipping Campden.

Details/brochure from 'Discover the Cotswolds', 2 School Cottages, Cider Mill Lane, Chipping Campden, Gloucestershire GL55 6HX. Telephone 01386 841441.

www.discoverthecotswolds.net

email: info@discoverthecotswolds.net

*l Holidays – Devon, Cornwall and beyond. This West Country specialist is virtually a
old name. They feature some real beauties, including houses right by the sea...*

*en-away properties where you'll hardly meet a soul during your stay and a number of
ses that will suit large groups...*

*its share of 'roses-round-the-door' thatched cottages, and places with historical
tions, such as the two amazing places above. Pages 201-203.*

*uth Holiday Homes, Devon. Super
rom many properties. Page 205.*

*Salcombe Holiday Homes. Reliable properties
in one of Devon's most-loved places. Page 191.*

Braddon Cottages, Devon. A dependable, peaceful escape from every-day cares. Page 188.

Wheel Farm, North Devon. A pool, a tenn court, near the sea but rural too. Page 18

The Swiss Chalet, Herefordshire. An impressive and unusual property: readers love it! Page 229.

Buckland, Worcestershire. One of our favourite Cotswold villages. Page 245.

Pekes, East Sussex. 'Incomparable', say readers. Also 'unique...great fun!' Page 218.

Owlpen, Gloucestershire. An unforgettal place:'rural England stands still'. Page

Poole Keynes, Gloucestershire. Two super finds, in a less famous corner of the county. Page 241.

The Old Dairy, Gloucestershire. The co a joy, the view a double-joy. Page 244.

h Country Cottages (main feature, Pages 250/251) also covers Scotland and Wales (there's rate brochure for Scotland). The organisation is now virtually a household name...

and above right, there's an extraordinary collection of cottages and fine houses that seem up the best of what's to be had, for example, in Cornwall and the Cotswolds...

Welsh programme is appreciated by the tourist board, and they've secured many ional' cottages, as above. Also above, right: a charming North Yorkshire cottage.

er the British Isles, their range is huge, but they are known for their properties of ter, historic interest and comfort. These two are in Cornwall and Dorset...

Vivat Trust, Shropshire. Some marvellous restorations, an inspiration to stay in. Page 26.

Heath Farm Cottages, Oxfordshire. Qui remarkable – a tour de force! Page 248.

'Village and Country', Co Clare. Stylish places in a sought-after location. Page 262.

Ballina, Co Mayo. Modern comfort, clean inexpensive, great for touring. Page 259

Cottages – main features on Pages 117 and 254/255 – is one of the three or four prominent agencies in the country. It has 'properties with facilities', many rural jewels...

several places ideal for extended families, such as this (above left) in rural Somerset and right) near the sea in Wales. This one sleeps up to twenty!

so many properties of character is this beauty near Barnard Castle, in much underrat-nty Durham and (above right) this country property, again near the sea in Wales.

l Suffolk you can stay in the wing of a handsome country house, above, and, in hire's Peak District, among so many possibilities, this charmer in the Hope Valley.

National Trust Cottages have come on in leaps and bounds during the past few years. As y might expect, virtually all their properties are full of character and rich in history...

By definition, properties tend to be in interesting locations. Those featured here are (top) Norfolk and, above, Scotland and Northern Ireland. Main feature: Pages 24/25.

Bruern Cottages, Oxfordshire. In a little known but handsome village setting village setting dominated by a great country mansion, these are like little palaces. Interiors are exquisite..

...with fine antiques, original paintings, expensive carpets and fabrics; gardens are in ke and there's a nice balance between keeping one's privacy and 'meeting new people'. Pa

...ry Holidays (main feature on Pages 252/253) have a bigger selection of individual ...es than any other operator, so holidaymakers needing variety tend to be regulars.

...ppreciate this fine mill in North Yorkshire, adjacent to a waterfall once sketched by ...' Turner, and this deeply rural property near Kendal, on the edge of 'the Lakes'.

...g people's dreams-come-true are such places as (above left) an unusual farmhouse in ...shire and, right, a beauty near Cheriton Bishop, in rural Devon.

...s this superbly well situated cottage in the West of Scotland, close to a sandy beach, and ...htful place in Naunton, near Bourton-on-the-Water, in the Cotswolds.

Colour section B, Page 7

With over 9,000 dream cottages...

ENGLAND • WALES • SCOTLAND • IRELAND • FRANCE

...where will you escape to next?

There has never been a wider choice of superb self-catering cottages for you to discover. Plan your escape now to some of the most beautiful properties situated in the most sought after locations.

All our cottages are regularly inspected and graded so you can always expect quality properties, with excellent facilities – a real home from home. From quaint, romantic hideaways in beautiful rural settings, to spectacular sea, lake and mountain locations, superbly appointed, many with pools, just waiting to welcome you.

Over 9,000 cottages @ one address
Visit www.cottages4you.co.uk where you can search through all of our properties, which will allow you to choose the one that is perfect for you. It's simple to use and many of our properties have a virtual tour, allowing you to discover your dream get-away before you leave home.

So visit www.cottages4you.co.uk now to discover your perfect holiday cottage

cottages4you

Poole Keynes, near Cirencester
Old Mill Farm

After the comparative hustle and bustle of nearby Cirencester we enjoy detouring to these quietly situated converted barns – at the end of a series of meandering country lanes. On two sides of the not-very-busy farmyard are four cottages **sleeping from 2/3 to 7** (all have space for a cot). We really liked – and have stayed in – *Thames Cottage*: it liter-

We've stayed several times, and love the quiet but not hard-to-find location...

ally backs on to the stream that is the infant River Thames. Stylish, comfortable, light and bright, it has some exposed stone walls, lots of pine. It has a double room downstairs, and the main (galleried) double has a five foot bed. Next door is *Granary*, the littlest, also with a five foot double and backing on to the stream: both cottages have a little balcony. We didn't see *Tuppenny Cottage* but met a family enjoying their stay in single-storeyed *Stable*, with french windows on to the yard and the biggest sitting room/diner. Dogs welcome. TVs. Linen, not towels included. Dishwashers in the larger cottages. Cost: £195 to £700. Details from Gordon and Catherine Hazell, Ermin House Farm, Syde, Cheltenham, Gloucestershire GL53 9PN. Telephone 01285 821255. Fax 821531.

www.oldmillcottages.co.uk email: catherine@oldmillcottages.fsnet.co.uk

---

Poole Keynes, near Cirencester map 9/523
Moondara/Island Lodge

These are quite extraordinary places. *Moondara* (**Colour section B, Page 2**) and *Island Lodge* (right) are traditional Finnish log houses on a private, peaceful, secluded 100 acre lake in the Cotswolds. It's a 'Site of Special Scientific Interest', mainly because of its over-wintering wildfowl, its nightingale colony and its (yes!) seventeen species of dragonfly. Coarse fishing is available (excellent pike, for exam-

Here are two delights, in a little-known corner of England. This is Island Lodge.

ple) and the property, which has a two mile perimeter path landscaped around it, comes with a four-man rowing boat. The path has superb lake views and is of course a vantage point from which to observe wildlife. Both properties have covered verandahs with memorable lake views and an open plan living room with woodburner. Moondara **sleeps 8** and costs between £690 and £1280 per week. Island Lodge **sleeps 4** and costs between £495 and £920. Short breaks available at two thirds of the weekly price. Dogs welcome. **'Visit Britain' Four Stars**. Further details from Log House Holidays, Poole Keynes, Cirencester, Gloucestershire GL7 6ED. Telephone 01285 770082 Fax 770053.

www.loghouseholidays.co.uk email: relax@loghouseholidays.co.uk

The Cotswolds and beyond
Rural Retreats*

We're gratified but never surprised when we hear from readers, as we so often do, about how much they've enjoyed Rural Retreats properties. The distinctive Rural Retreats style (always properties of character, often with historical associations, very well cared-for, a fine attention to detail) seems to suit them particularly well.

The many readers who have discovered Rural Retreats through *The Good Holiday Cottage Guide* won't be surprised to know that they only accept about one in four of the properties offered.

Being based at Moreton-in-Marsh, Rural Retreats are particularly strong in the Cotswolds, but their selection of over 400 properties now extends all over England, Scotland and Wales, from Cornwall to the Scottish Highlands.

On arrival, you'll be greeted with a complimentary hamper sitting on the kitchen table, a bottle of wine chilling in the fridge, and often a log fire waiting to be lit. Many of the properties are several hundred years old, so you can expect to find plenty of character too. And there are invariably nice interior touches like handsome table-lamps, expensive curtains, good quality rugs, pretty bedspreads and complimentary toiletries.

Another bonus is that at any time of the year you can choose which days of the week you want to arrive and leave (minimum stay is often only two nights). TVs, bedlinen, towels, electricity, fire logs and cots/highchairs are all included in the price; the only item charged extra is calls from the pay-phone. Dinner delivery to the door is often available too, and at some properties you can even arrange for an expert cook to take over the kitchen and prepare dinner.

The fine brochure simplifies the task of choosing where to stay by having very clear maps and an index which lists the properties by size, by whether they have ground-floor bedrooms and by whether dogs are

The Pendeen Lighthouse properties are an experience, not just 'a place to stay'!

Watermill Cottages: a great location, and each property with its own character.

allowed. And an 'activity' index shows those suitable for guests who want a swimming pool, a hot tub, tennis, fishing or cycle hire.

Some of the most interesting properties, thanks to Rural Retreats' partnership with Trinity House, are former lighthouse-keepers' cottages. Three of them, all single-storey, are in a group of four at the foot of the famous Pendeen lighthouse, just six miles north of Lands End. Built in 1900, it

242

was automated in 1994, but an attendant who lives in the fourth cottage conducts brief tours for the public four days a week, Easter to September. And you must be prepared for the fog-horn to sound when necessary! *Vestal* and *Solebay* cottages both **sleep 4**, *Argus* **sleeps 3**. Ref CW-032/3/4.

Two lighthouse-keepers' cottages ideal for keen golfers are situated beside the Cromer lighthouse on the north Norfolk coast, adjacent to the 18-hole Royal Cromer course. *Valonia* **sleeps 6** and *The Link* **sleeps 2**. Ref NO-034 & 051.

There are in fact now twelve sites, from Yorkshire to Cornwall and the Channel Isles, that feature lighthouse keepers' cottages.

Among Rural Retreats' many lovely old properties in the Cotswolds, the aptly-named *Cotswold Cottage* at Tetbury is a period semi-detached stone building, **sleeping 5,** with TV in each of the three bedrooms. Its gardens are unusual in that the front one has a pond and small waterfall and the rear one has a hot tub (for year-round use). Ref CO-163.

In the Peak District, walkers appreciate *Memorial Cottage* at Eyam as an ideal location. **Sleeping 2** plus a child, it is a Grade II listed stone terraced house a few minutes' walk from the centre of the beautiful unspoilt village, high in the moors of the National Park. Ref DE-024. Nearby, in a restored 18th-century cotton mill on the River Derwent, a spacious ground floor apartment **sleeping 4/6** is available. Each room is south-facing and has lovely views. Ref DE-025.

During 2006 we had glowing reports of, for example, *John Sparrow's House*, **sleeping 10**, one of the 'Watermill' cottages, in a notably pretty location – which is really saying something – in rural East Suffolk. In the Deben valley (the River Deben at Woodbridge being one of our favourite places in England) there are two other properties – *Tarka* and *Bluebell*, each **sleeping 4**. Refs SU023, SU022, SUO24.

And one regular readers has said he 'will definitely book' 200-year-old *Nuthatch* (Ref SH020) **sleeping 6**. Beautifully situated in an Area of Outstanding Natural Beauty in Shropshire, with views of Clunbury Hill, it has an open inglenook fire and many original features. Ref SH020.

Holcombe is near Hemyock, which has a pub, a post office, a shop and a 'chippie'.

Lochenkit is in a most desirable remote setting on the edge of the moors.

Further details from Rural Retreats, Draycott Business Centre, Moreton-in-Marsh, Gloucestershire GL56 9JY. Telephone 01386 701177.

www.ruralretreats.co.uk

email: info@ruralretreats.co.uk

Cleve Hill, near Winchcombe
The Old Dairy

One of our long-time Cotswold favourites.

Whenever we call in to see this outstandingly well-cared-for and characterful cottage we also build in time
to enjoy the view. For not only is this
property a delightful *tour de force*
done to a superb standard (**'Visit
Britain' Four Stars**), it also has an
amazing 180-degree panorama over
the Severn Vale to the Black Moun-
tains. After taking a narrow track off the Winchcombe/Cheltenham road,
one snakes past the owners' house, then climbs higher. We love the huge
sitting room, its woodburning stove and oak floor, the vaulted ceiling, the
gallery at one end. Downstairs, from that main room you go through to a
stylish kitchen. A good-sized bathroom leads to a pristine double bedroom
(ensuite). Upstairs are two twin rooms, and another bathroom. The house
is light and heated partly by solar panels.

Sleeps up to 8 (including the use of a futon). TV/video/DVD/CD.
Linen/towels included. Not suitable for pets. Cost: about £370 to £1200.
Details: Rickie and Jennie Gauld, Slades Farm, Bushcombe Lane, Cleeve
Hill, Cheltenham, Gloucestershire GL52 3PN. Telephone/fax 01242
676003. Mobile 07860 598323 and 07764 613284.

www.cotswoldcottages.btinternet.co.uk
also: **www.btinternet.com/~cotswoldcottages**
email: **rickieg@btinternet.com**

Bruern Cottages

The village of Bruern (near Chipping Norton, in Oxfordshire) is beautiful,
but notable (in our terms) for Bruern Cottages. Each is like a mini-stately
home, with open fires, soft and subtle lighting, deep sofas, fine paintings
and prints, many antiques, good quality rugs and carpets, five-foot four-
poster beds in several cases, show-house kitchens, the sort of bathrooms
you would find in discreet, expensive Mayfair hotels. Each has its own
character, as well as its own particular fans: they **sleep from 2 to 8**.

'Visit Britain' Five Stars. Not suitable for pets. Changeover day is either
Friday or Monday. Cost: about £550 (for the smallest cottage out of sea-
son) to £4750 (for the biggest in high season). Telephone 01993 830415.
Fax 831750. Mobile 07802 182092.

www.bruern.co.uk   email: enquiries@bruern.co.uk

Exhall, near Alcester
Glebe Farm

There's a skilful use of the available space in the conversion here of one-time barns that stand around three sides of a traditional farmyard. Of the ten properties, five are single storeyed cottages, *The Stable* is a sizeable, two storeyed, and chintzily comfortable house with lots of beams and lots of warmth (shower only, not bath). One of the cottages, *Mill Meer,* is suitable for people with limited mobility. Most recently

Neat and warm cottages well placed for Shakespeare Country and the Marches. There are two good pubs in the village, both serving food, and others just a short drive away...

available, within a handsome converted barn, are *Duck Pond* and *Goose,* deliberately made for flexibility. There are two apartments done to a very high standard in a separate, detached, one-time cartshed, called *The Granary* and *The Cart Hovel.*

One dog per cottage welcome. TV. All linen and towels, electricity and heating included. Cost: about £150 to £500. Details from Roger Arbutt, Glebe Farm, Exhall, Alcester, Warwickshire B49 6EA. Telephone/fax 01789 772202.

www.glebefarmcottages.net   email: enquiries@glebefarmcottages.net

---

Buckland, near Broadway   map 9/534
Hillside Cottage/The Bothy   Colour section B, Page 2

Buckland is one of our half dozen favourite Cotswold villages At the end of its picture-postcard street (it's a no-through-road) you continue uphill to locate three comfortable, private, self contained properties. Two are 'upside down' (first floor sitting rooms, from which you look down on the outer reaches of this leafy, honey-coloured village), the new one – *The Nook* (**sleeps 2**) – is on the ground floor, and can inter-

A lovingly cared for duo of properties in one of our favourite Cotswold villages.

communicate (to suit a larger family or a group of friends) with *Hillside* (**sleeps 4**). All are adjacent to but have separate entrances from the own-ers' home. We like the beamed ceilings, the open fires, the comparative roominess, the comfy sofas. One of the bedrooms in Bothy (also **sleeping 4**) has a four-poster. There is a good sized indoor heated pool available all day, and a garden with barbecue. A bonus for walkers: the Cotswold Way is yards from the cottages. TV with teletext. Linen/towels included. Dogs welcome. Cost: about £280 to £560. Details from Bob Edmondson, Burhill, Buckland, Worcestershire WR12 7LY. Telephone 01386 853426. Mobile 07811 353344.

www.burhill.co.uk   email: bob.e@tesco.net

245

The Cotswolds
Manor Cottages and Cotswold Retreats*

During 2006 we met the new owner of this highly regarded medium-sized agency, enviably based in the heart of sought-after Burford. 'Manor Cottages' are known for dealing almost exclusively with properties that offer 'the true Cotswolds experience': places of real character and, sometimes, historical associations, as well as picture-postcard locations.

We looked at a handful of typically chic properties, absolutely pristine inside and out but very much in keeping with their surroundings. Four of these stand together in the Oxfordshire-Cotswolds in the quiet, little-known but not remote village of Lyneham, near Burford. As neat and pretty as (four) maids-in-a-row, **sleeping 2, 3, 3 and 4**, they are contained within the building that was once the village school, and are little jewels.

Then, just over the border (some border!) in Wiltshire, at Luckington, we saw *The Forge*. This is also quietly situated, with owners conveniently at hand and with all the accommodation on the ground floor. **Sleeping 4**, it

'Maids in a row', in sleepy, little-known Lyneham, near Burford.

Gable Cottage, in Lower Quinton, is a classic of its kind, and sumptuous inside.

is expensively ultra-modern, with for example surround-sound TV and a cosy corner-sofa. Booking days are flexible.

We have also visited a couple of the agency's houses in the village of Lower Quinton, between Stratford-upon-Avon and Broadway. *Elmhurst* **(sleeping 9)** and *Gable Cottage* **(sleeping 7)** are real charmers, though different in character. The latter is a plushly comfortable jewel, a real no-expense-spared *tour de force*, in which the powerful (and very recent) combination of a specialist builder and an interior designer is a delight to see. Elmhurst is more farmhousey in character. We like the big family kitchen, the spacious bedrooms in most cases, the country antiques, the unfussy comfort.

Most properties sleep **from 2 to 4/6**, with a sprinkling of places that will take **7/9**, and three or four will **sleep 8/9**. Because of the location of the Cotswolds and the now established demand from London weekenders, among others, short breaks are often available at a sensible price.

Dogs and other pets are welcome in about half the properties. Brochure/details from Chris Grimes, Manor Cottages and Cotswold Retreats, Priory Mews, 33A Priory Lane, Burford OX18 4SG. Telephone 01993 824252. Fax 824443.

www.manorcottages.co.uk
email: chris.grimes@cottagesetc.com

Cottage in the Country*
(Incorporating Cottage Holidays)

This long established agency has as its main patch the Cotswolds, Oxfordshire and the Thames Valley, with a nod to Herefordshire, Shropshire, Buckinghamshire and Hertfordshire. It has always appealed to overseas visitors as well as holidaymakers from within the UK. Oxford, Stratford-upon-Avon, Ledbury and Windsor are among the places that attract. There are also houses within the Thames Valley, there are properties easily accessible by train from central London. The ones we know tend to be in the Cotswolds or Worcestershire or Herefordshire, where there are some real beauties.

They have a great choice, including three stunning cottages near Hereford, a real little jewel in pretty Swinbrook called *The Coach House* and (new last year) a lovely property a few miles from Henley-on-Thames with a huge sitting room with beams and a vaulted ceiling.

With **'Visit Britain'** gradings of **Two to Five**, and properties that are all known by the staff, this organisation comes highly recommended.

Details from Cottage in the Country, Tukes Cottage, 66 West Street, Chipping Norton, Oxfordshire OX7 5ER. Telephone: 0870 0275930. Fax: 0870 0275934.

www.cottageinthecountry.co.uk
email: ghc@cottageinthecountry.co.uk

Titley/Yarpole, near Leominster

Once part of a blacksmith's shop, in a rural part of one of England's prettiest counties, a semi-detached 400-year-old cottage in the village of Titley, in the heart of 'cider country' **sleeps just 2** in a double. The charming cottage **(map 9/515)** has that always-appealing combination of central heating and woodburner. for which all the fuel is included. Ref W41229. Neatly **sleeping 5**, a picture-perfect black and white cottage at Yarpole (the style is variously known as 'magpie' or even

A romantic hideaway in Titley, in one of "middle England's" quietest counties.

'licorice allsorts'!) is a good base **(map 9/502)** from which to explore the gloriously accessible Malvern Hills, the Welsh border country, 'Shakespeare Country' and the Cotswolds. It is for example only ten miles from much sought-after Ludlow. **Sleeps 5**.

Details of these and many others from Welcome Cottages, Spring Mill, Earby, Barnoldswick, Lancashire BB94 0AA. Brochures and bookings: 0870 197 6957.

www.welcomecottages.com

Swerford, near Chipping Norton
Heath Farm Cottages

These are almost 'in a class of their own'. We revisited two seasons ago, and, having inspected the latest property to become available, came away even more full of admiration. For this is a superlatively comfortable and thoughtfully equipped group of five cottages, which make an excellent base from which to explore the whole of the unspoilt Cotswolds, the glories of Oxfordshire and, further afield, Shakespeare Country.

There's a pretty, flower-filled courtyard with a mature water garden, 70 acres of meadows and woodland readily accessible, extraordinary views of large tracts of rural Oxfordshire from the courtyard and some windows of the five golden ironstone cottages, and exceptional interiors.

David Barbour, who with his wife Nena has created such a haven of comfort at Heath Farm, is a master craftsman with his own joinery business. For example, all the interior doors and the windows, the kitchen units and much of the furniture is hand-made *on site*: a joy to see. (In one of the larger properties, attached to the Barbours' own house, we admired handsome hand-made high backed dining chairs in elm from the farm itself.)

Beechnut and *Hazelnut* **sleep 2**, but both also have sofabeds. They are compact, comfortable and private, with rugs, expensive small sofas, cosy lamps, a skilful use of space. Across the courtyard are *Chestnut*, **sleeping 2** (but it also has a sofabed), and *Walnut,* **sleeping 4**. They are exceptional by any standards, with lots of space, a six foot double bed in the latter, rugs on slate floors. Walnut is a little palace, with a big sitting room, ceiling to floor windows, fabulous views (it's on two floors), a magnificent dining table, exposed stone walls, handsome beams, a superb bathroom/perhaps the most impressive shower-room we've ever seen! The most recently available cottage is *Cobnut*, **sleeping 4** in two ensuite twins/doubles (that is, zip-link beds). Among so many good things, there are extraordinary views from the master bedroom and a top of the range power shower.

All have open fires for which logs are provided. Cobnut is **'Visit Britain'** **Five Stars**, the others are **Four Stars**: we'd have thought Five throughout. Electricity, central heating, linen and towels included. Non smokers only. 'Sorry, no pets.' Cost: £276 to £658 (Christmas/New Year cost extra). Credit cards accepted. Details/brochure from David and Nena Barbour, Heath Farm, Swerford, near Chipping Norton, Oxfordshire OX7 4BN. Telephone 01608 683270/683204. Fax 683222.

www.heathfarm.com email: barbours@heathfarm.com

Award-winning properties, effectively all 'Visit Britain' Five Stars...

...are outstanding, among much else, for the craftsmanship of the interiors.

248

Churchill, near Chipping Norton
The Little Cottage

A long-time favourite with readers, not least because it fits so harmoniously into its villagey surroundings, this cosy and inexpensive cottage has a woodburner, oak beams, a neat sitting room enhanced by good quality, co-ordinated furnishings, adjacent to a well planned kitchen that leads to a pretty garden. There's lots of pine, a separate dining room, a metal, not plastic, bath in a good-sized bathroom

Neat and comfortable, and very reasonably priced for a popular location.

and a charming twin/double bedroom. Picturesque, quiet, little-known Churchill, on the eastern edge of the Cotswolds, has a fine church, a village green and a quantity of traditional, honey-coloured stone cottages, of which The Little Cottage (in the middle of a terrace of three and on a not very busy B-road) is one. '**Visit Britain' Four Stars**. Non smoking. Small TV/video. Laundry available (washer/drier). Not suitable for dogs. Central heating over which guests have control. Linen/towels included. Cost: £225 to £315 **for 2** plus cot. Short breaks off-season: three nights for £165. Details from David and Jacky Sheppard, Gables Cottage, Junction Road, Churchill, Oxfordshire OX7 6NW. Telephone 01608 658674.

www.littlecottage.co.uk

East Hagbourne
The Oast House, Manor Farm   map 9/548

Another 'cottage guide' fixture for over 20 years, with lots of praise from readers, *The Oast House* is quietly situated. On the edge of the village of East Hagbourne, below the Berkshire Downs and half way between the 12th century church and the farmhouse where owner Robin Harries lives, it is more spacious than its creeper-covered appearance suggests, and has five bedrooms. (The one on the ground floor can be used

Very much a family house, with a tennis court by arrangement.

for alternative sleeping arrangements.) The master bedroom has a five foot bed. The living room has a Victorian style gas fired stove as an appealing back-up to the central heating. On the ground floor there is also a separate dining room, a modern kitchen which includes a dishwasher, and a utility room with washing machine and drier, a shower and a third loo. **Sleeps 6/8**. TV/DVD/video plus satellite TV and freeview. Not suitable for dogs. '**Visit Britain' Four Stars**. Details are available from Robin Harries, Manor Farm, East Hagbourne, Oxfordshire. Telephone/fax 01235 815005.

email: manorfarm.easthag@virgin.net

English Country Cottages*

When 'ECC' was set up nearly thirty years ago, its aim was to provide 'superior and beautifully well-equipped holiday homes'. A clear measure of its undoubted success ever since is that over two-thirds of the bookings the company receives are from people who have holidayed with them before. Furthermore their reputation is by no means limited to the UK. Our own reader responses from the USA and Canada show a greater awareness of ECC than any other agency.

The cottages, including over 2500 available year-round, are spread not only all over England but also Wales. You'll find them located everywhere from picturesque villages to lonely clifftops. Big or small, smart or quaint, each is carefully described in the hefty 584-page brochure which is helpfully grouped into ten colour-coded regional sections, each starting with an introduction to the area.

'How will we find you?' asked visiting friends. They won't need a map! Ref CNN. Lighthouse Cottage is in Norfolk.

West Lynch, near Porlock in Somerset, is set amid stunning landscape and has far-reaching views. Ref EJL.

For people seeking a large property, the brochure has a useful index of those accommodating ten or more people. Properties with swimming pools are also listed, separated into private and shared ones. So no-one should have any difficulty in finding his or her own special 'treasure', whether for a full holiday or short break.

Last summer we had an idyllic week in Somerset staying with a group of friends at *West Lynch*, a beautiful thatched farmhouse at Allerford, close to Porlock. Owned by the same family for over 300 years, its rambling interior (**sleeping 11**) is interestingly furnished with both antique and modern items as well as some original art works. We found it a really relaxing place, though enlivened by some keenly contested table-tennis, and ideally located for walking on Exmoor or beside the sea. Porlock has a good choice of restaurants and one day we took a memorable steam train ride on the scenic 23-mile West Somerset Railway. Ref EJL.

The Granary, Gardener's Cottage, Dove Cote and *The Butler's Quarters* are the evocative names of four individually-styled restored cottages at Hopton Hall, a splendid mansion dating back to 1575, deep in the Derbyshire Dales near Wirksworth. **Sleeping 14, 8, 4** and **8** respectively, they share use of an indoor heated pool and gardens with children's play area and football and volleyball nets. Horse-riding, clay-pigeon shooting, golf, fishing and watersports are all available locally. Ref RAI, QVS, QVT and QVU.

We find North Wales wonderfully far from the hustle and bustle of city life, a feeling that becomes even stronger if we cross the Menai Bridge on to Anglesey. One of ECC's twenty or so properties on the island is *West Lawn*, a spacious detached bungalow (**sleeps 7**) with its own secure garden and direct access to Rhosneigr's vast sands. The beach, a popular venue for windsurfers, offers safe swimming as well as canoeing and sand-yachting. Riding, golf and sailing are available nearby, as well as Anglesey's castles, museums and nature reserves. Ref JAC.

Large groups can relax in rather imposing but also comfortable surroundings at *Arden House*, Church Stretton, in Shropshire, in a location (on a main road) that is excellent for exploring this green and wooded though often rather overlooked county. There's an open fire in both the sitting room and the dining room, each of which also has stone mullion windows and a wooden floor. There's a games room and, charmingly (via narrow and steep stairs), a small roof terrace. Ref RZ8.

Tuckenhay Mill, in South Devon, offers 21 properties to choose from. This is the shared outdoor pool. Ref FUB.

White Magpie Cottage, near Tunbridge Wells, enjoys panoramic views over gardens, ponds and lakes. Ref P12.

One couple we know has so much faith in ECC that they open the brochure at random and put their finger on a property. The first time either of them lands on a property for two, they book it. 'We've ended up in all sorts of lovely places and never been disappointed', they say. Last summer they chose *White Magpie Cottage,* in an area of Outstanding Natural Beauty at Lamberhurst, near Tunbridge Wells. It has a panoramic view over the gardens and the lake in the owners' 20-acre grounds. Ref P12.

In the Cotswolds, *Underwood Cottage* at Sheriff Lench, five miles from Evesham, is a spacious 19th-century detached house (**sleeps 8/9**) in secluded wooded grounds. From mid-May to mid-September, guests have exclusive use of its heated outdoor pool and sauna. Ref NYF. In Evesham itself, *Durcott Cottage* (**sleeps 2**) is a beautifully restored cottage featuring an elegant four-poster bed and cosy sitting-room. Ref NO6. For both of these, special rates apply during Cheltenham Race Week in March.

Greenwood Grange Cottages at Higher Bockhampton in Dorset are just two miles from Dorchester. **Sleeping 2 to 8**, they stand in peaceful grounds with two all-weather tennis courts, badminton and croquet lawns, a children's play area and Wendy house. Indoor facilities include a heated Roman-style pool, sauna, solarium and games room. Ref DGY-DUC.

Further details from English Country Cottages, Spring Mill, Earby, Barnoldwswick BB94 0AA. Brochures and bookings: 0870 197 6890.

www.english-country-cottages.co.uk

Country Holidays*

'Britain is filled with beautiful and enchanting places that you can't help falling in love with' is the message from Country Holidays. 'Whatever you want, we'll help you find the perfect cottage to make your holiday dreams come true'. True to their word, their 2007 brochure (628 pages!) certainly includes something for everyone. It offers more than 4000 cottages of every shape, size and age, spread all over England, Scotland and Wales, plus a few in Ireland, France and Spain. To help you make your choice, the properties are divided into 20 regional sections, each beginning with interesting suggestions for days out in the area.

Many of the properties are available at 2006 prices, many accept pets and many are available for short breaks. Each is inspected annually and graded to 'Visit Britain' standards and criteria which go from the 1-star 'Acceptable overall level of quality; adequate provision of furniture, fur-

Grade II listed Luntley Court, sleeping up to 15, is one of the finest houses in Herefordshire. Ref 13708.

Just outside the beautiful village of Burwash, in the High Weald of Sussex, this peaceful place is Ref 16700.

nishings and fittings' up to 5 stars for 'Exceptional overall level of quality; high levels of decor, fixtures and fittings, together with an excellent range of accessories and many personal touches'.

In addition, some properties have been given a Gold Award. Totally separate from Star gradings, these are awarded solely because holidaymakers have rated them as 'excellent overall' in customer satisfaction surveys.

If you fancy the idea of staying in a top class Five Star/Gold Award property, *Trelawn,* at Hayle, near St Ives in Cornwall could be just what you want. It's a spacious detached house **sleeping 13**, so ideal for families or large parties wanting to holiday together. The long sandy beach of Hayle Towans, good for surfing and sandcastles, is within a mile. Ref 15639.

Another large Gold Award property is *Luntley Court* at Dilwyn, near Hereford, which **sleeps 15**. Dating from 1674, this Grade II half-timbered mansion is one of the county's most beautiful buildings, noted for its oak panelling, original oak staircases and large galleried dining-hall. Its rural 10-acre estate is bordered by a small stream. 3 stars. Ref 13708.

Also Gold rated, but much smaller (**sleeps 4**), *Milk Lodge* is a converted milking parlour close to the beautiful village of Burwash, in the Ancient High Weald of Sussex. Graded 4-star, it is ideal for exploring the 1066 country or visiting the many National Trust castles and gardens in the area. Eastbourne, Bexhill and Hastings are within 20 miles. Ref 16700.

Chickens, pigs, sheep, goats, geese, ducks and horses help keep visitors entertained on the 10-acre *Werngochlyn Farm* at Llantilio Pertholey, near Abergavenny, in South Wales. Riding is available too (with instruction if desired) and also stabling for those who want to bring their own horse – and there's an indoor swimming pool. Accommodation is in four interesting barn conversions, all 2-star, **sleeping from 2 to 6**. Ref 6252/5.

A 'priest's hole', ideal now as a children's den, is one of the features of *Boshula*, a 400-year old cottage Grade II listed thatched cottage overlooking the village green at Hartest in Suffolk, eight miles south of Bury St Edmunds. The building, once the local bakery and beamed throughout, has been cosily converted to **sleep 7 to 9**. Ref 17212.

For families with lively children, *Whitmuir Hall,* near Selkirk, in the Scottish Borders, is ideal. (We stayed with a seven and a nine year old.) Originally an Edwardian manor house, its buildings have been skilfully converted into comfortable 3-star cottages and apartments **sleeping 2 to 6**. The 32-acre grounds include an indoor heated pool, sauna and games

Originally the old bakery overlooking the green, Boshula, at Hartest in Suffolk, is a thatched, beamed delight. Ref 17212.

Werngochlyn Farm has an indoor pool, and there's even stabling for visiting horses. Sleeps from 2 to 6. Ref 6252/5.

room. Instruction in abseiling and archery is available by arrangement and no fewer than eighteen golf courses are within easy reach. Ref 5309.

In the heart of the Norfolk Broads, *Deerfoot,* at Horning, is a comfortable 4-star detached house **sleeping 9** on the waterfront. It has a small garden with a decked seating terrace leading on to the river and a first-floor decked veranda. Fishing is available from the garden and a day cruiser (bookable in advance) can be moored there. There are plenty of walking and cycling trails nearby, and Norwich is just 11 miles away. Ref 19794.

Country Holidays also have a good choice for those who simply want a quiet retreat for two, or to escape alone – like a friend of ours who regularly seeks a little hideaway to work on her TV scripts. 'All I need is a bed, microwave and my laptop', she says. Her current favourite is the delightfully named *Pixie Cottage* (3 stars) in the picturesque Cotswold village of Naunton, five miles from Bourton-on-the-Water. A 17th-century Grade II listed building **sleeping 2**, it has a garden. Ref 11192.

Also **sleeping 2**, *The Old Church* – a very small one! – on the Isle of Skye is now a 4-star holiday home. Built in the mid-1800s, it has spiral stairs leading to a galleried area and to a small snug bedroom neatly fitted into the attic. The garden has a stone bridge over a stream. Ref 17488.

Details from Country Holidays, Spring Mill, Earby, Barnoldswick, Lancashire BB94 0AA. Brochures and bookings: 0870 197 6895.

www.country-holidays.co.uk

Blakes Country Cottages*

Blakes, with over 4000 properties on their books, including many still at 2006 prices, are a major-player on the self-catering scene. Their 2007 brochure divides England, Scotland, Wales and Ireland into 20 regions, making it simple to locate a property in a particular area. Moreover the indexing is helpfully designed to simplify finding a large property or one with a swimming pool.

In addition, each of the twenty sections starts with information about the area and tips for days out, including a specific recommendation from one of Blakes' local team. The brochure also shows whether a property is available for short breaks and – if so – for how many nights and at what times of the year.

Header bars against each property's details highlight important features

Delightful Ninham House, at Shanklin, a family house set in a wooded valley, is close to sandy beaches. Ref 19270.

Ivy Cottage and (above) The Coach House, near Newcastle Emlyn: a fine base for seeing South Wales. Ref 16267/8.

such as those that accept pets and those which can be checked out in more detail by a 'virtual tour' on the Blakes website.

As before, every property has been quality assessed using the Visit Britain criteria. Five stars mean 'exceptional' while, at the other end of the scale, 1-star cottages suit those, perhaps on a tighter budget, who are happy with somewhere simpler but still want to be assured of cleanliness and comfort. Some properties have also been given a Gold Award because previous holidaymakers rated them as 'excellent overall'.

One of the Gold Award properties is *The Mill* (**sleeping 6**) in the unspoilt Northumbrian village of Wall. Enjoying a beautiful setting on the banks of the Tyne, this 3-star detached stone building was originally a millhouse and is close to Hadrian's Wall and the Kielder Forest. Ref NN15.

Another Gold winner is *Heyhoe* at Walcott in Norfolk. This 2-star detached timber holiday bungalow (**sleeping 4**) is as near to the sea as it's possible to get, as it stands at the top of the sea wall just above a sandy beach. Eighteen miles from Norwich, it is also well placed for visits to Cromer, famous for its crabs, and Sheringham. Ref AB38.

Perfect for train lovers of all ages is a first-floor 4-star apartment (**sleeps 5**) in Kingsley & Froghall station, 10 miles east of Stoke-on-Trent. This replica Victorian building is on the five-mile plus Churnet Valley line which recreates the ambience of a 1950s rural railway, with trains hauled by gleaming steam locomotives. There are special Thomas Tank Engine days and even occasional ghost trains. For days out, Alton Towers and the glorious Peak District National Park are within a short drive. Ref 17343.

For lovers of the sea, the 3-star *Coastguard Cottage* is within 100 yards of the beach at Downderry near Looe on Cornwall's south coast. This cosy compact terraced building (**sleeping 5**) has a comfortable lounge with picture window and garden overlooking the beach. Ref 50100. Nearby at Polperro the Old Rectory has been divided into five beautiful 3 or 4-star apartments, all with evocative names – *Crow's Nest, Fisherman's Heights, Smuggler's Watch, Bosun's Retreat* and *Captain's Rest*. **Sleeping from 2 to 7/8**, each has a south-facing sun terrace looking down towards the picturesque fishing harbour. Ref 17576-80.

On the Isle of Wight at Shanklin, *Ninham House* (**sleeping 9/10**) is a delightful family home in a picturesque wooded valley with decorative lake. Built in 1904 it's been upgraded to provide comfortable accommodation (4-star). Guests have access to a heated outdoor pool, open from Spring Bank Holiday until September 6, toddlers' pool and games room

Gold Award property, The Mill, on the banks of the Tyne in Northumberland, is a haven of peace. Ref NN15.

The entire first floor of Montrose House (Ref B4706) provides an apartment with panoramic views of Loch Lomond.

provided for the nearby caravan park. Attractions like Carisbrooke Castle and Osborne House are within an easy drive. Ref 19270.

In South Wales, 3-star *Ivy Cottage* (**sleeps 4**) and *Coach House* (**sleeps 5**) stand in 5$^{1}/_{2}$-acre grounds at Cilwendeg, meaning "place to escape and seek refuge" at Drefach Velindre, about 12 miles inland from Cardigan. Hens, geese, ducks, goats, ponies, cats and dogs invariably enchant children staying there, though younger ones need to be carefully supervised as the grounds include a woodland lake and stream. Ref 16267-8.

At Erbistock near Llangollen, a 3-star converted water mill **sleeping 10** enjoys a spectacular setting on the banks of the River Dee. Surrounded by natural woodland, it boasts spiral staircases and a balcony outside the spacious living/dining room which overlooks the river and weir. Llangollen, home of the famous annual International Eisteddfod and noted for its canal basin and steam railway, is just ten miles away. Ref WN76.

Overlooking Loch Lomond, the grand *Montrose House* at Balmaha in Scotland has a spacious 4-star apartment available (**sleeps 8**), which fills the building's entire first floor. With wonderful views, it is excellent for walking, as the Ben Lomond mountain path and West Highland Walkway are in easy reach. The sheltered harbour at Balmaha is ideal for sailing and watersports, and an 18 hole golf course is within four miles. Ref B4706.

Further details from Blakes, Spring Mill, Earby, Lancashire BB94 0AA. Brochures and bookings: 0870 197 6896.

www.blakes-cottages.co.uk

Welcome Cottages*

'Pets go free' is just one of the reasons why this is such a successful agency (most of its properties accept them). Moreover, if you book to go with your pet between October and the end of March you get £25 off the cost of your holiday. Further inducements are that most off-peak prices have been pegged at last year's level and some properties offer a 20% discount to couples holidaying between October and May (including those accompanied by a small child up to the age of 5).

We know too that Welcome turns down around two-thirds of the cottages offered to it. Yet its properties, which are spread all over England, Scotland, Wales and Ireland, plus a good selection in France, remain notably affordable.

Welcome also has the advantage of having its own clear and simple

Handy for the Norfolk Broads, this little thatched gem sleeps 2. The North Norfolk coast is within easy reach. Ref W3645.

This bungalow near Amble, Northumberland, has a full size snooker table and a whirlpool bath. Ref W1766.

colour-coded grading system. This ranges from Comfortable ('plenty of creature comforts'), through Good Quality ('well appointed and well furnished') and Lovely ('handsome, harmonious and tasteful'), to – at the top – Beautiful ('beautifully decorated and furnished').

Among those rated 'Beautiful' is a 16th-century Grade II listed farmhouse **sleeping 8** at Cwm Main near Bala, North Wales. It's on a 100-acre farm where pheasants and ducks are reared. Lovingly restored, the original character is combined with modern facilities throughout. There's a wealth of huge beams and oak wall panels, two inglenook fireplaces and an impressive wooden spiral staircase. All four bedrooms have unspoilt views; one is en-suite with a four-poster. The beautiful Bala Lake (watersports, leisure centre and steam railway) is eight miles away. Ref W2399.

Much more modern but also rated 'Beautiful' is a magnificent bungalow (**sleeping 8**) at Radcliffe, half-a-mile from the fishing port of Amble, in Northumberland. In its own enclosed garden of over an acre, it has a delightful sunny conservatory and snooker room with full-size table. The area is renowned for its bare hills, rugged cliffs and sandy beaches, so there is plenty to explore nearby. Ref W1766.

In the Malverns, at Malvern Wells, the upper floors of the former bottling plant of the famous Malvern Water have been converted into a comfortable holiday home **sleeping 6** and graded 'Lovely'. On the ground floor, visitors still come to collect the pure mineral water which flows into it from a spring. Behind the 200-year old building, a terraced garden rises up the hillside and the kitchen/dining room leads on to a patio with its own private water source. There are views towards the Severn in the distance, and, from the Malvern Hills nearby, east to the Cotswolds, north to Shropshire and west to the mountains of Wales. Ref W8151.

One of our most memorable holiday experiences ever was waking up in the Ring of Kerry in south-west Ireland. It was our first visit and we had arrived after dark the previous evening. When we looked out of the bedroom window, the scenery was absolutely breathtaking. We knew we were going to have a wonderful week – and we did. A modern house (**sleeps 8**) on the Ring route near the lively little town of Caherciveen makes a good base, especially as the main rooms all have lovely views, some of the nearby River Fertha, some of rugged mountains. Graded 'Lovely', it is within three miles of a Blue Flag beach. Ref W31361.

A considerable number of thatched properties are on Welcome's books,

Created from the 19th century bottling plant of Malvern Water, this sleeps 6 in comfort and has wonderful views. W8151.

Original character blends with 21st century facilities in this listed Welsh farmhouse near Bala. Ref W2399.

including a charming old cottage with a pretty garden in the village of Ludham, 13 miles from Norwich and seven from the sea. The wildlife and windmills of the Norfolk Broads can be explored from nearby Potter Heigham and Wroxham; there are bird and seal colonies, stately homes and steam railways. Graded 'Good Quality', it **sleeps 2**. Ref W3645.

Eight miles north of Banbury, an open-plan studio apartment **sleeping 2** is available in the grounds of a private home in the beautiful conservation village of Wormleighton. Graded 'Good Quality', it's on the first floor of a small modern building, above a games room with table-tennis. Quiet and secluded, the property has a shared patio/lawned garden and boasts stunning views of the surrounding countryside beyond the Oxford Canal, a mile away. Ref W8300.

An artist friend of ours reckons that north-west Scotland is unbeatable for seascapes and mountains to paint, but its attraction for us is the scope for bird-watching and walking. Others we know go to fish or climb. At Laide, near Gairloch, a 'Beautiful' property (**sleeping 6**) is only yards from the shore and a small sandy beach. Built in the 1700s but lovingly renovated, it has original wood panelling in several rooms, a four-poster style box bed and even its own sauna. Ref W143.

Details from Welcome Cottages UK, Spring Mill, Earby, Barnoldswick, Lancashire BB94 0AA. Brochures and bookings: 0870 197 6957.

www.welcomecottages.com

Ireland

Of all the holiday destinations we feature, Ireland is the one that gets people wanting to go back. We've often heard people say 'The more I see of it, the more I like it.' It's probably Ireland's age-old charms that make this one of the most appealing destinations in Europe. We remember strolling through Killarney after dark, listening to traditional music being played in what seemed like every other pub, the sun setting over the bleakly beautiful coast of Connemara, and finding 'b and b' en route between cottage visits in a faded but still grand Georgian mansion. We think of the deep green of the countryside bordering the coast of North Antrim, of the mystical quality of the early-morning light over Lake Killarney, and of the wild blue mountains of Connemara. We are not fishermen, but remember seeing anglers' eyes light up over a candlelit dinner in romantic Delphi Lodge, among the hills on the Galway-Connemara border, when describing their day's battles with salmon. We hear from readers who enjoy 'two-centre' Irish holidays. One family, regular users of the book but first-time visitors to Ireland, stayed first in a thatched cottage at Kinvara, nicely poised for explorations of Galway and the Connemara National Park, and then had a week within the Ring of Kerry.

Note: when telephoning Ireland you should dial your own international prefix (eg 00) then 353 followed by the area code (eg 51, not 051), then the number. Within Ireland, however, you should prefix the area code with '0', eg 051. Note also: a small number of contact phone numbers in this section are UK ones.

Killarney, Muckross   map 10/562
Killarney Lakeland Cottages

Killarney is the most popular tourist destination in Ireland, and usually buzzes with life. Brian O'Shea's landscaped, well-spaced, villagey arrangement of white-painted and traditional-style cottages is in a quiet parkland setting seemingly miles from the town centre (though that's actually quite close). In two separate groups, each is surrounded by trees, a well planned distance from its neighbours. Every one has a peat

A great location, close to a famous town.

fire. The number each property sleeps varies **from 4 to 7**. There is access to two hard tennis courts, a good games room, bikes, and in each cottage TV with multi-channel reception and direct dial telephone. Not suitable for dogs. Cost: about €200 to €1000. Details/colour leaflet from Brian O'Shea, Killarney Lakeland Cottages, Muckross, Killarney, Co Kerry. Telephone (outside Ireland) – your international code plus (353) 64-31538, fax (353) 64 34113.

www.killarney.cottages.com

email:info@killarneycottages.com

Bansha
Lismacue Coach House

We loved this cosy converted coach-house attached to a Georgian mansion.

In a superb location for touring (the Glen of Aherlow, Tipperary, historic Rock of Cashel, and beautiful Cahir beyond it, Killarney, the Dingle Peninsula, Co Clare and more besides), here is a skilfully converted two storeyed coach house conversion attached to the owners' grand listed Georgian mansion, where very up-market 'bed and breakfast' is available. **Sleeping up to 7** in one double, two twins and a single, it has the advantage of a wood-burning stove and even a sauna. The single bedroom, conveniently for older or less able people, is on the ground floor. There is a covered garage.

Among comments from people who have stayed. Adam and Lucille Pauley, of Cambridge, Massachusetts, write 'a wonderful week in peaceful and scenic surroundings', and William Koyle of Orangeville, Ontario, said 'To look out on the Galtee Mountains from Lismacue has to be one of the best views in Ireland'.

Not suitable for dogs. Linen and towels included. Details from Kate Nicholson, Lismacue House, Bansha, Co Tipperary. Telephone (62) 54106.

www.lismacue.com

Ballina   map 10/563   Colour section B, Page 4
'The Holiday House'

It's a pleasant fifteen minute walk into lively Ballina alongside the River Moy.

Used occasionally by the Suffolk-based owners, this neat, modern, semi-detached house, just 45 minutes from Knock airport, makes a *notably inexpensive* base from which to explore much of the glorious west of Ireland. A town property but quietly situated on a little-used road that runs alongside the River Moy, it **sleeps 5** in a double, a twin and a single. It is well carpeted throughout, and as well as central heating there are *two* open fires – a great bonus for those so-enjoyable spring and autumn breaks. There is easy access to the river and walks along it (a fifteen minute walk to the town centre) and it's just eight miles from the fabulous sandy beach at Enniscrone. Fishermen will love this: among much else there's salmon fishing on the Moy from February to September. Cable TV, small 'music centre'; large storage shed for housing fishing gear. Not suitable for pets, and there are no special facilities for babies or small children. *Costs are very reasonable.* Details from Mr and Mrs Burke, 57 Head Lane, Great Cornard, Suffolk CO10 0JS. Telephone 01787 311626.

email: m.burke@amserve.com

The South of Ireland
Country Cottages in Ireland*

'The clock seems to tick slower here' says the Irish Country Cottages brochure. Rich in colour, it cleverly conveys the essence of what makes this beautiful and historic country so popular among travellers.

About 250 elite properties are featured, divided into five regional sections. At many during the off-peak seasons you can choose which day of the week to start and finish your holiday, and at some you can even get two weeks for the price of one. Furthermore, two adults can upgrade to a larger property for added comfort and get a 20% discount on it.

One of the remotest properties is *Aitin Aoibhinn* on the west coast island of Achill in Co Mayo. Though accessed by a bridge, the island has an unspoilt 'away-from-it-all' charm which often lures artists and writers. The property is a smart modern house, **sleeping 8,** with big windows to ensure that everyone enjoys the ever-changing views of the mountains and the sea, which is only 50 yards away. Ref YBBE.

Even closer to the sea, beside the Blue Flag beach at Duncannon on the east side of the wide Waterford Harbour in Co Wexford, is *Strand Court*, a newly-built first-floor apartment **sleeping 4**. Steps lead down from it

Remotely situated on the island of Achill, Co Mayo, this spacious modern house is just 50 yards from the sea. Ref YBBE.

The Old Monastery is an elegant Victorian property in secluded gardens at Cahersiveen, Co Kerry. Ref ZO3.

straight on to the sand. The nearby Hook Peninsula is known as the sunniest corner of Ireland, and the 12th-century lighthouse on its headland, still in operation, is open to visitors. Duncannon itself has an interesting maritime museum, a quaint fishing harbour and several pubs. Ref YTI.

For a large group, the *Old Monastery* at Cahersiveen in Co Kerry **sleeps 16**. Built in 1840 as a merchant's house, it was used by the Christian Brothers for over 100 years. Now fully renovated, but retaining old wood floors and stained-glass windows, it offers spacious and comfortable accommodation. Ancient castles, prehistoric burial grounds, standing stones and medieval crosses all wait to be explored nearby. It is also a good area for activities – you can enjoy walking, cycling, climbing, watersports, riding, tennis, golf and every sort of angling from wild salmon to shark fishing. Ref ZO3.

Details from Irish Country Cottages, Spring Mill, Earby, Barnoldswick BB94 0AA. Bookings and brochures: 0870 197 6891.

www.2007icc.co.uk

Connemara
Connemara Coastal Cottages*

Knowing how fond we are of Ireland, an American reader wrote to us to say how useful this guide had been in finding properties there of character, and described the locations she had loved most. We quickly realised that in most cases she meant Connemara: 'romantic sunsets over the water, endless beaches, marvellous seafood'. During our most recent Irish visit we spent time with a small, personally run agency we'd heard excellent reports of, and saw a good handful of the properties on their books. For example, two extremely comfortable cottages, pride and joy of the owners, overlooking the water at Cleggan village, and a thickly carpeted cottage (called *Doon House*) attached to the charming owners' house: rural views but, of course, not far from the sea, and a light, bright cottage conversion almost surrounded by water, with fabulous sea and mountain views, called *Ross Point*.

Among the properties we've had very good reader reports of is a modern bungalow in the centre of Cleggan, overlooking Cleggan Bay. **Sleeping 5**, it's just a short walk to the pub, a restaurant and shops. Don't miss a trip on the twice-daily ferry to Inishbofin. Ref 099.

Pets welcome in most. Details of these and other beauties in an excellent loose-leaf brochure from Julia Awcock, Connemara Coastal Cottages, Cloon, Cleggan, Co Galway. Telephone 353 95 44307.

www.cc-cottages.com   email: cccottages@eircom.net

'Some like it modern'. And most will appreciate the panoramic views.

The light, bright main bedroom (double aspect) is an attractive feature.

'In brief'

Grayling, at New Quay, on the coast of Co Clare, is one of our west coast favourites. **Sleeping 7**, the neat, tidy, detached white bungalow is a charmer – one of our best finds on a recent visit to the west of Ireland. Though it's very much a holiday home (**map 10/585**), it's of permanent-home standard. It is just five minutes' walk from a safe and little-used beach. Prices are very reasonable.

Details from Noel and Susan Callaghan, Ballytarsna House, Kilshanny, Co Clare. Telephone 353 65 7071055. Fax 7071717.

Bantry
Whiddy Holiday Homes

On board a small passenger ferry you cross beautiful Bantry Bay, fringed by green hills, to Whiddy Island. Ten minutes on the water, a world away. Depending on which of the three most appealing cottages is yours (usefully, their owners live on the island in summer), you might be driven a couple of miles along a bumpy track, past a freshwater lake

An outstanding quartet of spacious and comfortable cottages, with Shannon airport just an hour away.

with a rowing boat freely available to cottage guests, past hedges of scarlet fuchsia that are a summer trademark of the west of Ireland. All three are utterly quiet, all with sea views 'to die for'. Rowing on the lake, exploring every nook and cranny of the island by bike or on foot, climbing to the eerily beautiful, deserted Napoleonic fort, would fill a happy week or, in good weather, a fortnight of serious unwinding. Fishing and sailing can be arranged without difficulty. Linen and towels included. TV. Dogs welcome.

Booking details available from Greta Steenssens, Roddam 83-2880, Bornem, Belgium. Telephone: 00 32 3 889 61 11. Fax: 00 32 3 889 41 71.

email: walco.pottery@skynet.be

Ballyvaughan   Colour section B, Page 4
Village and Country Holiday Homes   map 10/573

At the heart of the 'character' village of Ballyvaughan, surrounded by the limestone hills of the Burren and on the shores of Galway Bay, these are some of the best self catering properties we know in Ireland. The enclave of well appointed cottages (each with its own garden, quiet and private) is located in a courtyard. The owners also have two apartments, bright, deceptively spacious, within a few yards of the courtyard cottages. All properties have quality fabrics

A rather pleasant decision for visitors to make: in the village or by the sea? Both sets of properties are quite outstanding.

and furnishings, easy-on-the-eye colours, well equipped kitchens. The houses **sleep 6**, **4 or 6** (there are two styles, plus the apartments). Cost: about €310 to €830. Details from George Quinn, Frances Street, Kilrush, Co Clare. Telephone (outside Ireland) – your international code plus 353 65 90 51977.

www.ballyvaughan-cottages.com
email: sales@ballyvaughan-cottages.com

Delphi, North Connemara
Boathouse Cottages/Wren's Cottage

We've stayed here twice, and would recommend it wholeheartedly as a place to unwind in beautiful surroundings. We love it, and would rate it among our favourite half dozen places in this guide.

Delphi is in a beautiful mountain setting, reminiscent of a idealised classical 18th century landscape: great looming hills, misty valleys, rushing rivers, dark woods.

Serious fishermen probably know Delphi, and walkers should consider it. It is a wildlife paradise, known for wild flowers, otters, peregrine falcons, pine martens and badgers. You will find it where western Mayo nudges into Connemara, a few miles north of Leenane.

Almost adjacent to elegant Delphi Lodge, the original four cottages (Boathouses) are very cosy, quite unpretentious, with deep chairs and sofas, lots of antique pine, big open fires (making them a most appealing choice for an autumn or winter break), traditional stone floors with rugs downstairs and carpets upstairs. These four are most attractively bordered by shrubs and old stone walls; two **sleep 4** in two twins, the other two **just 2** in a double bed.

During our most recent visit we saw a newly restored cottage, Wren's. On the approach road to Delphi Lodge, overlooking Finlough, in the Delphi Valley, it has a greater degree of privacy, and has been furnished and equipped to a very high standard. It **sleeps 6** in three bedrooms.

Boathouse Cottages are full of character and charm. We have met people in residence, and they have all loved their cottage and its romantic location.

Wren's Cottage, newly renovated, is the pride and joy of the Delphi ownership. Idyllically, it overlooks the lough, and is bound to attract a following of its own.

Linen/towels included. All cottages have telephone. Wrens has Sky TV. Not suitable for very young children or dogs. Cost: about €800 to €900 (c £533 to £600). Wrens €1250 (c £833). Details: Delphi Lodge, Leenane, Co Galway (postal district). Telephone 353 95 42222. Fax 42296.

Note: Excellent bed and breakfast accommodation is available in Delphi Lodge, and cottage guests may sometimes have candlelit dinners here, usually on a communal basis: such a bonus for lone travellers or people from overseas wanting to make new friends.

www.delphilodge.ie
email: stay@delphilodge.ie

Ireland Directory
Welcome Cottages*

There really is nowhere else like the Emerald Isle. We like it more and more each time we go. All its irresistibly beautiful corners are well represented in this exceptional selection of around 500 cottages there, each graded as Beautiful, Lovely, Good Quality or Comfortable.

Down in the south, 25 miles east of Cork, a detached modern cottage (**sleeps 8**) in the seaside village of Ballycotton is a 'Beautiful' property. Spacious and stylish, it enjoys stunning sea views over fields. The area is noted for its pubs and restaurants, including famous Ballymaloe House (6 miles), ideal for rounding off a day spent bird-watching, playing golf, fishing or just lazing on one of the area's numerous beaches. Ref 31010.

On the west coast, the breathtaking Ring of Kerry is one of the loveliest drives we know. A tastefully furnished bungalow (graded 'Lovely' and **sleeping 4**) is well placed for exploring it, just three miles from the lively village of Glenbeigh. Set in a peaceful scenic valley, soothed by the sounds of a nearby mountain stream, it is close to some of Ireland's highest mountains, yet there is a sandy beach only four miles away. Golf, horse-riding and fishing are nearby. Ref W31130.

Lovers of organic fare can book a comfortable modern bungalow (**sleeping 8**) on an organic working farm at Aclare in Co Sligo. It's graded 'Lovely' and the owners can supply guests with organic poultry and beef at very favourable prices. Golf, fishing and riding are available at Ballina, 15 miles to the west, while the Ox mountains to the north provide plenty of scope for scenic walks or drives. Ref W31296.'

In Co Cork, this (not featured) is only 4 miles from a Blue Flag Beach. Ref W31134.

Just outside Woodford, this is ideal for those seeking an active outdoor holiday.

A 'Lovely' former farmhouse, comfortably refurbished to **sleep 5**, on a mature 1-acre site in countryside near the village of Woodford between Galway and Limerick, is particularly well placed for those who want an active outdoor holiday. Golf, riding and pitch and putt are all within easy reach; a nearby oak forest nature reserve and the Slabh Aughty mountains provide plenty of possibilities for walkers; and the Shannon (6 miles) and Lough Derg offer boating, watersports and fishing. Ref W31233.

Details from Welcome Cottages, Spring Mill, Earby, Barnoldswick, Lancashire BB94 0AA. Bookings and brochures: 0870 197 6957.

www.welcomecottages.com

A broader view...

Readers of *The Good Holiday Cottage Guide* who stay in self catering properties abroad as well as in the UK were among the first to encourage us to widen our horizons, as did the noticeable number of UK cottage owners who *also* have properties to let overseas. For the moment we've confined ourselves to France, Italy and Spain, with a nod to Scandinavia and Cyprus plus, in Germany, Bavaria, and, in New England, Vermont. We'd be pleased to get more reader reports and recommendations of self catering properties in those and other countries.

One of our best recent discoveries were self-catering cottages on the Baltic islands of Bornholm (Denmark) Goland and Öland (Sweden) Åland (Finland) and Saaremaa (Estonia), which provide the same high standard of accommodation as those on the Scandinavian mainland.

The islands are memorable for their delightful scenery and fine bathing beaches. Except for Öland, which is connected to the Swedish mainland by a four and a half mile bridge across the sea, a holiday on the islands involves a ferry trip through one or more of the beautiful Baltic archipelagoes – a delight in itself...

More details from Scandinavian Holidays, 8 Boreham Holt, Elstree, Hertfordshire WD63QF. Telephone + 44 (0) 20 8953 8874.

email: info@scandinavianholidays.freeserve.co.uk

Denmark

Island of Fyn
Hindemae Mill

On the picturesque island of Fyn, this converted 200 year old mill, with an attached miller's cottage, provides comfortable and centrally heated accommodation for **up to 12 people** in six bedrooms, with three bathrooms. This year sees a super *It's a lovely introduction to Denmark...* new dining room/kitchen, washing machine and dryer. There is a cosy sitting-room off the dining/kitchen and a huge octagonal family room with squishy sofas and open fire. This room covers the entire ground floor area of the old mill. There's a games room. satellite TV, video games and small office with internet access. There is large garden surrounded by beechwoods, with lovely country walks. Two adult bikes are provided. Fyn has many sandy beaches, the nearest about five miles away. Access: via Copenhagen (90 minutes by motorway and road bridge) and Esbjerg (ferry from Harwich) also 90 minutes via motorway. By air from Stansted to Esbjerg. Cost: about £600-£1600 per week. Contact Victoria Sutherland: telephone 01855 811207. Fax 811338.

email victoria@torrenglencoe.com

Vence (Alpes Maritimes)
Villa Paradise

Recently constructed Villa Paradis (**sleeping 8**) has all the advantages of new fittings, uncluttered space and yet still with charm and character from the unusual furnishings, some from Morocco and many of them hand-cast pieces of unique wrought-iron. The bathrooms and showers are all tiled with hand-made tiles, and the wardrobe doors are North African hardwood, specially imported.

The house is on the outskirts of Vence, where there is a medieval walled 'cité', and, close by, other perched medieval villages such as St Paul de Vence and Tourrettes sur Loup. Sightseeing in the area reveals spectacular views along the Gorge du Loup. Within easy access to Nice, Cannes and the whole of the Côte d'Azur, the villa provides comfortable living, peaceful surroundings, unrestricted views and good accessibility.

Largely open plan on the main living area, there is a spacious salon with full width patio windows opening on to the pool terrace. French satellite TV, CD and DVD. New kitchen with maplewood and stainless steel fitments. On the same level are two bedrooms, one twin with shower room/WC en suite and a master double with views to the swimming pool. The first floor has two further bedrooms.

email: azuruk@boltblue.com

Vence/Grasse (Alpes Maritimes)
Villa La Salamandre

This villa (**sleeping 5 to 6**) is situated just outside Vence and ten minutes from St. Paul de Vence, with its famous restaurants, *jeu-de-boules* court and art galleries. It has a splendid view over the hills towards the mountains. The villa lies in a calm residential area and has its own private grounds with automatic gates and large private pool. The garden is immaculately maintained, and has a most beautiful rose garden.

The villa itself is on two levels. The main entrance door gives access to a hall with access via French doors to the living room on one side and the hall to the bedrooms on the other side. The living room has a sitting area with comfortable sofas and chairs around an open fire place with a TV with satellite and music system. On the other side is a large wooden dining table that seats six people with access to the covered veranda and garden. The kitchen is exceptionally well equipped.

On the same floor there are two bedrooms, each with a double bed. They share a bathroom There is also a study that can be made in another bedroom with single bed. On the upper floor there is another bedroom with a large comfortable single bed and nice views over the garden.

email: azuruk@boltblue.com

Hérault
Magalas

A fast, easy drive from Montpellier airport (80 km, much of it via motorway) brought us early on an October evening to the – for us! – unexpectedly ancient and absolutely charming hilltop village of Magalas. The origin of the name in the old local dialect is said to mean 'a pile of old stones'. But don't let that put you off: it's a delight, full of narrow, spiralling alleyways with sudden views of distant wooded hills and vineyards. It's especially deserted, silent and full of atmosphere after dark, with cats in the shadows and, if you're lucky, shafts of moonlight illuminating the half-hidden courtyards of 500-year old houses.

We knew our villa was in a small, new, residential development, but had assumed it was some way out of Magalas. In fact, it's just a very pleasant five minute walk from the house up towards the market square, close to which there are restaurants, bars, small shops, two bakers and a pâtisserie.

Though it's essentially 'practical' and designed for easy living and maintenance, it has certain very appealing features. For example, we

Easy, uncomplicated modern living on the edge of a fascinating ancient village...   *...with a really inviting sitting room that at any time is 'so nice to come home to'.*

liked the good sized sunken sitting room, more than adequate for the eight people the house sleeps. The October weather was very mild, but we eyed the (safely enclosed) fireplace with satisfaction, remembering the pleasures of other houses in rural France and the scent and instant heat from stores of olive wood: get it when you can. We also liked the first floor twin room (extra privacy, and an ensuite shower to boot), a bath and shower in the main bathroom, boules court at the rear, the swimming pool, by all accounts a serious sun-trap in summer. There's a spacious paved terrace with an awning. There's good touring from Magalas to, for example, the coast at Sète and Mèze, to the attractive town of Pezenas and the lower reaches of the Massif Central.

Cost: approximately £180 to £950. Further details from Tim and Jo Gray, Kembroke Hall, Bucklesham, near Ipswich, Suffolk IP10 0BU. Telephone 01394 448309.

email: tdgray@msn.com

Nérac
Moncaut

We stayed here recently, and were delighted by it. It's a 'Maison de Maître', which sits well back from a moderately busy road and is in fact hardly disturbed by traffic. It's a real family house, which is used from time to time by the owners themselves. and therefore functions properly! There's plenty of heating,

A fine, spacious, comfortable house of character, with an excellent pool and very well tended gardens.

instant hot water (two actual baths), a well equipped kitchen, a big outdoor pool – with shade – kept in tip-top condition by the efficient caretaker. He also looks after the six acres of grounds, within which there are separate sitting-out areas: we loved our *al fresco* meals on the shaded paved terrace outside the kitchen. The main, first floor bedrooms are spacious, even elegant. And the hall and the staircase are a joy. **Sleeps 10**. Ref DL22.

Though the surrounding scenery is not dramatic, it's pleasant, and we were deeply impressed by the virtually traffic-free minor roads. The country town of Nérac, fifteen minutes away by car, is a charmer, with lots of cafes and restaurants, plus boat trips and a preserved-railway jaunt. Details from Dominique's Villas: see Page 277.

Dinan (Brittany)
Moulin de Lorgeril

A reader from Suffolk who joined a family party staying in this 'really comfortable, really romantic' converted mill thinks 'cottage guide' readers will love it. The surroundings are peaceful – mainly woodland, fields and lakes. The main part of the house has a large sitting room cum diner with a stone fireplace and french windows, two bedrooms, a

Loads of character, and easily accessible from the UK while still 'very French'...

well equipped kitchen and separate stairs from the kitchen to that boon in wet weather – a games room. But the real attraction is the tower. On three levels, it has a sitting room with woodburner and french windows and stairs that lead to a double bedroom. From that there are further stairs to a fourth double bedroom with a sunken bath.

Cost: about £600 to £800. Details from Mrs P Lintern:

Telephone/fax 01749 342760.

Dordogne
Souillac Country Club

Readers quickly caught on to this much-admired enclave of properties, which we have featured for the last three years. Nestling in the hilly forests of the picturesque Dordogne valley, near the river/town of Souillac, this young-family-orientated club is a favourite all-year-round holiday destination for British and French alike. We know it well, and have found the staff, both English and French, most welcoming, with good suggestions of what to do and see in the region.

The scenery in this part of France is breathtaking, with deep gorges and castles perched on cliff-tops. It's most impressive in October, when mists rise up from the deep river valleys and the trees take on a multitude of colours. This is the land of foie gras and truffles, of honey and umpteen varieties of bread and mushrooms: British first-time visitors to the weekly market in nearby Sarlat are amazed by the local produce.

The detached houses (all privately owned and managed by the club when the individual owners are not in residence) have views of the eighteen-hole golf course and surrounding countryside. They are all spacious and fully equipped, with large patios, where in peaceful surroundings we enjoyed watching the sunset over a glass of wine.

The houses are in small well separated hamlets, with private swimming pools, and residents can also use the many central amenities, including two swimming pools, tennis, boules, golf, and in July and August the children can join in the fun at the Kids' Club. The excellent restaurant provides a welcome change from cooking at home, and the bar is a friendly meeting place after a game of golf or tennis.The whole region

The detached houses have views of the golf course and the surrounding country.

In a peaceful situation, 'they are all spacious and fully equipped'...

is a popular holiday destination. Apart from that beautiful scenery, medieval market towns and the numerous restaurants for which Périgord is famous, there's extra-good walking and horse-riding.

More information is available on 00 33 (0) 565 27 5600.

www.souillaccountryclub.com
email:rentals@souillac-countryclub.com

France – countrywide
Large Holiday Houses in France*

Much valued both by visitors to France and people in the industry, and from the same stable as the hugely successful *Large Holiday Houses in Scotland* (see Page 102), this is an impressive collection of chateaux, villas and farmhouses. It's an organisation larger groups should definitely check out.

For example, the medieval village of Vouvent, recently voted the most beautiful in France, is only about seven miles from *Les Tilleuls*, a lovely family home in the Vendée. Only an hour's drive from Poitiers (home of Futuroscope) and the coast, the setting is perfect for a secluded holiday. Among its many charms this lovely family home stands in a private two-acre garden. The 14m x 6.5m heated pool is surrounded by a large

Les Tilleuls: quiet and secluded, in a lovely area, with a super floodlit pool.

Chateau De Combecave: 'This has the makings of a holiday of a lifetime'.

patio area with mature palm trees. The pool is floodlit at night, making it an idyllic location for alfresco dining or – under the stars, during a hot summer holiday, a late night swim. **Sleeps 13 'plus 8'.**

Chateau De Combecave, at Touffailles, Tarn et Garonne, is a romantic and luxurious 18th century hillside chateau with a stone lined swimming pool, surrounded by extensive grounds, with spectacular views. This has the makings of a holiday of a lifetime: the chateau is exquisitely preserved and constructed of pale local limestone, with a roof of ancient terracotta tiles. Within 57 acres of woods and meadows, the chateau is surrounded by green lawns and shady trees. **Sleeps 11.**

For more of this, plus some simpler properties, visit the website:

www.LHHFrance.com
email: LHH@LHHFrance.com
Telephone 01381 610496

[All properties are inspected by, and carry the seal of approval of, Large Holiday Houses Ltd, but are booked direct with the owners.]

France – countrywide
The France Directory*

Whether you want to mingle with the celebrities on the smart Côte d'Azur or prefer a quiet hideaway by the Loire, you'll have no difficulty in finding just what you want in Welcome's colourful French brochure. It offers a wealth of choice, from cosy gîtes to luxury villas with pools, all helpfully grouped into the country's different regions from Brittany to the Languedoc.

In the Vendée, always a favourite area of ours because of its endless sandy beaches and excellent sunshine record, a lovely stone cottage (**sleeping 4**) tastefully created from a 16th-century barn is available at *Le Tablier,* near La Roche-sur-Yon. The lounge opens on to an attractive garden and the large decorative stone open fire, bread oven and cosy feeling. With a vineyard outside, and Les Sables d'Olonne about 25 miles away, this is a great spot to enjoy a relaxing holiday. Ref W9161.

Further down the west coast, in the little resort/fishing port of Capbreton, where we've had two excellent holidays, a first floor apartment (**sleeping 2/4**) is available in a residence partly built on sand dunes. Shops, restaurants and sandy beaches are all within a short walk, and the property has use of a shared swimming pool. Ref W12346.

Across in the south-east corner of France, a delightfully situated villa (**sleeping 5/6**) is tucked away at Montseret, near the beautiful village of Lagrasse, which is famous for its 11th century bridges and historic

Some impressive, sensibly priced properties, a skilful geographical spread.

Included in the portfolio are places we'll see for ourselves during 2007.

houses. The villa has its own pool, and the Mediterranean beaches are only 18 miles away. Narbonne, Perpignan and Carcassonne are within easy reach too. Ref W12534.

At Plevenon, on the north coast of Brittany, a pretty detached stone cottage (**sleeping 6/8**) has a downstairs master bedroom that opens on to the garden – and has a four-poster bed. A sandy beach is within 800 yards. Ref W12757.

Welcome French Cottage Selection, Spring Mill, Earby, Barnoldswick, Lancashire BB94. 0AA. Telephone 0870 242 3857.

www.welcomefrance.co.uk

France – countrywide
'Chez Nous'

'How could one govern a country that has over 2609 different kinds of cheese?' Charles de Gaulle is reputed to have said. Were he alive today, he might have added 'How can one choose a holiday cottage from the Chez Nous brochure when it contains such a wealth of delightful properties?'

In fact it's not a problem, as the 452-page brochure is helpfully divided into 17 geographical sections, each beginning with a description of the region and year-round temperature chart. Also there is also a very useful map on every second page showing the relevant area. And the company's website has extra photos of most properties.

Altogether it has over 7000 on its books, all independently-owned. A telephone call or email to the English-speaking owner enables you to find out all you want to know about it and the surrounding area, so you quickly get a real feel of the place. Then, having booked your accommodation, the exclusive Chez Nous travel service can arrange your journey.

One of our favourite parts of France is the Atlantic coast north of Biarritz. It offers the choice of the rolling waves that pound the long sandy sea beaches or the calmer waters of large inland lakes, also with sandy beaches. An attractive modern villa (**sleeping 12**) with its own pool is available in the attractive little town of Hossegor, where we once spent a memorable evening watching cyclists racing round and round the streets, all bunched terrifyingly close together. Feasting on the fresh

La Boursaie, Calvados, offers restored cider farm cottages in 100 acres of woodland, meadows and orchards. Ref 4485.

Close to Biarritz and sandy beaches, this modern villa with own pool is in Hossegor and sleeps 12. Ref 11850.

fish sold on the quayside in the picturesque little port of Cap Breton nearby is another happy memory. Ref 11850.

Further north in the Vendée, another of our favourite holiday areas, Le Moulin de la Roche, is a character farmhouse (**sleeps 8/10**) on the banks of a rver, with fishing on the doorstep. The large garden is fenced from the river and there is a heated pool, table-tennis and football to help keep all ages entertained. The nearby village of Tiffauges has shops and restaurants, or meals can be delivered. For days out, the Loire valley chateaux are full of interest.

In the Hautes-Pyrenees at Gerde, a small village near the elegant little spa town of Bagneres de Bigorre, there are stunning mountain views from the balcony of a neatly restored house **sleeping 8**. One of the three bedrooms has four single beds – an arrangement which would delight many children. Ref 2028.

La Boursaie is a former cider farmstead south-east of Caen. Five 16th-century half-timbered cottages have been restored to provide **accommodation for 2 to 7**. The 100-acre estate includes woodland, wildflower meadows and apple orchards with extensive views over a beautiful valley. Within easy reach are the D-Day beaches and museums. Ref 4485.

On the Côte d'Azur, three miles south of Cannes, a large villa (**sleeps 8**) occupies one of the most exquisite locations on the French Riviera, above the Bay of Theoule. The building matches the setting as it has a terrace and pool, all the rooms have panoramic sea views. The accommodation is spread over three floors but there is an eight-person internal lift. Luxury indeed: the makings of one of those never-to-be-forgotten holidays! Ref 11182.

A private south-facing terrace with stunning views of the Mediterranean, harbour and mountains is one of the delights of a top-notch modern first-floor air-conditioned apartment in the fishing port of Port Vendre, a few miles north of the border with Spain. Five minutes' walk from the beach, it **sleeps 2/6**. Just a mile north beyond a headland, another charming port, Collioure, has been a magnet for artists since Matisse settled there in 1905; it's also renowned for its anchovies – and we're talking about fresh ones! Ref 10307.

Fabulously placed on the French Riviera, this villa sleeps 8, and has terrace, pool, and panoramic sea views. Ref 11182.

A Pinarella at Monticello, on Corsica, has breathtaking coastal views to Cap Corse, big grounds and pool. Ref 15505.

The Chez Nous range also extends to Corsica where we have enjoyed several very happy holidays. Still largely untouched by mass tourism despite its many sandy beaches, the island has some superb scenery and you can take a breathtaking train ride through the mountains. A Pinarella is a massively-beamed stone house at Monticello, about 15 miles up the coast from Calvi in the north-west part of the island. **Sleeping 10**, it enjoys magnificent sea and mountain views. Ref 15505.

For a free copy of the Chez Nous directory, telephone 0870 242 3813.

www.cheznous.com email: enquiries@cheznous.com

France
Quality Villas

'Large enough to offer an unrivalled selection of villas throughout France and small enough to give you that personal service larger companies cannot match' is the proud boast of this family company, now in its 21st year as a French specialist. Their portfolio of luxury villas, farmhouses and chateaux have all been hand picked and personally inspected.

The amply-illustrated brochure is a joy to read. Page after page is filled with colourful photos and detailed descriptions of truly lovely properties, including many suitable for families or groups of a dozen or more. Moreover, the reservations team know each one personally so can advise about it and nearby towns and villages. What more could anyone want!

For example, *Bay View,* at Villefranche-sur-Mer, enjoys spectacular views down to the bay over the rooftops of this delightful old port. A

This beauty, called Bastide du Bois, sleeps 6 and is about 20 minutes from Grasse.

It's real, and you can stay here! It's the Château de la Rivière, in the Dordogne.

bright modern villa **sleeping 8,** with billiard table and kidney-shaped pool, it is ideally placed for exploring the coast, being just ten minutes' walk from Villefranche station, on the Monte Carlo-Nice-Cannes-St Tropez line. Ref PR590.

For those who prefer not to have a long journey after crossing the Channel, a château and farmhouse at St Maclou-la-Campagne can be booked separately or together. *Château de la Haye* **sleeps 12/14** (including 2/3 in a former carriage house), having been completely renovated to combine classic features with modern furnishings. *Ferme de la Haye* (**sleeping 10**) in the same grounds has been totally rebuilt, retaining only the original wooden frame. Because of the château's historic importance, the grounds are open to the public on Saturdays. Here you're well placed for visiting the D-Day landing beaches, the Bayeux tapestry and Monet's house and garden at Giverny. Ref 543/8

An infinity pool with lovely views from its sun-terrace is one of the delights of *La Vieille Ferme*, an old French farmhouse (**sleeping 6**) near the village of Saussignac, nine miles from Bergerac, in the Dordogne. Lovingly converted it has beamed ceilings, stone walls, terracotta floor tiles and antique furniture, paintings and tapestries. Ref PR541.

In Provence, *Domaine des Anges,* near Uzes, is a luxury property (**sleeping 18**) arranged around a wonderful garden courtyard amid vineyards and fields of wheat and sunflowers. It was built in 1840 but has been renovated by local craftsmen and decorated in a traditional but comfortable style to maintain its original splendour. Ref PR557.

Lovers of Art Deco are entranced by *Villa Mont St Clair*, in Sète, on the Languedoc coast, which **sleeps 6/7**. A spacious villa with green tiled roof, it has marble floors, Italian style ceilings and a grand staircase. The indoor heated pool and garden overlook the sea. Ref PR620.

Deep in the Vendée, you can holiday in *Château Xaintray*, a former medieval castle (**sleeping 14**) surrounded by an ancient moat where water lilies flower in abundance. Now a listed historic monument, nestling in 30 acres of woods and pastoral land, it has impressive stone walls, wooden beamed ceilings and immense fireplaces. The village of Coulonges-sur-l'Autize (six miles) has restaurants and a popular Tuesday farmers market. Ref PR635.

Villa Paradou, with 17th century origins, is near Arles, and sleeps six.

Villa Elegant, near Monte Carlo, is amazing even in Quality Villas terms.

At the southern end of the same coast, the long-established resort of Biarritz is famous for its beaches, fine shops, casino, aquarium and sea museum. *Brise Marine* is a traditional Basque villa **sleeping 4/5** on the cliffside at Bidart, five miles south, close to the Spanish border. Each room enjoys a magnificent sea view and there is a large deck above the small terraced garden which has direct access to the sandy beach below. The area is a golf and surfer's paradise, with twelve golf courses and wonderfully high waves for surfing and body boarding. Also available are wind-surfing, kite-surfing, hang-gliding, horse riding, mountain biking and hiking, or you can simply pamper yourself in one of the numerous thalassotherapy centres. Ref PR569.

Note: it is usually possible for most properties to offer maid service, a cook, a chauffeur and more.

Further details and a copy of that superb brochure from Quality Villas, 46 Lower Kings Road, Berkhamsted, Hertfordshire HP4 2AA. Telephone 01442 870 055. **www.quality-villas.co.uk**

Note: Quality Villas also has properties throughout Italy and Morocco:

www.qualityvillasitaly.co.uk and **www.qualityvillasmorocco.co.uk.**

Haut-Jura
Les Rousses Farmhouse Apartment

Roger Jones's Welsh properties (see Pages 164-166) have featured in this guide for many years, and he has brought the same energy and concern for his guests' comfort to his properties in mainland France and in Corsica – see below. Les Rousses, very close to the Swiss border, is compact but comfortable, at one end of a farmhouse now divided into five apartments. Charmingly, there is access via a wooden staircase to a garden area,

We see some fabulous locations in this job, but this really is something. And it's pretty nice in summer too!

and there are uninterrupted panoramic views across a wide valley to Les Rousses Lake, in a location known for its Alpine wild flowers. There's lots to do, including walking nature trails into Switzerland, golf (two 18-hole courses within sight of the apartment), exceptional ski-ing, fishing and sailing on the lake. And Les Rousses itself has restaurants, bars and shops. **Sleeps up to 4** in a double and a twin. Linen/towels not provided. TV/video. Bathroom with shower only. Cost: from about £195. Accessible by train and taxi, or about eight hours' drive from Calais. Details from Roger Jones, Flat B, The Old Granary, Tremadog, Gwynedd LL49 9RH. Telephone (01766) 513555.

Corsica
Calvi – La Reginella

Just add a glass of local wine, sit back and relax: this is the view from the balcony.

If a picture's worth a thousand words, we can relax for a moment: the view on the right is what you see from the balcony of this town centre apartment, which is on the third (top) floor of a building overlooking the bay and mountains beyond. Calvi is a chic place, with shops, restaurants and boutiques in walking distance of the apartment. Most appealingly, you can pick up a train here on a narrow-gauge railway that links coastal villages and beaches, with connections to Ajaccio, in the south, and you are just ten minutes' walk from the ferry point from where there are connections to Marseilles, Nice, Toulon and the Italian sea-ports.

Specifically, the apartment **sleeps 4** in a double and a twin, with a combined sitting room/diner and a balcony with a table and chairs, and those marvellous views. TV/video. Bathroom with bath and shower. Very well equipped kitchen: oven, microwave, fridge, freezer, washing machine, dishwasher. Cost: from about £195. Further details from Roger Jones, Flat B, The Old Granary, Tremadog, Gwynedd LL49 9RH. Telephone (01766) 513555.

France – countrywide
Dominique's Villas

Dominique's Villas is a medium-sized agency created 20 years ago by Dominique Wells. The agency is notable for its stylish and beautifully illustrated brochure that's highly professional but also has some charming personal touches. Its great strengths in the Dordogne, Provence and the Côte d'Azur – so much loved by Brits – help towards its popularity.

During a 2004 visit to a number of houses in the Lot et Garonne region, we were much taken with two that are somewhat different in character and location. First, we saw an isolated, utterly quiet, rambling, many roomed and beautifully restored house being spruced up, as it happened, for the owners due down for their own holiday. Gorgeous! **Sleeps 10**. Ref DL72. Then, in a busier location, in an extraordinary situation beside an ancient bridge and a dramatic weir, we visited an exceptional property that use to be a well known rural restaurant and hotel (there's a huge 'professional' kitchen'). **Sleeps – yes – 13.** Ref DL34.

We also stayed in a handsome traditional house (that is, not a conversion) **sleeping 10**. See Page 268.

During a 2004 visit we were much taken with 'Property No DL72', near Nérac.

Open the wine and get the cook-books out! This is the kitchen in 'Property No NR21'.

We remember a house in a hamlet on a hill that overlooks the Lot Valley – a comparatively little-known part of the country. There's a pleasant pool and 'country' furniture, along with antiques. Ref DL60. **Sleeps 6**. Just across the Channel, within easy reach of the ferry ports at Caen and Le Havre, we came across a gem. It's a beautifully renovated 18th-century farmhouse (**sleeping 9/10**) with idyllic views. Sandy beaches at Deauville and Trouville are within fifteen minutes' drive. Ref NR21. And, handy for the Cherbourg ferries, there's an enchanting 17th-century chateau (**sleeping 15**) in the village of Yvetôt-Bocage, just outside Valognes. It's perfect for children, as the grounds include a child-size manor house, a games room, swings and sandpit. A heated pool is a recent addition. Ref NR18.

Details/brochure from Dominique's Villas, The Plough Brewery, 516 Wandsworth Road. London SW8 3JX. Telephone 020 7738 8772.

www.dominiquesvillasco.uk
email: dominique@www.dominiquesvillas.co.uk

France Countrywide
French Country Cottages*

Glorious food and wine, spectacular chateaux, colourful markets, easy to reach. No wonder France is so popular with the British. From Brittany to the Languedoc, from Alsace to the Côte d'Azur, French Country Cottages has over 1200 cottages, villas and farmhouses, each selected for its own special character and charm.

In a remarkable brochure that bursts with colour, each property gets a detailed write-up and is illustrated with uniformly excellent photos. Plenty of local information highlights nearby beaches, towns and attractions too. Also, the brochure is helpfully split into thirteen regional sections, each prefaced with a short description of the area and a diagram showing the average daily temperatures from May to September.

French Country Cottages also has an excellent website which allows for hassle-free online browsing. You can use it to view additional photos and information, find a property on a map, check availability and make your booking online, all at your own pace.

The brochure also helps you find properties that accept pets or have swimming pools, complete with full details as to whether these are shared or private, and of their sizes.

Anyone who likes staying in a property with real character would be as delighted as we were with *Les Manis,* near Vimoutiers in Normandy, located just 25 miles south-east of the ferry port of Caen. This beautifully restored half-timbered three-storey house has exposed beams and

Le Pressoir is a most interesting conversion in the 'private and silent' grounds of a chateau. Surrounding the property itself are well kept lawns, a dovecote and a lake...

stonework throughout. Step into the garden and you are met by extensive grounds with a heated pool and glorious views over the surrounding Pays d'Aude. For days out, the D-Day beaches and Bayeux, with its famous tapestry, provide plenty to interest all ages. **Sleeps 6**. Ref F61114.

For its situation alone, *Le Cortal,* in the peaceful 12th-century village of Nohedes, near Prades, is unmissable. Perched on a mountainside at a height of 1000 feet in the heart of the Parc Naturel Regional of the Catalan Pyrenees, it is surrounded by spectacular scenery. The apartment, **sleeping up to 4**, is part of an old dry-stone house which was originally a sheep barn. It has its own private terrace and a pool shared with the owners. The coast, which curves down towards Spain in an almost continuous strip of sand, is about 40 miles away. Ref F66107.

For something really special, nothing quite beats a top-class property on the

French Riviera. *Soleil du Midi* (**sleeps 6**) is a beautiful three-storey villa built in the 19th century, very close to Monte Carlo and ten miles from Nice. It nestles on a hillside in the Basse Corniche, facing the Mediterranean and the delightful village and bay of Roquebrune Cap Martin. Decorated and furnished to a very high standard with marble or parquet floors throughout, the rooms are all bright and airy and have sweeping views of the sea. Each of the three bedrooms has its own bathroom. Outside there is a pretty terrace and swimming pool. Ref F06236.

Ideal for a couple, perhaps with a baby or small child, *Chinon* is a lovely apartment (**sleeps 2/3**) in the Loire Valley, named after the historic town nearby. It's on the upper two floors in a group of mellow stone ecclesiastical buildings dating from the 15th century. Great care has been taken to preserve the authentic atmosphere with old beams and an open fireplace. There is a private terrace, shared courtyard garden and pool. Ref F37121.

In the Vendee, a region where we have had several sun-blessed holidays, are five top quality properties (**sleep between 2 and 8/10**) in the grounds of the beautiful Chateau du Breuil near La Roche-sur-Yon. They have been cleverly created from the estate's old hunting lodge, stables and forge. Each has its own terrace or garden, but guests also have access to the chateau's grounds, which include extensive gardens, woodland, swimming pool and 18-hole golf course. Ref F 85137/8, 85157/8 & 85168.

Le Pressoir, a beautifully converted cider mill in the grounds of a private chateau, lies in the lush countryside of Picardy. The building's original ancient beams remain, set off by modern home comforts. The chateau's tranquil grounds feature well-tended lawns and a lake. **Sleeps 4**. Ref F 80103.

Chinon is a first-floor apartment in what was a 15th century ecclesiastical enclave.

Les Manis stands in extensive grounds with breathtaking views over countryside.

At the other end of the size scale, *Le Bastit* is an elegant house (**sleeps 20**) in the small village of St Medard, deep in the Dordogne, about 17 miles north of Bergerac. Very comfortably furnished, it is ideal for a group as it has ten en-suite bedrooms (five double, five twin), two living rooms and a dining-room big enough to seat everyone – with a cook available if required. It stands in a lovely garden with mature trees and large swimming pool (shared with another property). Ref 24181.

For a brochure or to make a booking, telephone 0870 197 6893; French Country Cottages, Spring Mill, Earby, Barnoldswick BB94 0AA.

www.french-country-cottages2007.co.uk

Tuscany
Tuscan Holidays

This hugely successful agency (a number of our readers, having 'discovered' it, go back to it year after year) is run by the people behind Heart of the Lakes/Cottage Life. That much-admired Cumbrian organisation has featured in every edition of *The Good Holiday Cottage Guide* since it first appeared in 1983.

Tuscany is a region of outstanding beauty, and a treasure trove of history and culture. The superb landscape embraces vineyards, olive groves and medieval villages, while a visit to the ancient cities of Florence, Pisa, Lucca and Siena is an essential part of any holiday. Tuscan Holidays offer over 120 villas in prime locations. A good number are either in or on the fringes of Chianti, perhaps the region's most beautiful area.

There are two apartments in the beautiful Casa Leopoldo, 20 miles from Pisa. *Part of La Sughera: a very flexible arrangement of apartments, a super pool.*

During 2006, for example, places within the agency's portfolio that caught people's eye were the apartments and barn at *La Ranocchiaia*, amid the picturesque hills between San Casciano and the village of Chiesanuova, just eight miles from Florence. This rural location is ideal for people looking for a quiet holiday but also within easy reach of Florence. Refs 180–183. Also, the two apartments in a superb 'tower house' called *Montioni*, in a beautiful location among the Florentine Hills of Chianti. The tower dates from the 12th century, and was *restored* in the 15th/16th centuries. In this case one is only about ten miles from Florence.

Among places readers have enthused about are a beautiful 18th century manor house called *Palazzo Rosardi*. **Sleeping up to 12**, it has fabulous panoramic views and a super swimming pool. Ref 490. Also, *La Villetta*, **sleeping 6**, near Castelfiorentino. They especially loved the blissful peace and quiet. Ref 270.

Among those we ourselves know is *Casa Fabia*, at Palaia, a delightfully restored old farmhouse on a hillside, with lovely views and plenty of scenic walks all around. It's on a 20-acre farm estate covered with vineyards and olives, so few guests leave without purchasing some of the owner's wine and olive oil. With two bedrooms (**sleeping 4**), it's not huge but has lots in its favour, such as the pretty sitting-room, a very convivial dining room/kitchen, a sunny terrace, a good size garden. Ref 240.

Down a quiet lane, though less hidden away than Casa Fabia, the lovingly restored 19th-century *Podere Le Murelle* cottage (**sleeping 2**) is on the outskirts of Palaia. Very comfortably furnished, it has superb views of the surrounding hills. Altogether it is a perfect romantic retreat, as the sole bedroom is particularly pretty, with its king-size double bed – ideal for honeymooners! Ref 140.

Also **sleeping 2** is *Casa Maria Luisa* at Castellina, in Chianti, about 19 miles from Pisa. This delightful mellow stone cottage is part of a beautiful old farmhouse: two sitting rooms, one with a dining area, and a kitchen with small Tuscan fireplace. There's a small, private back garden, a small downstairs shower room with W.C, a big double bedroom upstairs with views over the garden. a good bathroom, central heating and terracotta floors. There's a shared swimming pool in a neighbouring garden, and (of course!) a barbecue. Ref 410

Le Ginestruzze is one of the most-loved properties in this company's collection.

La Murelle is on the outskirts of the most attractive small town of Palaia.

We met two Australian families travelling together and staying at *San Angiola*, a big restored farmhouse (**sleeping 12/14**) near Terricciola. In the cool interior of the rambling house we admired spacious high-ceilinged rooms and very comfortable furniture of the old fashioned kind, especially several grand extra-large beds. There are six en-suite bedrooms, including one on the ground floor, and a seventh sleeping area (with its own shower room) on a galleried landing behind a screen. Ref 440.

Not far from here we discovered one of Tuscan Holidays most popular properties, *Fattoria Vallorsi,* in beautiful surroundings containing six apartments on a award winning vineyard. The apartments sleep between 2/4/6/7 or 9 people. Swimming pool, BBQ and children's play area. Ref 20– 25

Another property (**sleeping 10**) that has many fans is *Le Ginestruzze,* at Montespertoli, just 18 miles from Florence and 20 from San Gimignano. The large private swimming pool in the olive grove is always very well maintained. There are beamed ceilings, cool terracotta floors and, particularly in the bedrooms, some lovely old country furniture. Ref 100.

Details and a top-class brochure that gives admirably full details of every property is available from Tuscan Holidays, Fisherbeck Mill, Old Lake Road, Ambleside, Cumbria LA22 0DH. Telephone 015394 31120.

www.tuscanholidays.co.uk

Italy
Sunvil

Knowing our readers, we are not surprised they've responded to previous features about 'Sunvil Discovery', a company that arranges 'unpackaged holidays'. With 34 years' experience in a number of European countries, Sunvil has a wide range of holidays for the independently minded, with destinations slightly off the beaten track. Cottages, villas and apartments in Portugal, Greece, Cyprus and Madeira are also available, many of them all year round.

In Italy, for example, the lure of the medieval university town of Perugia is a strong one for many travellers. The smaller towns of Assisi, Gubbio, Todi, Spoleto and Orvieto are also worth exploring, and the surrounding Umbrian countryside of olive groves, vineyards and woods shelters lovingly restored farmhouses converted into cottages and apartments.

Not far away is one such farm; *Le Due Torri*, between Spello and Assisi, has two separate stone-built country houses, offering both self-catering apartments and 'b and b'. The main house, *Torre Quadrano*, has a

The Ospitalita Rurale and La Fattoria apartments are in tiny Montemelino...

The main house at Le Due Torri is proud of its 900-year-old watchtower!

medieval watchtower about 900 years old, a restaurant serving local cuisine, a swimming pool, and an apartment, *Il Fienile* (**sleeping 2 'plus 2'**), with a double bedroom, bathroom with shower, living room with double sofa bed and corner kitchenette. The second house, *Ponte Pazienza*, about 2km away, has two studios, a three one-bedroom apartments and a swimming pool. Both houses are beautifully furnished with fine antique pieces. Although the farm is mainly devoted to cattle breeding, it does produce its own virgin olive oil, honey and wine. Another farm property, *Ospitalita Rurale* and *La Fattoria di Montemelino*, in the ancient hill-top hamlet of Montemelino, 14km from Perugia, has been restored and converted to provide several apartments of various sizes. The old buildings, their wooden beamed ceilings, thick stone walls and open fireplaces have all been retained, and all apartments have outdoor furniture, well-equipped kitchens and enjoy access to the swimming pool.

Sunvil Discovery, Sunvil House, Upper Square, Old Isleworth, Middlesex TW7 7BJ. Telephone 020 8758 4722; Fax 020 8568 8330. **www.sunvil.co.uk email: discovery@sunvil.co.uk**

Italy: nationwide
Interhome

More than half a million clients annually, a good percentage of them regulars, surely 'can't be wrong'. Interhome, an extraordinary organisation, offers over 20,000 properties, each graded from one to five stars.

We've been especially impressed by the company's superb 'Prestige' brochure, featuring nothing but the very best four and five star holiday accommodation in grand castles and chateaux, fabulous houses, luxurious villas and top notch apartments, all in sought-after European locations (plus Florida). We haven't the space to do more than scratch the surface, so here's just a flavour of what the company offers in Tuscany.

Villa La Casina: very private, and most lovingly renovated by the owners.

Casa Pergolina: a fine 18th century house set off by olive groves and cypresses.

We liked the look of *Podere delle Rose*, Val d'Orcia, so much that we chose it for this year's cover! What a charmer, with its good sized pool, its open fire and that sense of history one associates with so many of Interhome's beautifully cared for and restored properties. Delightfully, there's outdoor seating in the shade of the forest. **Sleeps 6.** Ref i5377/600. Another property of character is *Casa Pergolina*, an 18th century farmhouse near S. Casciano set off by olive groves and cypress trees, also with an open fire. But who would be such a purist as not also to appreciate the swimming pool and the satellite TV? **Sleeps 7.** Ref i5274/820.

Villa La Casina, in Bucine, reached by a private road, is an old stone farmhouse renovated by the owners with great care. It has a woodburner, heating, stereo system and dishwasher. It is surrounded by a large well-kept garden with the swimming-pool shared with another house (i5238/845) about 50 yards away. **Sleeps 10.** Ref i5238/812.

All Interhome properties are available for viewing on a CD rom, available from Interhome Limited, 383 Richmond Road, Twickenham TW1 2EF. Write for any of Interhome's destinations (eg Austria, Switzerland, France, Germany, Portugal, Spain, Poland, Croatia) or, particularly, their new brochures: 'Solemar' and (as featured above!) 'Prestige', 'featuring top quality Four and Five star properties and City Apartments'.

Telephone 020 8891 1294. Fax 020 8891 5331.

www.interhome.co.uk email: info@interhome.co.uk

Tuscany: Casentino
Canova

This spacious farmhouse, recommended by a previous printer of this book, is close to the pretty town of Casentino. In spacious grounds among peaceful wooded and olive tree clad hillsides, and with its own secluded swimming pool, it **sleeps up to 12** – either as a whole or via two separate apartments **sleeping 4 and 8** people respectively. Specifically, there are two separate living rooms, six bedrooms and two bathrooms.

Though very pretty, this part of Tuscany, remarkable for its mountain scenery, is comparatively little known. But there is easy access to all the Tuscan 'favourites' such as Florence and Siena.

Details from Rebecca Rawlings. Telephone 020-7482 1663.

email: rebeccarawlings@hotmail.com

Tuscany/Umbria
Vintage Travel

Vintage Travel's Italian portfolio is concentrated in two popular regions, with access too to some famous places.

In Tuscany and Umbria there are about a dozen properties. In the former, Vintage Travel have taken the extraordinary medieval hilltop town of San Gimignano as their focal point. In the latter, most properties are within easy access of Perugia. We know these parts of Italy quite well, and 'Vintage' have the essence of them: almost without exception each property fits prettily into its surroundings, and panoramic views from the properties themselves are quite common.

As noted on other pages, the company's quite outstandingly good brochure is more like a coffee table book than a conventional brochure: quite inspiring. Though there is one modern house (25km from Perugia) that **can sleep up to 22**, most properties tend to be rustic and family-sized rather than palatial. Several have swimming pools – but this is the sort of villa/cottage collection in which the pool serves the property rather than the other way round. Altogether, very impressive.

Further details and a superb are brochure available from Vintage Spain Ltd, Milkmaid House, Willingham, Cambridge CB4 5JB. Telephone 01954 261431. Fax 260819.

www.vintagetravel.co.uk
email: holidays@vintagetravel.co.uk

Tuscany: Versilia
Il Castoro

Readers have recommended this, a rare chance for people who want to be in Tuscany to have a base by the sea. *Il Castoro* is situated on a small development just outside the village of Torre-del-Lago. It is one of the most appealing seaside resorts along the coast of Versilia – not a sleepy hideaway, but a lively resort likely to appeal most to youngish people. And if the occasionally frenetic atmosphere gets you down you can always escape into the hills or take a trip to easily accessible Florence, Lucca, San Gimignano and Siena.

The house **sleeps up to 7** in three double bedrooms and there is shared access for all residents on this complex to a swimming pool and tennis courts. (Music lovers should note that Torre-del-Lago is the place where Puccini wrote all his operas, which are performed every summer in an open air theatre.)

Cost: £350 to £700. Details from Mr N Castoro. Telephone 07979 528955. For a brochure: fax 020 8458 1394.

Tuscany: Posara
Watermill

Somewhat off the beaten track, only just outside the walled medieval town of Fivizzano in the district of Lunigiana, this privately owned watermill (it really is picture postcard stuff) stands beside the River Rosaro, in the small village of Posara. It's almost too good to be true: in a peaceful wooded valley

Five separate apartments in a very sympathetic conversion of this old mill.

with a background of rolling hills and mountain peaks, it has the big advantage of being within easy access of the sea – don't forget that inland Tuscany can get very hot in high summer – and the principal tourist attractions of this much loved region.

Specifically there are five self-contained apartments within the mill and it's possible to rent more than one at a time, so a group of **up to 16** can take the whole place.

There are secluded gardens extending for about a quarter of a mile beyond the millstream and around the mill there are grapes and vegetables for the use of guests. Add to this sunny terraces and millstone tables under the vines for eating outside.

Please note: during May and September there are painting courses based here. Further details of those or simply the accommodation from Bill Breckon or Lois Love. Telephone/fax 01466 751111.

Costa Blanca/Javea

It will be interesting to see whether our increasingly hot and dry summers will have any effect on the British love of 'the Costas', which is mainly driven by the weather. It has been reported that 60% of people in the UK would like to live all or part of the year abroad, and something like 50% of that number said they would choose to be on Spain's Costa Brava or Costa Blanca.

'Cottage guide' readers Eileen Robinson and Sally Martin have recommended a number of properties in this inescapably popular 'honeypot'. Not a place to get away from it all but as a colleague put it 'quite a good place to start getting to know holiday-Spain'.

1. Villa Alicia

Just five minutes' drive from Javea – shops, restaurants, discos and fine, sandy beaches – this is detached, comfortable and quietly situated among orange groves and its own well cared for gardens. There is a small but private swimming pool, a sitting room with satellite TV, a separate dining area and a very smart kitchen. **Sleeps 7**. Cost: £400 to £750.

Details from Mr Thomas McConkey. Telephone 0034 965 79 59 70.

email: tjmcconkey@yahoo.com

2. Villa Torre Wombata

This elegant stylish and extremely comfortable villa has been described as having the best view on the whole of the south coast. Though it looks

Villa Torre Wombata has been said to have the best view on the south coast... *...and they've said some pretty nice things about the interior too!*

huge, it does in fact only **sleep 6**, so it has the advantage of a degree of intimacy as well. South facing, with several terraces, a large floodlit swimming pool, a solar heated jacuzzi and sauna (all with the view of fishing port, the marina, Javea bay and mountains beyond), it has been furnished with great care and is, not surprisingly, unavailable to children under 12. Cost: about £625 to £1250.

Details from Liane Webster. Telephone 01273 833072.

Among other property recommendations that have come our way are:

*Casa Tranquila and Casa Barranca (Javea)

Both in the same ownership, these excellent properties have a big following among Brits wanting to be close to this popular resort but with a good degree of privacy as well. The former is in spacious gardens in very peaceful surroundings, just 1km from Javea. **Sleeping up to 7** in a double and two twins, it has a particularly charming and shaded good sized swimming pool. The latter is most impressive, **sleeping up to 11** in three doubles and two twins with a particularly appealing sitting room with satellite TV, a dining room just made for convivial get-togethers and a 'last word' kitchen.

Cost: (Casa Tranquila) £400 to £1050: Casa Barranca £600 to £2400. Details from Brian or Angela Liddy. Telephone 0115 989 9118.

*Casa Gisela (Jesus Pobre/Javea)

This is superbly well situated in the foothills of the Montgo mountains among pinewoods, vineyards and almond groves. Just ten minutes' walk from the famous but still very attractive classically Spanish village of Jesus Pobre, it is also just 8km from Javea. **Sleeping up to 10** in two doubles and three twins (and, note, three bathrooms), it has a pool side patio and terraces. Babysitting possible by arrangement; satellite TV; barbecue. Cost about £435 to £1150.

Details from Sheelagh Massey. Telephone 01904 468777.

*Villa Babar/Casa Felix (Benitachell)

Here are two absolute charmers, the first in a quiet new development, with fabulous views and with the advantage for wheelchair users of being all on one level. There's a south facing terrace and a private pool (which the master bedroom gives straight on to). **Sleeps 4**. Details from 01346 515262. The latter also has great views, and the advantage of a feature open fireplace. **Sleeps 4**. Details from 0034 96 6493074.

Casa Barranca sleeps up to eleven. There are manicured gardens and memorable views...

Casa Gisela is just ten minutes' walk from Jesus Pobre, but it's private too. It sleeps up to ten people...

Andalucia
Spain at Heart

This is a spectacular region of the country, with a huge variety of land-scapes: sandy beaches, stark mountains, green valleys, clusters of white-washed villages and rolling green hills. The Moorish and Roman legacy is everywhere, and music, dance and food are among many attractions.

Seville, Cordoba, Granada and Jerez add to the attractions of this vast region. The Spain at Heart brochure suggests properties to enjoy in winter: look for the *Winter Sun* coding. The Axarquia region, bounded by the coast and the Sierra de Tejeda, is getting more accessible, but remains suitably rural for walks, wildlife and uncrowded beaches.

The beaches of the Costa de la Luz really are among Spain's 'best kept secrets'...

La Teja: a cool, spacious interior, with a number of original features retained...

Casa Azul, near Competa (**sleeps 5/6**), for example, home of a sculptress, exudes a particularly welcoming atmosphere. It delights in a circular tower sitting room, a shaded pergola, terraces and private pool.

South of Antequera are remote villages and the impressive El Chorro Gorge. On the edge of El Torcal Natural Park stands *La Teja* (**sleeps 4-8/9**), a country farmhouse retaining many traditional features, while the bathrooms and the kitchen have been updated.

La Saucedilla, near Antequera (**sleeps 6**), also turns heads, with its baronial-style dining room decorated with antiques and the mantelpiece collection of wooden decoy ducks. *El Tornero,* near Aracena (**sleeps 6**) is remarkable for its lovingly tended gardens and the cottage overflows with character: beamed rooms, wooden floors, an open fire, antique bedsteads, a country-style kitchen and a terrace overlooking orchards and pastures below. *El Chopo,* near Cortes de la Frontera (**sleeps 8**), is a restored 17th-century farmhouse, hidden away in a tiny country hamlet. Sympathetically restored, comfortably furnished, El Chopo is also endowed with a large cobbled terrace shaded by a vine-covered pergola, and a pool offset by lawned gardens.

Spain at Heart, The Barns, Woodlands End, Mells, Frome, Somerset BA11 3QD. Telephone 01373 814222 (bookings); 01373 814224 (admin). Fax 01373 813444.

www.spainatheart.co.uk email: spainatheart@spainatheart.co.uk

Mallorca, Menorca and Javea
Villa Select

As travel writers we've long had a high regard for Villa Select, which has a fine reputation for holiday villas in Mallorca, Menorca and Javea (plus Cyprus – see Page 336 – and also Portugal). Every villa has its own pool. We also have a special affinity with the organisation, as it was set up in the same year (1983) as The Good Holiday Cottage Guide! Standards can be depended upon: beyond that it's really a question of whether one looks for something grand or on a smaller scale.

There are a number of properties big enough for two families to join together or one big extended family, such as the highly recommended *Es Pujol*, on Mallorca, just outside a picturesque village, handy for Cala D'or and just ten minutes' drive from beautiful beaches. It is a moneyed area, so be prepared for stylish living in this property. Among good things there is a covered terrace with spectacular views, a lovely beamed sitting room with an open fire for cooler evenings. **Sleeps up to 8**.

Other very large properties on Mallorca include *Casa Nova*, looking from its fine position across attractive countryside towards the Bay of Pollença. **Sleeping 10**, it has masses of space, and an excellent swimming pool. On a smaller scale, *La Serelleta*, **sleeping 4**, has absolute privacy, fabulous views and a open fire. *C'an Lloberina*, **sleeping 8**, is a traditional *finca* in the Colonya Valley, at least 200 years old, private and full of character.

Menorca is slightly more sophisticated, slightly more private, with some really stylish properties, outstanding among which is *C'an Xaloc*. This stunning property is in millionaire country. **Sleeping 12,** it has fabulous views, total privacy, peace and quiet.

In brief, much-loved Javea, on the Costa Blanca is a favourite destination, with some quite beautiful villas. We love their style: generally rather elegant, shaded by trees, shrubs and climbing flowers, often full of character and, of course, reliably comfortable.

Villa Select, Arden Court, Alcester, Warwickshire B49 6HN. For a copy of a stunning brochure, telephone 01789 764909. Fax 400355.

www.villaselect.com   email: holidays@villaselect.com

Son Cisterna (not featured) is simply (or not so simply) an amazing property.

C'an Xaloc is 'a stunning property in millionaire country'. It sleeps twelve.

Cyprus: 'island in the sun' – and how!

A recent mid-winter visit to Cyprus brought us into Larnaca airport on one of those tension-relieving, golden-glow Mediterranean evenings.

We checked our watches ('exactly four hours from London – not bad'), but might also have checked our pocket calendars. The temperature was 20°C: was this *really* January? We thought of the dusting of snow at Heathrow, the upturned collars in our local high street.

Though we were mainly there to check out self catering properties for later editions of this guide we also luxuriated in sumptuous seafront hotels where reception areas are measured in acres rather than square feet. These were the Amathus Beach Hotel at Limassol, and the Coral Beach Hotel at Paphos, where we loved watching the sun go down – always more quickly than we are used to in northern Europe – from our sea-view rooms.

Some of our party were first-timers in Cyprus. They loved the balmy winter weather but cringed at the thought of the much-vaunted 42°C at the height of summer. We were all bowled over by Paphos's Roman mosaics of circa 250-450AD, impressed by the surprisingly modern faces at our feet, one dark-haired beauty a spit of Alma Cogan ('Who she?' Ed). We were also awed by our guide Louisa's fluency in *five* languages: maybe Latin too – we forgot to check.

She was from the north of the island. As far as the south is concerned that's not so much a 'no-go' place for tourists as a 'we'd rather you didn't go'. But British travellers are famously curious. In rather sad tones Louisa reminded us to order 'Cypriot' or 'Greek' coffee if we wanted to avoid the ubiquitous Nescafe, never 'Turkish'.

We exclaimed over the rich, sweet Commandaria dessert wine we tasted at the winery in Omodos (it's used as communion wine: no wonder the orthodox priests look so contented). As we pottered around the village, we paid high prices for jars of honey that did however taste like the nectar of the gods. And the jars were pretty, and some of them contained almonds along with the honey.

Via olive groves, almond trees in early blossom, with sudden glimpses of the all-embracing sea far below, we drove on blissfully empty switch-back roads. From a point overlooking 'Aphrodite's Birthplace' among an outcrop of rocks in the sea we rememebered that in Cyprus, disbelief in legends must be suspended

We travelled via Episkopi's RAF base – a bit of Basingstoke under the sun – to Kourion's Greco-Roman theatre, seating 12500. We half-expected graffiti: 'If Zeus had wanted us all to sit here for hours he'd have given us smaller bottoms and bigger cushions'.

Then to 'the best seafood restaurant in Larnaka' for an array of hot and cold fish dishes. Every time we looked up a waiter swam into view with more. So fresh, I bet the chips on the children's menu arrive wriggling.

Tochni, Troodos, Pafos/Akamas
'Cyprus Villages'

The aim of this most interesting concept is to revive rural communities and preserve their traditional houses. Once-deserted or ruined houses have been converted for visitors seeking an alternative to purpose-built tourist facilities, and the villages are able to keep more of the

A typical Cyprus Villages summer scene...

younger generations in their communities, with new sources of income. Cyprus Villages' traditional accommodation is dispersed around several locations. Guests can experience the tranquillity of village life in an authentic Cypriot house. (There's a choice of studios, one-bedroom apartments, two-bedroom apartments and three-bedroom houses.) Swimming pools are provided for the exclusive use of guests, the majority of whom take advantage of low restaurant prices and eat out. Car hire is highly recommended, as local bus services are extremely sparse.

The Tochni Region is ideal for first time visitors to Cyprus or for guests who want to explore this beautiful island. Centrally located between Larnaka and Limassol and not far from the sea, this is the ideal region to combine exploring the countryside with relaxation on the beach.

Also featured are the Troodos Region (traditional, tranquil wine villages among the mountains) and the Pafos/Akamas Region (the rugged beauty of the Akamas peninsula, notably the massive mountainous pine forests).

Details/brochures from 01202 485012. 0r **www.cyprusvillages.com.cy**

Latchi/Coral Bay
Villa Select

Cyprus has never lost its longstanding popularity among British people. It seems immune to the fads and fancies that affect other tourist destinations. Villa Select (see Page 000), have some gorgeous villas notable for their pools, their spaciousness and reliable standards of comfort.

Mircini, in the Coral Bay area, is exceptional even in Villa Select terms!

Among others in two main locations are the sumptuous *Olive Grove*, notable for its rather stone archways and super pool and – yes! – hot tub. Air conditioning in most rooms. **Sleeps 8**. Another remarkable property among so many is the imposing *Mircini*, also **sleeping 8**, surrounded by banana trees and offering peace and quiet. All the bedrooms are air-conditioned at no extra charge. The excellent Coral Bay beach is close by, and there are sea views from the house. Contact details as on Page 314.

Bavaria: 'We got a little high'....

We thought we'd died and gone to brochure-heaven (*writes Bryn Frank*). Jagged snow-capped peaks against a sapphire sky, toffee-coloured cows watching us lugubriously across wild-flowery meadows, a sudden glimpse near Berchtesgaden of the Königssee below: scrubby cliffs sheering into the still, dark waters of the lake, famously so pure that sightseeing launches are electrically operated so as to keep it that way, with the added bonus of almost no engine noise.

As we cable-car'd it up to about 4000 feet, via summer pastures where the scent of new mown hay mingles with pine, we were surrounded by the rich local dialect. Bavarian is to formal 'High German' as clotted-cream-rich Devonian is to 'BBC English'.

After just a few days in Bavaria we began to feel quite light headed, and it wasn't just the height. There's something about the combination of high mountain air and chilled wine from small vineyards unknown outside Germany that hones the holiday mood. And the taste of local beer that beats the mass produced exports. I'm thinking about all those foaming *steins* we drained at a pint-sized beer festival in Ruhpolding. Litres come automatically: it's really not manly to whisper to the *dirndled* waitress 'Mine's just a small one'.

There was general agreement among us that the *Dirndl* is the most fetching national dress after the sari, though there were some who spoke up for the kimono.

In one mountain watering hole we got the best of both worlds – panoramic views, air good enough to bottle *and* good food and drink. For in Bavaria, at the beginning of time, God created great mountains, secret valleys, rushing streams and picture-windowed restaurants with log fires, antique decorative ceramic stoves, stags' heads, sepia hunting prints and home cooking.

Of course they were created for the view, but I like them when the mist closes in: eerie and beautiful. As people linger over a drink they tend to glance at the menu: 'Well, as we'll be here for a while, let's at least try a plate of *Bratkartoffeln* and *Spiegeleier*'. Which is fried eggs and fried potatoes. Sounds routine, but at its best, *haute cuisine*. Or perhaps something more substantial, like *Eisbein* (pigs' trotter) and sauerkraut, or wild venison with wild berries and potato dumplings .

Most south-easterly of all Germany's semi-independent States, bordered by Austria and the Czech Republic, dissected by great rivers, Bavaria likes to play the part of the simple peasant, but it is a prosperous place

As well as those lakes and mountains it suggests the lush green parks and the Baroque architecture of Munich, 'The Merry Widow' at the opera house, cycling in the English Garden: more an English parkland, a bit of 'Capability Brown' a long way from home. It's the weekend exodus, summer and winter, of Munich's sleek Mercedes, BMWs and Porsches to the Bavarian Alps, where against a backdrop of mountains ghosts steal between shadows cast by ancient street lamps, and the striking of elaborately decorated clocks emphasises the silence. The fondness for nostalgic, moody lighting in the depths of winter, sudden gales of laughter from a snug bar in some 400 year old tavern, perhaps a snatch of music from a 'squeeze box', an intense pride in community is all very Bavarian.

A good tourist map will mark 'The Romantic Road', threading its way mostly in Bavaria, roughly on a north-south axis to the west of Munich. It takes in Nördlingen, where you can walk all the way round a town of red and orange roofs, and Dinkelsbühl, as pretty as its name and best known for its annual children's pageant. Also, the sweetest tourist honeypot of them all, Rothenburg, like a set of wood-cuts from a well thumbed book of fairy tales brought to life.

If there is one 'must-see' on the Romantic Road it's near the southern end. Neuschwanstein Castle is a cross between a wedding cake of the embarrassingly elaborate variety and a five year child's idea of the sort of castle in which Rapunzel would choose to let her hair down. Though she'd have the luxury of a different tall turret for each week of the year. This was 'Mad', though actually just very, very eccentric, King Ludwig III's greatest fantasy.

But he had taste, as we discovered at Chiemsee, where on one of the wooded islands in the lake another of his three castles is a partial recreation of Versailles. It was a bonus to stumble across another island, the Fraueninsel – the name comes from the pretty convent, an oasis of peace and simplicity, never more so than when the day boats have left and the picture postcard village is left to its own devices.

Storm clouds came over (contrasting with an elaborate rainbow) as we sailed back to the shore: 20 minutes' worth of pure calm, with the bonus of a final glimpse of Ludwig's palace through an avenue of tall trees.

Due south of Munich the serious ski resort of Garmisch-Partenkirchen, is close to the foot of Germany's highest peak, the Zugspitze. From a little station near the main line from Munich the partly rack and pinion route climbs to the top of the dramatic mountain. One draws a veil over the fact that the peak is technically just inside Austria.

On an early summer Sunday evening Garmisch was all very genteel: Franz Lehar from the bandstand in the park, elderly ladies with pugs and poodles on the lead. And, of course, gooey-cake shops, which in southern Germany have an almost religious significance.

British eurosceptics suggest that greater federalism in Europe will lead to a loss of national identity. They have probably not been to Bavaria. A Texan once told me, 'We are Texans first, Americans second'. In this not-to-be-missed corner of Germany – in some ways it contains the essence of the country – they go one better: they are Bavarians first, Germans second, Europeans third.

Ruhpolding (Upper Bavaria)

Here's a useful base for discovering much of the best of Bavaria. (Berchtesgaden and Chiemsee, for example, are less than an hour's drive.). But families especially love the farm itself: archery, sunbathing on the lawn, or going on long walks with the llamas. There's a barbecue and the tepee has room for up to 20 people, is equipped with an open campfire, and in terms of visitors is ideal for informal socialising. Children, of course, feel particularly at ease on the farm. The playground with the big tepee offers lots of fun and excitement. Or let your children hunt around in the nearby wood, play with the animals, build a dam in the stream, play table-tennis or simply let them use their own imagination.

Vacation Villas International property number 2616.

Telephone: 49 (0) 8663 2762. Also 01438 869489.

Rothenburg
(recommended by readers)

Apartments at Haus Benji, Wiesenstrasse. 10 Adelshofen,

Rothenburg o.d.Tauber. Germany 91587

Telephone 49 (0) 9865 941 97 91

In a rural situation, close to Rothenburg, on 'The Romantic Road', there are suites and apartments with **Four tourist board Star**s.

Garmisch-Partenkirchen
(Upper Bavaria)

Here's a convenient holiday flat near the base of the 'Zugspitze' (the highest mountain in Germany), with impressive mountain views. The centre of Garmisch is just eight minutes away from the house, which is surrounded by a beautiful garden – the holiday flat is on the first floor, and is suitable for **2 to 4** people 'sleeping comfortably'. Light and sunny, it has a big living room, an open kitchen and dining area. Cable TV, radio, CD player. There are two bedrooms, and a bathroom with bath and shower, and there are three balconies.

A garage is available for a small charge. The flat is also handy for mountain railways and hiking paths ice-skating in the ice stadium nearby and tobogganing,

Cost: from about 50 Euros per day for two; 60 Euros per day for four.

Details from Familie Huff, Hubertusstrasse 46, D82131 Gauting. Telephone 49 (0) 89-85 06 293. Fax 49 (0) 89-85 06 293

Kaprun, near Zell am See
'Haus Fischer' (Interhome)

After a false start, when we found ourselves in the wrong apartment in the heart of this famous ski resort (all round skiing on the fabulous, dramatic Grossglockner, but lots to see and do hereabouts in the summer), we detoured 'up the hill' to the correct building. Excellent! It's always nice to be a bit 'out of town', to have your own space. With good views of the mountains and easy access to the village, this was a spacious, reasonably priced delight.

With Zell am See just ten minutes by car, cable cars within three minutes and the one that transports you to the peak of the Grossglockner just ten, it was a good find. We walked for many miles on mountain paths, cycled on hired bikes round the lake at Zell, went on a round-the-lake boat tour.

Specifically, our first floor apartment had a spacious double-aspect double-bedded sitting room, a good sized twin room, the option of a further twin, a kitchen-diner and – yes – a bathroom. For some people this is important, and it's not automatic. Soakers must check the small print: only a minority of holiday properties in Austria (and Bavaria) have a bath rather than or as well as a shower. Not that there's any shortage of water around! There's a shared balcony, use of a garden, with some outside seating, and, at the back of the property – which contains other apartments, though all with a good degree of privacy – there's easy access to a charming country lane that, with rural views all around and a panoramic one of most of Kaprun, takes one down into the (large) village centre. **Sleeps up to 6.** Ref A5710/222B

In the same ownership, and in the main street of the village, a newly and smartly renovated apartment house is better suited to people who don't want to trek up the hill. There are two apartments, each **sleeping 6.** Refs A5710/230B and A5710/230C.

All the Interhome properties are available for viewing on a CD rom, available from Interhome Limited, 383 Richmond Road, Twickenham TW1 2EF.

Telephone 020 8891 1294. Fax 020 8891 5331.
www.interhome.co.uk email: info@interhome.co.uk

Summer and winter, Austria is a playground for 'bon viveurs' and outdoor types alike...

Barnard, near Woodstock
Seven Hills (New England Country Homes*)

It was interesting, in the summer of 2006, to test the famously smooth organisational skills of the people behind this company, which is in the same stable as the much admired English Country Cottages. Having booked a handsome-looking house half hidden among wooded hills a few miles north of Woodstock, Vermont, we travelled via Boston to so-chic Lennox, in Massachusetts, then spent a few days in rural New Hampshire, before venturing into the real life picture-postcard that this little light-under-a-bushel state is.

Vermont had been a long-time 'must see' for us. We'd *expected* to find weatherboarded houses and delicate timber framed churches bright white against emerald village greens, leaves just beginning to turn, tumbling rivers. We hadn't expected the horse-drawn buggies, the home made ice-cream, the maple syrup fountains, a pace of life that makes rural Ireland seem positively hectic.

Seven Hills was a delight: very quiet, very private, with great sunsets to admire.   *Another Vermont charmer: West Hill Meadows, just outside the town of Ludlow.*

Conveniently for the purposes of this guide it was our holiday house that was the star of the trip. It's called *Seven Hills*, after the view from the back of the house. Though after a few glasses of local applejack – a roughish calvados – on the porch we always counted more. Actually, we counted more even while quite sober. Seven Hills (Ref WR02), however accurately named, was a delight, and if anything rather undersold in the thoroughly inspiring New England Country Homes brochure.

A nearby bonus was the country store in the hamlet of Barnard: on a cool, rainy Sunday morning the stove was warm, the bacon and eggs a must. In continual use since 1830, the photogenic store was a reporting centre for boys joining up to fight in the Civil War, in which Vermont lost a higher percentage of its troops than any other state in the Union.

In this southern half of Vermont there are several exquisite properties in the agency's portfolio, such as *Vista View*, at Killington (Ref GM112), *West Hill Meadows*, at Ludlow (Ref LW061), and *White Birches*, at Wilmington (Ref 070).

Details from **www.newengland-countryhomes.co.uk**   0870 192 1764.

Special Categories (UK/Ireland)

A quick reference

We're pleased when readers call us for extra information about cottages we feature. They ask all sorts of intriguing questions, but mostly it's things like 'This cottage looks nice, but can you confirm it has a swimming pool?' ... 'How far away is it from the sea?' ... 'There seems to be a railway station quite near, but are there taxis or will the cottage owners pick us up and take us back?' Listing such items as this is not, however, a value judgement, as many of our very best cottages scarcely score at all in these lists. **Please note that agencies are not included, as it is assumed that most of them can offer properties that include some or even most of the facilities featured.**

1.	*In or on the outskirts of a village or town.*
2.	*Beside a lake, a loch, a lough, a river, the sea.*
3.	*Within about five miles of the sea.*
4.	*Deeply rural and/or fairly remote.*
5.	*Home cooked food available (including freezer food).*
6.	*Access by rail or owner will collect from train.*
7.	*Owner/manager living on site or immediately adjacent.*
8.	*On working farm.*
9.	*Suitable for people with limited mobility.*
10.	*Suitable for the disabled (using ETC or RADAR criteria).*
11.	*Big houses, suitable for two or more families (say, 9/10).*
12.	*Swimming pool on site or immediately adjacent.*
13.	*Open fires/coal or woodburning stoves.*
14.	*Tennis court on site.*
15.	*Special play/entertainment facilities for children.*

* Asterisks mean the facility applies to some properties only.

NB: Some readers ask us to indicate cottages that are available for short breaks, but our records show that four out of five owners or agents offer this facility. It is worth phoning about short breaks even at the height of the season.

	1	2	3	4	5	6	7	8	9	10	11	12	13	14	15
East Anglia/E Midlands/Shires															
All Seasons	✓						✓								
Blue Barn Cottage				✓	✓		✓	✓			✓		✓		
Bones Cottage	✓		✓												
Bramble & Hawthorn				✓			✓		✓				✓		
Brancaster Farms Cottages			✓				✓	✓		✓•	✓•		✓	✓	
Carpenters Cottages, No.6	✓		✓												
Chantry	✓	✓													
Clippesby Holiday Cottages			✓		✓		✓		✓•	✓•		✓	✓•	✓	✓
Corner Pightle			✓										✓		
Dowagers Cottage, The	✓					✓	✓					✓			
Gladwins Farm				✓	✓	✓	✓		✓				✓	✓	✓
Grove Cottages, The			✓				✓								
Highland House		✓									✓				
Holly Farm	✓			✓			✓		✓		✓				
Ivy House Farm				✓		✓	✓	✓	✓	✓•	✓	✓	✓		✓
Jenny's Cottage	✓		✓										✓		
Little River View	✓	✓					✓								
Margaret's Cottage				✓	✓		✓					✓	✓		✓
Moorings, The	✓	✓									✓		✓		✓
Northernhay		✓									✓				
Orchard Cottage	✓												✓		
Peddars Cottage	✓						✓						✓		
Potash Barns				✓	✓				✓		✓		✓		✓
Stubbs Cottages			✓•	✓			✓	✓	✓•				✓•		
Sunnyside Cottage	✓		✓												
Vere Lodge				✓	✓		✓		✓		✓	✓	✓•	✓	✓
Vista/Carpenters Cottages	✓	✓											✓		
Willow Fen	✓	✓				✓									
Willow Lodge	✓	✓				✓			✓		✓				
Wood Lodge				✓							✓		✓		
Yorkshire and The Peaks															
Beech Farm Cottages	✓						✓		✓•		✓	✓			✓
Billy's Bothy				✓	✓	✓	✓		✓		✓		✓		
Cherry Tree/The Old House	✓•												✓•		
Cliff House	✓				✓		✓					✓	✓•	✓	✓
Cotterill Farm Cottages						✓	✓						✓•		
Cressbrook Hall Cottages		✓		✓	✓		✓		✓	✓	✓		✓		✓
Dalegarth & The Ghyll Cottages	✓					✓	✓		✓	✓		✓			
Dalehead Court	✓			✓		✓	✓								
Darwin Lake Properties		✓		✓			✓								
Dinmore Cottages							✓		✓	✓			✓		
Farsyde Mews Cottages		✓	✓		✓•		✓					✓•	✓•		
Fold Farm Cottages	✓			✓			✓	✓					✓		
Hartington/Courtyard Cottages	✓												✓		
Hayloft, The				✓			✓						✓		
Headon Farm Cottages				✓			✓						✓		
Hillside Croft	✓			✓	✓	✓			✓		✓		✓		
Knockerdown Farm Cottages	✓			✓			✓		✓		✓	✓	✓•		✓
Sarahs Cottage	✓					✓	✓								

	1	2	3	4	5	6	7	8	9	10	11	12	13	14	15
Sawdon Country Cottages	✓												✓	✓	
Shatton Hall Farm Cottages				✓			✓						✓	✓	
Shepherd's Cottage				✓									✓		
Swaledale Cottages	✓•			✓•			✓•				✓•		✓•		
Thiernswood Cottage	✓			✓•			✓•		✓		✓•		✓•		
Townend Cottage	✓						✓						✓		
White Rose Holiday Cottages	✓		✓•			✓	✓•		✓•				✓•		
Wrea Head House Cottages			✓			✓	✓		✓	✓	✓	✓			✓
York Lakeside Lodges		✓					✓			✓•					✓
Northumberland and Durham															
Akeld Manor & Cottages				✓	✓		✓				✓•				
Blue Bell Farm Cottages	✓	✓	✓			✓	✓	✓•							✓
Cresswell Wing				✓			✓				✓			✓	
Farne House	✓	✓										✓			
Holmhead Cottage	✓	✓				✓	✓	✓	✓		✓				✓
Old Smithy, The				✓			✓	✓	✓				✓		
Outchester & Ross Farm Cottages			✓	✓	✓		✓	✓	✓•				✓		✓
Pele Tower, The							✓						✓		
Shepherd's Cottage			✓	✓		✓	✓	✓	✓				✓		
Stables, The & The Byre				✓	✓	✓	✓	✓	✓				✓		
West Lodge/Stables/Coachhouse/Bee Cott			✓	✓	✓		✓				✓		✓		
Scotland															
Ardblair Castle Cottages							✓•	✓•	✓•		✓•				
Arduaine Cottages		✓		✓			✓								
Ardverikie Estate Cottages		✓•		✓			✓	✓•			✓•		✓•		
Arisaig House Cottages		✓	✓	✓		✓	✓		✓•					✓	✓
Attadale				✓		✓	✓	✓							
Balnakilly Log Cabins/Cottages		✓		✓			✓	✓	✓•	✓•	✓	✓	✓	✓	
Blairquhan		✓		✓			✓	✓	✓•		✓•		✓		
Bothy, The		✓		✓			✓						✓		
Captain's House, The	✓	✓		✓									✓		
Carna Farmhouse		✓		✓									✓		
Coruanan Farmhouse		✓		✓		✓	✓		✓				✓		
Culligran Cottages		✓		✓			✓	✓					✓		
Druimarbin Farmhouse			✓	✓		✓			✓		✓		✓		
Drumblair	✓						✓								
Duinnish Chalets			✓	✓			✓		✓						
Duncrub Holidays				✓	✓	✓	✓	✓•	✓•				✓•		
Duns Castle Cottages		✓		✓	✓		✓				✓		✓•	✓	
Easter Dalziel Cottages			✓			✓	✓	✓	✓						
Ellary Estate Cottages		✓	✓	✓			✓	✓					✓		
Glen Coe Cottages		✓	✓	✓					✓						
Isle of Carna Cottage		✓	✓	✓									✓		
Lorgba Holiday Cottages	✓	✓	✓		✓	✓	✓	✓					✓		
Machrie Hotel Lodges		✓		✓	✓		✓		✓						✓
Millstone Cottage		✓		✓			✓								
Muirhall Holiday Cottages						✓	✓						✓		
Parker's Retreat	✓						✓						✓		

	1	2	3	4	5	6	7	8	9	10	11	12	13	14	15
Penmore Mill		✓		✓			✓				✓		✓		✓
Pier Cottage/The Library		✓		✓									✓		
Rhuveag		✓		✓							✓		✓		
Seaview Grazings		✓													
Shore Croft		✓	✓	✓					✓				✓		
Speyside Holiday Houses	✓	✓							✓		✓		✓		
Tomich Holidays				✓			✓	✓				✓			
Torrisdale Castle Cottages		✓	✓	✓			✓	✓	✓•		✓•		✓•		
Cumbria/Lancashire															
Bailey Mill Cottage		✓		✓	✓	✓	✓	✓	✓	✓	✓	✓			✓
Bassenthwaite Lakeside Lodges		✓										✓			
Bowderbeck		✓		✓											
Croft House Holidays	✓•						✓•		✓•				✓•		✓•
Field End Barns		✓•		✓			✓		✓		✓		✓		
Howscales				✓		✓	✓		✓	✓					
Kirkland Hall Cottages		✓					✓				✓		✓		
Land Ends		✓		✓			✓		✓						
Long Byres				✓	✓	✓	✓	✓							
Loweswater Holiday Cottages	✓•	✓•		✓			✓		✓•				✓•		
Matson Ground Estate Cottages				✓•			✓•				✓•		✓•		
Meadowbank/Garden Chalet	✓								✓•		✓		✓		
Monkhouse Hill Cottages						✓	✓		✓•	✓•	✓•		✓•		✓
Mossgill Loft & Chapel	✓						✓						✓	✓	
No 4 Green Cross Cottages	✓					✓									
Old Coach House, The	✓								✓						
Wheelwrights	✓						✓		✓•			✓	✓•	✓	✓
Wales															
Aberdovey Hillside Village	✓	✓					✓	✓							
Beth Ruach		✓					✓		✓		✓				✓
Blackmoor Farm Holiday Cottages			✓				✓	✓							
Bryn Bras Castle			✓				✓								
Bryn-y-Mor		✓		✓					✓		✓		✓		
Clydey Country Cottages															
Cnewr Estate		✓•		✓				✓			✓•		✓		
Fron Fawr		✓					✓								
Gwynfryn Farm		✓			✓		✓	✓				✓	✓•		✓
Nantcol		✓	✓								✓		✓		
Pant Farm & Sanctuary Cottage		✓	✓•	✓			✓	✓					✓•		
Penbryn Bach Cottage		✓		✓			✓						✓		
Penwern Fach Cottages		✓					✓					✓	✓		
Portmeirion Cottages	✓	✓	✓										✓	✓	
Quality Cottages, Cerbid		✓		✓•			✓•	✓•	✓•				✓•		
Rhos-Ddu		✓		✓			✓	✓					✓•		✓
Rhyd-yr-Eirin		✓	✓	✓									✓		✓
Rosemoor		✓			✓	✓	✓		✓	✓	✓				
Talcen Foel		✓		✓									✓		
Trallwm Forest Cottages				✓	✓	✓	✓	✓			✓•		✓		
Trenewydd Farm Cottages			✓	✓			✓		✓	✓	✓	✓			✓

	1	2	3	4	5	6	7	8	9	10	11	12	13	14	15
Victorian Barn		✓		✓			✓					✓	✓	✓	
Y Bwthwn		✓		✓			✓					✓	✓	✓	
Y Llaethdy		✓		✓			✓		✓			✓	✓	✓	
West Country															
Badham Farm Holiday Cottages		✓	✓	✓		✓	✓		✓•		✓•			✓	✓
Bosinver Cottages			✓			✓		✓	✓•		✓•	✓	✓•	✓	✓
Braddon Cottages		✓		✓			✓				✓		✓	✓	✓
Butler's Cottage			✓	✓			✓	✓					✓		
Chapel & Hockadays Cottages	✓•		✓•	✓•		✓	✓•						✓•		
Chew Hill Farm Holidays				✓			✓	✓							
Cider Room Cottage				✓	✓		✓	✓							
Coach House Cottages				✓	✓	✓	✓				✓	✓	✓	✓	
Compton Pool	✓	✓	✓	✓			✓		✓			✓			
Dairy Cottages				✓	✓		✓	✓	✓•	✓•		✓			✓
Draydon Cottages				✓											
Duddings Holiday Cottages			✓	✓			✓		✓		✓	✓	✓	✓	✓
Fursdon				✓			✓	✓					✓	✓	
Glebe House Cottages	✓		✓		✓		✓								✓
Gullrock		✓	✓	✓			✓		✓						
Horry Mill Cottage				✓			✓	✓					✓		
Kirk House	✓	✓	✓								✓		✓		
Knowle Farm		✓•					✓•	✓•			✓•	✓•	✓•	✓•	✓
Manor Cottage				✓	✓	✓	✓						✓		
Marigold/Penny	✓	✓	✓				✓								
Mineshop Holiday Cottages		✓•	✓	✓			✓				✓•		✓		
Mudgeon Vean			✓	✓			✓	✓	✓				✓		
Old School Cottages, The		✓		✓									✓		
Oldaport Farm Cottages			✓	✓	✓		✓	✓	✓•						
Otter Falls				✓	✓		✓		✓•		✓•	✓	✓•	✓	✓
Pettigrew Cottage	✓	✓					✓						✓		
Pollaughan Cottages		✓	✓	✓	✓		✓	✓	✓•	✓•			✓•	✓	✓
Red Doors Farm Cottages				✓	✓	✓						✓	✓		✓
Rockford Lodge	✓	✓	✓												
Scoles Manor			✓	✓			✓		✓	✓	✓				
Sea Meads Holiday Homes		✓	✓				✓				✓				
St Aubyn Estates Cottages	✓•	✓•	✓•	✓•			✓•	✓•			✓•		✓•		✓•
Stowford Lodge Holiday Cottages				✓	✓		✓		✓			✓	✓		
Trefanny Hill			✓	✓	✓		✓		✓			✓	✓		✓
Tregeath				✓				✓					✓		
Trevarrow Cottage	✓	✓	✓										✓		
Trevorrick Farm Cottages			✓				✓		✓	✓		✓	✓		✓
Treworgey Cottages			✓	✓	✓	✓	✓		✓•		✓•	✓	✓•		✓
Wheel Farm Country Cottages			✓		✓		✓		✓•		✓	✓	✓•		✓
Wooder Manor			✓				✓	✓	✓•		✓•		✓•		
Wringworthy Cottages	✓		✓	✓		✓	✓		✓		✓	✓	✓		
South and South East															
Ashby Farms Cottages	✓•	✓•		✓•									✓•		
Coach House, The				✓		✓	✓						✓		

	1	2	3	4	5	6	7	8	9	10	11	12	13	14	15
Eastwell Mews		✓			✓	✓	✓		✓•	✓•		✓		✓	
Pekes				✓	✓		✓		✓•		✓•	✓	✓•	✓	
Cotswolds/Heart of England															
Barn, The				✓		✓	✓						✓		
Bruern Stable Cottages				✓	✓		✓		✓•	✓•	✓•	✓	✓	✓	✓
Cotswold Water Park		✓		✓			✓					✓		✓	✓
Docklow Manor							✓		✓			✓	✓•	✓	
Glebe Farm							✓		✓						
Hall Farm	✓					✓	✓	✓							
Heath Farm Cottages				✓			✓						✓		
Hillside Cottage/The Bothy	✓			✓			✓	✓				✓	✓		
Little Cottage, The	✓					✓	✓						✓		
Log House		✓					✓						✓		
Mainoaks Farm				✓									✓		
Oast House, The/Manor Farm	✓					✓	✓		✓						
Old Cottage, The	✓												✓		
Old Dairy, The						✓	✓				✓		✓		
Orangery, The	✓					✓					✓				
Orangery, The							✓		✓			✓	✓		✓
Owlpen Manor Cottages				✓	✓		✓	✓	✓		✓		✓•		
Stowford Lodge				✓			✓		✓			✓	✓		✓
Sutton Court Farm Cottages				✓	✓		✓		✓•				✓•		
Swiss Chalet, The		✓		✓		✓	✓		✓						
Ireland															
Delphi Cottages		✓		✓	✓								✓		
Holiday House, Ballina	✓	✓											✓		
Killarney Lakeland Cottages	✓					✓	✓	✓	✓		✓	✓	✓	✓	✓
Village and Country Holiday Homes	✓•	✓•	✓				✓		✓•				✓•		

'Sleeps five' (or six, or seven, and so on) usually means what it says, but double check this if you like lots of space...

East Anglia/ East Midlands/ The Shires

Numbers underlined on maps denote agencies (which in the main text are marked with an asterisk). With only a few exceptions the location marked on the map is the letting agency's headquarters, and it is normal for the agency to be strongly or even exclusively represented in that particular region. In the case of the larger regional and the main national agencies, no location reference is given.

Gainsborough
Caistor
58
60
56 Mablethorpe
Lincoln
Skegness
60
Notts
Lincolnshire
Nottingham
Grantham
Hunstanton
46 23 31
26
42
37
25
27 20
Kings Lynn
21
22
Leicestershire/Rutland
Leicester
Peterborough
49
Kettering
Cambs
Northants
Northampton
Newmarket 1
Milton
Bedford Cambridge
Keynes
Beds
Bucks
4
Herts
St. Albans
Oxford
High
Wycombe
Oxfordshire
Chelmsford
Greater London

28
47
38 40 Cromer
41
43
Fakenham 34
29
44
48 32 33 Great
36 35 Yarmouth
19 Norwich Lowestoft
Norfolk
Diss 12 Southwold
Thetford 5
18 7 9
Suffolk 8 10
Bury 8
St Edmunds 3 Aldeburgh
Ipswich
11
6
13 2 Harwich
Colchester
Clacton-on-Sea

Map 1

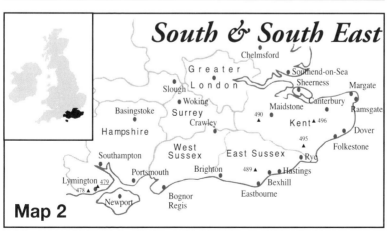

South & South East

Chelmsford
Greater
Slough London Southend-on-Sea
Sheerness
Woking Margate
Basingstoke Surrey Maidstone Canterbury
Crawley 490 Ramsgate
Hampshire Kent 496
Dover
495
West 489 Folkestone
Southampton Sussex East Sussex Rye
Portsmouth Brighton Hastings
Lymington 479 Bexhill
478 Bognor Eastbourne
Newport Regis

Map 2

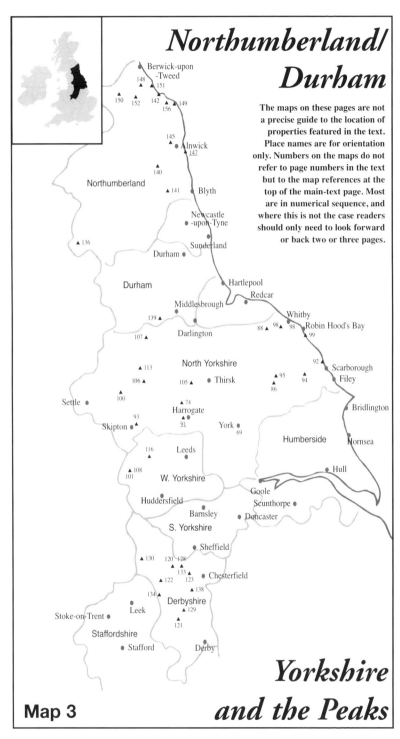

Northumberland/ Durham

The maps on these pages are not a precise guide to the location of properties featured in the text. Place names are for orientation only. Numbers on the maps do not refer to page numbers in the text but to the map references at the top of the main-text page. Most are in numerical sequence, and where this is not the case readers should only need to look forward or back two or three pages.

Berwick-upon-Tweed
148
151
150 152 142 149
156

Northumberland

145
Alnwick
147
140
141 Blyth

Newcastle-upon-Tyne
Sunderland
Durham

136

Durham

Hartlepool
Redcar
Middlesbrough
139
Whitby
107
Darlington
88 98 98
99

North Yorkshire
113
106 105 Thirsk
92 Scarborough
95 Filey
94
86
100
74
Harrogate
Settle
93 91
Skipton York
69
116 Leeds
Humberside Hornsea
108
101
W. Yorkshire
Hull
Huddersfield
Goole
Scunthorpe
Barnsley Doncaster
S. Yorkshire
Sheffield
130 120 128
133 Chesterfield
122 123
138
134
Derbyshire
Leek 129
Stoke-on-Trent 121
Staffordshire
Stafford Derby

Map 3

Yorkshire and the Peaks

Scotland

John o'Groats
Durness
Tongue
Thurso
Wick
Unapool
Kinbrace
Lybster
Lochinver
Highland
Ullapool
Lairg
Brora
Gairloch ● 204
Inveran
203 ▲
Invergordon
Dornoch
Isle of Skye
Lossiemouth
Macduff
Achnasheen
Cromarty
Nairn Elgin Buckie
Banff Fraserburgh
207 ▲ 195 185
189
Rothes
Kyle 199 168 ▲
Inverness
Peterhead
Huntly
Invermoriston
Grantown-on-Spey
Mallaig ● 201
Invergarry
Aviemore
Grampian
Aberdeen
▲ 196
Kingussie
Banchory
Fort William
Stonehaven
207 211 ▲ 198 202
209
Tobermory 212 183
Glencoe
Pitlochry ▲ 166
Brechin 182 Montrose
▲ 197
Mull
Tayside
▲ 164
Aberfeldy
200 ▲
Oban
165 ▲
Dundee Arbroath
▲ 217 Argyll
Perth ●
St Andrews
Callander
167 ▲
Stirling
Fife
Central
206 ▲
North Berwick
210 ▲
Dunoon
Dumbarton
Dunbar
Greenock
Glasgow
Lothian Edinburgh
Islay
Paisley
Eyemouth
215 ▲
181 ▲
154 ▲
218 ▲ Arran Irvine
Galashiels 153
Kilmarnock
Melrose ▲
Campbeltown
Prestwick
Ayr Strathclyde
Kelso
▲ 162
Borders
Girvan
Dumfries
and
Stranraer
Dumfries ● Galloway
Whithorn
Kirkcudbright

Map 4

Wales

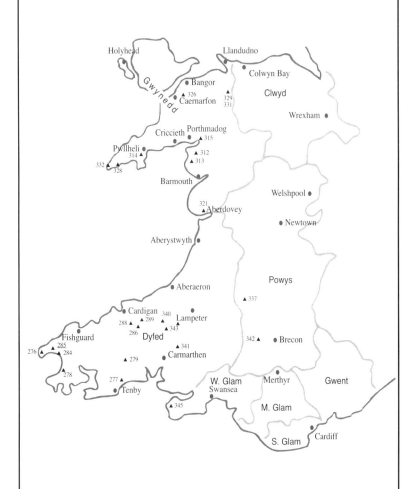

Holyhead

Llandudno

Colwyn Bay

Gwynedd

Bangor

▲ 326
Caernarfon

329
331

Clwyd

Wrexham ●

Criccieth

Porthmadog
▲ 315

Pwllheli
314 ▲

332 ●
328

▲ 312
▲ 313

Barmouth

Welshpool ●

321
▲ Aberdovey

Newtown ●

Aberystwyth ●

Powys

Aberaeron ●

▲ 337

Cardigan
288 ▲ ▲ 289
286

340
Lampeter ●
▲ 343

Dyfed

342 ▲ ● Brecon

Fishguard
285
276 ▲ 284

▲ 341
● Carmarthen

▲ 279

278

277 ▲
Tenby

W. Glam
Swansea

Merthyr ●

Gwent

▲ 345

M. Glam

S. Glam

Cardiff ●

Map 5

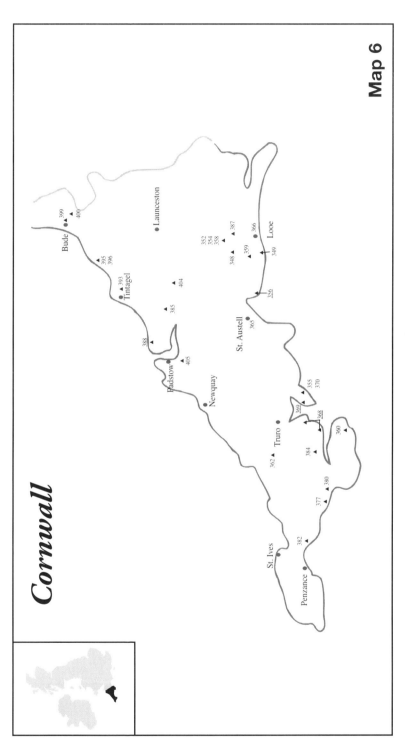

Cornwall

Map 6

Bude ● ▲ 399
▲ 400

● Launceston

▲ 395
396

▲ 393
Tintagel

▲ 404

352
354
358
348 ▲
▲ 359
▲ 387
● 366
Looe
349

388

▲ 385

356

▲ 405

St. Austell ● 365

Padstow ●

● Newquay

355
370
▲

369
368
360 ▲

362 ▲
Truro ●
384 ▲

380 ▲

377 ▲

St. Ives ● 382

Penzance ●

West Country (Devon, Dorset, Somerset, Wiltshire, Avon)

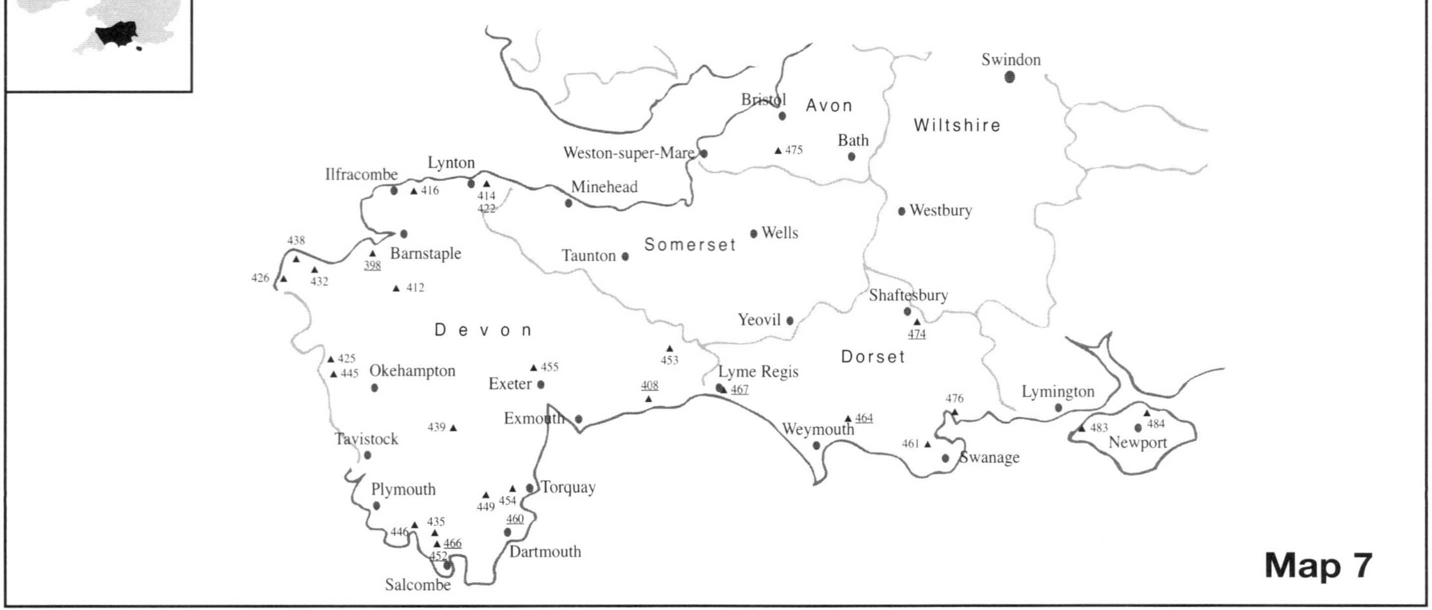

Map 7

Wiltshire

Swindon

Westbury

Avon

Bristol

Bath ▲475

Somerset

Weston-super-Mare

Minehead

Taunton

Wells

Yeovil

Dorset

Shaftesbury
474

Weymouth 464

461 ▲

Swanage
476

Lymington

483
484 Newport

Devon

Ilfracombe

Lynton
414
422

416 ▲

Barnstaple
398

412 ▲

438
432 ▲

426 ▲

425 ▲
445

Okehampton

439 ▲

Tavistock

Plymouth
444
435

452
466

Salcombe

Exeter ▲455

Exmouth

Torquay
449 ▲
454
460

Dartmouth

453

408

Lyme Regis
467

Cumbria/Lakes/ Lancashire

▲ 222

Carlisle
●
▲ 226

▲ 262

C u m b r i a
232
▲

Penrith
●
▲ 220

259
▲

254
▲

269 ▲ ▲
236

Keswick ●
▲ 252

246 ▲
▲ 248

▲ 265

Whitehaven

243 ▲ 258

● Windermere
▲
250

253
▲

244
▲

273 ▲ ▲ 274

● Kendal

▲ 268

Barrow-in-
Furness ●

● Carnforth

L a n c a s h i r e

● Blackpool

Map 8

309

Cotswolds/
Heart of England

Cheshire

Malpas ● ● Nantwich

Shrewsbury ●

Wolverhampton ●

Shropshire   W. Midlands

497   Oldbury ●
498 ▲   ● 507   Birmingham ●   ● Coventry

499 ● Ludlow   Kidderminster   Warwickshire   Rugby
502 ▲
Leominster ●   ▲ 521   ● Warwick
▲ 515

Worcester ●   ▲ 533

Herefordshire
▲
526   535 ▲   ▲ 534
Hereford ●   ▲ 538

514 ▲   ▲ 545   546

505 ▲   530 ▲
   ● Gloucester
Monmouthshire   ▲ 506   Gloucestershire   ● Oxford
      ▲ 529   ▲ 519
510 ▲   ▲ 511   501
      524
      523   ▲
        548
       Oxfordshire

Map 9

Ireland

Letterkenny
Londonderry
Donegal
Belfast
Killyleagh
Enniskillen
Armagh
Sligo
Dundalk
Ballina
563
Navan
Castlebar
Westport
580
Clifden
Athlone
Dublin
Dun Laoghaire
Galway
Port Laoise
585
573
Wicklow
Ennis
Carlow
Arklow
Limerick
Wexford
Tipperary
Waterford
581
Clonmel
Tralee
Killarney
562
Dingle
Cork
Bantry
572

Map 10

Listed below are brief details of cottages that appear on our associated website, www.goodcottageguide.com, but not in the guide itself.

Enquiries can be directed to info@goodcottageguide.com where an owner does not have their own email.

Walnut Tree Barn, Swanton Abbott, Norfolk. Barn conversion on village outskirts. Well placed for the Norfolk Broads and the coast. Sleeps 4. Telephone (01692) 538888, email: mark@citibuild.co.uk

Bosun's Rest, Blakeney, Norfolk. Fisherman's flint cottage; a stone's throw from the quay, log burning stove, modern appliances, sleeps 4. Telephone (02088) 662683, email: deborah.fitzpatrick1@btinternet.com

Plunketts Cottage in sought after Brancaster. Comfortable and well equipped sleeping up to 8. Close to stunning beaches, golf club and much more. Telephone (01485) 210892. email: roger.raisbury@btinternet.com www.brancasterstaithe.co.uk

Flagstaff House, Burnham Overy Staithe, Norfolk. Several properties with memorable coastal views. Sleep 2-11. Telephone (01278) 638637, email: admin@flagstaff-holidays.co.uk   www.flagstaff-holidays.co.uk

Lower Wood Farm Country Cottages, Mautby. Bordering Broads and National Park. Indoor heated pool and facilities ideal for families. Sleep 4-9. Telephone (01493) 722523, email: info@lowerwoodfarm.co.uk www.lowerwoodfarm.co.uk

The Grove Cottages, Cromer, Norfolk. (1/2 mile Cromer). Converted barns in 3 acre grounds. Heated indoor swimming pool. Sleep 2-6. Telephone (01263) 512412, email: thegrovecromer@btopenworld.com www.thegrovecromer.co.uk

Norfolk House & Courtyard Cottages, Docking (near Burnham Market and Brancaster), North Norfolk. Traditional properties in village. ETC 5 Stars. Telephone (01485) 525341, email: holidays@witleypress.co.uk

Wood Farm Cottages, near Holt, Norfolk. Converted barns and stables in secluded five acres. Children and dogs welcome. Telephone (01263) 587347, email: info@wood-farm.com www.wood-farm.com

Heron Cottage, Horning, Norfolk. Enviable position right on the Broads - rowing dinghy provided! ETC 5 Star. Sleeps 6. Telephone (07788) 853332, email: info@heron-cottage.com www.heron-cottage.com

Wensum View, Great Ryburgh, Norfolk. Spacious cottage for 8+2. Indoor heated pool. Magnificent scenery - a must for artists and anglers. Telephone (01328) 829288, email: wensumview@aol.com www.wensum-view.co.uk

4 The Courtyard, Snettisham. In conservation area 3 miles from Hunstanton and Sandringham. Close to countryside/beaches. Sleeps 4. Telephone (01406) 422569, email: jennifer.overson@ntlworld.com www.cottageguide.co.uk/4.thecourtyard

Anchor Cottage, Blakeney, Norfolk. Charming brick and flint cottage yards from the quay. Sleeps 6. Telephone (01462) 742245, email: anchor_cottage@hotmail.co.uk www.blakeneyhideaways.co.uk

The Old Bakery, a characterful and spacious family cottage in idyllic Blakeney on the North Norfolk coast. Sleeps 6. Telephone (01438) 869334, email: julian@godlee.com www.blakeneycottage.com

The Saltings, Blakeney. Child friendly, traditional cottage, open all year round. Sleeps 6. Telephone (07971) 798802, email: bcarroll@fleetmarsh.co.uk www.thesalting.co.uk

Kingfisher Lure, Wroxham. Ideal for couples or a small family. In quiet backwater with use of dinghy. Sleeps 4. Telephone (01923) 812912, email:info@wroxhamcottage.co.uk www.wroxhamcottage.co.uk

The Old Rectory Cottages, Flixton. Four delightful Victorian properties each sleeping 2. Well behaved dogs welcome. Telephone (01986) 893133, email: enquiries@oldrectorycottagesflixton.co.uk www.oldrectorycottagesflixton.co.uk

Bolding Way Holiday Cottages, Weybourne, North Norfolk Heritage Coastline. Four cottages sleeping 2-14 + cot + 2. Telephone (01263) 588666, freephone UK only 0800 0560996, email GHCG@boldingway.co.uk www.boldingway.co.uk

Hill Farm Holiday Cottages, Ashdon, Essex. Two adjacent cottages in quiet location with stunning views. Ideal for family and business groups. Telephone (01799) 584881, email: hillfarm-holiday-cottages@hotmail.co.uk www.hillfarm-holiday-cottages.co.uk

Old School Cottage, Norfolk/Suffolk/Cambs borders. Near Thetford Forest. Ideal for nature lovers, walkers and cyclists. Telephone (01953) 498277, email: oscott@clara.net   www.4starcottage.co.uk

Whitensmere Farm Cottages, Ashdon. Cambs/Suffolk/Essex borders. 3 well equipped barn conversions, 1 for disabled. Sleep 4-10. Telephone (01799) 584244, email: gford@lineone.net   www.holidaycottagescambridge.co.uk

Thaxted Holiday Cottages, Essex. In beautiful countryside, two cottages, each sleeping 4, plus B & B in converted stables. Telephone (01371) 830233, email: enquiries@thaxtedholidaycottages.co.uk www.thaxtedholidaycottages.co.uk

Epping Green, Essex. Modern 3 star bungalow sleping 2/4. Convenient for M25, M11, M1. 30 minutes to Stansted Airport. Telephone: (01992) 571828, email: enquiries@kingswayholidays.com www.ukholidaycottages.biz

The Cottage Collection. Superb selection of properties located in every area of Outstanding Natural Beauty around Great Britain. Telephone (01603) 724809, email: bookings@the-cottage-collection.co.uk www.the-cottage-collection.co.uk

Elms Farm Cottage, Fleckney. Comfortable, fully equipped cottage on working farm in the heart of rural Leicestershire. ETC 3 Star. Telephone (01162) 402238, email info@elms-farm.co.uk www.elms-farm.co.uk

Woodthorpe, Lincolnshire (near Alford). Attractive, well equipped cottages near superb sandy beaches. Sleep 2-6. Telephone (01507) 450294, email: enquiries@woodthorpehall.com www.woodthorpehall.com

Belleau Cottage, near Alford. Situated on the edge of the Lincolnshire Wolds, steeped in history and places of interest. Telephone (07984) 437517, email: dom@thepersuadersltd.co.uk www.belleaucottage.co.uk

Waingrove Farm Country Cottages, Fulstow, Louth. Award winning cottages offering a rural retreat in the heart of Lincolnshire countryside. Telephone (01507) 363704, email: ptinker-tinkernet@virgin.net www.lincolnshirecottages.com

Cliff Farm Cottage, North Carlton, Lincolnshire. Converted 19th century farm building with panoramic views across the Trent Valley. Telephone (01522) 730475, email: rae.marris@farming.co.uk www.cliff-farm-cottage.co.uk

Walnut Lake & Lodges, Algakirk. 4 star lakeside lodges in 10 acres of farmland with on site fishing. Telephone day: (07958) 362538, evening (01205) 460482, email: maria@walnutlakes.co.uk www.walnutlakes.co.uk

Kenwick Woods, Louth. Luxury Scandinavian lodges in mature woodlands with excellent leisure facilities. Telephone (01507) 353003, email: anna@kenwick-park.co.uk www.kenwick-park.co.uk

Keld Head, Pickering. Nine cosy stone farm cottages, by North Yorkshire Moors. Four-poster beds. Sleep 2-8 + cots. Telephone (01751) 473974, email: julian@keldheadcottages.com www.keldheadcottages.com

Burton, Turbine, Greystones, Charlie's Stables, Reeth. Stone-built cottages with views to the Pennines, ideal for the Yorkshire Dales. Sleep 2-5. Telephone (01748) 884273, email: cproctor@aol.com www.uk-cottages.com

Baille Hill House, York. Outstanding and sumptuously comfortable gem of a house, overlooking York's historic walls. Sleeps up to 10. Telephone (01845) 597660, email: enquiries@baillehillhouse.co.uk www.baillehillhouse.co.uk

Mel House Cottages, Pickering. 3 properties in extensive grounds. Perfect for York and Moors. Indoor pool. Suitable for mobility impaired. Telephone (01751) 475396, email: holiday@letsholiday.com www.letsholiday.com

Westwood Lodge, Ilkley - Yorkshire's original spa town. Superbly equipped cottages and apartments. M2 disability access award. Sleep 2-9. Telephone (01943) 433430, email: welcome@westwoodlodge.co.uk www.westwoodlodge.co.uk

Bottoms Farm Holiday Cottages, Oakworth. 3 olde worlde character cottages sleeping 4-6. Set in Bronte Country with spectacular views and walks. Telephone (01535) 607720, email: bottomsfarm@btinternet.com

Lilac Cottage, Aldbrough, East Yorkshire. A small charming cottage close to the coast. Sleeps 4. Telephone (01964) 527645, email: nick@seasideroad.freeserve.com www.dialspace.dial.pipex.com/town/walk/aer96/lilac-cottage

Rudstone Walk Farm Cottages, South Cave. Eleven cottages located close to East Yorkshire sandy beaches. Sleep 2-6. Telephone (01430) 422230, email: office@rudstone-walk.co.uk www.rudstone-walk.co.uk

2 Mouldgreave Cottages, Oxenhope. 18th century Grade II listed rural cottage close to historic Haworth and York. Sleeps 5. Telephone (01535) 642325, email: 2mouldgreave@lineone.net

Orchard Cottage, Goathland, North Yorkshire. Quiet location in popular moorland village. Sleeps up to 6. Telephone (01947) 896391, email: enquiries@theorchardcottages.co.uk www.theorchardcottages.co.uk

Cam Beck Cottage, Kettlewell, North Yorkshire. Idyllic 300 year old stone cottage with trout stream running alongside. Many walks from the door. Sleeps 4. Telephone (01132) 589833.

2 Penfold Yard, Richmond. A delightful stone cottage for 2+2 situated in the conservation area of this historic market town in the North Yorkshire Dales. Telephone (01268) 751036, email: susan.horton@southend.nhs.uk

Dales Holiday Cottages offer cosy cottages for 2 up to a splendid 16th Century building for 19. Telephone (01756) 799821, email: info@dales-holiday-cottages.com www.dales-holiday-cottages.com

Country Hideaways. 40 carefully selected properties in stunning locations in the heart of the Yorkshire Dales. Sleep up to 10. Telephone (01969) 663559, email: cottageguide@countryhideaways.co.uk www.countryhideaways.co.uk

Holiday Cottages in Yorkshire, Lancashire, Derbyshire and Cumbria. Over 200 properties from cosy cottages for 2 to spacious barns for 14. Telephone (01756) 700510, email: info@holidaycotts.co.uk www.holidaycotts.co.uk

Three traditional Dales stone cottages in beautiful Peak District National Park. Sleep 1 x 2 and 2 x 2+2. Telephone (07817) 900841, email: halleyr@aol.com www.thimble-cottage.co.uk

Mile House Farm Country Cottages. Four lovely Wensleydale cottages with spectacular views. Telephone (01969) 667481, email: milehousefarm@hotmail.com www.wensleydale.uk.com

1 New Leeds Cottage, Kettlewell, Upper Wharfedale. Comfortable one bedroom cottage ideally located for exploring the Yorkshire Dales National Park. Telephone (01132) 747924, email: Hilary_tucker@yahoo.co.uk

The Annexe, Acomb. Well furnished accommodation 10 minutes from York city centre. Double bedroom with cot/child bed available. Telephone (01904) 781985 or (07775) 771186, email: melia@theannexeyork.co.uk www.theannexeyork.co.uk

East End Cottage, Near Beverley. In pretty village of Walkington, East Riding of Yorkshire. Sleeps up to 4. Telephone (01482) 849809, email kay@jobber.karoo.co.uk www.eastendcottage.co.uk

Holiday Homes in Yorkshire. Over 80 superb properties throughout Yorkshire including the coast, Dales, Vale of York and North York Moors. Email: house-parties@globalnet.co.uk www.holidayhomesgroup.co.uk

Bradley Hall, near Ashbourne, Derbyshire. Highly individual, converted apartments with original features in rural surroundings. Sleep 4-9. Telephone (01335) 370222, email: michelle@pmwproperty.com www.ashbourneselfcatering.com

Badger, Butterfield and Bluebell Cottages, nr Buxton. Comfortable stone cottages in heart of the Peak District National Park. Sleep 6-8. Children & pets welcome. Telephone (01298) 872927, email: jan@cosycotts.com www.cosycotts.com

Holestone Moor Barns, Ashover. Two converted barns, one with wheelchair access, sleeping 4+baby and 12+baby, ideal family accommodation. Telephone (01246) 591263, email: HMbarns@aol.com www.hmbarns.co.uk

Tom's Barn & Douglas's Barn, Parwich, nr Ashbourne. Five Star 18th century limestone barns ideal for couples of any age. Telephone (01335) 390519, email: tom@orchardfarm.demon.co.uk www.tomsbarn.co.uk

Byanna Hall, Eccleshall, Staffordshire. 17th century manor house and butler's annexe. Sleeps 20. Telephone (01785) 850518, email: byannanivas@aol.com www.holiday-rentals.com/index.cfm/property/6416.cfm

Rushop Hall, Castleton. Three historic cottages sleeping 2, 4 and 6 in the Peak District National Park on the Pennine Bridleway. Telephone (01298) 813323, email: neil@rushophall.com www.rushophall.com

Ollerbrook Cottages, Edale Valley. Two 17th century cottages yards from the Pennine Way. Sleep 3 or 5. Telephone (01433) 670083, email: greenlees@ollerbookcottages.fsnet.co.uk www.ollerbrook-cottages.co.uk

Breamish Valley Cottages, Branton. Beautifully situated at foot of Cheviot Hills; half an hour from the Northumberland coast. Telephone (01665) 578253, email: peter@breamishvalley.co.uk www.breamishvalley.co.uk

Burradon Farm Cottages, Cramlington, Northumberland. Cottages sleeping 2-4. Fine views and ample parking. Good area for walking/cycling. Telephone: (01912) 683203, email: judy@burradonfarm.co.uk www.burradonfarm.co.uk

Beacon Hill Farm Holidays, Morpeth. Twelve superbly comfortable cottages on Northumberland farm with gym and other facilities. Telephone (01670) 780900, email: alun@beaconhill.co.uk www.beaconhill.co.uk

Britannia House and Cottage, Lindisfarne. Experience the magic of Holy Island; sandy beaches, castle and abbey. Sleep 6 and 4. Telephone (01289) 309826, email: ktiernan@onetel.net.uk www.lindisfarne-cottages.co.uk

Sandpiper Cottage, Low Newton, Northumberland. Delightful 18th century fisherman's cottage in outstanding coastal location. Sleeps 4+2. Telephone: (01665) 830783, email: sandpiper@nccc.demon.co.uk www.northumbria-cottages.co.uk

The Old Byre, Northumberland (near Hexham). Traditionally built farm-steading in 30 acres with panoramic views. Sleeps 6-9. Telephone (01434) 673259, email: enquiries@consult-courage.co.uk www.ryehillfarm.co.uk

Shilbottle Town Foot Farm & Village Farm, near Alnwick. Impressive cottages sleeping 2-12, free leisure facilities open all year. Telephone (01665) 575591, email: crissy@villagefarmcottages.co.uk www.villagefarmcottages.co.uk.

Laneside Cottage, Barnard Castle, Durham. A haven of tranquillity; former farmhouse with modern facilities and stunning views. Sleeps 8. Telephone (01833) 640209, email: teesdaleestate@rabycastle.com www.rabycastle.com

Kinlochlaich House, Appin, Argyll. Apartments/cottages within period house and grounds in spectacular Highlands. Telephone (01631) 730342, email: enquiries@kinlochlaich-house.co.uk www.kinlochlaich-house.co.uk

Achaglachgach Estate, South Knapsdale. Baronial mansion/cottages in secluded farm estate on shores of West Loch Tarbert. Sleep 4-14. Telephone (07770) 530249, email: Macleanh71@aol.com www.achahouse.com

Harrietfield Cottage, Roxburghshire. Two miles north of picturesque Kelso. Sleeps 2-5. Floors and Mellerstain Castles within easy reach. Telephone (01896) 831052, email: ncunnin640@aol.com

Crailloch Croft Cottages,Wigtownshire. 3 cosy cottages in peaceful countryside. Ideal base for local amenities and day trips to Ireland. Telephone (01776) 703092, email: viv@craillochcroft.freeserve.co.uk www.craillochcroftcottages.co.uk

Alvie Holiday Cottages, Kincraig. Traditional cottages with superb views of the Cairngorms combining tranquillity and sports activities. Telephone (01540) 651255, email: info@alvie-estate.co.uk www.alvie-estate.co.uk

Lochinver Holiday Lodges, Sutherland. Seven lodges by the sea, each sleeping 4. Scottish Tourist Board 4 Stars. Telephone (01571) 844282. www.watersidehomes@bushinternet.com

Tigh-a-Chladaich, Sutherland. Split level house on rocky promontory with spectacular coastal views. Sleeps up to 8 people. Telephone (01571) 844282, email: enquire@by-sea.co.uk www.by-sea.co.uk

Coillabus Cottage, Isle of Islay. Comfortable cottage on working hill farm on beautiful Mull of Oa. Open fire. Sleeps 2-6. Telephone (01315) 531911, email: holiday@islay-cottage.co.uk www.islay-cottage.co.uk

Armadale Castle, Isle of Skye. Six comfortable log cottages plus suite with sea/mountain views. Sleep 4-6. Telephone (01471) 844305, email: office@cland.demon.co.uk www.clandonald.demon.co.uk

Pirate Gows Chalets, Eday, Orkney. Five self-catering chalets virtually on the seashore. Beautiful surroundings and views. Telephone (01857) 622285, email: jan.crichton@btinternet.com www.takeabreak.com.au/pirategowschalets.htm

Crosswoodhill Farm Cottages, West Calder. Four exceptional homes on West Lothian hill farm. Visit their award-winning website for a wealth of details and photos, email: gchg@crosswoodhill.co.uk www.crosswoodhill.co.uk

Auchtermuchty Holiday Homes. Two warm and comfortable homes in small historic town of Auchtermuchty in the Kingdom of Fife. Sleep 5 and 6. Telephone (01337) 828496, email: elizabeth@auchtermuchty.com www.auchtermuchty.com

Binnilidh Mhor, Glenmoriston. Large and luxurious cottage for 2-6 near shores of Loch Ness with spectacular views. Suitable for guests with mobility disabilities. Telephone (01320) 340258. email: sheila@binmhor.co.uk www.binmhor.co.uk

Duirinish Holiday Lodges, Ross-shire. Nine lodges offering excellent self catering facilities for up to 4 or 6 on north-west coast of Scottish Highlands. Telephone (01599) 544268, email: sales@duirinishlodges.com www.duirinishlodges.com

Strathconon, Isle of Arran. Luxurious villa in sunny, secluded spot on outskirts of beautiful Whiting Bay. Sleeps 2-8. STB 4 stars. Telephone (01586) 830323, email: enquiries@arranselfcatering.com www.arranselfcatering.com

Dalhougal House Apartments, Croftamie. 200 year old refurbished apartments maintaining cosy Scottish atmosphere in Loch Lomond village. Sleep up to 4. Telephone (01360) 660558, email: dalhougal@croftamie.com www.dalhougal.com

Westloch House, Coldingham, Berwickshire. Ten character cottages sleeping 2 to 6. Coldingham Loch, known for its trout, is a stunning feature. Telephone (01890) 771270, email: westloch@hotmail.com

Leckmelm Holiday Cottages, near Loch Broom. Close to Ullapool, a lively fishing village on Scotland's scenic north west coast. Sleep 2 to 10. Dogs welcome. Telephone (01854) 612471.

Holiday Houses in Scotland. Some of the best self-catering houses and cottages in the most beautiful parts of Scotland. Tel. (01556) 504030, email: lettings@scothols.co.uk www.scothols.co.uk and www.discoverscotland.net

The Association of Scotland's Self Caterers. A comprehensive choice of carefully vetted properties throughout Scotland. www.assc.co.uk

Tigh-na-Mara, Dornie. This well equipped and welcoming property offers marvellous walks and wonderful scenery at the junction of three Lochs. email: nickgp@btconnect.com

Big Sky Lodges, Isle of Ord. Four luxurious detached log houses in glorious Scottish Highlands only 10 minutes from Inverness. Telephone (07752) 253376 Freephone 0800 6343524, email: angus@bigskylodges.co.uk www.bigskylodges.co.uk

Lorgba Holiday Cottages, Port Charlotte. Cottages sleeping from 2-5 beside safe and sandy beach on the beautiful Hebridean Isle of Islay. Telephone (01496) 850208, email: info@goodcottageguide.com

Brook House, near Keswick. Four 17th century stream-side properties in the delightful village of Bassenthwaite. Sleep 2-10. Telephone (01768) 776393, email: a.m.trafford@amserve.net www.holidaycottageslakedistrict.co.uk

Setrah Cottage, near Bassenthwaite. Charming cottage in quiet lane at the heart of Bothel Village. Excellent leisure facilities nearby. Telephone (01697) 320919, email: office@skiddawview.com www.skiddawview.co.uk

Barn House, Braithwaite. Traditional Lakeland Cottage, sleeps 2-6. Superb fells walks from the door and forest mountain bike trails. Telephone (01768) 778411, email: info@braithwaitefarm.wanadoo.co.uk www.barnhouseholidays.co.uk

Bridge End, Eskdale, Cumbria. Award-winning, characterful, Grade II listed cottages in small hamlet in valley beneath Scafell Pike. Telephone (08700) 735328, email: greg@selectcottages.com   www.selectcottages.com

The Orchards Apartment and Coach House, Eskdale. Ideal base to explore the Lake District; wonderful views over fells. Sleep 2-4. Telephone (01946) 723374, email: selfcatering@orchards-eskdale.com www.orchards-eskdale.com

Ashness Apartment, Keswick town centre. Beautiful apartment with views of Keswick and Derwent Water. Sleeps 6. Telephone (01768) 780855, email: info@ashness.net   www.ashness.net

Acorn Self Catering, Keswick. Three comfortable properties within five minutes of the town centre, sleep 6, 5 and 5. Telephone (01768) 480310, email: info@acornselfcatering.co.uk   www.acornselfcatering.co.uk

Richmond Cottage, Orton Hall. Peaceful relaxation in elegant wing of 17th century mansion in unspoilt Cumbrian countryside. Telephone (01539) 624330, email: info@stayinortonhall.com   www.stayinortonhall.com

Stonefold Cottages, Penrith. Three cottages within tastefully furnished 18th century stone building next to the Lake District. Telephone (01768) 866383, email: email@stonefold.co.uk   www.stonefold.co.uk

Fell View, Cumbria. Cottages/apartments in peaceful grounds close to Lake Ullswater, half a mile from Helvellyn. Pets welcome. Telephone (01768) 482342, email: enquiries@fellviewholidays.com   www.fellviewholidays.com

Green View Lodges, Welton. On northern edge of Lake District National Park, close to Scottish Borders, Scandinavian lodges sleeping 4 or 7. Telephone (01697) 476230, email: ghcg@green-view-lodges.com www.green-view-lodges.com

Staffield Hall, Kirkoswald, near Penrith. Seven elegant apartments in a magnificent mansion. Sleep 2 to 5 all with four poster beds. Telephone (01768) 898656, email: goodcotguid@staffieldhall.co.uk   www.staffieldhall.co.uk

Cumbrian Cottages. Cottages, apartments and houses in superb locations throughout the Lake District and Cumbria.   www.cumbrian-cottages.co.uk

Traditional Lakeland Cottages. An unrivalled selection of self catering holiday retreats within this beautiful corner of England.   www.lakelovers.co.uk

Penny Hill Farm Cottage, Eskdale. Once owned by Beatrix Potter and enjoying uninterrupted views of the Lake District fells. Perfect for couples. Telephone (01768) 776836, email: sally@hollinhead.co.uk www.hollinhead.co.uk/pennyhill

Lakeland Hideaways. Finest selection of cottages in and around Hawkeshead to suit every need. Telephone (01539) 442435, email: bookings@lakeland-hideaways.co.uk   www.lakeland-hideaways.co.uk

Sir Johns Hill Farm Cottages, Laugharne, Carmarthenshire, Wales. Three cottages in secluded location with views. Grazing for visiting horses. Telephone (01994) 427667, email: liz.handford@sirjohnshillfarm.co.uk www.sirjohnshillfarm.co.uk

Penffynnon, Aberporth. Characterful well-equipped properties by sandy beaches. Sea views. Dogs welcome by arrangement. Telephone (01239) 810387, email: tt@lineone.net   www.aberporth.com

Melin Llecheiddior, near Criccieth. 2 self catering cottages between the mountains of Snowdonia and the beaches of the Lleyn Peninsula. Telephone (01766) 530635, email: elen@whevans.freeserve.co.uk www.cottages-in-snowdonia.co.uk

Ffynnonofi Farm. Secluded farmhouse in North Pembrokeshire National Park with private beach. Sleeps 7-8 people. Telephone (01179) 268554, email: info@ffynnonofi.co.uk   www.ffynnonofi.co.uk

Carno Farmhouse and Little Barn, Libanus. WTB Grade 5/Disabled Access 2, sleeping 4/5 in the heart of the Brecon Beacons National Park. Telephone (01874) 625630, email: june.scarborough@lineone.net www.brecon.co.uk/local/carno

Wales Holidays. Around 550 properties throughout all areas of Wales, many in the Pembrokeshire and Snowdonia National Parks. Telephone (01686) 628200, email: info@wales-holidays.co.uk www.wales-holidays.co.uk

Cefnamwlch, one mile from Tudweiliog, Pwllheli. Three holiday homes on private estate within an area of outstanding natural beauty. Telephone (01758) 770209, email: cefnamwlch@hotmail.com www.cefnamwlch.co.uk

Walnut Tree Cottage, Pantygelli. WTB 5 Stars, pretty cottage with glorious views. Sleeps 4. Telephone (01873) 853468, email: enquiries@walnuttreeholidays.com www.walnuttreeholidays.com

Foxes Reach, Catbrook, near Chepstow. Traditional whitewashed stone character cottage. WTB 5 stars. Dogs/horses accepted. Telephone (01600) 860341, email: fionawilton@btopenworld.com www.foxesreach.com

Broomhill Manor, Cornwall (near Bude). 17 cottages and wing of manor house in beautiful 9-acre gardens. Sleep 2-6. Telephone (01288) 352940, email: chris@broomhillmanor.co.uk   www.broomhillmanor.co.uk

Houndapitt, Bude, Cornwall. Traditional farm cottages set in 100 acre estate overlooking Sandymouth Bay. Sleeps 2-9. Telephone (01288) 355455, email: info@houndapitt.co.uk   www.houndapitt.co.uk

The Old Farmhouse and Buttermill Cottage. Grade II listed farmhouse and barn conversion sleeping 6/2. Telephone (01288) 341622, email: helebarton@hotmail.com www.helebarton.co.uk

Fresh Breaks, Cornwall. High quality self catering accommodation with extremely comfortable furnishings, all in idyllic locations. Telephone (02089) 932628, email: bookings@freshbreaks.co.uk www.freshbreaks.co.uk

Barclay House, East Looe, Cornwall. Luxury cottages ETC 5 star. Restaurant, lounge/bar, heated swimming pool. Telephone (01503) 262929, email: info@barclayhouse.co.uk   www.barclayhouse.co.uk

Kennacott Court, Bude. Overlooking Widemouth Bay a variety of outstanding award winning cottages with excellent leisure centre sleeping 2-10. Telephone (01288) 362000, email: phil@kennacottcourt.co.uk www.kennacottcourt.co.uk

Treworgie Barton Holiday Cottages, St. Genny's. Nine superb character cottages in 36 acres of farmland and woodland setting within North Cornwall Heritage Coast area. Telephone (01840) 230233, email: info@treworgie.co.uk www.treworgie.co.uk

West Tremabe Cottages, Liskeard. Two beautifully converted and well equipped traditional Cornish stone barns, ideal for couples. Telephone (01579) 321863, email: christine.j.foster@btopenworld.com www.west-tremabe-cottages.co.uk

Trenant Park Cottages, near Looe. Four spacious cottages in a country park setting. Sleep 2-5. Five minutes from South Cornwall's superb beaches. Telephone (01503) 263639/262241, email: liz@holiday-cottage.com www.trenantcottages.com

Trevigue Wildlife Conservation, Crackington Haven. Luxurious coastal cottages surrounded by National Trust farmland in North Cornwall. Telephone (01840) 230418. www.wild-trevigue.co.uk

Cant Cove Cottages, Rock. Six exceptional 5 Key Deluxe cottages sleeping 5-8 in private 70 acre setting overlooking the Camel Estuary in North Cornwall. Telephone (01208) 862841, email: info@cantcove.co.uk www.cantcove.co.uk

Penrose Burden, St. Breward. Nine character cottages in peaceful, rural setting, sleeping 2-6 close to Bodmin Moor. Especially suitable for disabled people. Telephone (01208) 850277/850617. www.penroseburden.co.uk

Best Leisure. Superb accommodation in magnificent settings in Devon and Cornwall. Family owned properties highly graded by the ETC. Telephone (01271) 850611. www.bestleisure.co.uk

East Rose Farm, St. Breward, Bodmin Moor. Seven beautiful cottages in an Area of Outstanding Natural Beauty and Special Scientific Interest. Sleep 2-6. Telephone (01208) 850674, email: eastrosefarm@btinternet.com www.eastrose.co.uk

Court Farm Holidays, Bude. Excellent cottages, farmhouses and barn conversions with fantastic facilities. Sleep up to 17. Telephone (01288) 361494, email: mary@courtfarm-holidays.co.uk www.courtfarm-holidays.co.uk

Wooldown Farm Hol Cottages, Marhamchurch. Six stylish properties, sleeping 2-8, all with spectacular sea views towards Widemouth Bay and Bude. Telephone (01288) 361216, email: holidays@wooldown.com www.wooldown.com

Classy Cottages. A variety of individual and beautifully equipped properties, sleeping 1-16, in three stunning locations; Polperro, Lanlawren and Lansallos. Telephone: 07000 423000, email: nicolle@classycottages.co.uk

Rooky's Nook, Trewalder, Delabole. Luxury barn conversion for discerning couples. Deep in North Cornish countryside and close to beaches. Telephone (01840) 212874, email: info@rookysnook.co.uk www.rookysnook.co.uk

Trevornick Cottages, Holywell Bay. Three spacious, luxurious cottages in an idyllic setting, perfect for families. Dogs welcome. Telephone (01637) 830531, email: bookings@trevornick.co.uk www.trevornickcottages.co.uk

Looe & Polperro Holidays. Carefully selected cottages, apartments and bungalows in rural and coastal locations. Telephone (01503) 265330, email: info@looeandpolperroholidays.co.uk www.looeandpolperroholidays.co.uk

Northleigh Farm Holiday Cottages, near Colyton. Three ETC 4 Star barn conversions in the beautiful rolling countryside of the Coly Valley. Telephone (01404) 871217, email: simon@northleighfarm.co.uk www.northleighfarm.co.uk

Halcyon Cottage, near Honiton. Attractive cottage within easy reach of the East Devon Heritage Coast. Telephone (01404) 549196, email anne_biddle@lineone.net web.pncl.co.uk/molehayes/

Hill Cottage, Clawton, Devon. Large, private gardens, spectacular countryside views. 20 mins drive from beach. Sleeps 8, children welcome. Telephone (01409) 253093, email: lgsg@supanet.com www.selfcateringcottagesdevon.co.uk

Nature's Watch, Honiton. Two high quality cottages on the edge of the Blackdown Hills in Devon. Panoramic views and wildlife. Telephone (01404) 891949, email: enquiries@natureswatch.com   www.natureswatch.com

Kingston Estate, near Totnes. Beautiful cottages in glorious setting; easy reach of Dartmoor, sea and many attractions. Telephone (01803) 762235, email: info@kingston-estate.co.uk www.kingston-estate.co.uk

Beachcomber Cottage, Beer. Period stone cottage close to the beach and South Devon coastal footpath. Sleeps 6+cot. Children and pets welcome. Telephone (01298) 872927, email: jan@cosycotts.com www.cosycotts.com

Chalkway, Cricket St. Thomas. 19th century woodman's cottage sleeping 4 with panoramic valley views. Ideal for exploring Lyme Regis, East Devon and West Dorset. Telephone 0208 444 4296, email: elisabeth@thebuttonfamily.co.uk   www.westcountryhideaway.co.uk

Lancombe Country Cottages, near Dorchester. Five flint and brick cottages with breathtaking views. Indoor heated pool with sauna. Telephone (01300) 320562, email: info@lancombe.co.uk

The Quarterdeck, Dorset. Spacious family property with sea views close to splendid Swanage beaches. Sleeps 10. Telephone (01929) 553443, email: leanne@purbeckholidays.co.uk   www.purbeckholidays.co.uk

Country Ways, High Bickington, North Devon. Beautifully converted stone barns on small farm. Five cottages sleeping up to 21/28. Lovely gardens. Telephone (01769) 560503, email: country-ways@virgin.net www.country-ways.net

Widmouth Farm Cottages, North Devon. Nine cottages (sleeping 2-6) with spectacular views in secluded valley with private beach. Telephone (01271) 863743. email: holiday@widmouthfarmcottages.co.uk www.widmouthfarmcottages.co.uk

Exmoor Cottage Holidays. A group of four comfortable cottages with wood-burning stoves and private gardens. Children and pets welcome. Telephone: 01598 763320, email: enquiries@exmoorcottageholidays.co.uk www.exmoorcottageholidays.co.uk

West Banbury Farm, Broadwoodwidger. Ten cottages on Devon/Cornwall borders with many leisure facilities. Perfect for families or couples. Sleep 2-8. Telephone (01566) 784946 email: amanda@westbanbury.co.uk www.westbanbury.co.uk

Sweetcombe Cottage Holidays Ltd. Family run booking agency with a vast selection of cottages in East Devon. Telephone (01395) 512130, email: enquiries@sweetcombe-ch.co.uk www.sweetcombe-ch.co.uk

Coast & Country Cottages. Over 300 properties throughout beautiful South Devon. Short Breaks, Special Offers, Couples Discounts, Dog Friendly Properties Telephone (01548) 843773, email: suzanne@coastandcountry.co.uk www.coastandcountry.co.uk

Stable/Blackspur Cottages, Norton-sub-Hamdon. Excellent cottages sleeping 2-4 in peaceful Somerset village nestling beside Ham Hill Countryside Park. Telephone (01935) 881789.

The Old Stables and Barley Cottage, Chichester. Cottages on working family farm. Both sleep 4. Telephone (02392) 631382, email: carole.edney@btopen-world.com www.theoldstables.net and www.barleycottage.co.uk

The Thatched Barn, Broadwater, near Andover. Self catering or B & B. Sleeps up to 3 in peaceful village setting. Telephone (01264) 772240, email: carolyn@dmac.co.uk   www.dmac.co.uk/carolyn

The Barn at Bombers, Westerham. High quality 16th century barn conversions situated in open countryside. ETC 5 star. Sleep 6. Telephone (01959) 573471, email: roy@bombers-farm-co.uk   www.bombers-farm-co.uk

Fairhaven Holiday Cottages. Specialists in Kent and Sussex plus 2 Wiltshire farm cottages. Almost 100 properties. Sleep from 2-14. Telephone (01208) 821255. www.fairhaven-holidays.co.uk www.scottscastles.com

Westley Farm, Chalford. Five cottages on old-fashioned Cotswold hill farm. Views over the Golden Valley. Cirencester/Stroud 6 miles. Telephone (01285) 760262, email: cottages@westleyfarm.co.uk   www.westleyfarm.co.uk

Folly Farm Cottages, Tetbury. Twelve stone cottages nestling on 200 acre estate in the Rural South Cotswolds. Sleep 2 - 8. Telephone (01666) 502475, email info@gtb.co.uk www.gtb.co.uk

Grove House Holidays near Ledbury. Four holiday homes sleeping 2 -5 in country setting within easy reach of the Malvern Hills. Telephone (01531) 650584, email: ross@the-grovehouse.co.uk www.the-grovehouse.com

Combermere Abbey, Whitchurch. 11 cottages in stable block of 12th century Cistercian monastery on 1000 acre estate. Sleep 4-8. Telephone (01948) 662876.email: cottages@combermereabbey.co.uk www.combermereabbey.co.uk

Oatfield Country Cottages, Blakeney. Six cottages converted from Grade II listed 17th century farm buildings overlooking Gloucestershire's Severn Estuary. Ideal touring location. Telephone (01594) 510372. www.oatfieldfarm.co.uk

Wye Lea Country Manor, Ross-on-Wye. 5 Star accommodation with excellent facilities for the whole family in an area of outstanding beauty. Sleep 2-54. Telephone (01989) 562880, email: enquire@wyelea.co.uk www.wyelea.co.uk

Cotswold Property Lettings. Find the perfect holiday home from cosy   cottages to large period properties. All personally inspected. Telephone (01386) 858147, email: gill@cotswoldpropertylettings.com www.cotswoldpropertylettings.com

Courtyard Cottages, Upper Court, Tewkesbury. House and cottages in a splendid location with own lake in charming Cotswold village. Sleep 2-11. Telephone (01386) 725351, email: diana@uppercourt.co.uk www.uppercourt.co.uk

Bruern Holiday Cottages, near Chipping Norton, Oxfordshire. Eight award winning ETC 5 star rated cottages with exceptional interiors. Sleep 2-10. www.bruern.co.uk

Pooh Hall Cottages, Woodside, Shropshire. Three beautiful stone cottages sleeping 2 (adults only) with far reaching views over the Clun Valley. Telephone (01588) 640075, email: pooh-hall@realemail.co.uk www.pooh-hallcottages.co.uk

Largy Coastal Apartments. Five star accommodation on the beautiful Antrim coast with spectacular views over the Irish Sea. Telephone 0 2828 885635, email: gladyssmith@btopenworld.com www.ireland4you.freeservers.com

Grayling, County Clare. Bungalow finished to an impressive standard in an irresistible location close to Galway Bay. Sleeps up to 7. Telephone 00 (353) 65 7071055, email: info@goodcottageguide.com

'Do this...don't do that'

Some well-meant suggestions for owners and agents:

Do give detailed how-to-get-there instructions. Internet cartographic printouts are useful, and a bit of local information is a bonus ('Turn left *before* The Hinge and Bracket, not after'...'There's a hand made sign nailed to the dead elm tree'...)

Do let guests get their breath on arrival, get their bearings. Some well-meaning owners spend an hour telling people about eccentric previous guests and which cupboard the board games are hidden in when all the new arrivals really want to do is make a cup of tea and put their feet up.

Do take a deposit against damage and dirt. We wish everyone featured in this guide would do so, but few do. Inconsiderate tenants will thus be reminded of their responsibilities. (We've never heard of potential customers saying 'We won't go there because they want a deposit'...)

Do decide whether pets are welcome or otherwise. There are owners who'll accept cats but not dogs, and vice versa, and a number who'll accept everything except tortoises. Leaving the question of pets open to negotiation can mean trying to run with the hare and hunt with the hounds. Owners and holidaymakers end up on edge, wondering if that cute Border terrier ('Honest, we'll only bring one small dog') will have more impact on the furniture than a pair of elderly Dobermans (-men?).

Do include a folder with information about local pubs, restaurants and shops, including 'the nitty gritty': which fish and chips shops serve fresh, not frozen fish, which pubs have rude landlords, where there's an old fashioned ironmonger's that will sell you six odd nails or four candles...

Don't say 'Short walk to sandy beach', if that beach is really quicksand, and the nearest one to play ball games on is a fifteen minute drive.

Do by all means clean cottages to within an inch of their lives, but do leave salt cellars and pepper pots with their contents intact. It's something few tenants think to bring, and their absence has ruined many a fish supper!

Do let it be known in your brochure/fact sheet if any single beds are only 2 feet 6 ins wide or any 'double' beds are only four feet wide.

Do give guests control over the heating (and charge them accordingly). When a gale-force wind is blowing the sleet around, it is no consolation to be told when you enquire why the central heating does not appear to be working: 'Good Heavens, this is *June*!'

A

Abade Self Catering*	100
Aberdaron, Gwynedd	149
Aberdovey Hillside Village	146
Aberdovey, Gwynedd	146
Abergwesyn, Powys	155
Achahoish, Argyll	116
Achnamara, Ross-shire	110
Akeld Manor and Cottages	86
Akeld, Northumberland	86
All Seasons	61
Alnmouth, Northumberland	88
Amble, Northumberland	256
Ambleside, Cumbria	123
Appledore, Kent	219
Applethwaite, Cumbria	129
Ardblair Castle Cottages	96
Arden House	251
Arduaine Cottages	118
Arduaine, Argyll	118
Ardverikie Estate Cottages	106
Arisaig House Cottages	109
Arisaig, Inverness-shire	109
Ashby Farms Cottages	219
Ashwater, Devon	188
Attadale	107
Attadale, Wester Ross	107
Auchengray, Lanarkshire	94
Aultbea, Ross-shire	110

B

Badham Farm Holiday Cottages	162
Bailey Mill Inn	136
Bailey, Cumbria	136
Bainbridge, North Yorkshire	75
Ballina, Co Mayo	259
Ballyvaughan, Co Clare	262
Balnakilly Cottages/Log Cabins	98
Balquhidder, Perthshire	98
Bamburgh, Northumberland	88
Bamburgh, Northumberland	89
Bamford, Derbyshire	80
Bansha, Co Tipperary	259
Bantry, Co Cork	262
Barn, The	222
Bassenthwaite Lakeside Lodges	132
Bassenthwaite, Cumbria	132
Beadlam, North Yorkshire	66
Beal, Northumberland	91
Bee Cottage	91
Beech Farm Cottages	64
Beer, Devon	209
Belford, Northumberland	91
Beth Ruach	138
Biggin-by-Hartington, Derbyshire	82
Blackmoor Farm Holiday Cottages	139
Blairgowrie, Perthshire	96
Blairquhan	95
Blakeney, Norfolk	44
Blakes Country Cottages*	254
Blakes Country Cottages (Scotland)*	117
Blegberry Farm	189
Blisland, Cornwall	175
Blue Barn Cottage	61

Bluebell Farm Cottages	91	*Bylaugh Hall Cottages*	49
Boathouse Cottages/Wren's	263	Bylaugh, Norfolk	49
Boncath, Pembrokeshire	143		
Bones Cottage	54		
Boot and Shoe Cottage	85	**C**	
Borrowdale, Cumbria	130		
Bosinver Cottages/Lodges	164		
Botelet, Cornwall	156	Canon Frome, Herefordshire	229
Bothy, The	110	*Captain's House, The*	112
Bothy, The	245	*Carna Farmhouse*	114
Boughton Hall	43	*Carpenter's Cottage*	45
Bowderbeck	134	*Carpenters Cottages, No 6*	55
Bowsden, Northumberland	90	Carradale, Argyll	119
Braddon Cottages & Forest	188	Castle Acre, Norfolk	42
Braddon, Devon	188	*Cenarth Falls*	143
Bramble and Hawthorn	60	*Chantry*	57
Brancaster, Norfolk	44	*Chapel Cottages*	171
Brancaster Staithe, Norfolk	45	Charmouth, Dorset	214
Brechin, Angus	120	*Cherry Tree Cottage*	83
*Brecon Beacons Holiday Cottages**	153	*Chew Hill Farm Cottages*	215
Brendon, Devon	187	Chew Magna, Somerset	215
Brendon, Devon	188	Chiddingly, East Sussex	218
Briar Cottage	90	Chinley, Derbyshire	83
Brompton-by-Sawdon, N Yorks	63	Churchill, Oxfordshire	249
Bruisyard, Suffolk	36	*Cider Mill*	225
Bruisyard, Suffolk	37	*Cider Room Cottage*	192
Brundish, Suffolk	33	Cirencester, Gloucestershire	225
Bryn Bras Castle	151	*Classic Cottages**	176
Bryn-y-Mor	141	Cleeve Hill, Gloucestershire	244
Buckden, North Yorkshire	72	*Clematis/FellView/Well/Shepherd's*	75
Buckland, Worcestershire	245	*Cliff Cottage*	66
Bude, Devon	188	*Cliff House*	67
Bunkers Hill	43	*Clippesby Holiday Cottages*	53
Burnham Thorpe, Norfolk	43	Clippesby, Norfolk	53
Burnt Yates, North Yorkshire	71	*Clock House, The*	37
Burton-in-Kendal, Cumbria	134	*Clydey Country Cottages*	144
Butler's Cottage	180	*Cnewr Estate*	154
Buttermere, Cumbria	134	*Coach House Cottages*	157

Coach House, The	91		
Coach House, The	223	**D**	
Cockermouth, Cumbria	129		
Combe Martin, Devon	186		
Compton Pool Farm Cottages	204	Dalcross, Inverness-shire	104
Compton, Devon	204	Dalegarth & The Ghyll Cottages	72
Connemara Coastal Cottages	261	Dalehead Court	82
Connemara	261	Dales Holiday Cottages*	18
Corfe Castle, Dorset	210	Dalham Vale, Suffolk	27
Corner Pightle, The	43	Dartmouth Holiday Homes*	205
Cornish Holiday Cottages*	168	Dartmouth, Devon	205
Cornish Traditional Cottages*	178	Darwin Lake Cottages	80
Coruanon Farmhouse	115	Darwin Lake, Derbyshire	80
Cotswold Retreats*	246	Dedham Vale, Suffolk	32
Cotswold Water Park	225	Delphi Lodge	263
Cottage in the Country*	247	Delphi, Co Galway	263
Cottage Life/Heart of the Lakes*	123	Denton, Cambridgeshire	59
Cotterill Farm Holiday Cottages	82	Dervaig, Isle of Mull	113
Countisbury, Devon	185	Dinmore Cottages	71
Country Cottages in Ireland*	260	Discover Scotland*	121
Country Holidays*	252	Discover the Cotswolds*	232
Countryside Cottages*	57	Docklow Manor	230
Coverack, Cornwall	162	Docklow, Herefordshire	230
Crackington Haven, Cornwall	173	Dorset Coastal Cottages*	211
Crackington Haven, Cornwall	174	Dowager's Cottage	58
Cransford, Suffolk	37	Draughton, North Yorkshire	69
Cranworth, Norfolk	39	Druimarbin Farmhouse	115
Cressbrook Hall Cottages	79	Drumblair	94
Cressbrook, Derbyshire	79	Duloe, Cornwall	158
Cresswell Wing/Sawmill	87	Duloe, Cornwall	161
Croft Corner & Croftside	129	Duncrub Holidays	100
Croft House Holidays	129	Dunning, Perthshire	100
Crosby Garrett, Cumbria	137	Duns Castle Cottages	92
Croyde, Devon	182	Duns, Berwickshire	92
Culligran Cottages	104		

E

East Hagbourne, Oxfordshire	249
Easter Dalziel	104
Eastwell Manor, Kent	221
Eastwell Mews	221
Ebberston, North Yorkshire	67
Ecosse Unique*	99
Edwardstone, Suffolk	30
Ellary Estate Cottages	116
Elgol, Isle of Skye	112
Elterwater, Cumbria	128
Elterwater, Cumbria	131
English Country Cottages*	152
English Country Cottages*	250
Exhall, Warwickshire	245
Eyam, Derbyshire	82

F

Fairford, Gloucestershire	229
Falmouth, Cornwall	168
Farm and Cottage Holidays*	180
Farne House	87
Farsyde Farm Cottages	69
Fell View	75
Field End Barns	136
Fisherman's Quay	215
Fold Farm Cottages	71
Forgotten Houses	169
Fort William, Highland	115
Fowey, Cornwall	165
Fowey Harbour Cottages*	165
Frampton-on-Severn, Glos	226
Freshwater	208
Fron Fawr	143

Fulstow, Lincolnshire	60
Fursdon	207
Fursdon, Devon	207

G

Gairloch, Ross-shire	257
Garden Cottage	128
Gattonside, Roxburghshire	94
Ghyll Cottages, The	72
Gladwins Farm Cottages	32
Glaisdale Head, North Yorkshire	65
Glebe Farm	245
Glen Coe Cottages	108
Glen Coe, Argyll	108
Glen Strathfarrar, Inverness-shire	104
Golden Green, Kent	220
Goldhill Mill Cottages	220
Goodrich, Herefordshire	227
Gower Peninsula	152
Grange Farm Cottages	69
Graythwaite Farm	128
Graythwaite, Cumbria	128
Great Escape Holiday Co, The*	40
Great Hucklow, Derbyshire	78
Green Cross Cottages, No 4	134
Greenhead, Northumberland	84
Greystones	208
Greystones Farm Cottage	76
Grove Cottages	30
Gullrock	172
Gwarmacwydd Farm Cottages	141
Gwynfryn Farm Holidays	149

H

Hacheston, Suffolk	36
Hall Farm	231
Harehope Hall, Northumberland	87
*Harrogate Holiday Cottages**	70
Harrogate, North Yorkshire	70
Hartington Cottages	78
Hartington, Derbyshire	78
Hartland Point, Devon	189
Hawes, North Yorkshire	75
Hawthorn	60
Hayloft, The	78
Headon Farm Cottages	63
Healaugh, North Yorkshire	74
Heath Farm Cottages	248
*Helpful Holidays**	201
Heron Cottage	42
*Hideaways**	212
Higher Clovelly, Devon	189
Highland House	56
Hillside Cottage/The Bothy	245
Hockadays Cottages	175
Holiday House, The	259
Hollocombe, Devon	185
Holly Farm Cottages	39
Holmhead Cottage	84
Holt, Norfolk	55
Hope, Derbyshire	82
Hopworthy Farm	181
Horning, Norfolk	52
Horry Mill Cottage	185
*Hoseasons Country Cottages**	20
How Caple, Gloucestershire	225
Howscales	124

Hunstanton, Norfolk	50
Hunstanton, Norfolk	56

I

Interhome UK	19
*Ireland Directory**	264
Island Lodge	241
Isle of Carna Cottage	114
Isle of Carna	114
Isle of Mull	113
Isle of Skye	112
Isle of Wight	208
Ivy House Farm	39

J

*Jean Bartlett Cottage Holidays**	209
Jenny's Cottage	44
Jockey Cottage	27

K

Kettlewell, North Yorkshire	71
Killarney Lakeland Cottages	258
Killarney, Co Kerry	258
Kinlochlaggan, Inverness-shire	106
Kipscombe Farm	185
Kirk Cottage	66
Kirkland Hall Cottages	122

Kirkland, Cumbria	122	Lower Dinchope, Shropshire	223
Kirkmichael, Perthshire	98	*Lower House*	129
Kirkoswald, Cumbria	124	*Loweswater Cottages*	126
Knockerdown Farm Cottages	81	Loweswater, Cumbria	126
Knockerdown, Derbyshire	81	Luddenden Foot, W Yorkshire	76
Knowle Farm	206	*Lundy View*	189
		*Lyme Bay Holidays**	214
		Lyme Regis, Dorset	214
L		Lymington, Hampshire	217

*Lakeland Cottage Holidays**	130	**M**	
*Lakelovers**	127		
Lakeside Lodges	225		
Land Ends	124	*Machrie Hotel Lodges*	118
Langtree, Devon	184	Machrie, Isle of Islay	118
Langwith, Nottinghamshire	61	Maenporth, Cornwall	168
*Large Holiday Houses**	102	Maesycrugiau, Carmarthenshire	152
Library, The	113	*Mainoaks Farm*	227
Linzel Cottage	56	*Manor Cottage*	156
Lismacue Coach House	259	*Manor Cottages**	246
Little Cottage, The	249	*Margaret's Cottage*	36
*Little Holiday Houses**	103	*Marigold & Penny*	166
Little River View	52	*Marsdens Cottage Holidays**	182
Llanbedr, Gwynedd	145	*Matson Ground Estate Cottages*	135
Llanfallteg, Carmarthenshire	141	*Meadowbank/Garden Cottage*	128
Llanrug, Gwynedd	151	Membury, Devon	192
Lochaline, Inverness-shire	101	Milford-on-Sea, Hampshire	216
Lodge Cottage	36	*Mill Cottages, The*	229
Long Byres	125	Mindrum, Northumberland	90
Looe, Cornwall	165	*Mineshop Holiday Cottages*	174
Looe Valley, Cornwall	162	Modbury, Devon	192
Louie's Cottage	28	*Monkhouse Hill Cottages*	133
Louth, Lincolnshire	61	*Moorings, The*	58
Lovers Retreat	181	*Mossgill Loft/Chapel*	137
Lower Dinchope Big Barn	223	*Mrs. Jane Good (Holidays) Ltd**	34

Mudgeon Vean Farm Hol Cotts	171
Muirhall Holiday Cottages	94

N

Nantcol	145
National Trust Cottages	24
National Trust for Scotland, The	93
New Forest Cottages*	217
Newgale, Pembrokeshire	141
Norfolk Coast	54
Norfolk Country Cottages*	41
Norfolk Holiday Homes*	50
Northernhay/Highland House	56
Northumbria Coast & Country*	88
Norwich, Norfolk	58

O

Oast House, The	249
Offcote Grange Cottage Holidays	79
Offcote, Derbyshire	79
Old Coastguard Cottages, No. 3	208
Old Dairy, The	244
Old Farm Cottages	49
Old House, The	83
Old Mill Farm	241
Old School Cottages, The	173
Old Smithy, The	90
Oldaport Farm Cottages	192
Orangery, The	226
Orangery at Little Boynes	231

Orchard Cottage	59
Orford, Suffolk	34
Otter Falls	208
Outchester/Ross Farm Cottages	89
Owlpen Manor Cottages	228
Owlpen, Gloucestershire	228

P

Pant Farm	148
Parker's Retreat	120
Patton, Cumbria	136
Peak Cottages*	77
Peddars Cottage	42
Pekes	218
Pele Tower, The	89
Pelynt, Cornwall	160
Penmore Mill	113
Penny	166
Penrallt, Pembrokeshire	144
Penwern Fach Cottages	143
Pettigrew Cottage	167
Pier Cottage/The Library	113
Pollaughan Cottages	166
Polperro, Cornwall	166
Poole, Dorset	215
Poole Keynes, Gloucestershire	241
Port Gaverne, Cornwall	172
Portmeirion Cottages	151
Portmeirion, Gwynedd	151
Portscatho, Cornwall	166
Portscatho, Cornwall	167
Post Office Cottage	53
Potash Barns	33

Praa Sands, Cornwall	163		
Pwllheli, Gwynedd	149	**S**	
Pyworthy, Cornwall	181		
		Salcombe Holiday Homes*	191
Q		Salcombe, Devon	191
		Sanctuary Cottage	149
		Sarah's Cottage	76
Quality Cottages Cerbid*	142	Saundersfoot, Pembrokeshire	139
		Sawdon Country Cottages	63
		Sawdon, North Yorkshire	63
R		Sawmill Cottage	87
		Scalby, North Yorkshire	68
		Scarborough, North Yorkshire	68
Rattery, Devon	206	Scoles Manor	210
Ravenglass, Cumbria	129	Scorrier, Cornwall	180
Ray Desmesne, Northumberland	85	Scottish Country Cottages*	97
Recommended Cottage Holidays*	17	Seahouses, Northumberland	87
Reeth, North Yorkshire	74	Sea Meads Holiday Homes	163
Rhuveag	98	Seaview Grazings	111
Rhyd-yr-Eirin	145	Sebergham, Cumbria	133
Richards Castle, Shropshire	222	Sedbusk, North Yorkshire	75
Ring of Kerry. Co Kerry	257	Sedgeberrow, Worcestershire	231
Riverside Cottage	223	Sennybridge, Powys	154
Riverside Rentals	52	Shanklin, Isle of Wight	255
Robin Hood's Bay, N Yorkshire	69	Shatton Hall Farm Cottages	80
Robyn's Nest	148	Shaw End Mansion	136
Rockford Lodge	187	Shepherd's Cottage	75
Roseland Holiday Cottages*	167	Shore Cottage	101
Roseland Peninsula, Cornwall	167	Shore Croft	110
Rosemoor	140	Sleights, North Yorkshire	65
Ross Farm Cottages	89	Snape Castle	75
Rothbury, Northumberland	89	Snape, North Yorkshire	75
Rural Retreats*	105	Snowdonia Tourist Services*	150
Rural Retreats*	242	South Lodge	43
		South Raynham, Norfolk	46

Southfields Cottages	28	**T**		
Southwold, Suffolk	38			
Sowerbys Holiday Cottages*	54			
St Aubyn Estates	170	Talcen Foel	147
St Austell, Cornwall	164	Tal-y-Bont, Conwy	148
St David's, Pembrokeshire	138	Talkin, Cumbria	125
St Genny's, Cornwall	173	Tamar Lodges	189
St Issey, Cornwall	175	Thornham, Norfolk	56
St Martin, Cornwall	171	Three Mile Water, Inverness-shire	115
St Tudy, Cornwall	171	Throcking, Hertfordshire	28
Stables, The	91	Tides Reach	165
Staffin, Isle of Skye	112	Tintagel, Cornwall	181
Staithes, North Yorkshire	66	Tintern, Gwent	223
Stanbury, West Yorkshire	76	Toad Hall Cottages*	190
Stanhoe, Norfolk	53	Tomich Holidays	101
Stanton Lacy, Shropshire	224	Tomich, Inverness-shire	101
Stately Holiday Homes	22	Torrisdale Castle Cottages	119
Stein, Isle of Skye	112	Townend Cottage	66
Stoke Tye, Essex	28	Trallwm Forest Cottages	155
Stowford Lodge Holiday Cottages	184	Trefanny Hill	158
Straiton, Ayrshire	95	Tregarron	152
Stratton, Cornwall	181	Tregeath	181
Strontian, Argyll	111	Tremaine Green	160
Stubbs Cottages	60	Trevarrow Cottage	162
Suffolk Cottage Holidays*	31	Trevorrick Cottages	175
Suffolk Secrets*	38	Treworgey Cottages	161
Sunnyside Cottage	55	Treworgey Manor, Cornwall	157
Sussex Farm Holiday Cottages	44	Tunstead, Norfolk	49
Sutton Court Farm Cottages	224		
Swaledale Cottages	74		
Sweethope Crofts, 1 & 2	85	**U**	
Swerford, Oxfordshire	248		
Swiss Chalet, The	229		
Sykes Cottages*	21	Ullswater, Cumbria	135
		Undercroft, The	75
		Upper House	129

Upottery, Devon	208	*Windmill Cottage*	216
Upton-upon-Severn, Worcs	231	Wiveton, Norfolk	54
Uwchmynydd, Gwynedd	147	Wollerton, Shropshire	223
		Wood Lodge	37
		Woodbridge, Suffolk	31
V		Woodbridge, Suffolk	34
		Wooder Manor	189
		Wortham, Norfolk	39
Vere Lodge	46	*Wrea Head Country Cottages*	68
Village and Country Homes	262	Wrelton, North Yorkshire	64
Vista & Carpenter's Cottage	45	*Wren's Cottage*	263
Vivat Trust, The	26	*Wringworthy Cottages*	165
		Wycliffe, Co Durham	85

Y

W

		Yarpole, Herefordshire	266
Walwyn's Castle, Pembrokeshire	140	*York Lakeside Lodges*	62
Water House, The	43	York, North Yorkshire	62
Watermillock, Cumbria	124		
*Welcome Cottages**	152		
Well Cottage	75		
Wells next the Sea, Norfolk	57		
Welton-le-Wold, Lincolnshire	60		
West Burton, North Yorkshire	75	**Index (Overseas)**	
West Lodge	91		
Wheel Farm Country Cottages	186		
Wheelhouse	65	Denmark	265
Wheelwrights	131	France	266-279
White Rose Holiday Cottages	65	Italy	280-285
Whitby, North Yorkshire	65	Spain	286-289
Whiddy Holiday Homes	262	Cyprus	290-291
Widecombe-in-the-Moor, Devon	189	Bavaria	292-294
Windermere, Cumbria	127	Austria	295
Windermere, Cumbria	135	New England (Vermont)	296

'To do or not to do'

Some advice for self caterers...

Don't feel awkward about checking and re-checking details that are important to you (is the pond fenced, is there a noisy road, can a friend stay for a couple of nights?). Being a fusspot at the outset can save hassle at a later stage.

Do use the visitors' book, but find something more interesting to say than 'we had a lovely time'. Visitors' books full of chit-chat and advice can be fun, especially when a theme 'runs and runs'. Among our favourites were children's long-running observations of a 'family' of spiders in the shed.

Don't turn up with more people than you have actually booked for: this seems to annoy owners/agents more than orgies, murder and dogs being sick. And don't strip a car engine on the deep-pile carpet in the sitting room. (One reader did, at Chew Magna, near Bristol).

Don't take white rabbits to your cottage when they say 'No pets', even if you are a conjuror. Somebody did in the Peak District, and he was! And even if they do take pets, don't turn up with three Alsatians when you have had enough trouble persuading a cottage-owner to accept a Pekinese.

Don't be ashamed to have a good lie-in when you fancy it. It is something one can never really do in an hotel.

Don't arrive before 3pm unless you want to embarrass the cleaner, or, even worse, surprise the dowager duchess who owns the cottages on her hands and knees in the kitchen.

Do take a few favourite ornaments and, especially, books; these work wonders if you don't easily feel at home in strange houses. A pair of favourite bookends is a handy thing to pack.

Do feel free to move the furniture around (though most owners actually hate this), but do replace it as you found it. But do own up to breakages. Unreported objects missing or broken can be infuriating.

Do take hot water bottles, and maybe even a portable heater. Remember the old adage: 'my house is cosy, yours is warm-*enough*, his is freezing'.

Don't forget that a lot of excellent rural properties are still accessible by rail and that most owners will meet you at a convenient station.

Don't bottle up complaints and problems. Tell owners or agents about your worries on the evening of your arrival, if possible.